THE ROLLS-ROYCE 'B SERIES' ENGINE

IN NATIONAL SERVICE

ROLLS-ROYCE 'B SERIES' ENGINES IN BRITISH MILITARY VEHICLES

by
PAT WARE

•

WAREHOUSE
PUBLICATIONS

•

Published in Great Britain by Warehouse Publications.
© Copyright 1994 by Warehouse Publications.
First printed 1995.
ISBN 0-9525563-0-8.

All rights reserved. Apart from any fair dealing for the purpose of private study, research, or critical review, as permitted by the relevant parts of the 'Copyright and patents act 1988', no part of this publication may be reproduced or transmitted in any form or by any means, electronic, chemical, optical or mechanical, including photocopy, recording, or any information storage and retrieval system, without prior permission in writing from the publisher. All enquiries should be addressed to the Publisher.

Designed and produced by Warehouse Publications.
Page layout by Lizzie Ware.
Illustrations by Baxter & Brand, Radcliffe-on-Trent.
Text produced using 'Wordstar' V6.0; page layouts prepared using Aldus-Adobe 'PageMaker' V5.0.
Set in 10.5/11.5pt ITC New Baskerville by Tradespools, Frome.
Printed in England by Butler & Tanner, Frome and London.

For Ronnie

Published by Warehouse Publications
5 Rathbone Square, Tanfield Road, Croydon CR0 1BT.
Telephone: 0181-681 3031.
Fax: 0181-686 2362.

IN NATIONAL SERVICE
The Rolls-Royce 'B Series' in British military vehicles

CONTENTS

	FOREWORD	1
1	**THE 'B SERIES' ENGINE**	3
1.1	Introduction	5
1.2	Rationalised power	11
1.3	Technical data	27
2	**THE B40 ENGINE**	53
2.1	Austin 'Champ'	55
2.2	Land-Rover B40	67
2.3	Minor applications & prototypes:	71
	Jones KL 66 4/6 ton mobile crane	
	Auto Diesels 10kVA mobile generator set	
	Centurion bridgelayer	
3	**THE B60 ENGINE**	75
3.1	Daimler 'Ferret'	77
3.2	Humber 1 ton truck	89
3.3	Humber 1 ton armoured truck	101
4	**THE B80/B81 ENGINES**	113
4.1	Alvis 'Saladin'	115
4.2	Alvis 'Saracen'	125
4.3	Alvis 'Stalwart'	137
4.4	GKN 'Trojan' & Vickers 'Abbot'	157
4.5	Leyland 'Martian'	163
4.6	Thornycroft light mobile digger	175
4.7	Airfield vehicles:	179
	Alvis runway friction test vehicle	
	Alvis 'Salamander'	
	Douglas 10 ton fire tender	
	Douglas/BROS 'Sno-Flyr'	
	Douglas/Sentinel aircraft tug	
	Thornycroft 'Nubian' 3 and 5 ton fire tender	
4.8	Minor applications & prototypes:	189
	Albion 5 ton truck	
	BOC/Tasker 15 ton oxygen plant	
	Cambridge tracked carrier	
	Centurion ARV	
	Thornycroft 'Nubian' 3 and 5 ton truck	
	Vauxhall/Albion 3 ton truck	
	INDEX	199

From left to right
Graham Smith, Reg Spencer and Derek Wright of Rolls-Royce whom the author would like to thank for their encouragement and contribution to this book.

'Work till it hurts'... Ernest Walter Hives, later Lord Hives.
Managing Director, Rolls-Royce Motors, 1946.

FOREWORD

It is often the way that one's initial idea changes in the cold hard light of reality. This project was no exception and indeed, it did start life in a somewhat different form. However, as I got into the research work, it became obvious that, aside from the Army's own technical documentation, there was very little information available regarding the first generation of post-war British military vehicles.

It also became clear that there was an interesting story to tell.

Like many projects, the work seemed to have a way of expanding itself to match the time that appeared to be available, and it was simply in an attempt to prevent the work from running out of control that I started to concentrate on the Rolls-Royce 'B Series'. It seemed to provide not only an excellent focus, but also a way of dealing with many of my favourite vehicles... Stalwart, Ferret, Champ, Martian

Here then is an attempt to document the previously un-told story of the Rolls-Royce 'B Series' engines, and those post-war vehicles, mostly unsuccessful it has to be said, in which the engines were used. Many of the vehicles will already be familiar to most enthusiasts but I hope I have been able to shed at least some new light on them; some were new to me, and I only learnt of their existence as the project unfolded.

When researching information for a project of this nature, it is inevitable that there will be some errors and omissions in the final work. Much of the source information is 40 or 50 years old, and anyway was not committed to paper for the benefit of future researchers. Contrary to what one may want to believe, historic printed sources are not always reliable, and even the most diligent researcher must sometimes resort to informed guesswork. I ask for your indulgence if errors are evident, and I would welcome corrections, amendments and additional information.

Pat Ware
Croydon, 1995

MEMORANDA

Form of presentation
It was always my intention to produce a reference work which could be dipped into for specific information, and I did not intend that the book necessarily be read from cover to cover like a novel. I have presented the text in what I believe is an accessible form to reflect this, and included a comprehensive index.

Information
I would like to thank all those who patiently answered my questions and helped me with my research. The list includes, in alphabetical order:

Stephen Bagley; Museum of British Transport, Coventry
Brian S Baxter; REME Museum
John Breese
Tim Day
John Delaney; Imperial War Museum
Wally Dugan; Museum of Army Transport
Tim Fuggle; RR Motor Services
Peter Gaine
Derek Gilliam (Maj, retd); REME Museum
Graham Holmes; Tank Museum
Graham Smith; Roll-Royce Limited
Reg Spencer CBE; formerly of Rolls-Royce Limited
Mike Stallwood; RR Motor Services
Derek Wright; formerly of Rolls-Royce Limited

Lists of engines
I have used a summary of the Rolls-Royce production records as a source of information regarding the various marks and versions of the engines. There are cases where engine versions were produced which do not appear to have been used in any vehicles. For the sake of completion, I have not omitted these engines from the text.

Nomenclature
When I started this project, I was of the firm belief that there was a definitive description, or nomenclature, for each vehicle. As the work progressed, I realised that this was not the case: for example, FVRDE nomenclature was not the same as War Office nomenclature, and neither of them seemed to be absolute.

In the end, I took the easy way out and have included what seemed to be the most commonly-used nomenclature.

Documentation
Each chapter concludes with a list of technical publications and further reading. These lists are intended to be representative rather than comprehensive.

Equipment lists
Similarly, where lists of on-board equipment are included, these too are representative, not comprehensive.

FVRDE
Up until the mid-1950's, the Ministry of Supply maintained separate research and development bodies with executive responsibility for the design and specification, and testing of so-called 'fighting vehicles'.

In 1954, the two executives were merged to form the Fighting Vehicles Research and Development Establishment (FVRDE). Although not necessarily historically accurate, for the sake of convenience, I have tended to use this description throughout the text.

It is also perhaps worth pointing out that in 1972, FVRDE merged with the Military Engineering Experimental Establishment (MEXE) to form the Military Vehicles Engineering Establishment (MVEE), now renamed, yet again, simply as MoD Chertsey.

Photographs
I have tried wherever possible to use photographs which have not been seen before and I am grateful to those who allowed me access to their archives. Virtually all of the black-and-white photographs are contemporary to the development and service of the vehicles. The colour photographs were taken at many locations between 1980 and 1995, and I would like to thank all who allowed me to photograph their vehicles, albeit often unknowingly.

The following codes are used to indicate the copyright holders of the photographs:

BMIHT	British Motor Industry Heritage Trust/Rover Group
BTMC	British Transport Museum, Coventry
IWM	Imperial War Museum
MP	MotorPhoto
REME	REME Museum, Arborfield
RR	Rolls-Royce Limited
RS	Reg Spencer
TMB	Tank Museum, Bovington

CHAPTER 1

THE 'B SERIES' ENGINE

CONTENTS

1.1	Introduction	5
1.2	Rationalised power	11
1.3	Technical data	27

CHAPTER 1

CHAPTER 1.1

INTRODUCTION

In September 1944, a paper prepared for the War Office Policy Committee stated that within the Infantry Division there were nearly 55 different types of category 'B' transport vehicle, and close to 600 different types, makes and contracts within the Army as a whole. To make matters worse, many of these vehicles were based on commercial types, and thus were not properly suited to the needs of a mechanised army. And a large number were produced by companies outside the British Isles, who had no domestic production facilities at all.

By VE day, the total number of motor vehicles in service with all of the Allied armies exceeded one million.

Servicing and maintaining a fleet of this size and diversity cannot have been easy under any conditions. Try to imagine the logistical problems which this situation would create in peacetime, let alone whilst trying to provide supply, servicing and repair facilities for a rapidly-advancing army on the mainland of occupied Europe. Under these circumstances, even with the types of vehicle issued to individual units rationalised as far as possible, a field transport unit might have been required to carry spares for as many as 10 different types of vehicle and engine.

Anxious not to be faced with this sort of logistical nightmare in any future conflict, the Chiefs of Staff resolved that standardisation of transport vehicles was to be high on their future list of priorities. Even before WW2 had reached its conclusion, the War Office, together with the Ministry of Supply, which was the Government agency charged with the procurement of War Office vehicles, had approached the Society of Motor Manufacturers and Traders (SMMT), and begun to design and plan for a family of new standardised vehicles.

As the war in Europe came to a close, surplus vehicles from the existing inventory were disposed of, either through auction sales to civilians, or by government contract to the armies of friendly nations. Civilian operators were probably particularly pleased to be able to acquire surplus equipment since many had not been able to buy new vehicles since 1940.

In 1946, with vehicle stocks rationalised, to the admittedly somewhat uneasy peacetime levels, the Ministry felt that it was in a position to start putting the plan into effect. There was of course some degree of urgency, for not only were the remaining WW2 vehicles generally in poor condition, but there was every indication that the West would be at war with Russia within five years.

BRITISH MILITARY VEHICLES

Historically, British military vehicles are divided into three types, described as 'A', 'B' and 'C'.

Category 'A' covers armoured fighting vehicles (AFV's), generally designed to mount offensive weapons. The class also includes armoured personnel carriers, and AFV's which have been converted to other roles, such as armoured bridgelayers and recovery vehicles. 'B' vehicles are non-fighting transport vehicles. The 'C' category includes mobile plant such as cranes and earth-moving equipment.

The category 'A' vehicles obviously have no commercial equivalent and must be purpose-designed, while type 'C' vehicles, by their nature, tend anyway to be modifications of commercial designs, or to be mounted on 'B' type chassis.

Thus the plan for standardisation covered only the category 'B' vehicles.

Category 'B' vehicles

Towards the end of the war, the War Office had come round to the view that military vehicle design had become sufficiently divergent from mainstream commercial vehicles that all category 'B' vehicles should be purpose-designed by the government's own agencies. Apart from providing prototyping and manufacturing facilities, it was not felt that the commercial motor industry had much to offer in this design process.

This principle was tacitly set out in 'General Staff Policy Statement 35, Post-war design of 'B' vehicles', which was agreed and issued in June 1947. The document laid down general design parameters for the various types of vehicle, and actually opened with the words 'generally speaking, the standard commercial vehicle is unsuitable for Army use, and vice versa'.

However, it quickly became apparent that the country neither had the facilities to produce these vehicles, nor could it afford to have the entire fleet of wheeled military vehicles purpose-designed. Obviously a compromise was required. This led to the consideration of separating the 'B' vehicles into two groups: the general service vehicles, and the more specialised combat vehicles.

Investigation of this new principle continued until 1950 when a paper put before the Executive Committee Army Council (ECAC) went a little further, suggesting that the post-war 'B' vehicles be divided into three categories: 'combat' (abbreviated to CT), 'general service' (GS), and commercial' (CL). The split of vehicles between the three categories was projected as being CT 16%, GS 39%, and CL 45%.

Combat vehicles

The CT vehicles were defined by the War Office as 'specialised military vehicles with multi-wheel drive, manufactured from components not used for commercial purposes, and required to give the best possible load-carrying capacity and cross-country performance, with or without the appropriate guns or trailers'. It isn't in the definition but you can almost hear the unspoken 'regardless of cost'.

The category was to include a range of specialised soft-skin transport vehicles in five weight categories: 5 cwt, and 1, 3, 10, and 30 tons. There was also a requirement for a highly-specialised 60 ton tank transporter.

It was planned that all CT vehicles would be purpose-designed by the Fighting Vehicles Research and Development Executive (FVRDE) at Chertsey in Surrey. At the FVRDE site, the Ministry of Supply maintained comprehensive design and engineering facilities, as well as vehicle testing laboratories and test tracks.

General service and commercial vehicles

The 'GS' class comprised modified versions of standard civilian vehicles, for example down-rated commercial trucks with the addition of four- or six-wheel drive, heavy-duty wheels and tyres, and generally with FVRDE-standardised instruments, lighting and electrical equipment.

The 'CL' class consisted of essentially standard commercial designs.

FV NUMBERS

Each type of vehicle was assigned a standard model number, prefixed 'FV' (fighting vehicle): three and four figure numbers were used for (type 'A') AFV's; four figure numbers for CT vehicles; five figure numbers for GS vehicles; and six figure numbers for vehicles in the CL category.

The FV numbers were allocated in series to each vehicle type; for example the FV1800 series was assigned to the Austin 1/4 ton 'Champ' range, FV1600 series was the Humber 1 ton family, FV1100 series indicated the 10 ton Leyland 'Martian' range. The last two figures of the number assigned to individual vehicle types indicated the body design within the series; FV1801 is a cargo-bodied 'Champ', FV1802 has a utility body, and so on.

CHAPTER 1.1: INTRODUCTION

Heavy Tractor 6 x 6 Combat

Truck Combat ¼ Ton 4 x 4

THE ARMY'S NEW VEHICLES

The vehicles used by the Army are divided into three groups, Combat vehicles, General Service vehicles and Commercial vehicles. The Combat range consists of trucks, tractors, scout cars and the like, with "go-anywhere" performance. These vehicles are designed in their entirety for the Services to be used as fighting vehicles. As a result the performances of which they are capable are astonishing, whilst they fairly bristle with technical interest.

General Service Vehicles are for the less spectacular, but equally important, supporting roles. For the most part they are made of standard civilian parts adapted for Service use. They do of course differ in certain respects from vehicles of the same make to be seen on the roads. Most General Service trucks have cross-country tyres, some have 24 volt electrical systems and in all cases particular attention is paid to 100 per cent air-cleaning, for which purpose a special oil-bath air-cleaner has been developed. The Commercial Vehicles are standard "off-the-peg" vehicles for use in rear areas.

Particular attention has been paid to inter-changeability of parts. The majority of the Combat Vehicles have the "B" series engines, originally developed by Rolls Royce and now made by several manufacturers, and throughout the "B" series of engines pistons, piston rings, gudgeon pins, connecting rods and other parts are the same.

Since the war there has been continuous outcry about the tracts of land closed to the public for W.D. purposes. These photographs were taken at the Army Proving Ground, one of those disputed areas. But surely the work that has been done, the vehicles

Truck Combat 6 x 6 Field Artillery

Truck Combat 1 Ton 4 x 4

Leaflet produced by FVRDE in the early 1950's

THE ROLLS-ROYCE 'B SERIES' ENGINE

7

CHAPTER 1.1: INTRODUCTION

DESIGN AND PRODUCTION

The plan proposed that vehicle specifications and designs would be drawn up by FVRDE at Chertsey, and that development contracts would be placed with the motor industry.

Once development was complete, the manufacturing contract would be negotiated separately, perhaps with a different company. Throughout the life of a vehicle, usually the original developer, would be retained as 'design parent' overseeing modifications and ensuring that any proposed changes did not compromise the integrity of the original design. The problem of on-going manufacture of spares and replacements was not really addressed at this time.

It was intended that the purpose-designed combat vehicles in the four weight classes up to 10 tons, as well as certain of the GS vehicles, and the smaller vehicles in category 'A', would be powered by a family of standardised engines. This would reduce the need for extensive parts stockholding, as well as improving general reliability and maintenance standards in the field. By this means it was felt that the parts inventory could be reduced by a factor of at least 10, with attendant cost and efficiency savings. A high degree of standardisation also meant that cannibalisation of damaged vehicles, a practice widespread during WW2, could be used to keep other vehicles running in an emergency.

It was also planned that vehicle accessories such as ignition components, starters, generators, instrument clusters, switchboards, and lighting fittings should also be produced to standardised designs prepared by FVRDE.

Although this was as far as the formal standardisation went, with the benefit of hindsight, there appears to have been a common design approach running through most of the vehicles, presumably originating from the design team at FVRDE. Longitudinal torsion-bar suspension, for example was used on the 'Champ', the Humber, all of the Alvis six-wheeled vehicles ('Saladin', 'Saracen' and 'Stalwart'), and the FV432 'Trojan'. Outboard bevel boxes, and an H drive shaft layout was used in the final drive arrangement of the 'Ferret' and the Alvis range. The transfer case was integral with the rear axle, with a second prop shaft running the full length of the vehicle to drive the front axle, on both the 'Champ' and the Humber. Tracta-type constant velocity driveshaft couplings will be found on virtually the whole range. Most of the vehicles incorporated separate forward and reverse gears, making all of the speeds available in either direction.

This degree of standardisation, combined with specialised design must have seemed like a good idea at the time but

FV1800 Series, Austin 1/4 ton CT vehicle (IWM)

FV1600 Series, Humber 1 ton CT vehicle (MP)

FV1300 Series, Vauxhall 3 ton CT vehicle (IWM)

CHAPTER 1.1: INTRODUCTION

FV1100 Series, Leyland 10 ton CT vehicle (IWM)

FV1200 Series, Dennis/Leyland 30 ton CT vehicle (TMB)

in practice was far more expensive and difficult to administer than might be imagined. It was quickly found that for example the trucks in the CT category offered very little real benefit over the GS vehicles. Without the advantages of volume production, but with a very high level of technical complexity, the CT vehicles were often two or three times the cost of the equivalent GS type.

However, development of both CT and GS vehicles continued throughout 1951, and in the case of the purpose-designed CT range considerable difficulties were experienced. In fact, serious doubts were beginning to emerge as to the value of the CT family at all, and in September 1951 the Quarter Master Corps (QMC) proposed that no further orders for CT vehicles be placed. The proposal was discussed at some length but was not approved, and ECAC confirmed that the plan was to continue, albeit somewhat simplified.

Several weight classes and types of vehicle were abandoned altogether. Very few vehicles, for example, were constructed in the 3 ton CT category and those that were built were considered too complex and unreliable, and the class was not developed beyond the prototype stage. The 30 ton artillery tractor project was put on hold subject to further discussion, but at a price of £20,000 each it seemed unlikely that there would be any further progress. The 60 ton tank transporter was abandoned without any prototypes having been produced.

Even those vehicles which had been approved for production were not spared, and a working party was set up with a view to simplifying, and thus reducing the costs of the 1/4 ton 'Champ' and the 1 ton Humber.

In 1955, a research paper considering the future of the CT range of vehicles stated 'there is no doubt that the Combat range has had an unfortunate history. Of the three types so far produced, only one - the 1 ton vehicle - can be regarded as successful, and even this vehicle suffered from serious defects when it first appeared... All the vehicles so far produced have proved infinitely more costly than was at first conceived... The final verdict on the Combat range will almost certainly be that the design is too complex, causing difficulty in maintenance, that they are unreliable in service, and that they are much too costly'.

Over a period of 10 years, only the 'Champ' and the Humber had been produced in quantity. The Ministry was beginning to admit that perhaps the original specifications were too exacting and that it was not a good idea for the design work to have been carried out by FVRDE. By the mid-1950's, it was being suggested that perhaps the wealth of expertise available within the commercial motor industry should not have been so lightly disregarded.

During 1955 and 1956, officials at the War Office were beginning to draw up and circulate papers outlining new 'B' range vehicle policies. Gradually a consensus began to emerge. It was recognised that the GS vehicles had been far more successful at every level than had originally been envisaged, whilst the Combat range had not worked out as had been hoped. One paper actually stated 'the Army has got to discard the Combat range'.

The new policy plans proposed that the motor industry be more involved with the design stages. The SMMT were to be approached with an outline specification for a new range of improved GS chassis, and the industry was to be asked to produce prototypes which FVRDE would assess.

There was the inevitable to-ing and fro-ing but the die was cast and by 1956, the CT classification was abandoned,

CHAPTER 1.1: INTRODUCTION

and those vehicles which had been produced were regraded from CT to GS status.

Huge sums of money had been spent with really very little to show for it. For example, more than £1 million had been given to Austin in capital assistance for the 'Champ' project, and a third of a million spent on rectification work; £1.1 million had been given to Humber in capital assistance for the 1 ton truck. During the years 1950-55, the Army had spent a total of £30 million a year on 'B' type vehicles, and yet of the original five weight categories, vehicles were only produced in three of them, and by all accounts these were far from satisfactory.

STANDARDISED POWER

However, all was not lost. Although the CT concept had proved a failure, on the plus side, there was no doubt that the concept of 'standardised power' did have something going for it.

It had always been proposed that the CT vehicles, and some vehicles in the GS and AFV categories would be powered by a standardised engine. The engine policy was enshrined in the 1947 issue of 'General Staff Policy Statement 35', which included the words 'all specialist type of vehicles should as far as possible, use a standard engine...', and went on to describe 60, 90 and 180bhp engines.

In 1944/45, at the time this programme was conceived, the Ministry of Supply had commissioned Rolls-Royce to undertake further development work on a standardised military petrol engine. Work had started in 1943 under the direction of the company managing director, W A (Roy) Robotham - also known to his friends and confidantes as 'Rumpty'.

The engine was to be manufactured in four-, six- and eight-cylinder versions, and was intended to power vehicles ranging from around 2 tons unladen weight up to more than 20 tons.

The brief called for the highest standards of design and engineering excellence with a view to achieving a high degree of reliability. The engines were intended to provide a target life of at least 100,000 miles to first major overhaul, with 80% life following overhaul. Maximum power was to be achieved within the smallest possible physical dimensions and weight, and the engines were intended to run on low-grade fuels without undue loss of efficiency. Finally, there was to be maximum component interchangeability between the versions.

The result was the Rolls-Royce 'B Series' of standardised engines...

CHAPTER 1.2

RATIONALISED POWER
B40, B60, B80, B81

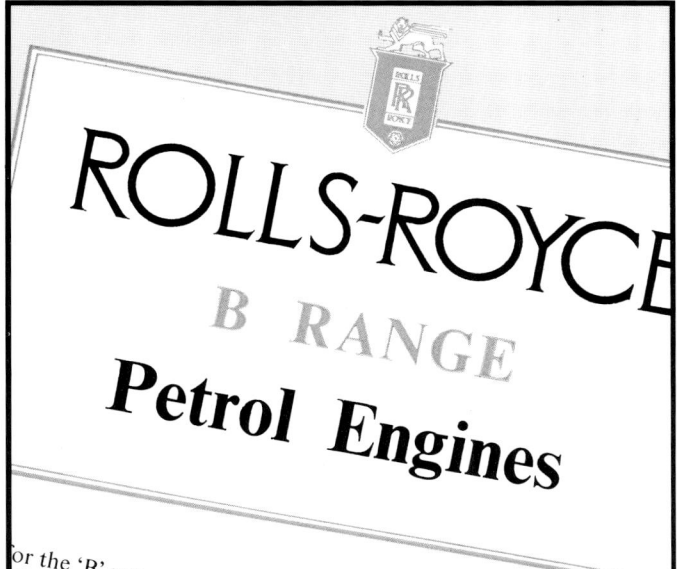

The original concept behind the rationalised 'B Series' was to produce a family of high-quality, long-life, four-, six- and eight-cylinder military petrol engines with a common bore and stroke, and a high degree of interchangeability of components across the range, regardless of the number of cylinders.

'B Series' engines were intended for use in the new CT class of post-war military vehicles which were under development by the FVRDE at Chertsey (see Chapter 1.1), as well as in the smaller AFV's such as the 'Ferret' and 'Saladin'. Between them, the engines were designed to cover a power range of between 75 and 160bhp, and later, with the commercial B81 unit, up to 235bhp.

Some commentators at the time stated that work actually began in 1940, and whether or not this is true, the project was certainly underway before the end of the War. By late 1943 or early 1944, W A (Roy) Robotham, who was Chief Engineer of Rolls-Royce at the time, had installed an eight-cylinder version of the pre-war 4.25 litre six-cylinder engine in a standard WW2 tracked 'universal carrier', and subsequently in the CT24 and CT25 versions of the 'Oxford' carrier which was being considered as a possible replacement. This engine should probably be considered as the father of the 'B Series' project.

Robotham demonstrated the engine to the Ministry of Supply, successfully 'selling' them the idea and securing funding for a substantial development programme, and also at the same time, picking-up the 'Oxford' tracked carrier development project referred to above.

Early versions of the eight-cylinder B80, Mk 1 engine were also installed in a variety of existing military trucks during the mid-1940's for field trials.

Although the engines were primarily intended for military applications, it was also anticipated by Rolls-Royce that they might be suitable for commercial fleet users.

OVERVIEW

The 'B Series' family consists of a range of basically-similar four-, six- and eight-cylinder engines, with the six- and eight-cylinder versions available with alternative bore dimensions. The larger-bore versions of the six-cylinder engines (B61/61SV), and the high-power version of the large-bore eight-cylinder engine (B81SV) were never used in British military applications, but were much favoured by commercial users.

THE ROLLS-ROYCE 'B SERIES' ENGINE

CHAPTER 1.2: RATIONALISED POWER

The smallest of the range, the four-cylinder B40 unit, had a swept-volume capacity of 2838cc; the six-cylinder B60, measured up at 4256cc; and the massive straight-eight B80 and B81 versions, had capacities of 5675cc and 6516cc respectively.

The design was extremely straightforward and even at the end of WW2, these engines might have been considered conventional, and perhaps even a little old fashioned. The emphasis was always on reliability and engineering excellence rather than technical innovation for its own sake.

All of the engines were petrol-fired and water-cooled, with overhead inlet valves and side exhaust, and were normally-aspirated through a side-draught (B40 only) or dual down-draught Solex carburettor. Wet- and dry-sump versions were available of each basic design, and the units were waterproofed for deep-water wading, with all electrical equipment radio-screened.

Close to 85% of the wearing parts, as well as many minor components, were common across the entire range. In contemporary sales literature, Rolls-Royce stated that of 207 different parts required by the engines, 184 were common to all versions. As well as reducing the need for extensive parts stockholding, this meant that in an emergency, it was possible to cannibalise engines in stock or in the workshop, in order to keep vehicles running under all conditions.

NOMENCLATURE

Each variation of the engine was assigned an internal Rolls-Royce specification number by the Development Department, prefixed 'PL' or 'CL' according to where the work was done, and given a unique designation code for identification outside the Company.

For example, internal specification PL6615 would have been identified externally as a 'B40, No 1, Mk 2A/4' engine; specification CL3377 was a B60, Mk 5K; while CL3847 was a 'B81, No 1, Mk 8B/2'.

The internal specification numbers were simply assigned in numeric sequence and have no inherent meaning; the external designation, however, provides basic identification and descriptive data, which can be decoded as follows:

Prefix code
Code letter 'B' indicates the parent company: Rolls-Royce Limited.

Numeric code
The numeric code denotes the number of cylinders; four, six or eight: and the bore size; '0' indicates 3.50 inches, '1' indicates 3.75 inches.

Original B80 prototype engine installed in running chassis (RR)

Albion FT15N 6x6 artillery tractor used as mobile B80 test bed (TMB)

Leyland 'Hippo' Mk 2 used as mobile B80 test bed (RR)

CHAPTER 1.2: RATIONALISED POWER

Type number
The type number indicates the fuel system: 'No 1' means petrol burning with a conventional carburettor.

Mark designation
The 'mark' number indicates differences in major constructional features as listed below, regardless of the number of cylinders.

Mk 1	Original Bentley engine using 'car' crankcase; only used for prototype work.
Mk 2	Cast-iron crankcase, aluminium cylinder head, fully machined crankshaft, wet sump.
Mk 3	Cast-iron crankcase, aluminium cylinder head, fully machined crankshaft, dry sump.
Mk 4	Cast-aluminium crankcase, aluminium cylinder head, fully machined crankshaft, wet sump; no series production.
Mk 5	Simplified version of Mk 2, with UNF screw threads, cast-iron cylinder head, forged crankshaft and connecting rods.
Mk 6	Simplified version of Mk 3, with UNF screw threads, cast-iron cylinder head, forged crankshaft and connecting rods.
Mk 7	High-power engine, UNF screw threads, cast-iron cylinder head, forged crankshaft and connecting rods, wet sump; high compression ratio. B81 units only.
Mk 8	High-power engine, UNF screw threads, cast-iron cylinder head, forged crankshaft and connecting rods, dry sump. B81 units only.

Notes:
A zero following the mark number, eg Mk 50, indicates an engine intended for commercial applications.

An oblique and figure one (/1) following the mark number suffix code, eg Mk 5H/1, indicates that the engine is fitted with a 305mm twin-plate clutch and ventilated clutch casing.

Suffix code
The final suffix letter denotes the detail variations made to the basic engine specification to meet the needs of the particular application. These suffix codes were allocated in alphabetic sequence to each engine series as the modifications were specified by the development department, and there is not necessarily any significance to the codes, one engine model to another.

Typical variations cover:

Inclusion of pipework and nozzles for Ki-gass cold start equipment. Orientation of carburettor air horn.

B40, Mk 5A engine installed in Austin 'Champ' (IWM)

B60, Mk 5A engine installed in Humber 'Pig' (TMB)

B81, Mk 8A engine installed in Alvis 'Salamander' (BTMC)

THE ROLLS-ROYCE 'B SERIES' ENGINE

CHAPTER 1.2: RATIONALISED POWER

Provision of power take-off, type of clutch or fluid power coupling.
Type and orientation of the sump.
Type of clutch housing.
Use of engine speed governor.
Type of inlet and exhaust manifolds.

DEVELOPMENT

The key dimensions of the six-cylinder 'Derby' Bentley 4.25 litre OHV unit (bore, stroke and cylinder centre-to-centre), originally introduced in 1936, were chosen as providing a suitable basis for the design of the new engine. Work had begun well before the war was over, and by offering the design to the Ministry of Supply, and receiving their sanction for the development work, Roy Robotham hoped to steal a march on his competitors once the war was over. As a matter of principle, Rolls-Royce undertook no motor car production during either WW1 or WW2, but it was always Robotham's intention that the work on the 'B Series' could also spin-off into a new passenger car engine.

The design team was headed by Charles Jenner (Jnr), who had the distinction of having actually worked with Sir Henry Royce, and included Jack Birkenshaw, who was responsible for the camshaft design, Jack Phillips, Les Robinson, and George Griffiths. The FVRDE project leader was Doug Miller and relations between the Rolls-Royce design team and the FVRDE personnel remained excellent throughout all stages of the project.

In 1946, a young Reg Spencer returned to the Company from military service, and was also assigned to the team. Reg was to remain with the 'B Range', as Rolls-Royce men described it, in one capacity or another for all of his working life.

The first engine to be produced was the B80, Mk 1, and as an engineering apprentice Reg Spencer had already had the dubious pleasure of machining the first B80 block back in 1944 on a Richards horizontal boring machine, a task which took two whole weeks.

The basic design was extremely versatile: the block, cylinder head and crankshaft design were capable of adaptation to provide closely-related four-, six- and eight-cylinder units, and the units were capable of adaptation to both wet- and dry-sump versions.

The resulting engines were suitable for the widest range of military applications. 'B Series' engines were used in both automotive and static plant applications, and quickly acquired a reputation for reliability, both for being able to provide instant full power virtually from a cold start, and for their ability to withstand rough usage over long periods without damage.

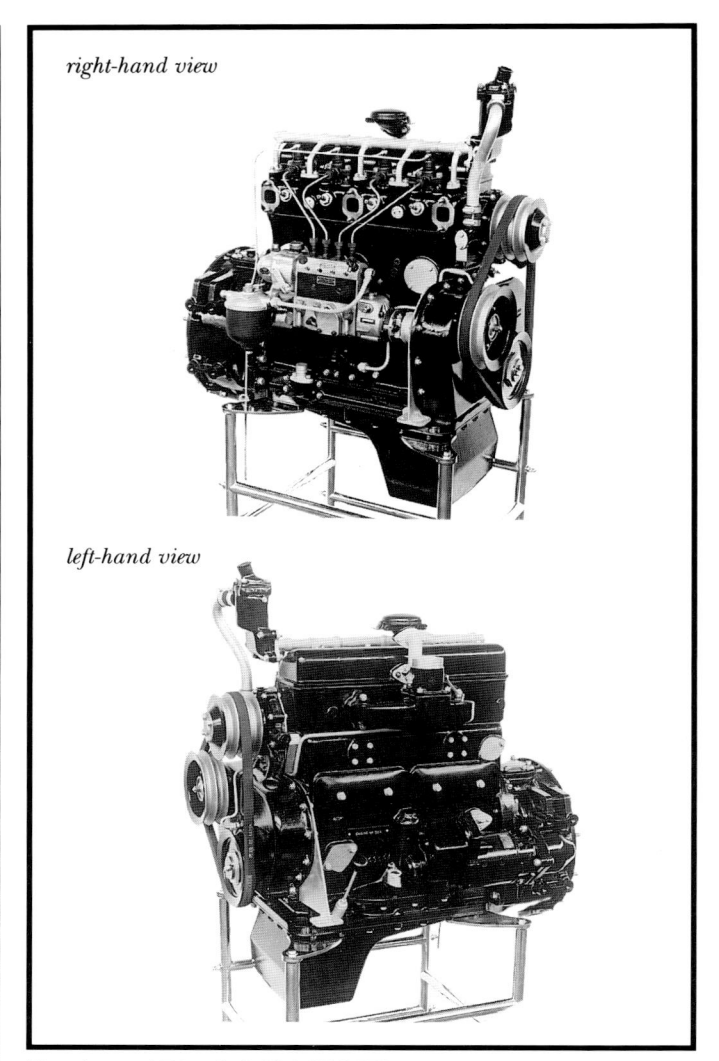

right-hand view

left-hand view

Experimental Ricardo B40 36X OHV diesel (RR)

Ricardo B40 36X diesel installed in Austin 'Champ' (RR)

CHAPTER 1.2: RATIONALISED POWER

Ricardo B40 36X diesel in Austin 'Champ', showing fan detail (RR)

Some idea of how seriously the military authorities took the issue of reliability can be illustrated by the fact that the design specification called for the (B81) engines to be able to withstand a continuous seven-day test run (168 hours) at full power without failure or damage. This was achieved, but only through the use of 'Brightray' exhaust valves and valve seat inserts.

Unfortunately there was a price to pay for this level of reliability.

The initial cost of the engines was high, and in addition, the units exhibited a prodigious appetite for petrol. For example, in 1952 the B40 unit installed in the Austin 'Champ', when purchased under a contract calling for literally thousands of units, cost the government close to £200 without tax - more than £2600 in today's prices. To help put this into context, at the time of its launch, the retail price for a complete Series 1 Land Rover was only £450. Derek Wright, retired Engineering Manager of what subsequently became the Rolls-Royce Specialised Engines Division, recalled that at one time, they had a rule of thumb which said that the engines cost a 'pound a pound'... and these were heavy engines!

However, by the standards laid down by the Ministry of Supply, the engines proved extraordinarily successful, remaining in service for close to 50 years.

DESIGN

The initial design work was carried out at the old Clan Iron Foundry at Belper in Derbyshire, where Rolls-Royce had established a research and experimental establishment. Belper, of course, was not far from the Derby factory where, until 1950, Rolls-Royce and Bentley motor cars were produced.

A vital part of the design brief was that the engines should be able to combine adequate power with low-down torque, particularly when running on low-grade fuels, (and remember, this was at a time when 72 octane was considered the norm).

Two man-years' work with single-cylinder experimental units went into the optimum design of the combustion chamber in order to satisfactorily control detonation. Particular attention was paid to the question of lubrication and cooling, with the intention of providing reliability under all kinds of operating conditions and in all kinds of climates, and Rolls-Royce enlisted help on optimum oil temperatures and wear rates from Shell Research at Thornton.

The design brief also called for the carburettor and induction system to permit operation in the ambient temperature range -40 to +50 degrees Celsius. In other words, vehicles were required to operate in conditions ranging from Arctic to Equatorial with equal efficiency and reliability. A cold room was installed at Crewe to ensure that engines would indeed start at these temperatures.

The inlet over exhaust (IOE) valve configuration was selected as allowing the use of the largest possible inlet valves, providing adequate breathing, while also allowing the use of durable exhaust valve seats, and at the same time, still retaining a compact design.

The IOE valve arrangement also gives a good 'squish' area in the combustion chamber, and better controls the build-up of residual heat around the exhaust ports. Unlike OHV configurations, the heat is contained within the mass of the crankcase and is more easily dealt with by the better flow of coolant in the crankcase water jacket.

CHAPTER 1.2: RATIONALISED POWER

Dimensions

The centre-to-centre dimension for adjacent bores was standardised at 4.15 inches, a figure which had some considerable historical significance at Rolls-Royce. In a paper presented to the Institute of Mechanical Engineers on 10 June 1963, Harry Grylls, who was Chief Engineer of the Motor Car Division of Rolls-Royce at the time, traced this figure directly back to the 50hp engine used in the 'Silver Ghost' in 1919.

For B40/60/80 engines, the bore and stroke were 3.50 x 4.50 inches, giving a bore to stroke ratio of 1:1.3. For the B61/81 units, the bore was increased to 3.75 inches and the bores were 'siamesed', leaving only 0.4 inches of metal, without a full water jacket, between adjacent cylinders; the stroke remained at 4.50 inches, giving a ratio of 1:1.2.

If Henry Royce would have been pleased to see that his bore-to-bore dimension of 4.15 inches was still being adhered to some 35 years on, he would have been positively delighted with this approach to standardising the bore and stroke across a range of engines. In 1904, when designing his 10, 15, 20 and 30 hp cars, he had chosen to use the same range of dimensions for the pistons, cylinders and valves.

The selection of a relatively long-stroke was intended to reduce the physical length of the units for a given capacity. The degree of success achieved can be judged by the fact that the straight-eight version, for example, was hardly any longer than the V12 installed in the contemporary Rolls-Royce 'Phantom III' motor car.

BSF/UNF

In accordance with pre-war practice, engines up to Mk 4 employed 'BSF' (British Standard Fine) thread forms, combined with BSW/BSF hexagon bolt head sizes. Engines from Mk 5 through to Mk 8 employed the standardised UNF (Unified National Fine) threads, and AF hexagon dimensions, based on the American NC and NF thread forms.

For this reason, the early units were sometimes described as 'BSF' engines, while the later variants were described as 'UNF'. The letters 'UNF' will be found cast, as rumour would have it, on Rolls-Royce-built engines, or pressed, on Austin-built (see page 18) engines into the rocker gear cover - or maybe this is another of 'those stories' that seem to abound whenever Rolls-Royce is involved.

However, as always, it's not quite that simple, and in fact the so-called 'UNF' engines incorporated a number of redesigned features intended to suit them better to a hard military or commercial life.

right-hand view

left-hand view

Experimental Ricardo B80 48X supercharged OHV diesel (RR)

B80, Mk 6A engine being fitted into Alvis 'Saladin' (BTMC)

B81, Mk 8A engine being fitted into Alvis 'Salamander' (BTMC)

Alvis 'Salamander' chassis showing rear engine configuration (BTMC)

Examples include forged connecting rods, built-in power take-off facility, cast-iron cylinder head, and a generally more-rugged all-round design, albeit, some said at the expense of the smoothness of the original 'BSF' engines.

Accessories
Standard 'FV-pattern' military accessories, such as distributors, starters and generators were designed and developed at FVRDE, and manufactured by companies such as AC-Delco, Lucas, Simms and CAV, specifically for use with these engines.

Both the engine and accessories were waterproofed for deep-water wading, with the electrical systems screened to prevent HF and VHF radio interference.

Prototypes
Prototypes of the engine were constructed and given exhaustive trials in a variety of different chassis, running under various load configurations and ambient conditions.

Test-bed operation, combined with the use of experimental vehicle installations, allowed the Rolls-Royce engineers to simulate constant running under a variable load, and to measure the performance of the engine under the most arduous and prolonged operating conditions. Reg Spencer recalled that the first, admittedly non-empirical, measurement for any engine under load on the test bed was to see how much of the exhaust pipe was glowing red hot! Not a serious statement of course, but it does help to demonstrate just how hard these test engines were expected to work.

In publicity material, Rolls-Royce claimed that the engines had been tested for more than 1,000,000 road miles and over many thousands of miles of cross-country work.

Once the development work was sufficiently advanced, trials were conducted at the Ministry of Supply FVRDE proving grounds at Chertsey in Surrey where 'B Series' engines were tested in a variety of war-time vehicles.

Documentation produced at the time is deliberately unclear as to exactly which of the newly-designed military vehicles were involved. Experiments certainly covered various weight classes and, among others, engines were installed in a number of existing chassis, including a recovery vehicle and trailer, staff car, and 15 cwt and 3 ton trucks of both 4x4 and 6x6 configuration.

Photographs of early test installations showed a variety of WW2 military vehicles, including the Austin K5 4x4 three-tonner, the Morris C8 4x4 15cwt, a 6x6 version of the Scammell 'Pioneer' (a prototype for the post-war 'Explorer', which incidentally, was ultimately to use a Scammell/Meadows petrol engine), an Albion FT15N 6x6 artillery tractor, and the 10-ton 6x6 Leyland 'Hippo'. As has already been mentioned, the engine was also fitted in the CT24 and CT25 versions of the developmental 'Oxford' carrier.

Military acceptance
Following the FVRDE tests, some work was still required to render the engines suitable for deep-water wading, and for operation in extreme conditions. However, in November 1946, the War Office, together with the Ministry of Supply, officially adopted the 'B Series' as standard in all wheeled combat (CT) vehicles, as well as for AFV's with all-up combat weights to about 16 tons.

Although obviously not suitable for the heavier tracked vehicles, 'B Series' engines were also installed in some prototype and experimental light-armoured tracked vehicles.

CHAPTER 1.2: RATIONALISED POWER

PRODUCTION

Series production began in 1948 with the Mk 2A engines.

The B80 units for the pre-production Leyland 'Martian' were the first engines to be produced, followed by B60 engines initially destined for the 'Ferret', and then the B40 for the 'Champ'. Although, in fact, the first application of a B40 engine was in driving a generator set at Duffield Bank House in Derbyshire, where Rolls-Royce maintained research and conference facilities.

For the first two years of the engine's manufacturing life, the design facilities remained at Derby, although all of the 'B Series' engines were produced at Crewe. The factory at Crewe had been turning out 'Merlin' engines since the beginning of the war, and had produced more than any other manufacturer, but the motor car side of the business had remained at Derby until 1950.

Initially, the block and head castings were produced by Leyland Motors in Lancashire. When the number of engines required was reduced, Leyland were not able to maintain the logistics of manufacturing a smaller number, and other suppliers had to be found. Discussing production some 40 years later, Reg Spencer recalled that it was extremely difficult to maintain the necessary quality after Leyland dropped out, and Rolls-Royce often became involved in additional remedial work.

After manufacture, regardless of whether the engines were destined for immediate installation, or were for 'stock', all units had their apertures sealed and were 'tropicalised' (so-called 'Level J' packaging) before crating.

By 1963, Rolls-Royce stated that more than 30,000 'B Series' engines had been produced, and by 1964, this figure had risen to 38,000. Total (military) production numbered more than 40,000 units of all types.

Although the B40 had been dropped from the range by the early 1960's, the other versions remained in the Rolls-Royce catalogue well into the 1970's and even into the 1980's, only gradually being superseded by the move towards more-powerful diesels, and multi-fuel units. Even in 1995, Rolls-Royce are still able to provide limited technical support, and as recently as 1991, new blocks were still being manufactured for the Ministry of Defence. The Company was undertaking engine rebuilding work during the 1960's and 70's, and at the time of writing, some parts for most of the models remain in stock at Crewe.

Manufacturers

Rolls-Royce were the original designers, and remained the design parent for the 'B Series' throughout its life. However, as with the FVRDE vehicle development and

Four B80 engines used to provide power for 'hoverlift' trailer (RS)

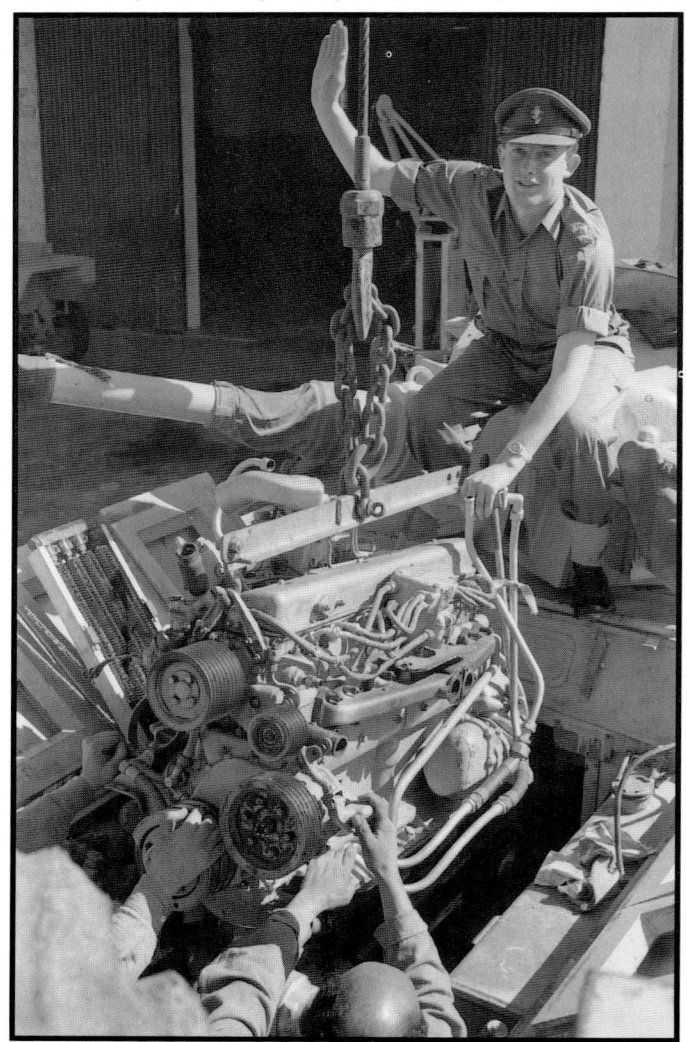

B80, Mk 6A engine being removed from Alvis 'Saladin' (IWM)

CHAPTER 1.2: RATIONALISED POWER

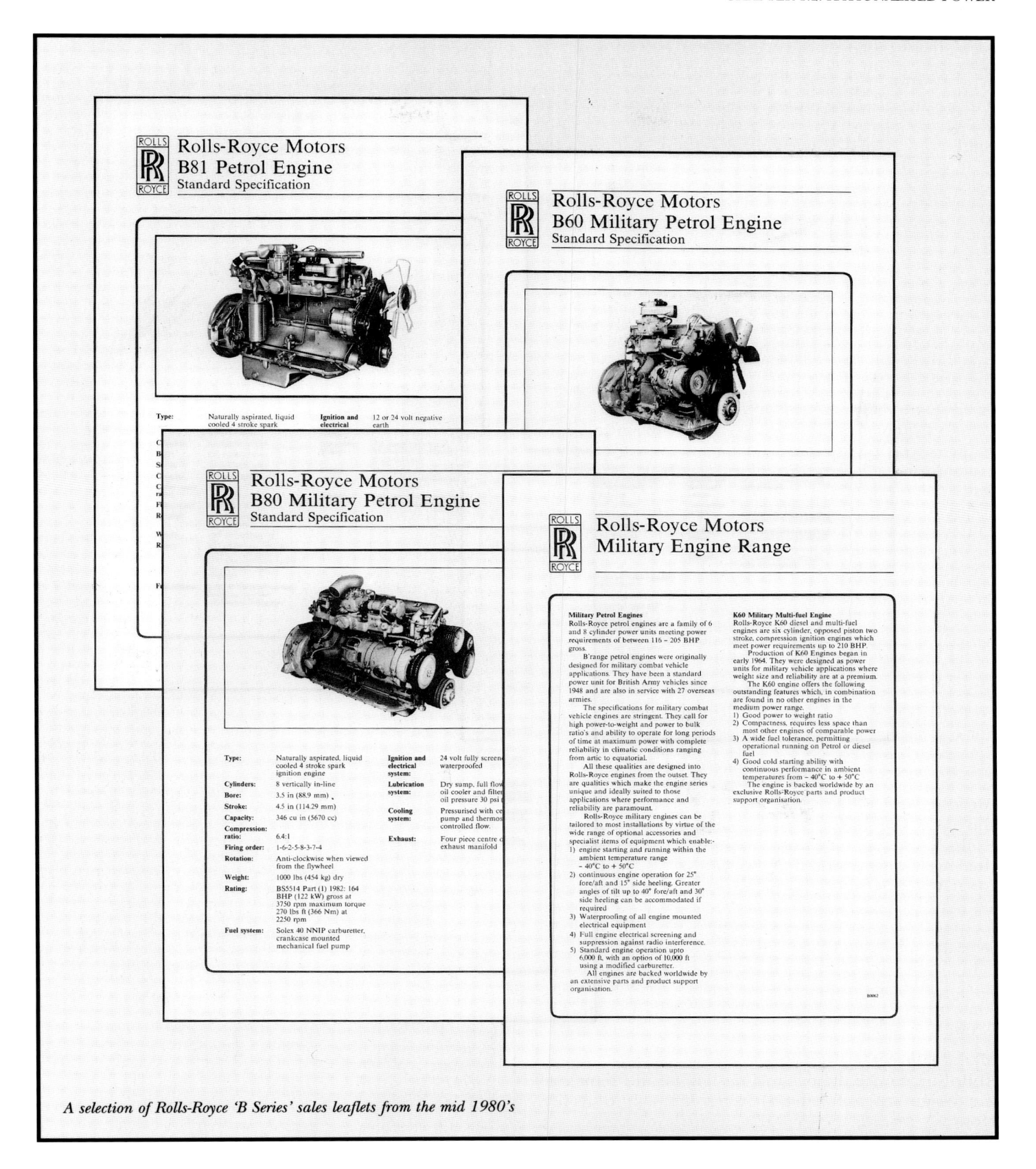

A selection of Rolls-Royce 'B Series' sales leaflets from the mid 1980's

THE ROLLS-ROYCE 'B SERIES' ENGINE

manufacturing programme, the intention was always that other companies would bid for manufacturing contracts, producing the various versions of the engines to the specifications and tolerances laid down by Rolls-Royce. Once volume production got underway, what actually happened was somewhat different.

The Ministry of Supply awarded contracts to Rolls-Royce for the manufacture of early B40, Mk 2A, 2A/4, and 2B engines, some B40, Mk 5A engines, and all of the B60 units required for the Humber 1 ton and 'Ferret' vehicles. Austin, by then part of the newly-formed British Motor Corporation, bid successfully for the manufacture of B40, Mk 5A and B80/81 units.

With the cancellation of the requirements for the 3 ton CT and 5 ton GS classes of vehicle (see Chapter 4.7), the number of B80 units required was much reduced, leaving Austin rather out on a limb as regards their sizable production capacity. The decision was taken to revert production of the B80, and ultimately the B81 engines, to Rolls-Royce at Crewe, leaving Austin with only the contract for the B40, Mk 5A.

So, although it is true to say that Rolls-Royce constructed examples of all of the 'B Series' variations, they were not the sole manufacturer of the B40.

However, should the subject of engine manufacturer come up for discussion, many military vehicle enthusiasts become misty-eyed and talk about the 'Rolls-Royce-engined Champ' without understanding the true situation. There is little doubt that Rolls-Royce built all of the early Mk 2A, 2A/4 and 2B engines installed in the 'Champ', in its predecessor the 'Mudlark', and in the largely-experimental Land Rover B40. They also built some of the Mk 5A units destined for 'Champs' and for various other B40-engined equipment.

It is equally certain that Austin manufactured 15,000 of the B40, Mk 5A engines used in the 'Champ'. Since this was most of the total B40 production, far from being Rolls-Royce engined, most 'Champs' were far more prosaically engined by Austin themselves, albeit to a Rolls-Royce design.

The Rolls-Royce-built engines can be identified by their four-figure serial numbers; Austin-manufactured units have five-figure numbers. It is also said that Rolls-Royce-built engines have a factory-applied glossy black paint finish, while Austin-built units are finished in the standard 'Ministry' pale blue/green. Engines are certainly encountered in these alternative finishes, but as regards identifying the manufacturer, this is just another of 'those stories'. Aside from Austin, no other manufacturers were involved.

TABLE 1. ENGINE APPLICATIONS

Engine mark*	Vehicle description and FV number	
B40 engines		
B40 Mk 2A/4	Wolseley 'Mudlark'	FV1800
B40 Mk 2A	Austin 'Champ'	FV1801
B40 Mk 2B	Land Rover B40	FV18001
B40 Mk 2D	10kVA mobile generator set	FV2401
	Temperature airfield ground unit**	-
B40 Mk 2E	Anti-aircraft gun project**	-
B40 Mk 2F	Jones KL66 4/6 ton crane	FV11103
B40 Mk 2G	Flame thrower project**	-
B40 Mk 5A	Austin 'Champ'	FV1801
		FV1802
B40 Mk 5E	Vickers medium anti-aircraft gun**	-
B40 Mk 5F	Jones KL66 4/6 ton crane	FV11103
B40 Mk 5H	10kVA mobile generator set	FV2401
B40 Mk 5P	Centurion bridgelayer	FV4002
B60 engines		
B60 Mk 2A	Humber 1 ton truck	FV1600
		FV1601
		FV1602
		FV1604
	Humber armoured truck/ APC	FV1611
		FV1612
		FV1613
B60 Mk 3A	Daimler 'Ferret'	FV701
B60 Mk 5A	Humber 1 ton truck	FV1601
		FV1602
		FV1604
	Humber Malkara supply truck	FV1621
	Humber armoured truck/ APC	FV1609
		FV1611
		FV1612
		FV1613
B60 Mk 5C	Thornycroft crash tender pump	FV14161
B60 Mk 5D	HML airfield hydraulic power unit**	-
B60 Mk 5F	Humber 'Hornet' Malkara launcher	FV1620
B60 Mk 5K	Humber Malkara test truck	FV1622
B60 Mk 5G	Vernon generator set**	-
B60 Mk 6A	Daimler 'Ferret'	FV701
		FV703
		FV704
		FV711
		FV712
B60 Mk 6A/L	'Vigilant' AFV	-

CHAPTER 1.2: RATIONALISED POWER

B80 engines		
B80 Mk 1B	'Oxford' CT24/CT25 tracked carrier	-
B80 Mk 1C	Marine application	-
B80 Mk 1D	Albion 6x6, 5 ton truck	FV14001
		FV14004
		FV14103
	Leyland 'Hippo' Mk 2	-
	Vauxhall 3 ton truck	FV1301
		FV1313
	Thornycroft 4x4, 'Nubian'	FV13403
	Thornycroft 6x6, 'Nubian'	FV14101
		FV14103
B80 Mk 2A	Leyland 'Martian'	FV1100
B80 Mk 2D	Thornycroft 4x4, 'Nubian'	FV13403
	Thornycroft 6x6, 'Nubian'	FV14101
		FV14103
B80 Mk 2F	'Cambridge' tracked carrier	FV401
B80 Mk 2H	Leyland 'Martian'	FV1103
B80 Mk 2K	Douglas/BROS 'Sno-Flyr'	-
B80 Mk 2P	Centurion ARV winch	FV4006
B80 Mk 3A	Alvis 'Saladin'	FV601
	Alvis 'Saracen' APC/ACoP	FV603
		FV604
B80 Mk 5C	Douglas/Sentinel aircraft tug	-
	Aldous Mk VII harbour tug**	-
B80 Mk 5D	Thornycroft 4x4, 'Nubian'	FV13403
	Thornycroft 6x6, 'Nubian'	FV14101
		FV14103
B80 Mk 5F	'Cambridge' tracked carrier	FV401
		FV402
	Thornycroft 4x4, 'Nubian'	FV13403
	Thornycroft 6x6, 'Nubian'	FV14101
		FV14103
B80 Mk 5H	Thornycroft 'Nubian' water carrier**	-
B80 Mk 5L	Heavy ferry pontoon raft	-
B80 Mk 5N	Douglas/Sentinel aircraft tug	FV2241
B80 Mk 5P	Centurion ARV winch	FV4006
B80 Mk 5Q	Thornycroft 4x4, 'Nubian'	FV13403
	Thornycroft 6x6, 'Nubian'	FV14101
		FV14103
B80 Mk 6A	Alvis 'Saladin'	FV601
	Alvis 'Saracen' APC/ACoP	FV603
		FV604
		FV610
		FV611
B80 Mk 6D/L	Alvis 'Saladin'	FV601

B81 engines		
B81 Mk 2H	Leyland 'Martian'	FV1103
B81 Mk 5A	City Electric airfield power unit**	-
B81 Mk 5G	Vernon 50kVA generator set**	-
B81 Mk 5H	Leyland 'Martian'	FV1103
		FV1110
		FV1119
		FV1121
		FV1122
B81 Mk 5K	Leyland 'Martian'	FV1119
B81 Mk 5M	BOC/Tasker 15 ton oxygen plant	FV3523
B81 Mk 5Q	Thornycroft 4x4, 'Nubian'	FV13403
	Thornycroft 6x6, 'Nubian'	FV14101
		FV14103
B81 Mk 5R	Thornycroft 6x6, 'Nubian'	FV14161
B81 Mk 7D	Thornycroft light mobile digger	-
B81 Mk 7F	Tracked carrier**	FV421
B81 Mk 7H	Douglas 10 ton fire tender	FV11501
B81 Mk 7K	Thornycroft 6x6, 'Nubian'	FV14161
B81 Mk 7P	Thornycroft 6x6, 'Nubian'	FV14151
B81 Mk 8A	Alvis 'Salamander'	FV651
		FV652
	Alvis runway friction test vehicle	FV652***
B81 Mk 8B	Alvis 'Stalwart' HMLC	FV620
		FV622
		FV623
		FV624
B81 Mk 8F	GKN 'Trojan' Mk 1, APC	FV432
B81 Mk 8G	GKN 'Abbot' self-propelled gun	FV433

* No commercial applications are included.

** Vehicle applications marked with an asterisk are included for the sake of completion only: no additional data on these vehicles is available in this book.

*** Modification.

CHAPTER 1.2: RATIONALISED POWER

TABLE 2. PRODUCTION DATA				
Mark variations*	Number produced**:			
	B40	B60	B80	B81
Mk 1C	-	-	1	-
Mk 1D	-	-	67	-
Mk 2A	30	260	69	-
Mk 2A/4	1483	-	-	-
Mk 2B	54	-	-	-
Mk 2C	-	-	2	-
Mk 2D	9	-	297	-
Mk 2E	7	-	-	-
Mk 2F	18	-	11	-
Mk 2G	8	-	-	-
Mk 2H	-	-	25	-
Mk 2K	-	-	-	-
Mk 2P	-	-	100	-
Mk 3A	-	34	275	-
Mk 4	No series production units made			
Mk 5A	17363***	4440	-	8
Mk 5C	-	25	145	-
Mk 5D	-	5	108	-
Mk 5F	41	9	16	-
Mk 5G, 5G/1	-	308	-	105
Mk 5H, 5H/1	84	-	237	1010
Mk 5K, 5K/1	-	11	-	386
Mk 5L	-	-	259	-
Mk 5M	-	-	-	8
Mk 5N	-	-	137	-
Mk 5P	40	-	282	-
Mk 5Q, 5Q/1/2/3	-	-	22	143
Mk 5R	-	-	-	26
Mk 6A, 6A/L	-	9395	1518	-
Mk 6D/L	-	-	1131	-
Mk 7D, 7D/2	-	-	-	5
Mk 7F	-	-	-	5
Mk 7H	-	-	-	2
Mk 7K	-	-	-	141
Mk 7P	-	-	-	15
Mk 8A, 8A/1	-	-	-	221
Mk 8B, 8B/1/2	-	-	-	1082
Mk 8F, 8F/2	-	-	-	812
Mk 8G	-	-	-	9
Totals	19137	14487	4702	3978

* There are places where the alphabetic sequence of variations is not complete: references which appear to be missing can be explained by the fact that other versions (not listed) were specified and detailed by Rolls-Royce, but no actual engines were produced.
** All military variations have been included in the table for the sake of completion, regardless of whether the application is dealt with in this book. However, commercial variations are not included.
*** Figure given is grand total, which can be broken down as total built by Rolls-Royce 2263, Austin, 15,000.

TESTING and ACCEPTANCE

Type testing schedules were laid down by the Ministry of Supply in the original specification documents.

During production, a resident FVRDE representative was on hand to sign-off the engines as they were completed. Virtually all 'B Series' engines were signed-off by either Wally Arnold or John Bushell who were assigned to Crewe for this purpose.

EXPERIMENTAL DEVELOPMENT

It is inevitable during an extended development and manufacturing cycle that one or two 'blind alleys' might be explored and this project was no exception.

In view of the possible difficulties caused by the inherent weight of large cast-iron engines, tests were conducted as early as 1947 on the suitability of cast aluminium for the block. An eight-cylinder unit was cast in aluminium and equipped with dry cylinder liners to give the standard 3.75 inch bore. The experiment was considered sufficiently successful for the War Office to order six similar B60 engines. Although these engines were used only for development work, there is some evidence that the Mk 4 engines, which never did go into production, were to be manufactured in aluminium.

Perhaps as part of a 'what if' project, in 1952, one of these six early experimental engines was also successfully run with the dry liners removed and with special 3.625 inch pistons running directly in the aluminium bores. This work was not pursued beyond the experimental stage.

In response to a projected military need for a low-profile engine, experiments were conducted on a B60 unit with the stroke shortened to 3.60 inches, giving a bore to stroke ratio of 5:4. To counter the shorter stroke, the engine was run at 125% of the standard rev limit, allowing the power output to be maintained at 190bhp. Unfortunately, the vehicle project for which this was destined was cancelled and the engine work subsequently abandoned.

Another oddball appeared in 1951, when the Rolls-Royce development engineers specified and produced one example of what might be described as a B41 engine. This had a bore of 3.75 inches but, unlike the standard designs, was a wet-liner unit. However, for whatever reason, the experiment was not continued.

In 1962, Reg Spencer was involved in a research project aimed at producing a lightweight, hydraulic-tappet replacement for the B60, of about 4 litres capacity, which could perhaps be used in the FVRDE project for the range of aluminium-armoured vehicles which ultimately was to result in the Alvis CVR(T) family. In the event, this engine, which was known at Rolls-Royce as 'Snippet', was not taken up by the Ministry (who preferred the Jaguar XK design) but led directly to the F60 unit fitted into the Vanden Plas 4 litre 'R' (see 'Commercial applications', below).

Experimental OHV direct-injection, glow-plug diesel conversions of both B40 and B80 units were produced in conjunction with consultant engineer Sir Harry Ricardo, whose company had carried out a considerable amount of early research work on cylinder head design, particularly for diesels. Described as 'Ricardo' 36X and 48X diesels, the B40 unit was normally aspirated, while the B80 was supercharged. Photographs exist showing the B40 engine installed in an Austin 'Champ'.

In all probability these engines, which were commissioned by FVRDE, were lacking the power and flexibility of later, more-modern diesel designs, and were not successful. Again, the work was not continued but in a sense, by embracing diesel power, the 'B Series' engines had already been visited by their ultimate fate.

APPLICATIONS

All of the initial design specifications for the vehicles themselves were handled by FVRDE. In consultation with the design team at Rolls-Royce, FVRDE decided which engine was most appropriate for each application. Close contact was maintained between all three parties during the development phase for any vehicle.

Table 1 lists all of the military applications.

OTHER MILITARY APPLICATIONS

The British Army was the major buyer for 'B Series' engines during their long production life, but Rolls-Royce were also keen to exploit the world-wide military sales potential. During the late 1950's and early 1960's, the Company mounted an export drive targeted at other possible military customers.

The sales programme met with some degree of success. For example, rear-mounted B81, Mk 80F engines were used by Leyland Motors to power the SP 12-3 ('Schutzenpanzer Lang') armoured personnel carrier built for the German Bundeswehr. Designed by Hispano-Suiza as a private venture, the SP 12-3 was part of a family of vehicles which also included an ambulance, command and fire control vehicles, anti-aircraft tank, TOW missile launcher, and mortar carrier. Examples were also constructed by Hanomag and Henschel, with all production being carried out between 1958 and 1962.

And again, for the West German Bundeswehr, B60 engines were installed by the French Hotchkiss company in the HS 30 tracked cargo carrier based on the similar 'Schutzenpanzer Kurt' chassis.

A number of B81, Mk 80K engines were supplied to Volvo in Sweden for installation in the Bv 202 over-snow tracked carrier. Although this type of vehicle was used by the British Army, for example in Norway, the more usual specification was for a Volvo engine. It is not known whether the use of the B81, Mk 80K engine (which was an engine with a commercial specification), was a British Army experiment which was not deemed successful, or whether these vehicles were intended for another end user.

Marine applications

Although outside the scope of this book, it is perhaps worth mentioning that the B80, Mk 5C and Mk 5L engines were used in two military vessels: the so-called motor tug, and the heavy ferry, respectively. The heavy ferry was particularly interesting in that it employed four B80 engines, one installed at each corner.

Although not strictly speaking a marine application, twenty-five B60, Mk 5C engines were supplied for use as pump engines on Royal Navy fire tenders (see Chapter 4.7).

COMMERCIAL APPLICATIONS

The design of the 'B Series' was very loosely based on an existing passenger car engine which had been used in pre-war Rolls-Royce and Bentley models. After the war, a variation of the engine was also employed in 'civilian' form in the Mk VI Bentley, and the similar Rolls-Royce 'Silver Dawn', introduced in 1946, and remaining current until 1952, as well as in the Rolls-Royce 'Silver Wraith' 4.25 litre, produced from 1946 to 1951. Although close to the B60 in specification, and often described as such today, this engine was never referred to as a B60 by Rolls-Royce.

Rolls-Royce had announced at the press launch of the 'B Series' engines in 1948 that they did not intend these engines be used in motor car chassis. Having made the announcement that further motor car applications were not envisaged, considerable efforts were made to sell the concept of 'rationalised power', and the whole family of power units to the commercial fleet market for use in other manufacturer's chassis. Presumably it was felt that this would help recover the development costs should the military orders not measure up to the quantities promised; this was probably a wise move since within three years, the numbers of B80 units required were reduced by the cancellation of the FV1300 series 3 ton, and FV14000 series 5 ton chassis.

The sales effort met with a considerable degree of success and typical commercial applications included fire appliances and heavy trucks. There were also examples of applications in aircraft ground power units, static plant of various descriptions, gritters and snow ploughs, and a small number of passenger buses and coaches.

The commercial engine range was actually larger than that standardised by the British Army and included B60, B61, B80, B81, and the higher-power B81SV variants. All commercial applications were given a zero suffix to the 'mark' number (eg, B81, Mk 50F).

Most commercial applications employed the B60 and the sister B61, which the military did not use, but the other variations also enjoyed limited application in civilian life. The engines were particularly favoured by fire appliance manufacturers and Dennis, Douglas and HCB-Angus, for example, were users of the B60/61 and B80/81 units. In fact, the first public appearance of a 'B Series' engine was a B81 installed in a Dennis F14 fire appliance. ERF and Thornycroft also fitted B80/81 engines to their truck chassis.

Strangely, in direct contradiction to the original application policy, Rolls-Royce themselves used one of these engines in a motor car chassis, manufacturing a total of 16 'Phantom IV' limousine chassis between 1950 and 1956 which used what was described as a B80, Mk X engine. This appears to have been the basic B80 unit with an aluminium, rather than cast-iron cylinder head, Stromberg carburettor, and standard commercial accessories. Other variations of this engine were used to power Dennis F7 fire appliances, but the use of the 'Mk X' nomenclature is a little mystifying. Presumably 'X' was used as a type designation to avoid confusing Mk10 with Mk 1O, ie Mk 'ten' vs Mk 1 'commercial'... but if this is the case, it is hard to understand why the Mk X *was* essentially a commercial engine... or was it simply that somebody in the sales office employed Roman numerals, rendering Mk 10 as Mk X.

Perhaps the most interesting commercial application of the engine was the use of four B81 units, in about 1967, to power the fans in a 'hoverlift' heavy transport trailer. The project originated when Wynn's, the heavy haulage company, were trying to find a way of avoiding spending £50,000 on rebuilding a bridge which was of insufficient capacity to bear the weight of a heavy transformer being delivered from the makers, AEI, to a power station in North Wales. The fans were installed in a separate blower vehicle which was coupled to the trailer by flexible ductwork, and sufficient pressure was generated to spread the weight of the trailer and transformer sufficiently so that the bridge did not need to be rebuilt.

Gas-burning versions
'B Series' commercial engines were also developed to operate on either natural gas or propane, and in this form were installed in stand-by generator sets, as well as vehicles such as refuse collectors, skip lorries, milk tankers, etc.

These engines can be identified by the inclusion of a 'G' suffix to the type code; eg, B61G, B81G.

F60 engine
Despite many stories which persist to the contrary, the F60 engine (or FB60 as it was sometimes known) used in the BMC-produced Vanden Plas 'R' 4 litre saloon was not a 'B Series' engine.

Although the lightweight aluminium-alloy F60 had the same bore as the B61, it actually shared more features with the Rolls-Royce aluminium V8 and was developed specifically for high-performance motor car applications. Only ever series-manufactured in one version, with a 3.75 inch bore, and a stroke of 4.60 inches, the F60 had a swept volume of 3909cc. A little-known experimental twin-cam derivative was also produced, known as the G60, and originally destined for the Austin Healey 3000.

The F60 had no components in common with its more restrained 'B Series' cousins.

Diesel wins the day
Unfortunately, in the long run, even for the most enthusiastic commercial fleet operator and supporter of the 'rationalised power' concept, the units were probably too expensive to buy, and too thirsty to run.

It was to little avail that Rolls-Royce attempted to counter this line of argument by pointing out, quite correctly, that running costs should be judged on the basis of horsepower-hours delivered against the initial outlay, and not simply on the purchase price. Whilst this argument might have convinced an accountant, it cut little ice with the cost-conscious fleet operators.

Perhaps the last commercial application was the fire appliance where instant starting, rapid production of full power, acceleration and speed are more important than economy. However, even for these applications, by the late-1960's, diesel engines had become more powerful, flexible and fuel-efficient, and sadly, the day of the large petrol engine had come and gone - taking the commercial 'B Series' with it!

Although its days were largely over, there is little doubt that the Rolls-Royce 'B Series' was the last, and possibly the finest, large commercial petrol engine.

CHAPTER 1.2: RATIONALISED POWER

They weren't always reliable... (IWM)

... a 'Stalwart' REME fitters' vehicle lifts a 'Saladin' engine (BTMC)

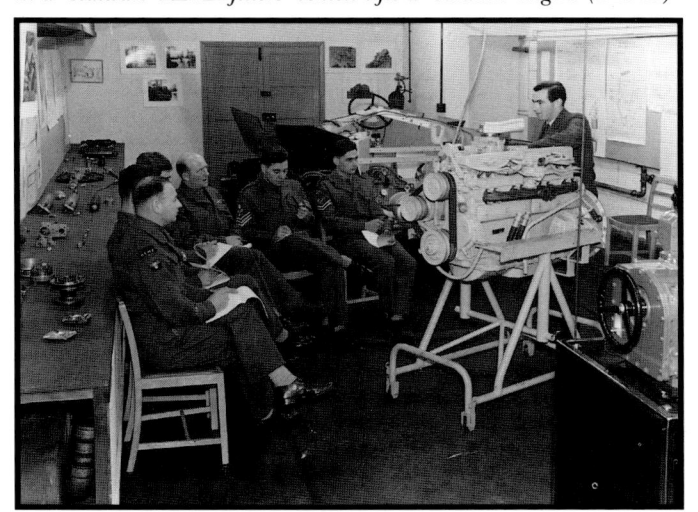

Alvis tries to show REME the way (BTMC)

REPLACEMENT

The same arguments and logic which led to the development of the 'B Series' remain as valid today as they were 50 years ago. However, it can be argued that the enormous variety of military vehicles encountered at the end of WW2 no longer exists.

Despite the problems encountered with the CT vehicle concept, standardisation has finally been achieved by rationalising the vehicle makes and types, and the notion of installing the same type of engine in a wide variety of chassis has fallen by the wayside.

So the 'B Series' has more-or-less finished its days in service and if there is a present day replacement, the choice is either the Jaguar 4.2 litre XK straight-six, or the Rolls-Royce K60 multi-fuel engine. The Jaguar is installed in the Alvis 'Fox' and in the 'Scorpion' family (which also includes the alliterative 'Scimitar', 'Spartan', 'Sultan', 'Samaritan', 'Striker,' and 'Samson' vehicles), while the K60 is used in the GKN-built FV432 (which started life with a B81) and its derivatives.

Since the FV432 is already on the disposal list, and the 'Fox' is likely to be replaced in the next few years, the pace of technological change suggests it is doubtful that either the Jaguar XK or Rolls-Royce K60 engines will be able to match the 'B Series' for longevity.

Unlike the 'B Series', neither of these power units seems likely to still be giving service in the year 2020, some 50 years after their introduction.

CONCLUSION

Regardless of the considerable advances in automotive technology in the last two or three decades, the 'B Series' has remained in service with the British Army, and with close to 30 other armies in some 75 countries worldwide, for almost 50 years. Indeed, at the time of writing (1995), the odd 'B Series' engined 'Ferret' or 'Saracen' can still be found, perhaps tucked away in a base workshop, or standing proudly to attention as a gate guardian.

During their considerable service life, these engines have been used to power a diverse range of equipment, from modest, relatively lightweight vehicles such as the Austin 'Champ', through cranes and tugs, armoured vehicles such as the 'Ferret', 'Saracen', and 'Saladin', up to the massive 8000 lb recovery winch of the 'Centurion' armoured recovery vehicle (ARV).

Rolls-Royce 'B Series' engines have both met and exceeded their design brief admirably, with many units going on to well over 200,000 miles or more before requiring major attention.

DOCUMENTATION

Bibliography

The History of a Dimension. Grylls, S H. London, Institute of Mechanical Engineers, June 1963.

The Magic of a Name. Knockolds, Harold. London, G T Foulis, 1949 (and earlier editions).

CHAPTER 1.3

TECHNICAL DATA
B40, B60, B80, B81

The Rolls-Royce 'B Series' engines were designed, almost regardless of cost, to provide maximum reliability, combined with adequate reserves of power and a long working life. The engines were intended for the widest range of military applications in so-called 'combat' vehicles and AFV's. It was the Ministry of Supply's intention that the combination of standardisation and long-term durability would greatly simplify the supply and maintenance logistics. In this assumption, they were broadly correct.

It is apparent when looking at, or working on these engines that no shortcuts were taken in the design process, and as one would expect from any Rolls-Royce product, the engineering and quality are superb, with all components produced to the highest possible standards. This commitment to quality is always evident in use. Idling is quiet and smooth, and there is very little mechanical noise even at high revolutions. The power is developed relatively low-down in the rev range and the engines pull extremely well from rest in any gear.

The whole engine has that elusive 'carved from the solid' feel.

The Rolls-Royce quality philosophy also manifests itself in the way the engines are assembled, and in the obvious care which has been taken in the design and manufacture of all of the components, even simple items such as clips, brackets and supports.

DESCRIPTION

BSF/UNF

During WW2, the English and American screw-threaded fasteners were produced to different standards. The British threads were based on the 'Whitworth' BSW/BSF system, while the Americans had standardised on the 'National Fine' (NC) and 'National Coarse' (NC) threads. This must have created considerable confusion whenever motor workshops were required to work on both British and American vehicles.

In accordance with the British industry standards, the early engines, up to Mk 4, employed BSF Imperial thread forms. However, in 1951, following the general trend in the British motor industry towards so-called 'unified' threads, the decision was taken to bring the 'B Series' into line with current practice, and later engines employed the new UNF/UNC fasteners, the dimensions of which were based on the American 'National' system.

For a period, components with both thread forms would have been in use at the same time, both in the Rolls-Royce factory and in REME workshops, and obviously this would have been a potential source of problems. In an attempt to overcome this, fasteners with a unified thread were identified by means of interlocked rings stamped on the faces of nuts, and by a small shoulder machined onto the ends of studs and bolts.

At the same time as the thread forms were changed, the crankshaft design was modified and the cylinder heads were produced in cast-iron rather than aluminium-alloy. Various other modifications were made, either to simplify the manufacturing process, or to reduce costs (see Chapter 1.2).

Because of the differences in thread form, early units were sometimes designated 'BSF' engines, while the later units would have been described as 'UNF'.

Crankcase and cylinder block
The cast-iron crankcase and cylinder block were formed as a single casting, with the water jacket core plugs screwed into place.

An integral water jacket allowed coolant to circulate around the cylinder walls, although on B81 (and the commercial B61) engines the bores were 'siamesed' and there was no full water jacket between the pairs of bores. A tubular gallery was installed longitudinally in the left-hand side of the block, drilled to direct coolant around the exhaust valve ports, which of course were also situated in the block.

The cylinder bores were machined into the block casting and dry-fitted with thin-wall wearing sleeves. The sleeves were hydraulically-pressed into the upper ends of the bores to provide a durable wearing surface at the point where the maximum piston thrust occurred. Originally, the sleeves employed on the B40/60/80 engines were just 57mm long, and were manufactured from 'Brichrome' alloy (30% chrome iron) with a wall thickness of 1.57mm.

These short 'Brichrome' sleeves stood accused of causing ring breakage, and for this reason were superseded in production by full-length high-phosphorous cylinder liners (which had always been fitted to B81 units); earlier engines were subsequently upgraded by the installation of these full-length liners on overhaul. Engines which were fitted with the full-length sleeves included an 'F' code following the mark designation; eg, Mk 5A-F.

Two removable tappet chest covers provided access to the exhaust valve gear.

Crankshaft
Engines of Mk 1 through Mk 4 used a fully-machined

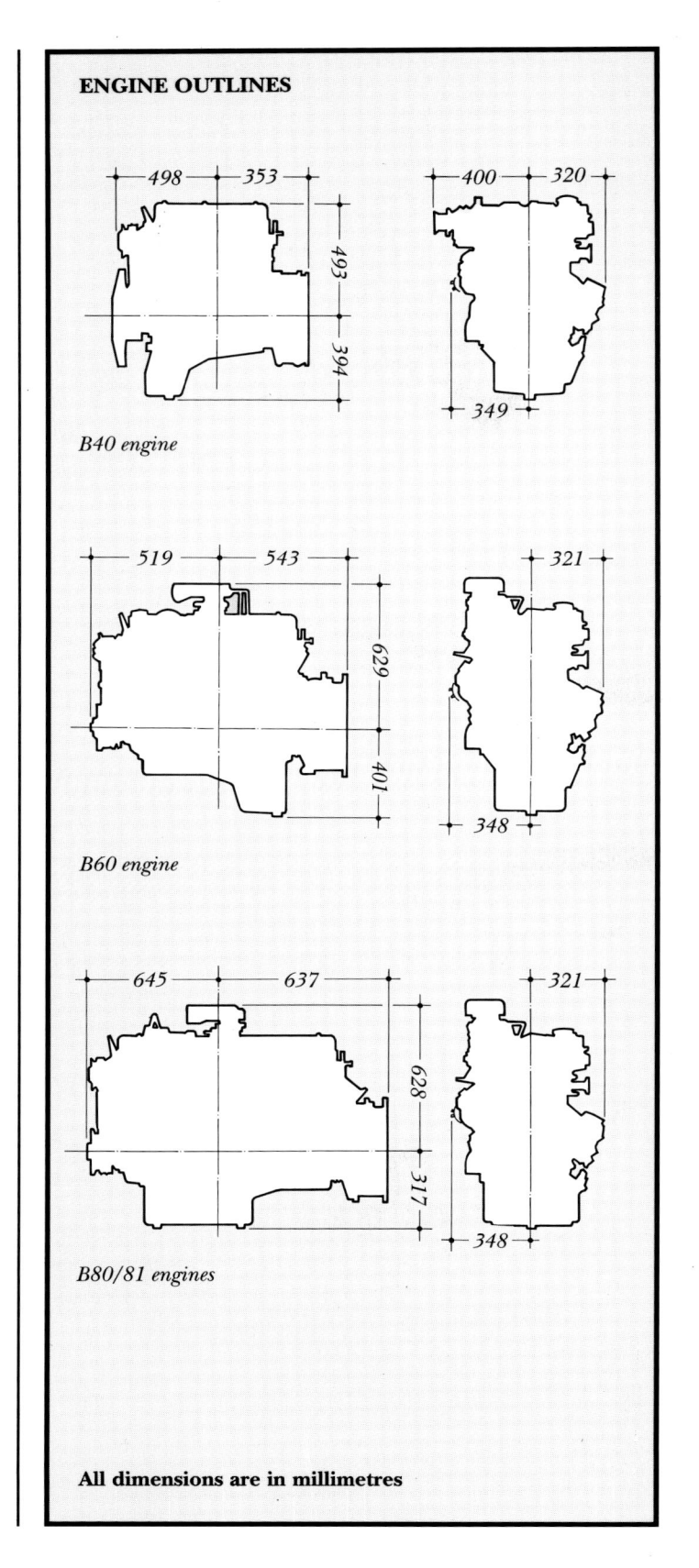

ENGINE OUTLINES

B40 engine

B60 engine

B80/81 engines

All dimensions are in millimetres

CHAPTER 1.3: TECHNICAL DATA

SPECIFICATION

Dimensions and weight

	B40	B60	B80	B81
Overall installed dimensions (mm):				
Length	851	1062	1282	1282
Width	720	669	669	669
Height*	887	1030	945	945
Dry weight (kg)	295	372	454	458
Key internal dimensions (mm):				
Bore	88.9	88.9	88.9	95.25
(inches)	3.50	3.50	3.50	3.75
Stroke	114.3	114.3	114.3	114.3
(inches)	4.50	4.50	4.50	4.50
Swept volume (cc)	2838	4256	5675	6516

* Standard wet sump: figures will vary for other sump configurations.

Performance

	B40	B60	B80	B81
Gross output, uninstalled:				
Bhp at 3750rpm	80	130	165	195-220
Torque (lbs/ft)	138	209	280	330-350
Compression ratio	6.4:1	6.4:1	6.4:1	6.4:1*
Firing order	1342	142635	16258374	16258374
Timing (degrees):				
Ignition (ATDC)**	6/2	6/2	8/TDC	2/TDC
Valves, standard camshaft:				
inlet opens (BTDC)	16	16	16	16
inlet closes (ABDC)	84	84	84	86
exhaust opens (BTDC)	60.5	60.5	60.5	61
exhaust closes (ABDC)	31.5	31.5	31.5	42
Valves, camshaft FV143624:				
inlet opens (BTDC)	-	-	-	11
inlet closes (ABDC)	-	-	-	91
exhaust opens (BTDC)	-	-	-	55.5
exhaust closes (ABDC)	-	-	-	25
Fuel consumption, maximum demand (litres/hr):				
at 3000 rpm	25	39	52	62-64
at 3750 rpm	29	45	61	74-82
Oil capacity (litres):				
Standard wet sump	8	11.33	11.33	11.33

* Certain B81 engines have 6.5:1 and 7.25:1 compression ratio.

** According to mark of distributor fitted.

---

forged crankshaft of heat-treated EN19 steel, with 'Nitrided' (nitrogen-hardened to VPN570 minimum) main bearing and crank pin journals, and integral crank counterweights. The main journals were concentrically bored for lubrication, with the bores blanked-off by shaped washers at the ends.

Mk 5 and later engines, had a simplified drop-forged crankshaft, again with 'Nitrided' bearing surfaces and integral counterweights. Lubrication of the bearing journals was effected by means of holes drilled through the journal into the crank webs, closed at the webs by press-fitted plugs.

Crankshaft bearings
Both types of crankshaft were supported in indium-flushed, thin-wall steel-backed bearings, with a lead-bronze lining. The indium was provided to protect the bearing against corrosion, while the lead-bronze material formed the actual wearing surface. Crankshaft end thrust was taken by split steel-backed lead-bronze thrust washers, fitted either side of the centre main bearing.

To reduce torsional vibration to the minimum, the crankshaft in the four-cylinder engine ran in five main bearings; the six-cylinder unit had seven; the eight-cylinder units, nine.

Crankshaft seals
The crankshaft had a rubber lip-type oil seal fitted into the timing gear housing at the nose end; with an Acme left-hand thread seal at the flywheel end.

Crankshaft damper
In order to further reduce unwanted vibration, the six- and eight-cylinder engines had an external bonded steel-and-rubber friction damper mounted on the nose of the crankshaft, and contained within the lower belt driving pulley.

The damper was not fitted to any of the B40 units.

Connecting rods and pistons
The connecting rods were I-section chrome-molybdenum steel forgings, either fully-machined, or drop forged to size. Each rod was drilled through from big end to small end for lubrication purposes, and a small hole cross-drilled through the rod, directed oil onto the cylinder wall.

The rods were originally weighed and graded in steps of one ounce and colour-coded accordingly; the weight was etched on the radius at the big end. Sets of rods for any particular engine were balanced to within one ounce (28g) per set.

Light aluminium-alloy 'Wellworthy' or 'Aerolite' pistons were employed, tin-coated to a depth of 0.0075mm. The pistons were of solid-skirt design in 'BSF' engines, T-slot split-skirt type in 'UNF' units, and were machined slightly elliptical, with the greater diameter being across the thrust face. Three grooves were provided above the gudgeon pin, fitted with two compression rings (three on B81 engines), one of square section, one of L section, and a 'Duaflex' oil scraper ring. The top ring was chromium-plated.

Although pistons were available in oversizes of 0.010, 0.020, and 0.040 inches for use in rebored units, the inherent durability of the engines was such that it is doubtful any of these were used in any quantity. This is nicely borne out by anecdotal evidence: in the days when smokers outnumbered non-smokers, it was apparently common to find a new, and oversized, 'B Series' piston serving as an ashtray beside most drawing boards in the Rolls-Royce design and engineering departments.

The gudgeon pin was of hollow heat-treated steel, fully-floating in the piston. Aluminium plugs were installed in the ends of the pin to prevent possible damage to the cylinder walls.

Cylinder head

On so-called 'BSF' engines (ie, Mks 1 through 4), the cylinder head was of aluminium-alloy with screwed S65 nickel-chrome steel inserts for the inlet valves, and bronze threaded inserts for the sparking plugs.

On engines of Mk 5 through to Mk 8, the cylinder head was of cast-iron with machined inlet-valve seatings, and with the spark-plug tappings threaded directly into the casting. The use of a cast-iron head on a cast-iron block was intended to avoid problems with differential expansion, giving more even heating of the engine and tending to provide more efficient sealing at the gasket.

The combustion chambers were formed in the cylinder head, and both types of head were jacketed, with cored-in passages for the circulation of cooling water.

A thick copper-asbestos-copper gasket provided a seal at the cylinder head joint.

The aluminium and cast-iron cylinder heads were not interchangeable, nor were their head gaskets.

Camshaft

The camshaft was of nickel-steel, designed to provide low-lift, combined with a long-duration of valve opening.

For the eight-cylinder engines, there were two alternative profiles for the inlet and exhaust cams. The standard camshaft (FV143278) allowed the inlet and exhaust valves to remain open for 102 and 103 degrees of crankshaft rotation respectively, while for camshaft

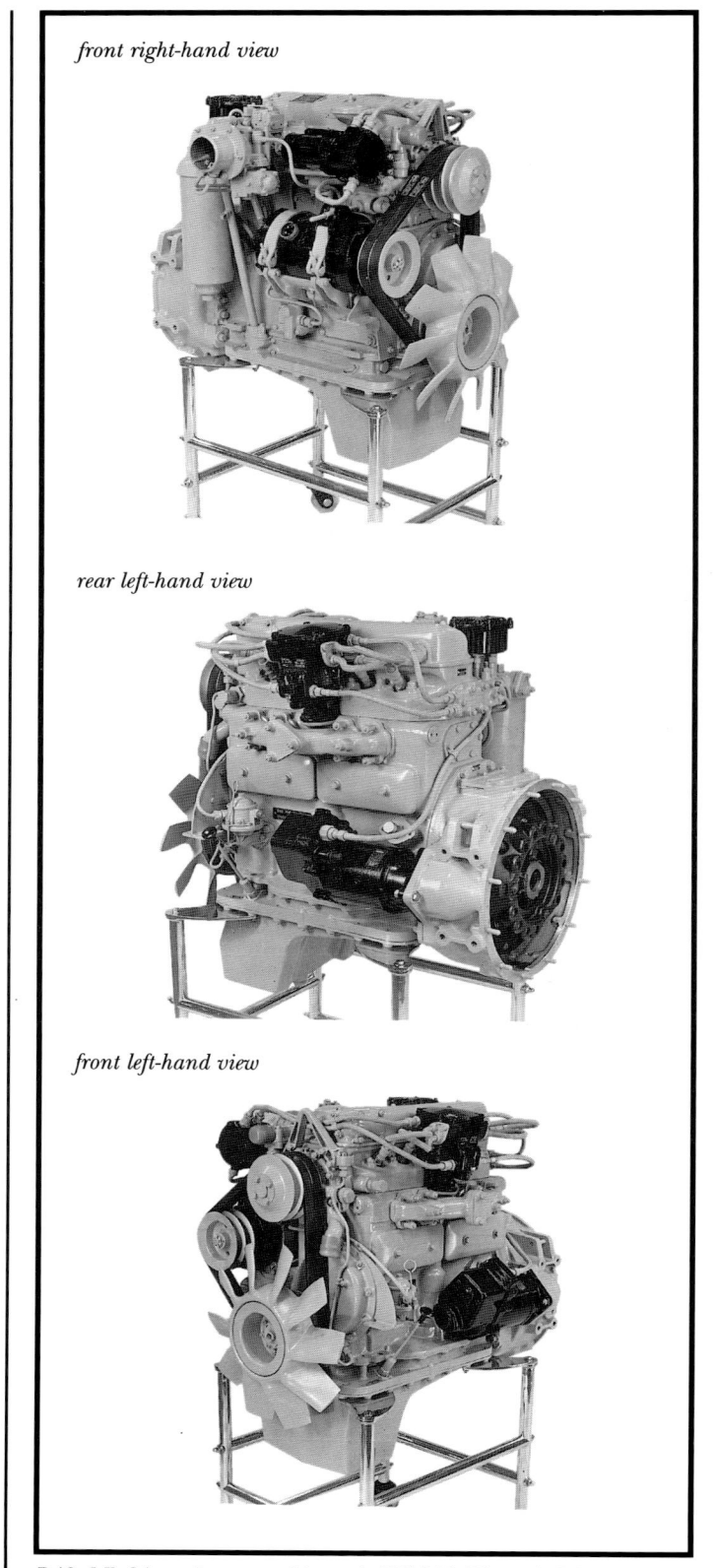

front right-hand view

rear left-hand view

front left-hand view

B40, Mk 2A engine as used in early FV1801 'Champ' (RR)

B40, Mk 5A engine as used in FV1801 'Champ' (RR)

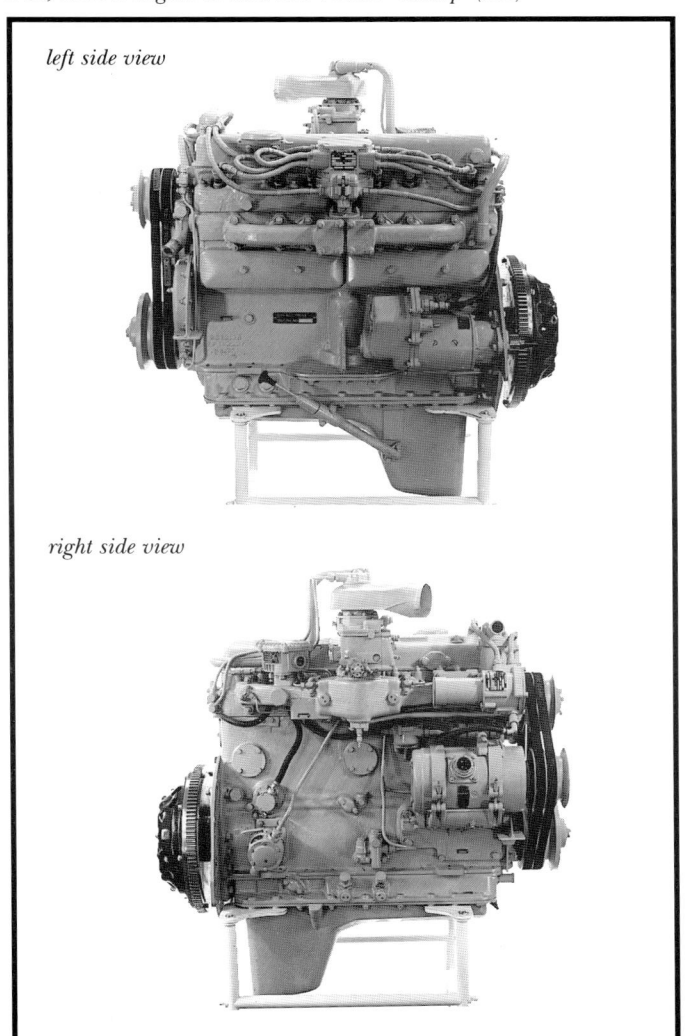

left side view

right side view

B60, Mk 5A engine as used in FV1600 series Humber (RR)

FV143624, the figures were 102 and 80.5 degrees, but with the valves opening some 5 degrees later in the cycle.

The shaft was gear-driven, and supported in thin steel-shell white-metal lined bushes offering a large bearing surface. The bearings, which were drilled for lubrication, were hydraulically-pressed into the crankcase; there were four bushes on the B40 and B60 units, and five on the B80/81.

In addition to the valve cams, the camshaft included an eccentric for driving the fuel pump, and spiral gears for the oil pump, distributor, and tachometer.

Valve gear
The valve configuration was inlet over exhaust (IOE), with two large-headed poppet valves per cylinder. Both the inlet and exhaust valve tappets were adjustable in the normal way. The rockers were of solid cast construction, fitted with a phosphor-bronze bush.

Inlet valves
The inlet valves were set into the cylinder head, operating in cast-iron valve guides. The double valve springs were retained by split conical wedges, and a rubber seal on the valve stem prevented oil running back down the guides.

Exhaust valves
The exhaust valves were set into the cylinder block. The valves themselves were 'Stellite' tipped and seated, running in replaceable phosphor-bronze guides, with a single valve spring.

On B81 engines, the exhaust valves were coated with 'Valray' metal to provide extra resistance to the build-up of corrosive combustion products.

The valve stems were fitted with rotators. These were originally of the 'free-release' type but were superseded later in production by a 'positive-release' design.

Timing gears
The camshaft gear, which was produced in either aluminium-alloy or cast-iron, was spigoted to the camshaft; the alloy gears were intended for all applications except those where a mechanical speed-limiting device was fitted to the engine. A substantial bronze thrust plate was fitted to the crankcase behind the gear. The camshaft driving gear was machined onto the crankshaft.

For those engines provided with an 'Iso-Speedic' mechanical governor, the power take-off for the governor was incorporated in the timing chest, or wheel case as Rolls-Royce called it.

Fuel system
All 'B Series' engines were normally-aspirated, and were originally designed to burn petrol of 68-70 minimum

octane rating (RON). As the quality of fuel improved during the 1960's, and particularly for the higher compression ratio versions, this figure was increased to 80-86 octane.

Although not specifically designed to run on unleaded fuels, according to a Rolls-Royce technical bulletin, the standard exhaust valves and seats could withstand the effects of unleaded fuel for restricted running, without modification. In fact, during the 1950's, the Company were claiming that 'prolonged running could be undertaken on *heavily leaded* fuels without ill-effect'. Providing suitable valves and guides were used, it was suggested that engine life running on unleaded fuels would be four times that achieved on heavily-leaded fuels. This is particularly ironic in the light of modern thinking regarding the effects of unleaded fuels on unprotected valve seats.

To provide rapid warm-up and efficient fuel vapourisation, the inlet manifold was heated by the engine coolant. Alternative types of coolant jacket, long and short, were used on the B80/81 engines, according to the application.

Fuel pump
The fuel pump fitted to the B40 engine was a standard AC Type U, diaphragm-action mechanical pump.

The B60 and B80/81 engines employed a David 'Korrect' P12A Mk 2B, P50/1, P50/2, P51/1 or P51/2 self-priming mechanical fuel pump, also having a diaphragm action. Unusually, the pump was mounted vertically on the crankcase, with the plunger bearing directly on the camshaft at one end, and operating the flexible diaphragm at the other.

Carburettor
Alternative types of carburettor were fitted according to the engine configuration. The B40 engines employed a side-draught Solex type 40 WNHEO/2; all B60 and most B80/81 engines were fitted with a dual-downdraught Solex type 40 NNIP or 40 NNIP/3. The two versions of the 40 NNIP were virtually identical, but the 40 NNIP/3 had an automatic choke. B80, Mk 7 and 8 engines had a Solex 48 NNIP twin-throat downdraught carburettor with manual choke.

The Solex 40 WNHEO/2 used on the four-cylinder engines was an alloy-bodied waterproofed carburettor comprising three basic units. The main carburettor consisted of a conventional choke tube, of 40mm diameter, together with metering jets for normal running; a vacuum pump accelerator device ensured smooth acceleration and full-throttle power; and a separate starting device provided easy starting at temperatures below -18 degrees Celsius.

B80, Mk 2H engine as used in early FV1103 'Martian' (RR))

front left-hand view

front right-hand view

B80, Mk 5H engine as used in FV14103 'Nubian' (RR)

CHAPTER 1.3: TECHNICAL DATA

left side view

front right-hand view

B81, Mk 5R engine as used in FV14161 'Nubian' (RR)

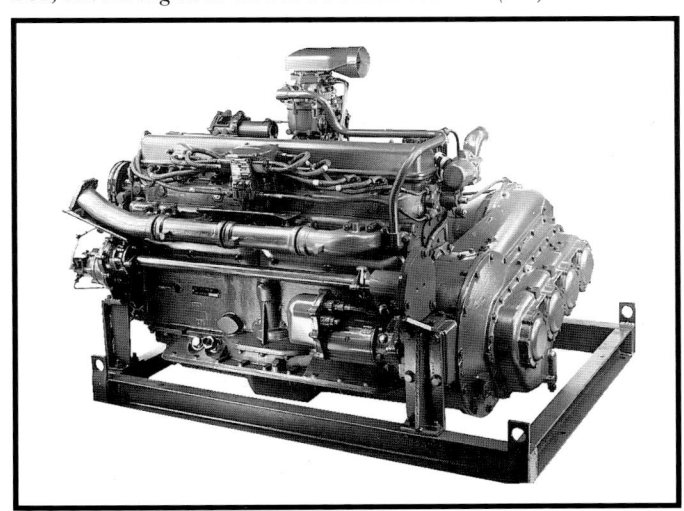

B81, Mk 8F power pack as used in FV432 'Trojan' (RR)

The Solex 40 NNIP and 48 NNIP units fitted to the larger engines were dual-downdraught cast-iron bodied carburettors, also waterproofed for wading. Two float chambers were fed through a single needle valve to two choke sets, each of 40mm or 48mm diameter, according to model, and through metering jets. The mixture was automatically enriched when required, either from twin accelerator pumps or from a single economy jet which served both chokes. One four-position starting device was provided, common to both throats, and a manually-operated adjustment on the carburettor body allowed automatic correction for the effects of oxygen starvation at higher altitudes.

Early prototype B80 engines (Mk 1D) were fitted with a Carter WCD 583S or WED 578S dual-downdraught carburettor, with each choke supplying fuel to four cylinders; photographs also exist of development engines fitted with SU carburettors.

Ki-gass cold start device

The Ki-gass cold-starting equipment was designed to inject an atomised high-volatility fuel, such as ether, directly into the inlet manifold to facilitate starting under extreme low-temperature conditions. Similar equipment was used on the 'Merlin' aircraft engine.

The priming pipework, non-return valve and atomisers for the Ki-gass system were fitted as standard to the inlet manifolds of engine models as follows:

B40 Mks 2A/4 and 5A.
B60 Mk 5A.
B80 Mks 2P, 3A, 5C, 5D, 5P, 6A, and 6D.
B81 Mks 5H and 5K.

The pipework and non-return valve only was fitted to engines B60 Mks 3A and 6A.

The final components of the system included a hand priming pump and fuel tank which would have been fitted elsewhere on the vehicle. However, very few of the production vehicles appear to have been fitted with either the pump or the Ki-gass reservoir.

Lubrication system

In the standard wet-sump configuration, oil was taken from the sump and delivered by high-pressure pump to the main oil gallery in the crankcase, and then to the high-pressure side of the relief valve. The valve controlled the pressure in the lubrication system at about 241kN/sq m.

Most military applications employed a simple low-oil pressure warning light, with the pressure reading taken as near to the main bearings as possible.

THE ROLLS-ROYCE 'B SERIES' ENGINE

From the gallery, the oil was fed to the main bearings, camshaft bushes, and to the driving gears for the oil pump and distributor. From the main bearings, drillings conducted the oil to the big ends, the small ends, and through a spray jet to the cylinder walls.

Where a two-speed generator was fitted, a high-pressure oil supply for the generator gearbox was taken by flexible pipe from the main gallery, with a separate return to the sump.

The low-pressure side of the relief valve was connected by external pipes and oilways to the rocker gear and to the timing gears.

In the dry-sump engine, oil was drawn from a tank by the pump and delivered to the oil filter; oil circulation was the same as that already described for the wet sump design. Excess oil was returned by the combined scavenge/pressure pump, via the oil cooler, to the tank.

Oil cooler
For most applications, B60 and B80/81 engines were fitted with a gilled-tube external oil cooler, interposed between the oil pump and the filter, and located in a convenient under-bonnet position.

Oil pump
Alternative types of oil pump were used according to the sump configuration; both types of pump were gear-driven directly from the camshaft.

The wet-sump engines employed a conventional alloy-bodied spur gear-type pump.

On dry-sump engines, a gear-type pressure pump on the delivery side was combined in a two-part casing with a gear-type scavenge pump designed to return oil from the shallow sump to the tank. The angle of the pump gear teeth was designed so that there was no compression of the oil during pumping.

Oil filter
Oil filters were of two types, supplied either by Tecalemit (paper element), or British Filters (felt element); the elements were interchangeable, though the housings and gasket arrangements were different.

Oil entered the filter bowl directly from the sump, and was circulated through the element via the oil-pressure relief valve to the main gallery. The filter was of the by-pass type and if it became clogged with sediment, the by-pass valve opened to allow unrestricted flow.

Oil-pressure relief valve
The oil-pressure relief valve was mounted externally on the right-hand side of the crankcase for easy access, and consisted of two spring-loaded valves in series, designed to open at 241kN/sq m and to close at 24kN/sq m.

Alvis show how to check the tappet clearances (BTMC)

AC fuel pump on B40, Mk 5A engine

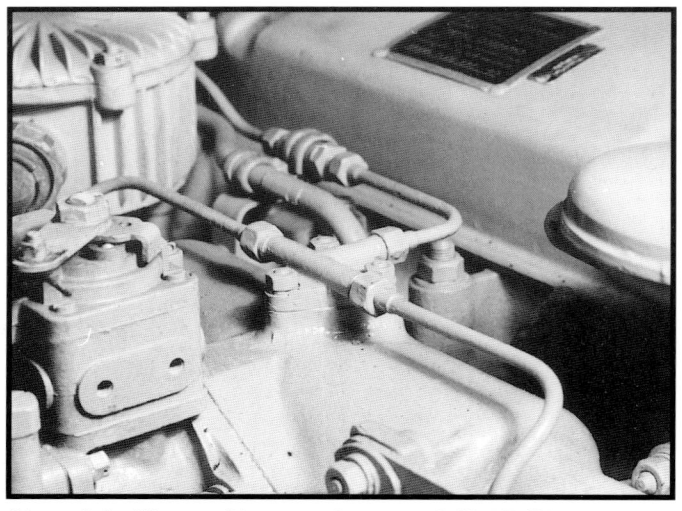

Pipework for Ki-gass cold-start equipment on B40, Mk 5A engine

CHAPTER 1.3: TECHNICAL DATA

Solex 40 WNHEO/2 carburettor as used on B40 engines

Solex 40 NNIP carburettor as used on B60/80/81 engines

Water pump on B40, Mk 5A engine

Sump design
The well reservoir of the standard wet-sump system was designed to allow continuous operation at the extreme angles likely to be encountered during serious off-road use. Full lubrication was maintained at up to 25 degree forward/backward tilt, and 15 degree tilt from side to side. A modified deep-well wet sump allowed these angles to be increased to 40 degrees and 30 degrees respectively.

The dry-sump system allowed operation at more extreme angles, whilst maintaining the minimum height dimension.

In both cases, the sump was attached to the crankcase via an adapter plate which had pipe unions and adapters mounted to it for oil supply and return. The use of this adapter plate allowed the sump to be readily reversed, or replaced with one of a different configuration, as well as permitting easy conversion from wet to dry sump.

Cooling system
The engines were water-cooled in the conventional manner with coolant designed to circulate by pump-assisted thermo-siphon action through passages formed in the castings around the cylinder bores, the combustion chambers and the valve seats.

The flow of coolant passed from the bottom of the radiator through the water pump into the gallery in the cylinder block, and thence into the cylinder head, and induction manifold. From the manifold it was either returned to the top of the radiator through the thermostat, once the engine reached normal operating temperature, or back through the pump during the warming-up period. On the B81 (and commercial B61) engines, the cylinders were 'siamesed' and the flow of coolant between adjacent bores was restricted.

The normal operating temperature was 70-75 degrees Celsius. The cooling system was pressurised to 7kN/sq m, raising the boiling point to 115 degrees Celsius.

Water pump
The water pump was mounted on the front of the cylinder block, with a vane-type rotor driven by tandem belts. Water was prevented from seeping into the bearings by either a packless gland, or a 'Flexibox' gland.

In some applications, the water pump driving pulley was also provided with flanges for driving ancillary equipment.

Fan
On B40, Mk 2A/2F and Mk 5A/5F/5H engines, in order to help maintain a low profile, the 10-bladed alloy cooling fan was mounted directly to the nose of the crankshaft, rather than on the water pump. Drive was transmitted via

CHAPTER 1.3: TECHNICAL DATA

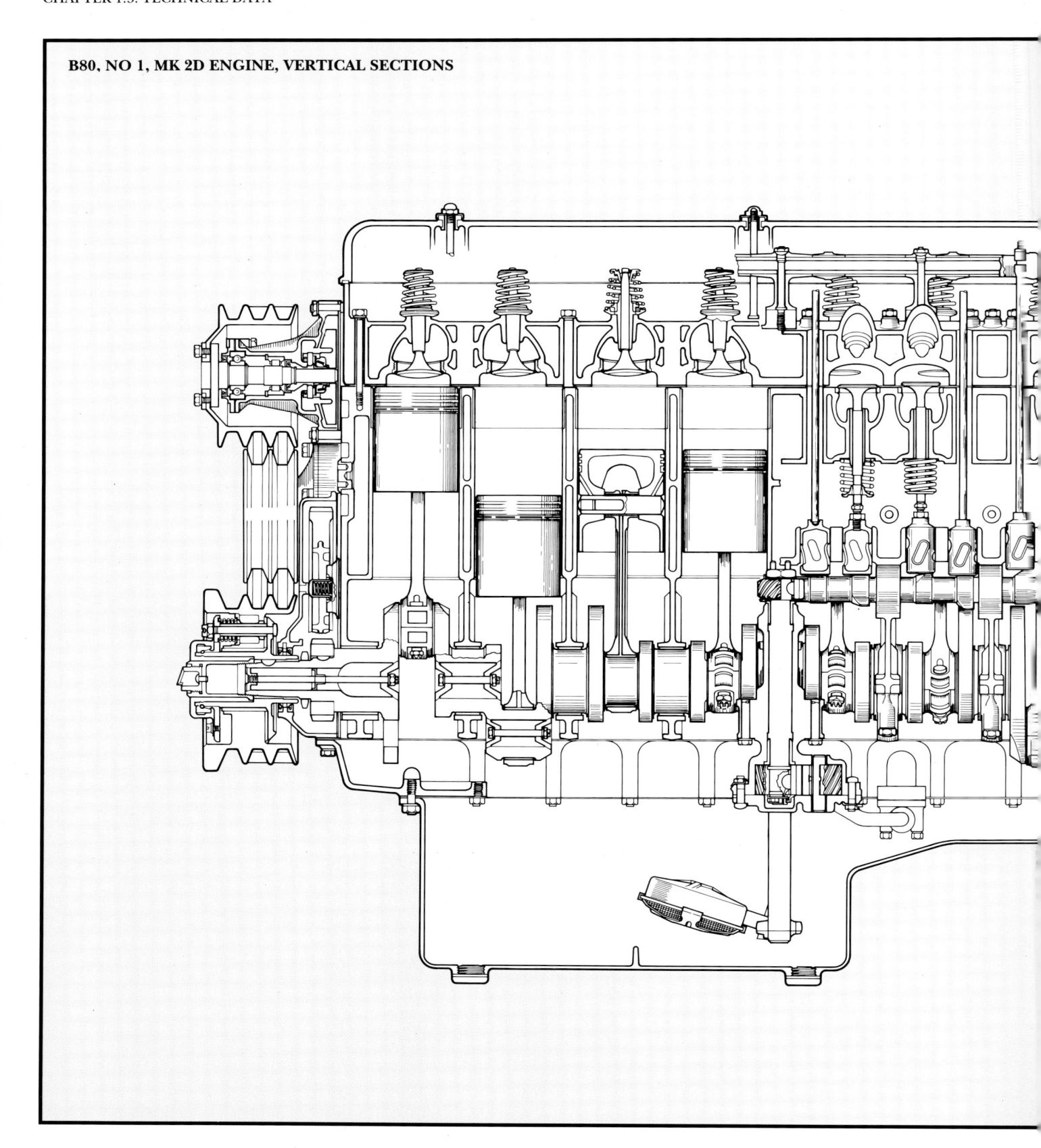

B80, NO 1, MK 2D ENGINE, VERTICAL SECTIONS

CHAPTER 1.3: TECHNICAL DATA

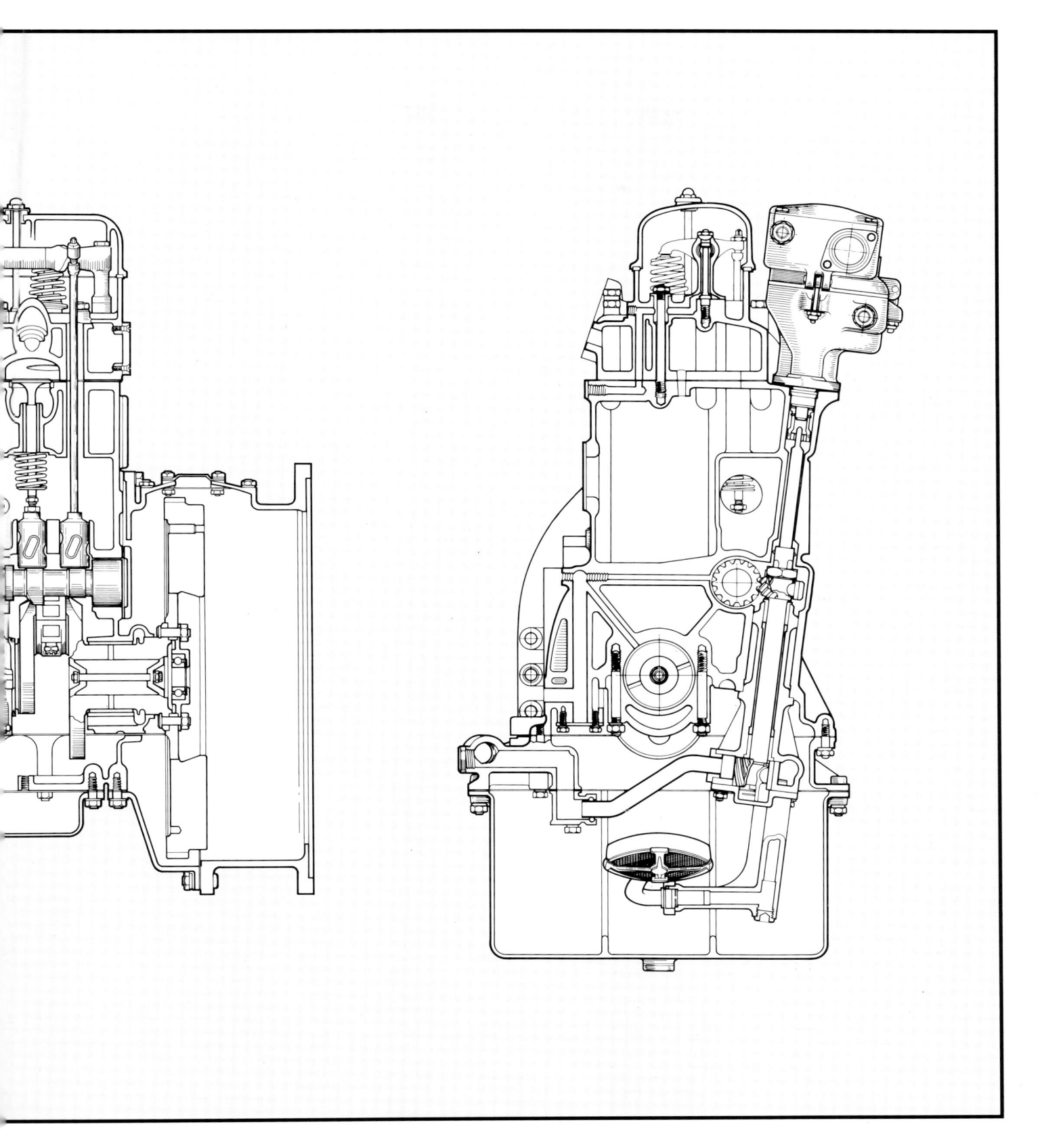

a belt and friction clutch which stopped the fan from rotating should it meet any sort of obstacle; this prevented the fan from drowning the engine during wading.

On the B40, Mk 2B engine employed in the Land Rover, a five-bladed fan was mounted on a flange on the water pump, and again, driven by tandem belts.

On most B60 and B80/81 engines, a 10-bladed alloy fan was installed in a shaped radiator cowl. The fan was mounted on a flange on the water pump, belt-driven by tandem belts from the crankshaft pulley.

In the Alvis 'Saladin' and 'Stalwart' applications, twin alloy cooling fans were installed side-by-side in the radiator cowl, mounted on idler shafts, and belt-driven from the water pump.

The fan belts were tensioned by adjusting the generator position in the normal way. In those applications where no generator was installed, a belt-tensioning device was fitted in its place.

Thermostat
The thermostat was a conventional bellows-type unit, produced by Smiths Industries, and employing a mushroom valve to restrict the water supply. As the valve opened, it progressively closed the by-pass aperture. Later models had a jiggle pin and bleed hole in the valve head to reduce the engine warm-up time.

The thermostat was designed to open and close in the temperature range 70-75 degrees Celsius.

Power coupling
Vehicles with a conventional gearbox, and those engines installed in static plant, were provided with a standard clutch and flywheel; engines fitted to vehicles with pre-selector gearboxes employed a Daimler 'fluid flywheel' or torque convertor.

Those engines used to drive the hydraulic pumps in the 'Centurion' bridgelayer vehicles had no clutch; a short propeller shaft was attached to the flywheel, connecting the engine to the hydraulic pump.

Clutch and flywheel
The B40 engine was fitted with a 305mm Borg and Beck dry-plate clutch; on B60 engines, the clutch was 280mm diameter.

B80/81 engines employed a 280mm or 305mm twin dry-plate clutch, consisting of two driven plate assemblies. The clutch was fitted to the splined end of the gearbox driven shaft, consisted of a cover assembly bolted to the flywheel, two friction plates, and an intermediate pressure plate.

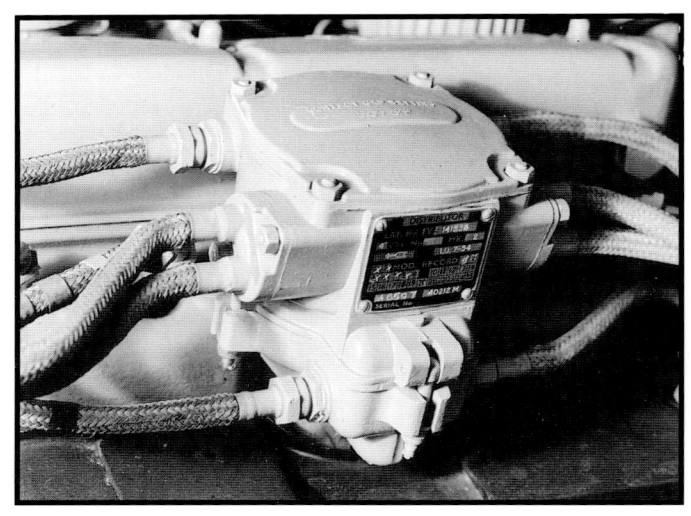

Distributor on B40, Mk 5A engine

Ignition coil

Ignition filter

Spark plugs 'No 1, Mk 1'

Generator 'No 1, Mk 1'

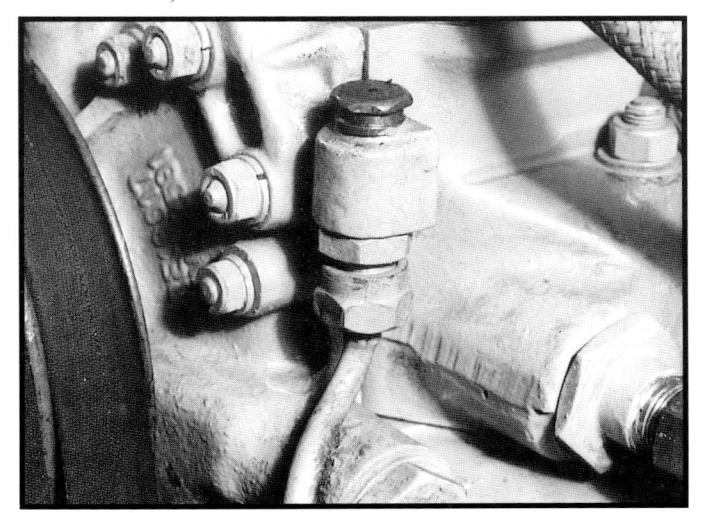

Timing case fording seal lubricator

On those engines equipped with a clutch, the flywheel was a heavy steel casting, machined on one surface to provide a clutch facing, and fitted with a shrunk-on starter ring. The flywheel was balanced, off the engine, at the time of manufacture.

Torque convertor

The engines installed in all vehicles equipped with the Wilson epicyclic pre-selective gearbox, for example the 'Ferret' and 'Stalwart', were fitted with an open-circuit, fluid flywheel, or hydraulic power coupling.

The unit consisted of three major components: the front casing, which was bolted to the engine crankshaft; the rear casing, or impeller, which was bolted to the front casing and formed the driving member; and the runner or driven member, which was splined to the gearbox input shaft. The runner and rear casing consisted of bowl-shaped castings of aluminium-alloy divided by radial ribs or vanes to form cells for the transmission fluid.

The whole assembly was contained within a housing bolted to the crankcase and gearbox assemblies, and the coupling was filled to a predetermined level with transmission fluid.

As the rear casing rotates under engine power, the oil contained in the cells is thrown outwards by centrifugal force, filling the corresponding cells in the runner and exerting force on the sides of the vanes. This tangential force causes the runner to rotate in the same direction as the rear casing, transferring motion to the gearbox input shaft. As oil enters the outer edges of the runner cells, it displaces oil from the inner edges into the rear casing. For circulation of the transmission fluid to be established, and thus for the coupling to operate, there must be a difference in speed between the two members: this is referred to as the 'slip'.

The unit is completely automatic in operation. With the engine idling, there is maximum slip, and negligible power is transmitted to the fluid: the vehicle can be held against the brakes, or allowed to creep forward. As the engine speed rises, the fluid exerts a progressively greater pressure on the driven member, until the two parts of the coupling are rotating almost as one. However, even at maximum power, there is still a slip factor of approximately 2%.

The hydraulic coupling is an extremely efficient and reliable component with a minimum of wearing parts. It is, however, liable to damage from excessive heat if allowed to slip unnecessarily, for example by driving in too high a gear with the engine labouring, by leaving the vehicle idling in gear for long periods, or by towing an excessively heavy load.

Electrical equipment

The engine electrical equipment consisted of the ignition system, starter, generator, water temperature sender, and oil pressure switch. All components were waterproofed, tropicalised, and screened and filtered to reduce electrical interference to wireless signals.

Alternative marks of most units were available, and these were normally interchangeable as a complete unit.

Ignition system

The ignition system consisted of a conventional coil and distributor design, with all of the equipment waterproofed and fully-screened against radio interference on both HF and VHF wavebands (to FVRDE Specification 2051).

The system also included an electrical filter unit, installed on the induction side of the crankcase, designed to suppress interference to radio signals.

Distributor

Despite its unorthodox appearance, the distributor was fully conventional, and was driven by the camshaft through a shaft extension on the oil pump drive. The direction of rotation was clockwise. The distributor body was sealed against the ingress of water, with the cap further protected by a screwed metal enclosure.

Twin contact-breaker points were fitted to the distributors used on six- and eight-cylinder engines. Automatic advance and retard of the spark was handled by a centrifugal rolling-weight mechanism. For six-cylinder engines, the operating range was 0 to 20-25 degrees on early distributors, and 0 to 20-22.75 degrees on later models; for eight-cylinder engines, the range was 0 to 14-15.5 degrees.

On the engines intended for most of the purely-automotive applications, the rotor arm incorporated a centrifugal earthing facility designed to short out the HT spark when a predetermined number of revolutions of the distributor was reached; the usual setting was equivalent to an engine speed of 3750rpm (plus or minus 100rpm).

The distributors used on B40 and B80/81 engines shared the same cap, but on the (B40) four-cylinder version only four of the eight electrodes were used.

Distributors were manufactured by either Lucas (No 1, Mk 2) or Delco-Remy (No 1, Mk 1 or Mk 2/1).

Ignition coil

Although all of these engines were designed for use with 24V military electrical systems, the low-tension side of the coil operated at 12V via a ballast resistor. The resistor was contained in a junction box mounted on the rear end of the inlet manifold, and was shorted out during

'Saracen' undergoing wading trials (REME)

'Mudlark' undergoing trials in the Chertsey wading tank (IWM)

Engine service record and container tube

starting, making the full 24V available for the strongest possible spark.

In addition to the ignition system, this junction box was also used as a connection point for the starter solenoid and oil pressure switch.

Coils were supplied by Lucas or Delco-Remy.

Sparking plugs
The military designation for the plugs was 'No 1, Mk 1', or 'No 1, Mk 1/1'. These were long-reach (19mm), three-piece, demountable 14mm threaded plugs, with a built-in resistor to reduce burning of the electrodes. Both types of plug were screened against radio interference.

In order to extend their working life and to provide the maximum reliability, the plugs incorporated platinum (4% tungsten) electrodes. On the 'No 1, Mk 1' plug, the centre electrode was of platinum, while on the 'No 1, Mk 1/1', it was the earth electrode.

The ignition leads were insulated with 7mm 'Neoprene' rubber, and were housed in special 'Toplock' braided conduit, designed to both exclude water and to provide radio screening. Screwed connectors were used at the plug and distributor terminations.

Starter motor
Two alternative types of starter were fitted, described in that inimitably prosaic military way as 'Starter, No 1', available in 'Mks 1-4, Mks 2/1 and 3/1', and 'Starter, No 2', Mks 1A, 1A/1, 1B and 1B/1'.

Manufactured by either CAV or Simms, the complete units were fully interchangeable, but individual components of one manufacturer could not be used with starters produced by the other. Both types were similar, and consisted of a waterproofed or semi-waterproofed, tropicalised 24V four-pole series-wound motor, with a solenoid-operated pre-engaged pinion.

The design provided for a relatively-slow, but positive engagement with the engine before full power was applied. A light coil pulled the pinion into engagement and allowed slow rotation; a heavier coil held the pinion in and allowed full power to be applied.

The drive was transmitted through a spring which both assisted engagement between the flywheel and pinion, and protected the motor against shocks due to torque reversal as the engine fired.

The pinion had either 11 teeth ('No 1' starters) or 13 teeth ('No 2' starters), and was manufactured from either aluminium-bronze alloy or steel.

Generator
Like the starter, alternative types of generator were fitted, manufactured by either CAV or Simms. Later engines were fitted with a CAV alternator, and many earlier installations were modified retrospectively.

The generator was mounted on a substantial cradle bolted to the crankcase, with a separate adjuster strut bracket. The driving belt tension was adjusted by means of a threaded strut.

DC generators
For applications with a low power requirement, 'Generators No 1, Mks 1 and 1/2', and 'No 2, Mks 1, 2 and 2/1' were employed; for applications where a higher output is required, the 'Generator, No 4, Mk 1' was fitted. All three were relatively massive machines, particularly the 'No 1' and 'No 2' units when their size is compared to their relatively modest power output.

'Generators, No 1, Mks 1 and 1/2' were shunt-wound single-speed units with a rated output of 12A at 28.5V. The units were both waterproofed and tropicalised.

Similarly, 'Generators, No 2, Mks 1, 2, and 2/1', and 'No 4, Mk 1' were waterproofed, tropicalised shunt-wound machines, but were equipped with an automatic (centrifugal) epicyclic gearbox. At low operating speeds, the generator output was maintained at 25A for the 'No 2' machines, and 75A for the 'No 4' (at 28.5V); the gearbox automatically changed gear at 1800-2000rpm (pulley speed) to prevent excess output. The generator gearbox was connected to the engine lubrication system and pressure fed from the oil pump.

The two-speed generators were designed for use where there was likely to be a heavy power requirement during periods whilst the vehicle was stationary. Examples would include FFW/FFR vehicles where radio operation created a considerable drain on the batteries, or armoured vehicles such as the 'Saladin' where the turret was operated electrically.

Alternators
Alternative types of alternator were installed; the largest of these being the 'Alternator, No 10, Mk A'. This was a high-output machine, semi-waterproofed designed to give a maximum of 90A, 24V and 1A, 28.5V at rotation speeds of 1900-9250rpm. An integral silicon diode rectifier system converted the ac output to dc.

Oil pressure switch
A pressure-operated switch was spigoted to the inlet side of the engine crankcase, and connected to a 'low oil pressure' warning lamp on the driver's switchboard.

The switch was adjustable, but was normally set to operate at 21-83kN/sq m.

Ancillary components
Speed limiter
The engines employed in most of the automotive applications were fitted with a centrifugal earthing device built into the rotor arm, designed to automatically inhibit the HT spark when a predetermined number of revolutions of the distributor was reached. For most applications, the unit was set at 3750rpm, plus or minus 100rpm (engine speed); on B80, Mks 2H, 5H, and 5L, and B81, Mks 2H and 5H, the setting is 4000rpm, plus or minus 100rpm.

The Leyland 'Martian' recovery vehicle (see Chapter 4.5) was fitted with both an ignition speed limiter, set at 4000rpm, and a mechanical governor set at 3750rpm (see below).

Engine governor
Engines intended for static plant applications, and for applications such as heavy lifting, were fitted with an 'Iso-Speedic' centrifugally-operated mechanical governor which was driven off the camshaft gears, and designed to maintain the engine at any predetermined speed between 2000 and 3750rpm, plus or minus 100rpm. A control facility was also available which provided a degree of adjustment.

Power take-off
The larger and heavier vehicles, such as the 'Stalwart', 'Martian', 'Saladin' and 'Saracen' were fitted with hydraulic power-assisted steering. The power for the steering system was derived from a hydraulic pump, belt-driven at half engine speed from a power take-off installed on the exhaust side of the engine.

The engine power take-off on the 'Stalwart' and 'Martian' was also used to drive the brake compressor.

COMPONENT INTERCHANGEABILITY

The design brief originally called for some 85-90% of wearing components to be interchangeable across the whole range and by and large, this was achieved. Each engine required in the order of 207 different parts; of these, some 184 components were common to the three basic types of engine.

Shared components included the pistons and piston rings (not interchangeable between B40/B60/B80 and B61/B81); connecting rods; valves (inlet valves not interchangeable on B40/B60/B80, and B61/B81), valve springs, and rocker arms; timing gears, of which there were two types, and timing chest cover; the oil pump and filter; the generator and starter motors; the water pump (although there were several pulley designs); ignition equipment, including the coil, distributor, ignition leads, and plugs; and many brackets and minor components.

The commitment to commonality was taken very seriously and, for example, an ingenious approach to the distributor design meant that, by using dual contact-breaker points, the same cap could be used for both the four- and eight-cylinder versions.

And of course, virtually all the special tools were equally suitable for working on the four-cylinder units, as they were for working on the six or eight; see 'Special tools', below.

WATERPROOFING

All of these engines were waterproofed (or splashproofed) for wading to a depth of around 2000mm by sealing the electrical components in watertight compartments, by raising the various engine vent lines and air intakes above the waterline, and by employing waterproofed and semi-waterproofed starters and generators. In addition, in armoured vehicles, the hull usually provided a complete enclosure for the engine from below, which helped to keep the water out.

In order to help prevent water from entering the timing case at the crankshaft pulley oil seal, a special fording seal configuration was provided, designed to be filled with grease (similar seals were also provided at the vehicle gearbox and axle shaft oil seals). The seal consisted of a pair of conventional lip-type oil seals installed back-to-back, with the space between filled with grease; over-enthusiastic use of the grease gun tended to lift the lips of the seals and to cause oil leaks at this point.

Of course, none of this meant that the vehicle could be waded to 2000mm without additional preparation since other areas such as axle and gearbox breathers, and ancillary electrical equipment would be vulnerable to the ingress of water.

As a further aid to wading for the Austin 'Champ', where the engine compartment was effectively open from below and the engine was close to the waterline, the B40 engine was also provided with a friction clutch drive for the fan designed to disengage if the fan met any obstacle. This would prevent water from being thrown all over the engine during deep-water wading. Curiously, this fan was also employed in a number of other B40 applications, such as the Jones KL 66 crane, even where the height of the engine installation compared to the wading depth might have rendered its use unnecessary.

Some startling period photographs exist which show vehicles travelling virtually completely submerged, sometimes with only the driver (in some cases wearing frogman's clothing), and the air intake exposed above the waterline.

ENGINE LIFE

In recognition of the very considerable mileages available from these engines, which in some circumstances could exceed 300,000 miles, it was REME policy not to 'waste' potential engine life. During base overhauls, 'B Series' engines were never simply rebuilt (ie, rebored and reground) regardless of condition.

The stated repair policy was that if at all possible, all 'B Series' engines received by base workshops were to be returned to a fit state by 'specified repair'. Complete overhaul was only to be only carried out where examination showed this to be necessary. Unlike 'overhaul' which meant that every part of the engine had been replaced or reclaimed in some way to return the unit to as near as possible its original condition, 'specified repair' did not involve the complete stripping and examination of all of the parts of an engine but only those components which had failed or were not operating within tolerances.

The 'base standard' for overhaul stated that the engine performance should be of the same order as new, with the durability not less than 80% (of that when new).

Engines which were returned to service after either overhaul or specified repair did not lose their identity or history. Mileage figures were transferred to the parent system log book, or entered on the service record certificate (see 'Engine service record', below) of those engines destined for storage.

In view of the exceptional service life available from these units, and the stated repair policy, it is somewhat ironic that heavier vehicles were often disposed of after a lengthy military career, with just a few thousand miles, or in some cases less than a thousand miles, showing on the odometer.

Testing
Before overhaul, components such as the cylinder head, crankshaft and flywheel would be magnetically crack-tested, and then de-magnetised. Connecting rods would be checked for straightness. The block and head would be thoroughly de-greased before being cleaned of internal rust and scale, and pressure-tested for porosity.

After overhaul, or after any specified repair intended to return the unit to 'Class 1' standard, REME policy called for the engines to be bench-tested for a total of two hours, including a five-minute run at 4000rpm.

During the test, the power and torque curves were measured and the engine was checked for leaks, noise, oil pressure, oil consumption, oil temperature, water temperature, and fuel consumption. Tuning and minor rectifications were carried out on the test bench, but if any major faults were encountered, the engine was returned to the workshop.

Engine service record
Unlike, for example the engine of a Land Rover or contemporary Humber 'Super Snipe' staff car which was considered to be 'disposable', REME rated the 'B Series' engines sufficiently significant to warrant detailed record-keeping during the life of the unit. In accordance with normal practice for major equipment items, every engine was accompanied by a manufacturer's approval certificate. This certificate stayed with the unit, and served as a record of modifications and major overhaul work carried out on the engine during its life.

Printed on linen-backed paper and signed by the inspecting engineer, this certificate was rolled up and stored in a water-tight tube, normally bolted to the thermostat housing.

SPECIAL TOOLS

Aside from considerations of cost and stockholding, another of the major advantages of standardisation was that whatever tools were required for, say the four-cylinder engine, would work just as effectively with the eight.

The engines were relatively conventional in design and assembly techniques, and the minimum of special tools were required. The following were listed in the various EMER's:

Camshaft tools
Drawbar for fitting and extracting camshaft bushes
Reaming bar and reamers for camshaft bushes

Extractor tools
Extractor for coolant pump bearings
Extractor for crankshaft damper
Extractor for fan pulley, water pump rotor and dynamo pulley
Extractor for rear main bearing cap
Extractor for thermostat
Extractor for wheelcase dowel

Miscellaneous tools
Box spanner for crankshaft damper retaining nut
Drain plug tool
Clutch alignment mandrel
Core plug spanners
Piston ring compressor
Timing lamp

Valve tools
Valve holder
Inlet valve compressor tool
Inlet tappet spanners, internal and external

Reamer for inlet valve guide, 0.3441in
Exhaust valve compressor tool
Exhaust tappet spanner
Locking plate for exhaust tappet
Reamer for exhaust valve guide, 0.3759in

DOCUMENTATION

Technical publications

Technical handbooks
Data summary: Rolls-Royce B Series engines, all marks. EMER Power S520.
Technical description:
B Series engines. EMER Power S522.
B40 engines. EMER Power S522/1.
B60 engines. EMER Power S522/2.
B80 engines. EMER Power S522/3.
B81 engines. EMER Power S522/4.

Engine build-up data
Engine, 4-cylinder, SI, type B40:
No 1 Mk 2A/4. EMER Power A267/1.
No 1 Mk 5A. EMER Power A267/2.

Engine, 6-cylinder, SI, type B60:
No 1 Mk 2A. EMER Power A267/3.
No 1 Mk 5A. EMER Power A267/4.
No 1 Mk 3A. EMER Power A267/5.
No 1 Mk 6A. EMER Power A267/6.

Engine, 8-cylinder, SI, type B80:
No 1 Mk 2D. EMER Power A267/7.
No 1 Mk 5D. EMER Power A267/8.
No 1 Mk 3A. EMER Power A267/9.
No 1 Mk 6A. EMER Power A267/10.
No 1 Mk 6D. EMER Power A267/11.
No 1 Mk 2P. EMER Power A267/12.
No 1 Mk 5P. EMER Power A267/13.
No 1 Mk 5C. EMER Power A267/14.
No 1 Mk 5L. EMER Power A267/15.

Engine, 8-cylinder, SI, type B81:
No 1 Mk 5H. EMER Power A267/16.
No 1 Mk 5K. EMER Power A267/17.

Parts lists
Illustrated parts list:
Engine B40 No 1 Mk 5H installed in generating set, AC, 10kVA, No 1 Mk 1. WO 12838.
Engine B80 No 1 Mk 1D, Mk 2D, Mk 5D installed in truck, 3 ton GS cargo, Thornycroft TF/B80; and truck GS FD arty 4x4 Thornycroft TF/B80. WO 12850.
Engine B40 No 1 Mk 2F, Mk 5F installed in crane, truck-mounted, 4 ton, Jones KL66/Albion; and crane, truck-mounted, 6 ton, Jones KL66/Albion. WO 12841.

Other parts lists are combined with the documentation for the vehicle in which the engine is fitted.

Repair manuals
Unit repairs: R: Rolls-Royce B Series engines, all marks. EMER Power S 523
Field repairs: Rolls-Royce B Series engines, all marks. EMER Power S 524/1.
Base repairs: Rolls-Royce B Series engines, all marks. EMER Power S 524/2.
Base standard: engine, Rolls-Royce B Series, B40, B60, B80, B81. EMER Power S528.

Inspection standards
REME Central Inspectorate: inspection standards for Rolls-Royce 'B' Series engines (all marks). REME code 9/B/RR/Gen/2.

Modification instructions
B Series engines. EMER Power S527.
B40 engines. EMER Power S527/1.
B60 engines. EMER Power S527/2.
B80 engines. EMER Power S527/3.
B81 engines. EMER Power S527/4.

Miscellaneous instructions
B Series engines. EMER Power S529.
B40 engines. EMER Power S529/1.
B60 engines. EMER Power S529/2.
B80 engines. EMER Power S529/3.
B81 engines. EMER Power S529/4.

Miscellaneous documents
Iso-Speedic governors. EMER Power M314.

Blinking in the summer sunshine, a reconditioned B60 engine, probably a Mk5A for a Ferret, is removed from its crate. Note the harmonic balancer on the crankshaft nose, and the multi-groove crankshaft pulley, intended to drive the generator and water pump and, occasionally, other accessories. The carburettor is complete with intake horn, and the coil and ignition filter are also fitted. The engine is finished in the distinctive 'ground equipment blue', used for all of the later 'B Series' engines.

A B60 Mk 5A engine complete with Wilson pre-selective transmission. Although the engine is complete with all its accessories, including an alternator rather than a dc generator, the starter motor is not fitted and can just be seen laying on the pallet behind the transmission. Note the three visible coupling flanges which form connections for the H configuration driveshafts running to the front and rear axles.

Above. An FV1801 cargo 'Champ' with the top erected. Note the pick-axe helve strapped to the body side, with the head stowed on the front wing. A .303 Lee Enfield rifle is fitted to the left-hand rear passenger's gun clips. A small stowage satchel is fitted to the backrest of the front passenger's seat. The small spotlight fitted to the scuttle was not original equipment.

Left. Close-up view of the 'Champ' left-hand antenna mount. These mounts also carried the rear lights and thus were installed on both cargo and FFW/FFR variants. Although not original equipment for the 'Champ', these Lucas rear lights and indicator lights were fitted to the vehicles during their service career, and were also used on all of the FVRDE-designed British military vehicles of the 1950's and 1960's, regardless of size. Similarly, the red painted fuel filler cap was standard equipment on most of the vehicles described in this book. The black painted water can was standard equipment for the 'Champ', in place of the more usual fuel container.

The same 'Champ' seen from the front. A GS shovel is strapped to the body side, and the tube laying across the offside front wing is the snorkel in its stowed position; the tube would be raised to the upright for wading. The yellow disc below the headlight is used for the bridge classification; a number rarely appeared on lightweight vehicles.

Unlike the WW2 Jeep, the top of the 'Champ' could be folded without being removed from the frame. The yellow fitting below the rear lights is a waterproof cover for the trailer socket. The spare wheel could also be mounted on the ribbed bonnet top.

An FV4002 'Centurion' Mk 5 bridgelayer with the bridge in the travelling position; the leading edge of the bridge is facing the camera. The 'Centurion' bridgelayer used a B40 engine to drive the hydraulic system. This vehicle serves as an eye-catching 'sign' and gate guardian at the Tank Museum, Bovington.

THE ROLLS-ROYCE 'B SERIES' ENGINE

Left. Close-up view of FV701 Mk 2 'Ferret', showing .30 calibre Browning machine cannon installed in a small rotating turret. This photograph also shows the driver's windshield, complete with its tiny wiper, installed in the opened hatch. The stalks protruding from the top of the turret support the turret door in the open position.

Below left. An FV701 Mk 2 'Ferret' awaits a private owner. The driver's hatch is closed.

Below. A hinged stowage basket installed over the engine compartment cover. These baskets were generally used for the personal effects of the crew, making conditions somewhat more pleasant in the cramped fighting compartment.

Above. **An FV701(E) Mk 2 'Ferret'** with 7.62mm GPMG installed in the turret. At the front the vehicle carries sand channels, and a stowage basket is fitted over the engine compartment.

Above right. **An FV701(C) Mk 1 'Ferret'** with a .303 Bren gun fitted to a pintle on the turret edge. The tube installed across the front of the vehicle is used to carry radio antennae sections, and beneath that can be seen the pick-axe helve. Smoke-grenade dischargers are mounted on each front wing.

Centre right. **An FV701(E) Mk 2 'Ferret'** seen from the rear showing the large amounts of kit these vehicles were expected to carry. A machine gun tripod is strapped to the nearside engine cover; a rope, tent and reel of cable are carried on the offside cover. Anti-tank rocket containers are hanging from the turret sides. Jerry cans for water and fuel, together with a cooker and cooking containers are strapped to the rear wing and stowage box.

Bottom right. **An FV701 Mk 1 'Ferret'** similarly festooned with kit. Note the generally lower profile of the turretless Mk 1 variant.

THE ROLLS-ROYCE 'B SERIES' ENGINE

Left. **An FV1609 Mk 1 Humber 'Pig'.** *This photograph shows the vehicle in its original armoured APC form, complete with stowage boxes around the rear wheel arches, and roof-mounted escape hatches. Note the canvas cover for the rear compartment extends down to partially cover the armoured side panels. Only the wire guards around the headlights are not original.*

Top right. **An FV1611 Mk 2 Humber 'Pig',** *unusual for not having served in Northern Ireland, and thus never having been up-armoured. The rear stowage boxes are still in place and the roof escape hatches are open.*

Top far right. **Close-up view of FV1611 Mk 2 'Pig'.** *This one has clearly been up-armoured several times; note the general crudity of the construction. Vision blocks have been installed in the windshield and side window covers.*

An FV1611 Mk 2 'Pig' slowly returns to the soil. This vehicle shows how the rear stowage boxes were cut away so as not to provide opportunities for booby-trapping. The angled projection just below the vision block on the nearside door provides a support for the window cover in the open position.

THE ROLLS-ROYCE 'B SERIES' ENGINE

Above. A rare FV1620 'Hornet' Malkara launch vehicle. The two anti-tank missiles are raised into the launch position. Note the plethora of stowage boxes installed on the vehicle; the box on the offside front wheel arch may not be original.

Above right. Close-up view of the launch arm and missiles on the FV1620 'Hornet'. The arm was hydraulically raised and lowered, and the missiles could be launched from inside or outside the vehicle. A joystick control was used, together with an optical sight, to guide the missiles to their target.

Right. An FV1611 Mk 2 Humber 'Pig'. This vehicle shows the front cow catcher used for removing barricades, the remains of the rear stowage boxes still used as rear light mounts, the armoured top flap above the rear doors, and the armoured plate hanging below the rear body to protect the occupants legs as they leave the vehicle. Note how a Vent-Axia fan has been installed in place of one of the rear compartment vision ports.

THE ROLLS-ROYCE 'B SERIES' ENGINE

Left. An FV1604 Humber wireless vehicle bristling with antennae and lamps, and fitted with a roof-mounted machine gun ring. Note the black painted water container mounted ahead of the radiator.

Above. An FV1601 Humber cargo truck, very-professionally converted to an airfield fire tender. The ladders seen above the vehicle belong to something parked behind it. This picture was taken at Duxford in the early 1980's and it is not known whether the vehicle was a one-off or part of a series.

Left. An FV1604 Humber wireless vehicle, somewhat more-modestly equipped. The canvas flap below the rear windows is used to cover the junction between the penthouse tent and the side of the vehicle; racks below this flap are used to store aerial mast sections or the framework for the tent. The protruding cover behind the cab provides access to the batteries. The domed cowl mounted on the scuttle is the carburettor air intake; this would have been removed and replaced by a snorkel during wading.

CHAPTER 2

THE B40 ENGINE
B40 Mk.1 to B40 Mk.5

CONTENTS

2.1	Austin 'Champ'	55
2.2	Land Rover B40	67
2.3	B40: Minor applications & prototypes:	71
	'Centurion' bridgelayer	
	Jones KL66 4/6 ton mobile crane	
	Auto Diesels 10kVA mobile generator set	

DATA SUMMARY

Dimensions and weight
Overall installed dimensions
Length: 851mm.
Width: 720mm.
Height (with standard wet sump): 887mm.

Dry weight: 295kg.

Performance
Bore: 88.9mm, 3.50in.
Stroke: 114.3mm, 4.50in.
Swept volume: 2838cc.

Compression ratio: 6.4:1.
Firing order: 1342.

Gross output, uninstalled: 80bhp at 3750rpm.
Gross torque, uninstalled: 209 lbs/ft.

Fuel consumption, maximum demand: 25 litres/hr at 3000 rpm; 25 litres/hr at 3750 rpm.

PRODUCTION SUMMARY

Mark	Qty	Vehicle and FV number	
B40, Mk 2 engines:			
Mk 2A	30	Wolseley 'Mudlark'	FV1800
Mk 2A/4	1483	Austin 'Champ'	FV1801
Mk 2B	54	Land Rover (B40)	FV18001
Mk 2D	9	10kVA mobile generator set	FV2401
		Temperature airfield ground unit	-
Mk 2E	7	Anti-aircraft gun project	-
Mk 2F	18	Jones KL66 4/6 ton crane	FV11103
Mk 2G	8	Flame thrower project	-
B40, Mk 5 engines:			
Mk 5A	17363	Austin 'Champ'	FV1801 FV1802
Mk 5E	-	Vickers medium anti-aircraft gun	-
Mk 5F	41	Jones KL66 4/6 ton crane	FV11103
Mk 5H	84	10kVA mobile generator set	FV2401
Mk 5P	40	'Centurion' bridgelayer	FV4002
Total	**19137**		

CHAPTER 2.1

AUSTIN CHAMP
FV1801, FV1802

During the 1930's and through the early years of WW2, the British Army had used near-standard commercial vehicle designs such as the Austin, Hillman and Standard utilities as light field cars, or 'tillys' as they became known. However, none of these vehicles possessed any significant off-road capability and when, under the WW2 Lend-Lease programme, supplies of Willys and Ford Jeeps were made available, the Army was impressed by the versatility and performance of what was essentially a new class of military vehicle.

The War Office and Ministry of Supply resolved that, once WW2 was over, or at least nearing its end, development work would begin on a new all-British replacement for the ubiquitous Jeep.

By the mid-1940's, the Fighting Vehicles Research and Development Executive (FVRDE) at Chertsey had begun to draw up the design brief for a new light, 4x4 field car. Rather than simply replacing the Jeep, which the FVRDE regarded as highly conventional, the new vehicle was planned to offer a far higher degree of sophistication, and was to be capable of adaptation to a variety of specialised roles. The project, designated FV1800, eventually led to the production of the Austin 'Champ'.

Unfortunately, the 'Champ' was not to repeat the success of the simple and versatile Jeep. A victim of changing circumstances, by the time the first production 'Champs' were delivered, the Army had decided that perhaps such a sophisticated vehicle was not required after all, and that the simpler and cheaper Land Rover would be acceptable in most roles. Measured against the new, simplified Army requirement, the 'Champ' was seen as expensive, and was beginning to be described as 'over-complicated'; it was also apparently not reliable. Whilst all of this might well have been the case, it could be argued that the vehicle was really being soundly criticised for embodying the technology necessary to meet its original design brief.

OVERVIEW

The FV1801 'Champ' was a small, lightweight field car intended for use as a radio reconnaissance vehicle, for passenger and cargo carrying over improved and unimproved roads, and for specialised roles such as field ambulance, machine gun platform, and signal cable laying duties.

In its radio role, the 'Champ' was fitted with a two-speed

CHAPTER 2.1: AUSTIN CHAMP

generator, extra batteries and associated wiring for use with wireless sets, such as the No 19 set, dating from WW2, or the British Army's new range of 'Larkspur' VHF radio sets, introduced in the late 1950's.

The standard FV1801 vehicle accommodated a crew of up to five men, or the driver and a 5cwt (250kg) load; a standard towing hitch allowed its use with a laden 10cwt (500kg) trailer (usually the FV2301A trailer), or other towed equipment. With reduced performance, the 'Champ' could also tow a 25 lb field gun, or battalion anti-tank gun such as a Mobat etc.

A utility version (FV1802) was also planned, with increased carrying capacity, and with rear bodywork more like that of the Land Rover. Although a number of prototypes were produced, the FV1802 never made it to series production.

The basic layout followed that of the WW2 Jeep, with a front-mounted engine driving the rear wheels for normal road use, or all four wheels to provide greater traction across country.

DEVELOPMENT

The FV1800 project was one of the first of the new family of post-war CT category military vehicles. The project was intended to build on the strengths of the Jeep and to provide a versatile and sophisticated vehicle which, as well as providing general transport, would be able to fulfil a variety of specialised roles. These were to include, for example, field ambulance, radio reconnaissance vehicle, and mobile gun platform.

The vehicle was to incorporate a more powerful engine than the WW2 Jeep. Independent suspension on all four wheels would be provided to give enhanced off-road capability. There was to be full waterproofing and radio suppression of electrical equipment, and mechanical components were to be sealed to allow wading to a depth of 760mm without preparation. The electrical system was designed to operate on 24V with a high-output twin-speed generator provided on vehicles designed for the radio role.

Finally, there was to be seating for a five-man crew with better stowage facilities than was offered by the Jeep.

The design authority was vested in the Nuffield Organisation, and the eventual design team included Charles (Rex) Sewell of FVRDE, whose credentials included a period of working with W O Bentley, and Freddie Henry from Austin. Alec Issigonis, who later was to design the Morris Minor and the Mini, was also involved in the general layout, and in the design of the torsion bar suspension system.

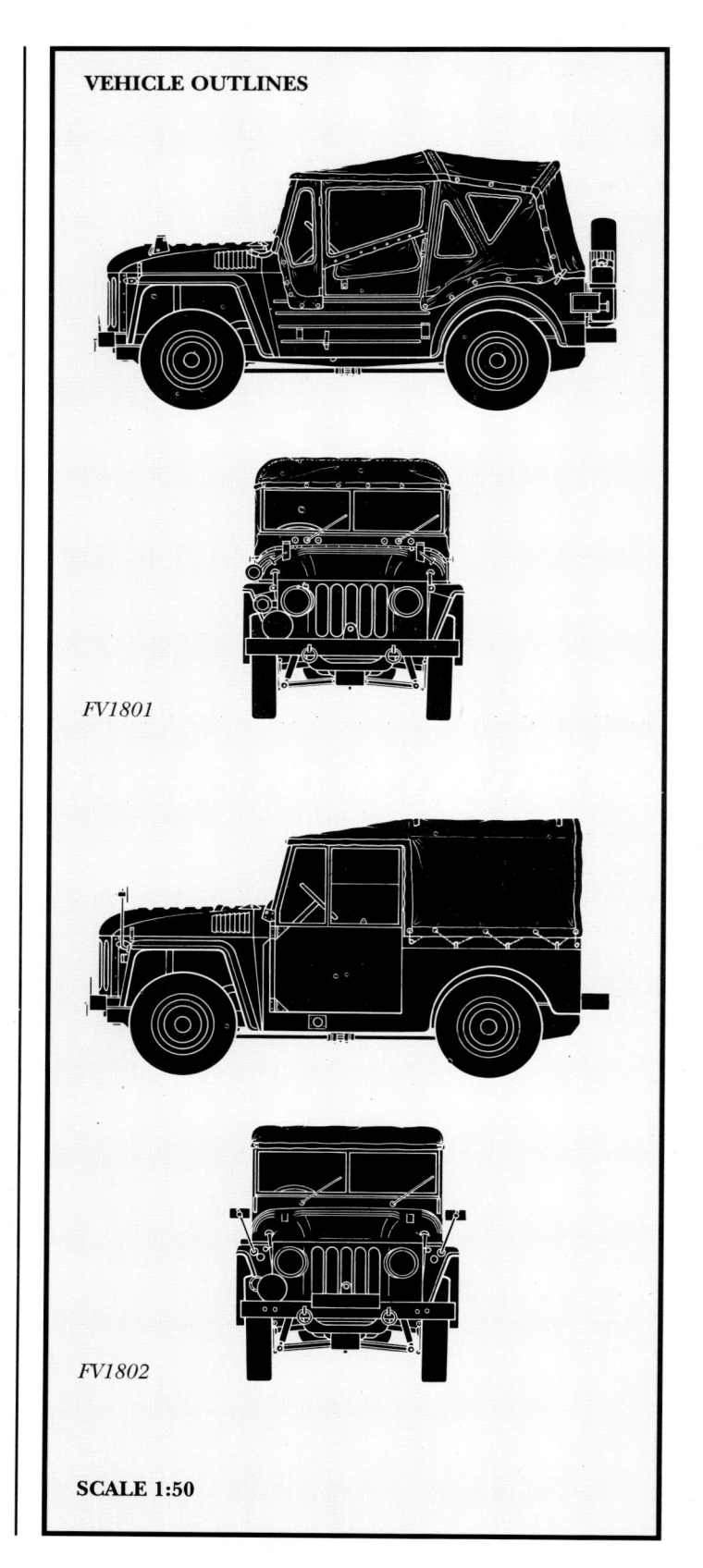

VEHICLE OUTLINES

FV1801

FV1802

SCALE 1:50

CHAPTER 2.1: AUSTIN CHAMP

SPECIFICATION

Dimensions and weight

	FV1801	FV1802
Dimensions (mm):		
Length*	3670	3658
Width	1559	1651
Height:		
6.50 tyres, top in place	1854	-
top and windscreen folded	1372	-
7.50 tyres, top in place	1880	1828
top and windscreen folded	1397	1397
Wheelbase	2134	2134
Track, laden:		
6.50 tyres, front/rear	1213/1232	1213/1232
7.50 tyres, front/rear	1238/1257	1238/1257
Ground clearance:		
6.50 tyres, front/rear	254/292	254/292
7.50 tyres, front/rear	292/311	292/311
Weight (kg):		
Gross laden weight:		
FV1801(A)	2032	2320
FV1801(A)i	2138	-
FV1801(A)ii	2127	-
FV1801(A)iii	2151	-
FV1801(A)iv	2036	-
Unladen weight:		
FV1801(A)	1664	1702
FV1801(A)i	1769	-
FV1801(A)ii	1758	-
FV1801(A)iii	1807	-
FV1801(A)iv	1667	-

* Length of ambulance vehicle FV1801(A)ii, 4197mm; length of cable laying vehicle FV1801(A)iii, 3861mm.

Bridge classification: solo, 3; with trailer, 3.

Performance
Maximum speed: on road (solo), 98km/h; on road with trailer, 72km/h; cross country (solo), 33km/h.
Fuel consumption: 0.13 litre/km, on road.
Maximum range: 700km, on road.

Approach angle: 45 deg.
Departure angle: 35 deg.
Side overturn angle: 45 deg.

Turning circle: 10.668m.
Maximum gradient: 36%.
Fording: unprepared, 914mm; prepared, 1831mm.

Capacity
Maximum load: 250kg.
Maximum towed load: 500kg.

The requirement for a light 4x4 field car was first issued by the War Office in November 1944, and by 1945 three hand-built prototype vehicles had been produced by Nuffield Mechanisations. Known as the 'Gutty', there were minor differences in the vehicles, one-to-another, but all featured stressed-skin monocoque body construction, and were fitted with an 1800cc flat-four engine. It is interesting to compare these features to Issigonis' early plans for the 'Mosquito', the forerunner of the Morris 'Minor'.

Extensive trials were undertaken at Chertsey and elsewhere, but the vehicle was not yet close to its final form. Further development was clearly required, and although the lineage from one vehicle to another can be clearly demonstrated, the 'Gutty' should not really be considered the forefather of the 'Champ'.

In 1948, the vehicle had been redesigned and by 1949, three more prototypes had been produced, by now equipped with the recently-available B40, Mk 2A engine. Dubbed the Wolseley 'Mudlark', the second incarnation of the project incorporated all of the mechanical features subsequently to be used in the production version, albeit with minor body styling variations which included flat side panels and bulbous rounded wings.

These prototypes were approved and an initial contract was placed for 12 vehicles. The Rolls-Royce production records show that 30 examples of the B40, Mk 2A engine variation were constructed, and since it was not used in any other vehicle, it is reasonable to assume that more than the 12 vehicles called for by the contract were constructed.

Reviewing this prototype vehicle in its 23 June issue of 1950, the 'Autocar' magazine described it as 'the new light 4x4 with which the British Army has planned to replace the Jeep'.

In 1951, one of these pre-production 'Mudlark' vehicles was sent to Aberdeen Proving Ground in the USA for assessment, subsequently being passed to the Ford Motor Company. Documentary evidence exists that this vehicle remained in the USA for two years, but there is no record of its ultimate fate.

Production
In 1952, the Nuffield Organisation and the Austin Motor Company merged to form the British Motor Corporation and the newly-formed Corporation put in a bid to the Ministry of Supply for the manufacture of 15,000 FV1801 vehicles. The Rover Company also tendered for the work, intending that the vehicles be built alongside the Land Rovers at their Solihull plant (now wouldn't that have been interesting!). But in the end, the production contract was awarded to the new BMC organisation.

CHAPTER 2.1: AUSTIN CHAMP

More than £1.5 million pounds was awarded in capital assistance to help set the project up. Production was to be managed by the former Austin Motor Company, with the production line established in an old wartime 'shadow' aircraft factory at Cofton Hackett, in Yorkshire.

By late 1952, the Army had begun to accept deliveries of the vehicle, and production continued until 1955. Although the original contract called for 15,000 vehicles, it was cancelled before production was complete and in all only some 12,000 units were produced. The original price of the vehicle was £1100, rising to £1300 by 1954, and the total value of the contract was £16 million.

Alongside the 'Champs' constructed for the British Army, some 400 vehicles were delivered to the Australian Army.

The 'Champ' was never to fulfil its promise and in less than 15 years most had been demobbed and sold.

Technical problems

Almost from the first year in service, technical problems were encountered which led to vehicles being taken out of use.

The 'Champ' was not popular: the services complained that it was 'too heavy and too big... it was difficult to get in and out of... it was unreliable... and was too costly to be regarded as expendable'. There were recurring problems with the steering and the axles. One War Office official writing in 1955 stated that 'it is disliked by users as much for its design as for its many serious defects... there seems little future for this vehicle as at present designed'.

By December 1952, there had been 102 separate criticisms of the vehicle, of which 35 were considered major defects. The most serious of these was with the steering gear, which exhibited fatigue fractures of the steering shaft, and with the combined back axle and transfer gears, which failed to carry the loads for which they were designed.

The rear axle problem was sufficiently serious to affect the vehicle's operational readiness and a sum of £288,000 was allocated for modifications. Various opinions exist today as to the exact nature of the problem. One story claims that the case hardening of the pinion was faulty and that this led to premature wear and ultimately to catastrophic failure (although, if true, this would have been a relatively easy fault to put right). Another view says that the axle lubrication system was not adequate, and that the needle roller bearing carrying the reverse shaft (which was installed in the rear axle casing) was starved of oil when the vehicle was reversing, leading to its rapid disintegration.

Whatever the reason, it seems that it was going to cost big

Nuffield Mechanisations 'Gutty' prototype (IWM)

FV1800 Wolseley 'Mudlark' (BMIHT)

FV1801(A) cargo 'Champ', middle of production run (IWM)

CHAPTER 2.1: AUSTIN CHAMP

FV1801(A) cargo 'Champ', early vehicle (IWM)

FV1801(A)i FFW/FFR 'Champ' with No 19 set (TMB)

FV1801(A)ii 'Champ' field ambulance conversion (IWM)

money to put the 'Champ' right. In all, a total of 305 modifications was required to vehicles that had been issued, at a cost of some £45 per vehicle.

It was also suggested at the time that the 'Champ' was over-designed and that it presented REME with a maintenance and repair nightmare. This is partly borne out by the fact that manufacturers other than Austin, who were approached regarding possible production of the 'Champ', turned it down on the grounds of its 'complicated design and radical departure from normal commercial practice'. Certainly, the vehicle was complex and sophisticated, both for its time, and when compared to the rugged simplicity of the WW2 Jeep which it superseded, and the Land Rover which was to replace it.

Perhaps Britain's conscript army of the 1950's was not sufficiently well-trained to maintain such a vehicle. The waterproofing and radio-screening cannot have helped; all electrical components for example, are in sealed enclosures which call for careful dismantling and reassembly in order to continue to perform properly. However, these comments apply equally to any of the CT class of vehicle and these problems were not apparent with other vehicles of this category.

It is clear that there many problems with the 'Champ'. Some commentators have suggested that, despite the expenditure of a further £369,340 on modifications, no fully satisfactory solution was found. Whatever the reason, the 'Champ' retains its bad name to this day and is still often dismissed as simply unreliable.

Replacement and disposal

The 'Champ' remained in uniform from 1952 to about 1966 and was effectively replaced in British Army service by the Land Rover, and perhaps, in certain roles, by the 'Ferret'. Neither of these, however, was a direct replacement.

By 1966 virtually every 'Champ' had been withdrawn from front line service and either disposed of, or passed to the TA volunteer reserve force. Perhaps the writing was already on the wall when, in March 1965, EMER A089 'Miscellaneous instruction 13' dictated that all existing 'Champ' EMERS were cancelled and should be destroyed.

NOMENCLATURE and VARIATIONS

All of the production FV1801 vehicles were manufactured under a single contract which called for 15,000 units. However, the contract was terminated before completion and the total number of vehicles actually delivered is believed to be 11,732. Although there were minor variations in detailed design, and in the versions of component assemblies fitted, no major design

CHAPTER 2.1: AUSTIN CHAMP

modifications were made and no further development was undertaken once delivery was complete.

In 1954, a small number of utility prototypes were produced with a 5/10cwt (250/500kg) capacity body and a hinged tailgate: there was no series production of this version, which was designated FV1802(A). The prototypes were most likely assembled by hand and period photographs show considerable detail variations, one to another.

No other factory variations were produced: those variations which did exist were retrospectively modified in Army workshops, and the vehicle could be returned to its basic role by simply removing the modification fittings.

In 1955/56, all versions were regraded from CT to GS classification when the CT concept was virtually abandoned.

The 'Champ' name
As a matter of record, the vehicle was never officially called 'Champ'. The model was designated WN1 by Austin, and FV1801/1802 by the military authorities.

The name 'Champ' was used by Austin for the much-simplified commercial variation, also designated WN2 or WN3, according to version. For some reason the name stuck, and all FV1801/1802 vehicles and derivatives tend to be described as 'Champs'.

Variations
FV1800. Truck, 1/4 ton, CT, cargo, 4x4
Wolseley 'Mudlark' pre-production vehicles. (The 'Gutty' prototypes were probably not allocated an FV number.)

FV1801. Truck, 1/4 ton, CT, cargo/FFW, 4x4, Austin, Mk 1
FV1801(A). Basic cargo version described as a light truck with a high cross-country performance.

FV1801(A)i. Basic cargo vehicle modified for FFW/FFR role (normally at the factory, but occasionally as a unit modification) by the inclusion of two additional batteries beneath the passenger seat, with a two-speed generator and matching control panel (designed to prevent the vehicle batteries from being discharged by the radio equipment), and a radio connection box. The vehicle was screened against both HF and VHF interference.

FV1801(A)ii. Basic cargo vehicle modified as a field ambulance by the addition of two stretcher frames and extended hood frame and hood. Similar to the WW2 Jeep-based field ambulance.

FV1801(A)iii. Basic cargo vehicle modified for telephone cable laying in the field by the addition of cable drum mounting equipment at the rear which allowed the cable to be paid-out with the vehicle moving. The vehicle has sufficient capacity to carry drums containing either

FV1801(A)iii 'Champ' cable layer with signals trailer (IWM)

FV1801(A)iv 'Champ' .50 calibre gun platform (IWM)

FV1802(A) 'Champ' utility vehicle (IWM)

FV1801(A) heavily-modified utility-bodied 'Champ' (IWM)

FV1801(A) 'Champ' with Straussler high-flotation wheels (IWM)

FV1801(A) 'Champ' with FV1 'Chobham magnetic compass' (TMB)

800m or 1600m of cable. Additional stowage was sometimes provided for ladders etc, and the spare wheel was re-located to the bonnet top. In this role, the vehicle was not fitted with a hood.

Telephone cable laying vehicles would normally be used in conjunction with a 10cwt (500kg) trailer, used to carry spare cable drums.

FV1801(A)iv. Basic cargo vehicle modified to mount a .50 calibre water-cooled Vickers machine gun in front of the co-driver, for example for use by the Long Range Desert Group (LRDG). Additional modifications included the fitment of applique frontal armour to the radiator and scuttle area. In this role, it was not possible to fit either a windscreen or a hood.

FV1802. Truck, 1/4 ton, CT, utility, 4x4, Austin, Mk 1
FV1802(A). Up-rated 5/10 cwt (250/500kg) version with wider, seven-seater utility bodywork.

Major differences compared to the FV1801 version include redesigned rear bodywork with fully enclosed wheels, modified front wings including side stowage lockers, flashing direction indicators, removable doors with sliding Perspex windows, hinged and removable tailgate. Only prototypes were built and the exact number is not known.

A REME document, entitled 'Technical inspection instruction: B series vehicles; post-war range', in editions dated 1952 and 1957, lists, in addition to the basic FV1802 vehicle, FFW/FFR, ambulance, cable laying and machine gun mount versions (ie, FV1802(A)i, ii, iii, and iv modifications, as described for FV1801). Although it is perfectly logical that these versions should have been planned, it is odd that the descriptions persisted in print for five years, whilst there is no evidence that the vehicles ever actually existed.

Admiralty vehicles
In 1952, some 30 standard FV1801 units were specially modified in naval workshops to provide a simple utility vehicle. Most of the bodywork behind the scuttle and windscreen was cut away and replaced by a basic flat-panelled body with a hinged tailgate and a tubular frame over the cargo area, designed to support a tilt. The windscreen itself was replaced by a fixed, single-light design.

It is unclear as to why this work was carried out in the way it was, and why fully-assembled vehicles were modified rather than having the vehicles supplied in partly-assembled form from the factory.

Factory modifications
In the early 1950's, Rolls-Royce constructed an experimental OHV direct-injection, glow-plug diesel

CHAPTER 2.1: AUSTIN CHAMP

version of the B40 engine in conjunction with the Ricardo Company, and installed it into a 'Champ' for evaluation. Known as the 'Ricardo' 36X diesel, photographs of the 'Champ' and the engine appear in Chapter 1.2.

Workshop modifications

Period FVRDE photographs show a strange, square utility-bodied 'Champ' with a fully-enclosed front end, and with rear bodywork not unlike that of the FV1802 version. The vehicle has every appearance of having been carefully-built, rather than simply cobbled together like some prototypes. Possibly it was a pilot vehicle for the utility 'Champ' project, but no annotations appear with the photographs. In 1966 this vehicle was described as being beyond economic repair and was scrapped. Its use remains a mystery.

During the Aden crisis in 1958, a number of 'Champs' were modified to allow easier loading by having the rear panel cut away and the spare wheel mounted on the right-hand side panel.

'Champs' were also used in various experimental roles; for example, vehicles were often pressed into service as 'guinea pigs' for FVRDE projects.

At least one vehicle was fitted with high-flotation Straussler wheels intended to provide enhanced mobility in soft swampy country.

The gyroscopic Sperry 'Chobham self-correcting magnetic compass' type FV1 was installed in a 'Champ', in at least two versions, for feasibility trials. This device was intended to give reliable magnetic readings from moving vehicles by countering the effects of the mass of ferrous metal of the vehicle itself.

Photographs exist of a vehicle with a battalion anti-tank weapon attached to a hefty frame installed in the rear compartment.

COMMERCIAL VARIATIONS

Austin had contracted with the Ministry of Supply to share the tooling costs in return for Ministry consent for the production and manufacture of commercial versions of the vehicle. This consent was granted, and in addition to the standard WN1 FV1801/1802 vehicle, three other versions exist.

The WN2 model was identical to the standard WN1 version but was fitted with the engine of the contemporary Austin A90 motor car in place of the Rolls-Royce B40. This was intended to be offered to military customers outside the UK.

With similar bodywork but otherwise much simplified in every way, a standard commercial version (properly

FV1801(A) 'Champ' and trailer rigged for air dropping (REME)

FV1801(A) 'Champ' after air dropping mishap! (REME)

FV1800 Wolseley 'Mudlark' entering the FVRDE wading pit (IWM)

called WN3 'Champ') was produced, with 12V electrics, and again, with the A90 engine.

There was also a military version of the WN3 model (designated FV1801/WN3) which had the simplified bodywork and electrical specification of the standard WN2 civilian model but was fitted with the B40 engine. This was also intended for military customers.

Although demonstration vehicles were supplied to FVRDE for assessment, as well as to many of Britain's former colonies, neither the WN2, nor the FV1802/WN3 versions were purchased by the British Army.

DESCRIPTION

Engine
Rolls-Royce B40, No 1, Mk 2A/4 (early production), or Mk 5A; wet sump.
Capacity: 2838cc.
Bore and stroke: 3.50 x 4.50in.
Power output: 80bhp (gross); 69bhp (net) at 3750rpm.
Maximum torque: 138 lbs/ft (gross); 115 lbs/ft (net) at 2150rpm.

Detail variations
Distributor limiter set at 3750rpm (crankshaft speed); oil filter mounted on crankcase; cooling fan mounted directly to crankshaft nose via slipping clutch to prevent drowning the engine during wading; conventional clutch housing; Ki-gass pipework and nozzles fitted (Mk 5A engines only); centre outlet exhaust manifold; horizontal inlet manifold with vertical carburettor flange.

Transmission
Driving through a 250mm Borg and Beck single dry-plate clutch, power was taken through a five-speed gearbox to the combined back axle and transfer gears. Forward and reverse gears were separate, housed within the back axle, making all five gears available in both forward and reverse.

From the back axle, an open prop shaft ran the length of the vehicle to drive the front axle. Engagement and disengagement of the front axle was effected by a simple dog clutch, controlled manually by a lever.

The transfer box ratios were 1.127:1 in forward gears, and 1:1 in reverse. The gearbox contained no low ratios and first gear was not normally used for road work, being retained for steep gradients or tricky off-road terrain.

The axles, which were very similar in design, front and rear, featured hypoid bevel drive to fully-floating halfshafts, with 80mm Tracta type constant velocity joints, interchangeable front-to-rear and side-to-side.

Suspension
Almost unheard of in passenger cars in 1952, let alone in four-wheel drive vehicles, the 'Champ' had independent suspension at all four wheels by means of longitudinal torsion bars with assistance from rubber compression buffers at the wheel stations. The suspension movement was handled by transverse upper and lower wishbones running in large surface oil-bath bearings.

Large telescopic hydraulic dampers were fitted vertically above each wheel.

All suspension components, including the torsion bars, which were not pre-loaded from new, were interchangeable left-to-right and front-to-rear, and the rubber-mounted axles could easily be dismounted complete with the suspension units.

Steering gear
Steering was by helical rack and pinion, again an advanced feature for its time, with the rack mounted behind the engine. A 250mm diameter sprung steering wheel provided 2.7 turns from lock to lock, and was easily removed by means of a large wing nut to reduce the overall height for shipping, or to ease access into the relatively small-bodied transport aircraft of the 1950's.

The suspension and steering design was excellent and off-road the 'Champ' provided a superb ride with precise positive steering, free from road shocks and kick-back.

Braking system
Lockheed hydraulic brakes were fitted at all four wheels with the hand (parking) brake acting mechanically on the rear wheels only by means of wedge expanders. Cast-iron drums, 305mm diameter x 44mm width, gave a total of 0.04sq m of braking area for each wheel.

Front brakes were of the twin-leading shoe pattern; rear brakes were leading and trailing.

The brakes were not waterproofed although a removable rubber wading cover was provided for the fluid reservoir.

Road wheels
Wheels were steel 4.50E x 16in or 5.50F x 16in with 6.50x16 or 7.50x16 cross-country type tyres respectively. The original tyres were Dunlop 'Trakgrip' pattern but many 'Champs' were later fitted with simple non-directional (NDCC) 'bar grip' tyres. Bar-reinforced non-skid chains could be fitted to the tyres to improve traction.

A single spare wheel was carried, mounted on the rear of the vehicle.

Chassis
The all-steel body was bolted to a cruciform chassis frame formed from two box-section side members

meeting at the centre, and welded to provide a rigid mounting for the torsion bars. The front and rear footwell floors were welded to the frame along with the inner scuttle, inner front wings and battery boxes to provide additional stiffness.

On the utility FV1802 version, the rear floor was removable.

Bodywork
On FV1801 vehicles, the simple bodywork was open, in similar style to a Jeep but with removable wings at both front and rear. The rear body panel, which normally carried the spare wheel, was fixed and, inevitably this caused loading difficulties. The bodies were constructed by Fisher & Ludlow.

The bodywork on FV1802 was fitted with a full-width rear section with a hinged and removable tailgate, rather more like a Land Rover; the spare wheel was stored inside the vehicle, behind the front seats.

A one-piece windscreen was used, with two separately-glazed lights, able to be opened on a top-hung hinge, or folded flat onto the bonnet.

The rear-hinged bonnet was a one-piece pressing with reinforcing ribs which allowed it to be used as an additional cargo platform or spare wheel mounting.

In the standard FV1801 version, the two separate front seats could be lifted and tilted to allow access to the battery boxes or storage compartments below. The rear seat had a three-part hinged back rest which could be folded down and used as a load platform; the rear seat base could also be swung forward to provide a full-length load platform in the rear. The utility FV1802 version had seating provision for three at the front, with detachable squabs providing two additional seats on the each wheel arch at the rear.

Weather equipment
A full length PVC Rexine hood was fitted with a small rear transparent panel. Unlike a Jeep, the top did not need to be removed and was easily stowed by folding. If the side enclosure was in place, the front section of the hood could be folded back whilst leaving the supports and the rear section in place.

For FV1801, a full set of removable PVC-covered doors and side curtains was available to provide a complete winter enclosure; whilst the FV1802 version was provided with removable metal doors, fitted with sliding/removable windows.

Stowage
Standard provision was made for stowing items such as the pioneer tools, personal weapons for the crew, jerry cans etc using clips and brackets on the inside and outside of the vehicle. Lockable tool compartments were provided in the rear wheel arches, and there was a large stowage bin beneath the driver's seat on cargo vehicles (on radio vehicles, this compartment was used to house the additional batteries).

The driver's seat had a small brown Rexine satchel attached to the back rest.

Electrical equipment
Hoping to avoid the cold-weather starting problems inherent with the 6V Jeep, the 'Champ' was specified with a 24V negative-earth electrical system from the outset. All electrical components were waterproofed and radio-screened.

The cargo version had two 12V 38Ah waterproof batteries in series, housed under the passenger's seat. Alternative versions of generator were installed, either No 1, Mk 1 or No 1, Mk 2/1; both were designed to produce 12A at 28.5V maximum.

On the FFW/FFR version, there were four 12V 40Ah batteries, also waterproof, with the additional pair being under the driver's seat and intended to power the radio equipment. The generator was either a No 2, Mk 1 or No 2, Mk 2 machine; both were automatic two-speed generators, with a maximum output of 25A. The two-speed facility was designed to produce higher outputs at idle, and at low engine speeds.

Winch
Provision was made for mounting a winch over the fuel tank well behind the rear seat. The power take-off was designed to attach to the rear axle in place of the cover plate, with the forward-reverse control also used to control the winch. Although at least one of the User handbooks describes the fitment and operation of a 'Turner 1 ton winch', there is some doubt as to whether a suitable unit was available, or ever actually fitted.

Wading
The first 5439 vehicles were issued with a snorkel fitted to the engine air intake. With the snorkel raised, and with suitable preparation, this allowed the vehicle to wade to a depth of 1980mm.

All standard FVRDE-designed electrical equipment was waterproofed and wading covers were provided for the brake master cylinder, clutch housing, generator control panel, and for the combined horn push/dip switch. In addition, the crankcase and fuel tank breather lines were vented into the snorkel air-intake elbow, and the engine cooling fan was driven through a friction clutch designed to disengage if an obstruction were met.

In April 1956, units with 'Champs' were instructed to

remove the snorkel and return it to stores. Subsequently, snorkels were to be drawn from stores if conditions dictated that wading might be a mission requirement.

However, wading was a reality, and many period photographs exist which show 'Champs', snorkel raised, travelling otherwise completely submerged.

ARMAMENTS

A machine gun pintle mount, designed to accept a .303 Bren, or water-cooled Vickers machine gun, was fitted into the scuttle forward of the passenger, and concealed by means of a simple clip-on cover. The separate gun pintle, which was designed to both traverse and elevate, was a slide-fit into the mount.

Clips were provided inside the vehicle for Lee Enfield No 4 SMLE rifles: four rifles on FV1801 vehicles, three on FV1802.

ANCILLARY EQUIPMENT

The War Office stowage sketch (WO 17940), dated October 1952, lists the following on-board equipment for the basic FV1801 cargo 'Champ':

Mechanics tools
Jack, with adaptor
Starting handle

Pioneer tools
Matchet
Pick axe head
Pick axe helve (carried separately)
Shovel

Drivers and crew equipment
Camouflage net, woodland, Mk 3, 4270x4270mm
Haversack (pattern 37) containing 2 blankets, brown, single, 2286x1525mm (4)
Large pack containing ground sheet, Mk 8 (4)
Rifles, no 4 Lee Enfield (4)

Other equipment
CTC fire extinguisher
First aid kit, large
Jerry can, water
Non-skid chains (4)
Tow rope

This equipment was either attached to the outside of the vehicle using various clips and brackets provided for that purpose, or stowed in the tool bins in each rear wheel arch.

RADIO EQUIPMENT

The FFR/FFW version of the 'Champ' was designed as a field communications vehicle. During its early years of service it was used with WW2 vintage equipment such as the No 19 or No 22 sets, whilst in subsequent years, it was fitted with 'Larkspur' equipment.

Radio 'Champs' were designated FFW (fitted for wireless), which meant that the vehicle was designed and prepared to receive radio equipment; or FFR (fitted for radio), which meant that radio sets had actually been installed. FFW-designated vehicles were supplied suppressed against electrical interference, and with a connecting box and aerial mountings ready for the user to install multi-purpose and specific radio kits.

The basic radio was installed on a rail-mounted carrier fitted across the body immediately behind the rear seat. The backrest to the seat was often removed and replaced with a simple plywood-backed squab which allowed easier access to the radio. The connecting box for the radio was installed in the left-hand rear footwell, while the control box was fitted to the shelf in front of the passenger. The aerial tuner unit was installed on top of the left-hand front wing, with the aerials themselves mounted on top of the purpose-designed rear light boxes; the right-hand box was always used for the HF aerial.

A typical standard 'Larkspur' station installed in a 'Champ' might comprise a single HF or VHF set, or two radio sets, together with the control harness, aerial tuner, junction boxes, and any ancillary equipment necessary to allow switching between the sets.

'Larkspur' radio stations in 'Champs' might include an HF/VHF combination such as C13/C42; or the C42/B47, C45/C45 and C42/BE201 VHF/VHF sets. Hybrid combinations such as 19HP/C45 were also being installed in the late 1950's.

DOCUMENTATION

Technical publications
User handbooks
Provisional user handbook: truck, 1/4 ton, cargo/FFW, Austin. WO codes 17759, 17807, 17826.
User handbook: truck, 1/4 ton, cargo/FFW, Austin. WO code 11780.

Technical handbooks
Technical description: truck, 1/4 ton, cargo/FFW, Austin. EMER D572, D573.
Waterproofing instructions: truck, 1/4 ton, cargo/FFW, Austin. EMER D575, WPF instruction no 1.

Servicing details
Servicing schedule: truck, 1/4 ton, cargo/FFW, Austin. WO code 12278.

Parts list
Illustrated spare parts list: truck, 1/4 ton, cargo/FFW, Austin. WO code 13577.

Repair manuals
Unit repairs: truck, 1/4 ton, cargo/FFW, Austin. EMER D574, Parts 1 and 2.
Field repairs, base repairs: truck, 1/4 ton, cargo/FFW, Austin. EMER D575.

Modification instructions
Truck, 1/4 ton, GS, 4x4, Austin. EMER D577, instructions 1-62.

Field inspection standard
Truck, 1/4 ton, GS, 4x4, Austin. EMER D578.

Miscellaneous instructions
Truck, 1/4 ton, GS, 4x4, Austin. EMER D579, instructions 1-12.

Stowage
Stowage sketch: truck, 1/4 ton, cargo and FFW, Austin. WO code 17940.

Radio installation
User handbook: radio installation in FFR 'B' Vehicles. WO code 12798.
User handbook: wireless station C45 in trucks, 1/4 ton, CT, FFW, 4x4, Austin; or trucks, 1/4 ton, GS, 4x4, Ford/Willys or Land Rover. WO code 11852.
Technical handbook; technical description: wireless stations 19HP/C45-24V in truck, 1/4 ton, CT, FFW, 4x4, Austin. EMER M402.

Bibliography
The Champ Enigma. Gowers, Gus. Chelmsford, privately published, 1995.

The Mudlark in Maryland. The story of project TT1-719. Hitchens, Mike and Patrick Hargreaves. Thornton, Colorado USA, Army Motors no 45, 1988. ISSN 0195-5632.

MV1. Truck, 1/4 ton, GS, 4x4, cargo and FFW, Austin. London, ISO Publications, 1984.

CHAPTER 2.2

LAND ROVER B40
FV18001

The story of the development of the Land Rover is probably sufficiently well known to require no more than a short summary.

Maurice Wilkes, director and technical engineer of the then-independent Rover Company, had purchased an ex-army American Jeep for use on his farm in Anglesey, a role which it performed admirably. As the Jeep began to wear out, he realised that there might be a demand for a similar, but purpose-built vehicle, for use on and around, not only his farm but others as well. Perhaps this could help see his company through what was proving a particularly-difficult time. By 1947, a prototype had been put together using a war-surplus Jeep chassis with engine and running gear from the Rover 10 car. To make the vehicle suitable for world-wide markets at minimal cost, the prototype had a central driving position.

This is how the project began, but it was a quirk of fate which determined one of the Land Rover's key features, a feature which contributed to its long-term durability. Unable to gain a government permit for the purchase of steel because the company had no export orders, Rover turned to 'Birmabright' aluminium alloy, the sales of which were not controlled, for constructing the bodywork.

The rest, as they say, is history.

What is less well known is that the military authorities were among the first buyers. Despite the development of the FV1800 project (see Chapter 2.1), there was considerable curiosity to see how this new, Jeep-like machine would perform. In 1948, the Ministry of Supply purchased 52 Land Rovers for appraisal, and in 1949, a further 1878 vehicles were purchased.

The Army classed the Land Rover as a GS or CL vehicle and it was thus not seen as a rival to the FV1800 project. However, it was expected to be able to pull a fully-laden 5cwt trailer, or to tow the 25 lb field gun. Uncertain as to whether the relatively-small 1595cc Rover engine would be satisfactory for these more arduous tasks, and in the interests of the engine standardisation policy, in 1949 it was arranged that Rover would fit the B40 engine into a number of vehicles.

It was not simply a matter of pulling out one engine and installing the other, considerable modification was required to make the big Rolls-Royce engine fit. Once the work was complete, one of the B40-equipped vehicles was trialled at Chertsey together with a standard Series 1

CHAPTER 2.2: LAND ROVER B40

Land Rover and a Wolseley 'Mudlark', the forerunner of the 'Champ'.

History tells us that it was the standard Land Rover which emerged victorious from these trials, so presumably the B40-engined conversion must be seen as one of those brave experiments which might have created a real winner, but which in practice led nowhere at all.

OVERVIEW

The Land Rover was a small, four-wheel drive utility vehicle intended for use in a variety of roles. Typical uses included radio reconnaissance, general transport for personnel and light cargo, and a variety of logistic support tasks. By installing the standardised B40 engine, the Army hoped to provide the vehicle with enhanced off-road performance, and to increase its all-round versatility.

The general layout followed that of the WW2 Jeep on which it was closely modelled. A front-mounted engine was arranged to drive through a unitary-constructed gearbox and transfer case to the rear axle, with the front axle engaged only for increased performance over difficult terrain.

A simple open body provided accommodation for a crew of two or three persons in the front, with a small cargo area to the rear; additional seating for four persons could also be provided on the rear wheel arches. Full weather protection was available, and unlike the WW2 Jeep, the Land Rover was provided with hinged metal doors with windows, and a drop-down tailgate.

DEVELOPMENT

The Rolls-Royce engined Land Rover was an attempt at producing a hybrid vehicle, halfway between the relative simplicity of the Land Rover and the standardised sophistication of the 'Mudlark'.

The result was an impressive, almost dangerous, road machine which had acceleration and top-end performance figures that were closer to the later Series III Land Rover. However, bearing mind the cart-spring suspension system, and general lack of sophistication of the early Land Rover, it should not really be a surprise that adding another 100 kilos of weight over the front axle, did nothing for its performance off road.

The experiment cannot have been cheap either, the B40 engine cost nearly £200 at a time when the whole Land Rover was only priced at £450.

Production

A prototype was produced by Rolls-Royce, presumably simply to prove the feasibility of the project. This must

VEHICLE OUTLINES

SCALE 1:50

SPECIFICATION

Dimensions and weight
Length: 3683mm.
Width: 1588mm.
Height: 1930mm.
Wheelbase: 2209mm.
Track: 1270mm.
Ground clearance: 216mm.

Weight: 1765kg, laden; 1380kg, unladen.
Bridge classification: 2.

Performance
Maximum speed: 98km/h, on road; 25km/h, cross country.
Fuel consumption: 0.12 litre/km, on road.
Maximum range: 230km, on road.

Turning circle: 11.44m.

Capacity
Maximum load: 250kg.
Maximum towed load: 500kg.

have been accepted by the Ministry because a further 33, or possibly 34, standard vehicles were supplied to a London engineering firm, Hudson Motors Limited, straight off the production line, for the conversion work.

The standard engines were removed by Hudsons and replaced by the Rolls-Royce B40, Mk 2B engine; 54 engines of this type were produced especially for this project. The original Land Rover engines were returned to the factory.

A considerable amount of re-working was required to make the conversion successful. For example, in order that the sump would clear the differential casing, the front axle was moved forward by 25mm (giving an 81 inch wheelbase), and was mounted on stronger springs. The transfer gear ratios were changed to keep the tractive effort at approximately the same figure as the standard Land Rover. Finally, the brakes were beefed-up to be able to cope with the additional weight.

The standard 250mm clutch of the B40 engine was retained, and this necessitated a new bell housing, together with modified linkages. Changes were required to the chassis cross members, the propeller shaft was lengthened, and the battery re-positioned beneath the passenger seat. The size of the radiator was increased and the cooling system pressurisation increased.

Although this is not evident in the photograph of the Rolls-Royce prototype, it was not possible to close the bonnet completely and, even with rubber blocks holding it up by 25mm or so, a hole still had to be cut in the bonnet to clear the cap.

Along with these other changes, the B40 engine added more than 100kg to the weight of the standard machine.

Replacement and disposal

The experiment was not considered a success and within 12 months most of the vehicles had been disposed of. In time, the 'Mudlark' became the 'Champ', remaining in service until 1966. Ironically, the standard Land Rover went from strength to strength, ultimately replacing the 'Champ' and remaining in service to this day.

Two of these vehicles are known to remain, one is in private hands, the other, subsequently converted to a Royal review vehicle, is at the Museum of Army Transport at Beverley.

NOMENCLATURE

FV18001. Truck, 1/4 ton, GS, cargo, 4x4, Rover, Mk 1.

The original, unmodified version of this vehicle was classified as 'CL'.

Rolls-Royce constructed prototype vehicle (RR)

One of the production B40-equipped Land Rovers (BMIHT)

View of the B40, Mk 2B engine (BMIHT)

DESCRIPTION

Engine
Rolls-Royce B40, No 1, Mk 2B; wet sump.
Capacity: 2838cc.
Bore and stroke: 3.50 x 4.50in.
Power output: 80bhp (gross); 69bhp (net) at 3750rpm.
Maximum torque: 138 lbs/ft (gross); 115 lbs/ft (net) at 2150rpm.

Detail variations
Oil filter mounted on crankcase; deep sump; cooling fan mounted on water pump; conventional clutch housing; centre outlet exhaust manifold; horizontal inlet manifold with vertical carburettor-mounting flange; 12V electrical equipment.

Transmission
The engine drove through the standard Borg and Beck 250mm clutch of the B40, to a four-speed gearbox with reverse, and a two speed transfer case; synchromesh was provided on third and fourth gear. The front and rear driven axles were of the spiral bevel type, connected to the transmission by open Hardy Spicer shafts: the front axle was fully floating, the rear axle semi-floating.

Suspension
The live axles were suspended on semi-elliptic leaf springs, with hydraulic telescopic shock absorbers.

Steering gear
Burman Douglas worm-and-nut steering was employed, with the tie rod installed in front of the axle in the same style as a WW2 Jeep. The sprung steering wheel gave 2.5 turns from lock to lock.

Braking system
Girling hydraulic brakes were installed, with 250mm drums front and rear. The mechanical handbrake operated on the transmission via a 225mm drum at the rear of the transfer case.

Road wheels
Standard WD pattern 4.50E x 16in split-rim wheels were fitted, mounting 6.50x16 Dunlop 'Trakgrip' cross-country type tyres.

Chassis
The chassis was of all-welded steel design, with deep channel-type side members, and five main cross members. All cross members were boxed-in for strength. Some modification was made to the chassis cross members to accept the B40 engine.

Bodywork
Aluminium-alloy open bodywork was fitted, with hinged/removable doors and tailgate, and fully-enclosed wings. The simple, flat windscreen did not open but was designed to fold onto the bonnet in the style of the WW2 Jeep.

Weather equipment
Complete weather-proof enclosure was provided by means of a canvas tilt supported by a simple metal frame.

Electrical equipment
The starter and generator were standard commercial types, and the 12V electrical equipment of the original Land Rover was retained.

DOCUMENTATION

Bibliography
The Inch War. Hutchings, Tony. London, Classic and Sportscar magazine, June 1982.

Profile: Land Lords. Cooke, Bob. London, Classic and Sportscar magazine, October 1989.

B40: MINOR APPLICATIONS & PROTOTYPES
FV2401, FV4002, FV11103

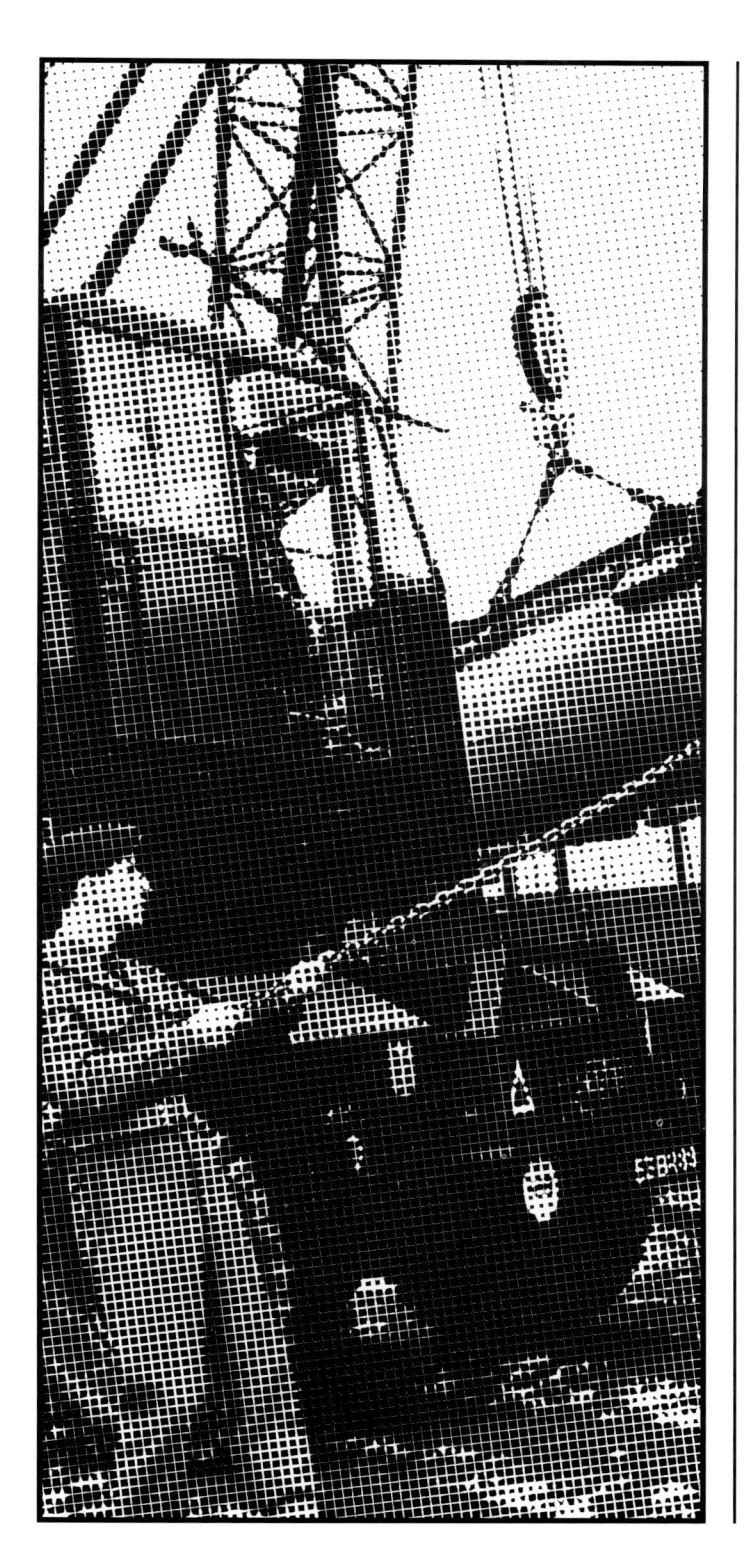

Between them, Rolls-Royce and Austin constructed a total of 19,137 B40 engines of various marks. Of these, the 'Champ' and Land Rover B40 accounted for nearly 99% of the production, a total of some 18,930 units. The balance of 207 engines were fitted into various experimental projects and low-volume production vehicles.

The most significant of these applications was the hydraulic system of the 'Centurion' bridgelayer, for which 40 engines were supplied. Other installations included the Auto Diesels 10kVA mobile generator set (84 engines); and the Jones KL66 mobile crane (59 engines). This chapter examines these minor applications in a little more detail.

Other applications which have been identified, but where no additional detail is to hand, include an airfield ground air-conditioning unit produced by Temperature Limited, a flame thrower project, and a medium anti-aircraft gun, possibly manufactured by Vickers. These last three projects used less than 25 engines, and none was pursued beyond the experimental stage.

'CENTURION' BRIDGELAYER

Design work on the 'Centurion' main battle tank began in 1944, with prototypes being delivered to Germany in May 1945, just too late to be battle tested. Variously produced by the Royal Ordnance Factory Leeds, and by Vickers and Leyland Motors, the tank was developed over 15 or so years into a total of 13 marks, and saw service with roughly a dozen armies. Production was completed in 1961 and the 'Centurion' was superseded by the 'Chieftain' which began to enter service in 1967.

Aside from the main battle tank, variants included an armoured recovery vehicle (ARV), beach armoured recovery vehicle (BARV), armoured vehicle Royal Engineers (AVRE), and two types of bridgelayer.

Although all 'Centurion' variants were powered by Rolls-Royce 'Meteor' petrol engines, 'B Series' engines were also used to drive auxiliary systems. The hydraulic power for the bridge-launching system of the Mk 5 bridgelayer employed a B40 engine; the motive power for the winch on the 'Centurion' ARV was derived from a B80 unit, and this is dealt with in Chapter 4.8.

Description
Based on the Mk 5 'Centurion' chassis, the 'Centurion' bridgelayer is used to launch, and recover a Class 80 No

6 single-span tank bridge, with a maximum width of 13.725m, across a river or ditch. Pressure in the hydraulic launch system is generated by a B40, Mk 5P engine driving a Towler high-pressure pump and single hydraulic ram.

Designed by FVRDE to War Office specifications, the first prototype was produced in 1960, with trials commencing in 1961.

The basic tank chassis was stripped of the turret and main armament in order to provide a mounting for the bridge unit which, in the travelling position, lays back across the hull. The bridge is of portal frame design with two arched trackways and a flat underside. Although normally carried fully assembled, the bridge actually consisted of four separate sections, and could be broken down for transport on 3 ton trucks.

Separate decking panels were carried on the side of the vehicle which could be laid by hand to fill the space between the trackways and provide a full-width deck. Spare portal frames were also carried.

The vehicle was provided with a jib assembly which was used to assemble the bridge sections. The launching mechanism consisted of a launch arm which carried the bridge, a roller frame which supported one end of the bridge on the ground, and a hydraulic ram.

The launching operation was electrically controlled by solenoid-operated valves, and was carried out from inside the armoured hull by one operator. During the launch and recovery cycles, the bridge was turned through 180 degrees on the ram; a counterweight on the opposite end of the vehicle hull ensured stability during this operation. The actual launching took just 100 seconds, and the bridge could be made ready for use within two to three minutes of the unit being positioned at the obstacle.

Nomenclature
FV4002. Bridgelayer, Centurion, Mk 5.

Dimensions and weight
Overall dimensions, vehicle and bridge:
Length: 16,318mm.
Width: 4267mm.
Height: 3889mm.

Overall dimensions, bridge only:
Length: 15,850mm.
Clear span: 13,720mm.
Width: 4267mm.
Height: 1370mm.

Weight: unladen, 48,864kg; laden, 60,960kg; bridge only, 7000kg.

FV4002 'Centurion' Mk 5 bridgelayer in action (IWM)

FV11103 Jones KL66 Mk 2 crane on Albion chassis (IWM)

Auto Diesels 10kVA mobile generator (TMB)

Bridge classification: 60.

Bridging performance
Maximum hydraulic pressure: 3kgf/sq mm.
Fording: 1067mm.
Maximum bank-to-bank height differential: 2440mm.
Maximum permissible fore and aft tilt: 15 degrees.
Maximum lateral tilt: 6 degrees.

Documentation
User handbook: bridgelayer, Centurion Mk 5. Army code 13382.

Illustrated spare parts list: bridgelayer, Centurion Mk 5. Army code 11195.

JONES KL66 4/6 TON MOBILE CRANE

Where purpose-built bridgelayers were not available or for whatever reason, were not appropriate, bridge construction in the field was carried out using commercial cranes adapted for use on rough terrain. The Jones KL66 crane, with a capacity of up to 6 tons lift was available mounted on a heavy truck chassis for this purpose.

Manufactured by K&L Steel Founders and Engineers of Letchworth, the Jones KL66 mobile crane employed a B40, Mk 2F or Mk 5F engine, with 'Iso-speedic' governor, as motive power for hoisting, slewing and derricking. Three prototypes were produced in 1953, and the complete crane-and-truck assembly was demonstrated at the 1954 British Military Vehicle display at Chertsey mounted on an Albion WD/HD/23, 6x4, 10 ton chassis, and designated FV11103. It is difficult to ascertain exactly how many were constructed, but the Rolls-Royce production records show that a total of 59 engines were supplied for use in this application.

The crane itself was available in three versions, designated as either Mk 1, Mk 2 or Mk 3. The Mk 1 had a 35ft lattice jib giving a maximum hoisting capacity of 4 tons, or alternatively, a 25ft straight channel jib with a capacity of 6 tons. The Mk 2 was available only with the straight channel jib. The Mk 3 was a four-wheeled, self-propelled version of the Mk 2.

The engine and its associated machinery were mounted on a revolving frame, which was totally enclosed by a steel superstructure. A glazed cab was provided for the operator, and all of the crane operations were controlled from the one driving position. The jibs were provided with visual load-and-radius indicators, together with 'Wylie' safe load indicators.

Drive from the engine was taken through a three-speed gearbox, and all crane operations were available through the three gear ranges.

Wire rope of 14mm diameter (6/25 construction) was used for derricking operations; 16mm rope (6/37 construction) for hoisting. A single sheave block was employed which could easily be adapted to three-part, two-part or single rope operation for the 25ft jib, or two-part and single rope operation for the 35ft jib.

Nomenclature
FV11103. Truck, 10 ton, 6x4, GS (Albion), crane, GP.

Dimensions and weight

	25ft jib	35ft jib
Overall dimensions, including truck chassis* (mm):		
Length:		
less jib	8230	8230
jib projecting to rear	1463	1737
jib stowed	1074	1098
Width:		
overall	2510	2510
superstructure only	2440	2440
crane overhang, slewed 90 deg	650	650
Height:		
jib fully raised	9750	12,800
jib stowed	4120	3990
maximum height of lift, at hook	7010	9450
Weight (kg)	19,610	19,914

* All dimensions refer to crane mounted on Albion chassis.

Bridge classification: 20.

Crane performance
Hoisting (third gear): 12.2m/min on three-part rope; 18.3m/min on two-part rope; 36.6m/min on single rope.
Derricking (third gear): 6900mm radius to 27,500mm radius in 20 secs.
Slewing (third gear): 2.5rpm.

Documentation
User handbook: crane, truck-mounted, 4 and 6 ton, KL66, Mk 1, and crane, truck-mounted, 6 ton, KL66, Mk 2. WO code 18476.

Servicing schedule: crane, truck-mounted, 4 and 6 ton, KL66, Mk 1, and crane, truck-mounted, 6 ton, KL66, Mk 2. WO code 10387-1.

Illustrated parts list: crane, truck-mounted, 4 and 6 ton, KL66, Mk 1, and crane, truck-mounted, 6 ton, KL66, Mk 2. WO code 11227.

AUTO DIESELS 10kVA MOBILE GENERATOR

The Auto Diesels mobile generating set was designed to provide a three-phase power and lighting supply for industrial uses in REME workshops and Light Aid Detachments (LAD). Three prototypes were produced in 1953, and a total of 84 machines was produced.

The equipment consisted of a B40, Mk 2D or Mk 5H engine driving a three-phase, four-pole alternator through a helical reduction (1.5:1) gearbox. The machinery was installed on a skid-type under-base complete with switchboard, exciter control panel, fuel tank, toolbox and tools, and all ancillary equipment. The complete unit could be mounted on a modified Brockhouse (FV2401A/5) 1 ton two-wheeled military trailer chassis, fitted with a metal canopy and canvas side curtains.

The alternator, supplied by McFarlane Engineering, was of the 'Magnicon' revolving field type, producing three-phase supplies rated at 415/240V 50Hz and 208/120V 60Hz. Maximum output was 10kVA.

Nomenclature
Generating set, AC, 10kVA, 415/240V 50Hz, 208/120V 60Hz, 3 phase, No 1 Mk 1, trailer-mounted.
FV2401(Q). Trailer, 1 ton, 2W/1L, 10kVA, single-phase generator.

Dimensions and weight
Overall dimensions, including trailer chassis:
Length (including drawbar): 3365mm.
Width: 2288mm.
Height: 2593mm.

Weight: 2122kg.
Bridge classification: 3.

Overall dimensions, skid-mounted equipment:
Length: 2364mm.
Width: 1093mm.
Height: 1524mm.

Weight: 1384kg.

Electrical performance
Power output: 10kVA at 0.8pf, 415/240V 50Hz, at 2250rpm (engine speed), phase amps 13.8A; or 10kVA at 0.8pf, 208/120V 60Hz, at 2700rpm, phase amps 27.6A.
Efficiency on full load: 0.78 at 0.8pf.
Fuel consumption on full load: 9-10 litres/hr.

Documentation
Technical description: generating set, AC, 10kVA, 415/240V 50Hz, 208/120V 60Hz, 3 phase, No 1 Mk 1, trailer-mounted; McFarlane electrical equipment. EMER CO12/1.

User handbook: generating set, AC, 10kVA, 415/240V 50Hz, 208/120V 60Hz, 3 phase, No 1 Mk 1, trailer-mounted. WO code 11193.

Illustrated parts list: generating set, AC, 10kVA, 415/240V 50Hz, 208/120V 60Hz, 3 phase, No 1 Mk 1, trailer-mounted. WO code 11227.

Plant servicing schedule: generating set, AC, 10kVA, 415/240V 50Hz, 208/120V 60Hz, 3 phase, No 1 Mk 1, trailer-mounted. WO code 11031.

CHAPTER 3

THE B60 ENGINE
B60 Mk 2, Mk 3, Mk 5, Mk 6

CONTENTS
3.1	Daimler 'Ferret'	77
3.2	Humber 1 ton truck	89
3.3	Humber armoured truck	101

DATA SUMMARY

Dimensions and weight
Overall installed dimensions
Length: 1062mm.
Width: 720mm.
Height (with standard wet sump): 1030mm.

Dry weight: 372kg.

Performance
Bore: 88.9mm, 3.50in.
Stroke: 114.3mm, 4.50in.
Swept volume: 4256cc.

Compression ratio: 6.4:1.
Firing order: 142635

Gross output, uninstalled: 130bhp at 3750rpm.
Gross torque: 209 lbs/ft.

Fuel consumption, maximum demand: 39 litres/hr at 3000rpm; 45 litres/hr at 3750rpm.

PRODUCTION SUMMARY

Mark	Qty	Vehicle and FV number	
B60, Mk 2 engines:			
Mk 2A	260	Humber 1 ton truck	FV1600
			FV1601
			FV1602
			FV1604
		Humber armoured truck/APC	FV1611
			FV1612
			FV1613
B60, Mk 3 engines:			
Mk 3A	34	Daimler 'Ferret'	FV701
B60, Mk 5 engines:			
Mk 5A	4440	Humber 1 ton truck	FV1601
			FV1602
			FV1604
			FV1621
		Humber armoured truck/APC	FV1609
			FV1611
			FV1612
			FV1613
Mk 5C	25	Thornycroft crash tender pump	FV14161*
Mk 5D	5	HML airfield hydraulic power unit	-
Mk 5F	9	Humber 'Hornet' Malkara launcher	FV1620
Mk 5G	308	Vernon generator set	-
Mk 5K	11	Humber Malkara test truck	FV1622
B60, Mk 6 engines:			
Mk 6A	9395	Daimler 'Ferret'	FV701
			FV703
			FV704
			FV711
			FV712
Total	**14487**		

* Powered by a B81, Mk 5Q or Mk 5R engine, see page 179.

CHAPTER 3.1

DAIMLER FERRET
FV701, FV703, FV704, FV711, FV712

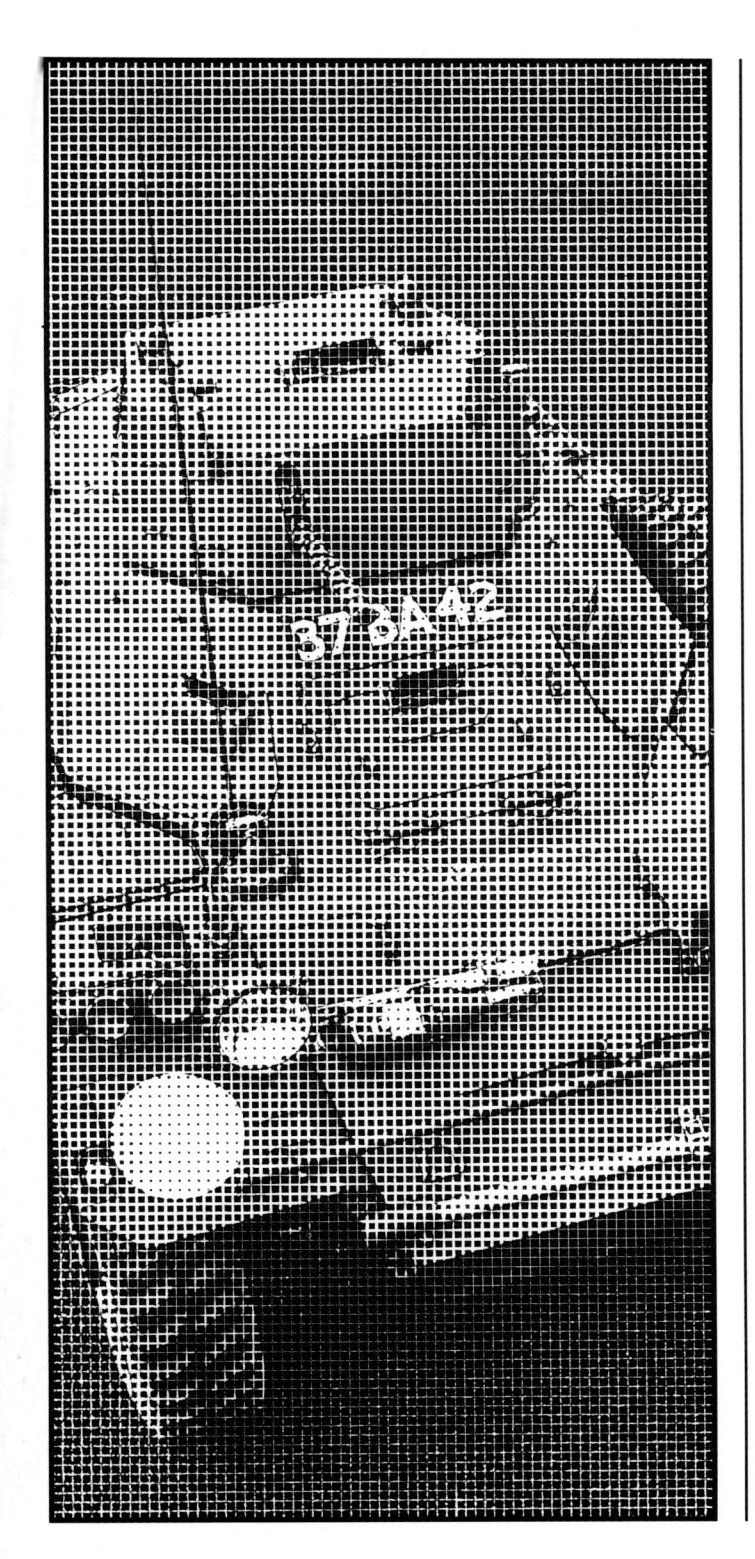

The British Army is among the best-equipped, most-professional fighting forces in the world. It is surprising therefore, that the 'Ferret' armoured scout car, which was originally accepted into service in the early 1950's, should have remained at its post for so long. In fact, for more than 40 years.

Maybe it is testament to the soundness of the original design brief and the success with which the Daimler Company was able to fulfil it. Or, maybe it is witness to the fact that 'real' war, fought by men with mud on their boots and guns in their hands, has changed rather less since 1950 than the complex technology suggests, and the strategists would have us believe.

Whatever the reason, without doubt, the 'Ferret' was one of the most successful wheeled armoured vehicles of all time.

OVERVIEW

The 'Ferret' was a small four-wheeled, low-silhouette (less than 1750mm high in Mk 1 form) armoured scout car with permanent all-wheel drive and excellent cross-country capability. It was intended for use on improved and unimproved roads, and in some versions had limited amphibious capability. The hull armour ranged in thickness from 12 to 16mm, sufficient to provide protection against machine-gun and small-arms fire, and shell splinters.

A rear-facing, rear-mounted engine was arranged to drive to a unit-construction, centrally-mounted five-speed pre-selector gearbox, differential and final drive, with drive shafts arranged in an H configuration, driving separately to each wheel. This arrangement allowed the driver to sit between the drive shafts and helped to maintain a low profile.

The vehicle was manufactured in open and closed versions. The Mk 1 'Ferret' was an open-topped light liaison vehicle, armed with a machine gun; the Mk 1/2, and Mks 2-5 reconnaissance vehicles were fitted with a turret, in the case of the Mk 2/6 and Mk 5 versions, mounting anti-tank missiles, in other versions mounting a machine gun. Mk 4 and Mk 5 vehicles also had larger wheels and improved amphibious capability.

The liaison versions were designed for a crew of two, a commander/gunner (or controller) and a driver; reconnaissance vehicles were intended to be manned by a crew of driver, gunner and commander. The interior

CHAPTER 3.1: DAIMLER FERRET

was not particularly spacious and, with all hatches closed down, even the two-man crew must have found conditions extremely cramped.

'Ferrets' were always considered to be air portable, even in the days when this was not considered the norm and when aircraft such as 'Beverleys' were used. Experiments were also carried out with air-dropping of 'Ferrets' by platform and parachute cluster.

Although only lightly-armed, the 'Ferret' was never intended to engage enemy fire - in fact, it could be argued that if a 'Ferret' came under fire it had failed in one of its major objectives. However, with a power to weight ratio of around 30 bhp/tonne, it was fast, highly mobile and extremely effective in its chosen roles.

DEVELOPMENT

During WW2, Daimler had produced the BSA-designed 'Dingo' armoured scout car. A fast, quiet and highly manoeuvrable vehicle, the 'Dingo' was enormously successful in its intended light reconnaissance role, well-suited to hit and run raids, airfield or fuel dump interdiction operations, 'behind-the-lines' intelligence gathering, and similar exercises. The 'Dingo' philosophy was to get in, do the job, and get out as quickly, and with as little fuss as possible.

When WW2 came to an end, the War Office and the Ministry of Supply set about developing specifications for new equipment, putting into practice the logistic lessons that had been learned during six years of conflict (see Chapter 1.1).

Unlike the Americans, the British Army had always been keen on wheeled armoured vehicles, and as part of the post-war military vehicle programme, there was to be a new light-armoured scout car or reconnaissance vehicle. The new scout car was intended to replace the highly-successful 'Dingo', and was to take its place alongside the other new post-war combat vehicle designs.

The specification was drawn-up in 1947 and a development contract was let to the Daimler Company of Coventry the following year. The vehicle was to follow the general design and layout of the 'Dingo', but was to incorporate the latest automotive thinking, including the use of the standardised engine. At the same time, the opportunity was taken of upgrading the hull ballistics. A prototype appeared in 1950.

The first vehicle in its definitive form was the Mk 1, FV701(C). This was somewhat inappropriately dubbed 'Fieldmouse', and it wasn't until the second vehicle was produced, the Mk 2, FV701(E) variation, that the name 'Ferret' was adopted. When series production got

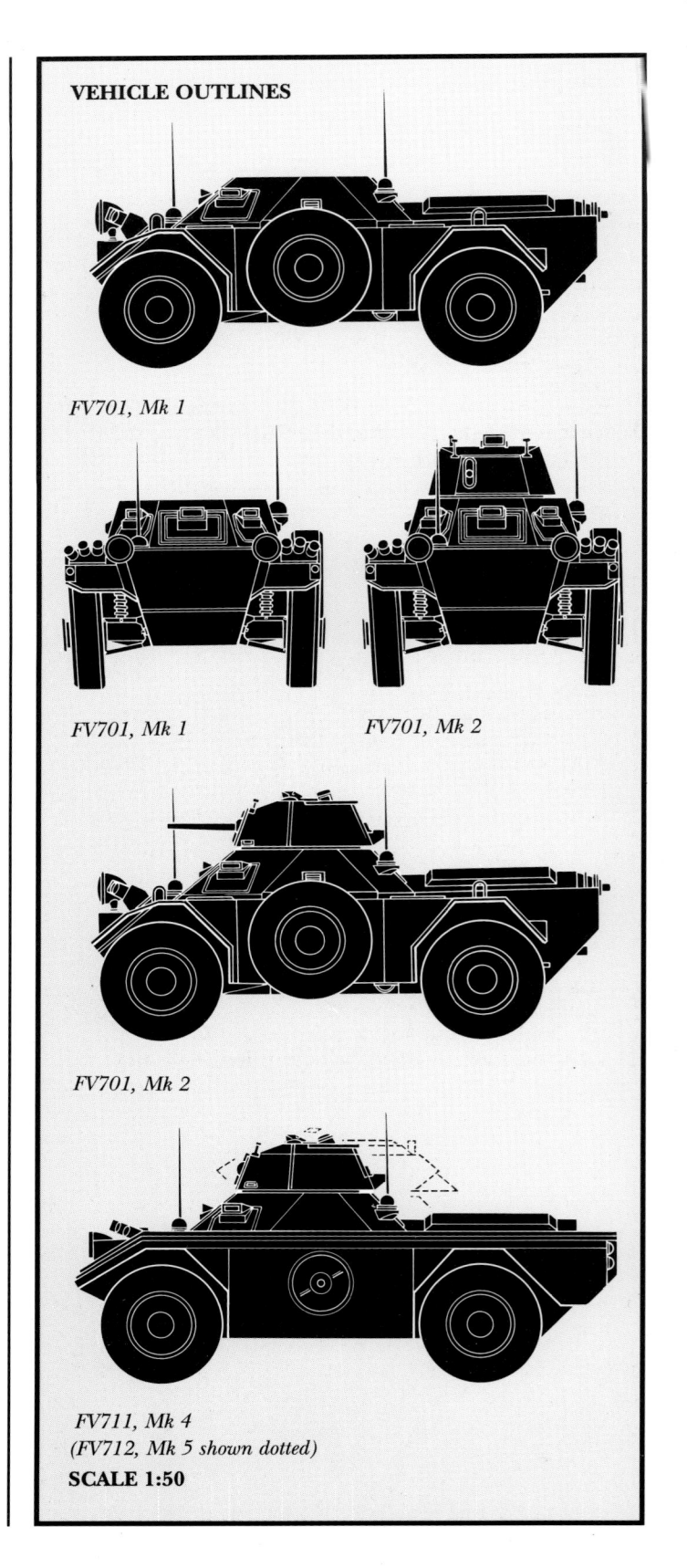

VEHICLE OUTLINES

FV701, Mk 1

FV701, Mk 1   *FV701, Mk 2*

FV701, Mk 2

FV711, Mk 4
(FV712, Mk 5 shown dotted)

SCALE 1:50

CHAPTER 3.1: DAIMLER FERRET

SPECIFICATION

Dimensions and weight

	Mk 1	Mk 1/2	Mk 2	Mk 3, 4, 5
Dimensions (mm):				
Length	3835	3835	3835	4095
Width	1905	1905	1905	2134
Height	1448	1651	1879	2336
Wheelbase	2286	2286	2286	2286
Track	1539	1539	1539	1750
Ground clearance	330	330	330	432
Weight (kg):				
Combat weight	4210	4370	4500	5400
Unladen weight	3510	3660	3680	4725
Bridge classification	4	4	4	5

Performance

	Mk 1	Mk 1/2	Mk 2	Mk 3, 4, 5
Speed (km/h):				
Maximum, on road	93	93	93	80
Average, off road	40	40	40	40
Maximum, in water	-	-	-	4*
Angle of operation (deg):				
Approach angle	60	60	60	55
Departure angle	50	50	50	47
Entry to water	-	-	-	25*
Departure from water	-	-	-	25*

* Mk 4 vehicles only.

Fuel consumption: 0.31 litre/km, on road.
Maximum range: 306km, on road; 160km, off road.

Turning circle: 11.58m.
Vertical obstacle: 406mm.
Ditch crossing (trench) with channels: 1220mm.
Maximum gradient: 46%.
Maximum gradient for stop and restart: 30%.
Fording: unprepared, 910mm; prepared, 1524mm.

---

underway, it was the Mk 2 vehicles which were delivered first.

Although the hull ballistics were better than the 'Dingo', some additional work was conducted with a view to making further improvements. In 1957, for example, armour-proving and anti-tank trials were conducted at FVRDE, and in 1967, up-armouring trials. These trials led to the production of the Mk 1/1, and Mks 2/3-2/5 versions.

Considering that the first 'Ferrets' were accepted for service in 1951, and there was very little subsequent re-development (as opposed to simple upgrading), Daimler made a remarkable job of the design work in a space of just three years.

Production

The post-war procurement procedure for military vehicles normally separated the design/development, and manufacturing phases of a project, but in this case, Daimler were also awarded the contract to manufacture the 'Ferret'. Production began in 1952, and was spread over 20 years, with the last vehicle entering service in 1971. A total of 4409 'Ferrets' was produced, including those which were supplied to overseas customers. This compares to a production total of 6626 for the WW2 'Dingo'.

By far the majority of the production total went into service with the British Army, but 'Ferrets' have also been used by the armies of more than 30 countries, including Bahrain, Burma, Burundi, Cameroon, Canada, Central African Republic, France, Gabon, Gambia, Ghana, Indonesia, Jordan, Kuwait, Libya, Madagascar, Malaysia, New Zealand, Nigeria, Portugal, Qatar, RSA, Rhodesia, Saudi Arabia, Somalia, Sri Lanka, Upper Volta, Yemen, and Zambia.

Faced with the uprising in Algeria, the French purchased a number of Mk 1 and Mk 2 'Ferrets', initially as an interim measure, but they were sufficiently impressed with the vehicle to consider producing a version under licence. There was considerable resistance from the French arms industry, and ultimately it was decided that the 'Ferret' was insufficiently armed, and the Panhard AML (automitrailleuse legere - light-armoured car) was chosen as a replacement.

In 1955, the Australian Army hosted joint armoured-vehicle trials of both 'Ferrets' and 'Saracen' APCs, presumably with the intention of perhaps buying quantities of each. The trials, which included wet/hot, dry/hot and road use phases took place at Innisfail and Mt Ina in Queensland. In the event, no 'Ferrets' went into service with the Australian Army.

CHAPTER 3.1: DAIMLER FERRET

Replacement and disposal

In the same way that the 'Ferret' replaced the 'Dingo' as a front line vehicle, the intention was that it would, in turn, be replaced by the new 'Combat vehicle, reconnaissance, wheeled' (CVR,W) and related 'Tracked' (CVR,T) range.

The 'wheeled' range included the more-advanced aluminium-armoured, Jaguar-engined 'Fox' and 'Vixen' vehicles, both of which were based on the general hull design of the Mk 4 'Ferret'. With its larger turret and powerful 30mm Rarden cannon, the 'Fox' was to fulfil the reconnaissance role, whilst the similar 'Vixen' was to provide the liaison vehicle. However, the 'Vixen' project was cancelled as part of the defence cuts of the early 1970's, and although the 'Fox' had already been accepted into service in 1970, in practice, it proved rather less than satisfactory.

If proof were needed that the 'Ferret' rates as one of the most successful vehicles of its type ever produced, it is surely evidenced by the fact that, around the world, a small number of 'Ferrets' soldier on, virtually unchanged - 40 years after their introduction!

NOMENCLATURE and VARIATIONS

The 'Ferret' was produced in five Marks, most with minor variations. The Mk 1/2 and Mk 2 versions were the most numerous: the Mk 3 version was produced only as a prototype.

FV701. Car, scout, 4x4, liaison, Ferret, Mk 1
FV701(C), Mk 1. Open-topped liaison vehicle; designed to mount a .30 Browning or .303 Bren.

FV701(J), Mk 1/1. Up-armoured version of Mk 1, with thicker side and rear hull plates incorporated during manufacture (see also Mk 3).

FV701. Car, scout, 4x4, floating, Ferret, Mk 1/3
As standard Mk 1/1, but fitted with rubberised-fabric collapsible flotation screen and tubular frame, and with a raised, sealed air intake duct enclosing the engine compartment. Also occasionally described as Mk 1/1 'floating'. Production limited to pilot vehicles only.

FV701. Car, scout, 4x4, reconnaissance, Ferret, Mk 2
FV701(E), Mk 2. Reconnaissance vehicle; fitted with two-door rotating turret, mounting a .30 Browning.

FV701(E), Mk 2/1. Reconnaissance vehicle; fitted with two-door rotating turret, mounting a .30 Browning; additional stowage for .303 Bren.

FV701(E), Mk 2/2. Reconnaissance vehicle; fitted with armoured extension collar (between the hull and turret), for better observation, and three-door rotating turret,

Mock-up of Mk 2 'Ferret' at FVRDE (IWM)

Prototype of FV701(C) Mk 1 'Ferret' (TMB)

FV701(C) Mk 1 'Ferret' production vehicle (IWM)

CHAPTER 3.1: DAIMLER FERRET

FV701 Mk 1/3 floating 'Ferret' with screen and air duct (TMB)

FV701(E) Mk 2 'Ferret' (TMB)

FV701(E) Mk 2/2 'Ferret' with extension collar (IWM)

mounting a .30 Browning. This was a local modification undertaken in the Far East.

A second variation on this theme was intended to produce an open-topped liaison vehicle with better observation, and consisted of the Mk 2/2 vehicle with the rotating turret removed and a machine gun ring and pintle mount for a .30 Browning installed directly to the turret collar. Although the increased height allowed easier observation from the vehicle, it also had the disadvantage of making the vehicle more visible.

FV701(H), Mk 2/3. Up-armoured version of Mk 2, with thicker side and rear hull plates incorporated during manufacture.

Also existed as Mk 2/4, which was an up-armoured version of Mk 2, with retro-fitted applique plates to the sides and rear of the hull and turret.

FV701(H), Mk 2/5. Up-armoured version of Mk 2/1 vehicle to bring it up to the standard of the Mk 2/4, with retro-fitted applique plates to the sides and rear of the hull and turret.

FV701(H), Mk 2/7. As Mk 2/6 but with missiles removed: in other words, returned more-or-less to Mk 2/3 configuration.

FV701(H), Mk 2/8. As Mk 2/3 but fitted with 7.62mm general-purpose machine gun (GPMG).

FV703. Car, scout, 4x4, reconnaissance/guided weapon, Ferret, Mk 2/6
As Mk 2/3 but with two BAC 'Vigilant' wire-guided anti-tank missiles fitted to the turret sides; two 'reload' missiles were carried on the hull side in place of the spare wheel.

FV704. Car, scout, liaison, Ferret, Mk 1/2
Reconnaissance vehicle; as Mk 1/1, but with fixed turret having a two-part hinged roof.

Car, scout, reconnaissance, Ferret, Mk 3
As Mk 1/3 reconnaissance vehicle (also sometimes referred to as Mk 1/1 'floating'), but fitted with larger (11.00 x 20in) wheels and tyres; and with new watertight stowage bins.

This was to be the first vehicle of the improved 'Ferret' design but in the event, only prototypes were constructed and there was no series production of the 'improved' turretless vehicle. However, the Mk 3 provided the basic hull design for Mk 4 and Mk 5 vehicles (and the later 'Fox' and 'Vixen').

FV711. Car, scout, 4x4, reconnaissance, Ferret, Mk 4
The so-called 'big-wheeled Ferret' with a new hull design derived from the Mk 3; reconnaissance vehicle (improved

CHAPTER 3.1: DAIMLER FERRET

version of Mk 2/3); fitted with two-door rotating turret, mounting a .30 Browning; 11.00 x 20in wheels and tyres; watertight stowage bins; and with a collapsible flotation screen permanently attached to the hull.

FV712. Car, scout, 4x4, reconnaissance/guided weapon, Ferret, Mk 5

Similar to Mk 4, with flotation screen, but with a completely redesigned aluminium-armoured turret (produced by Alvis, and the first use, incidentally, of aluminium armour in a British AFV), mounting two twin-launchers for 'Swingfire' anti-tank guided missiles; two 'reload' missiles are carried in an armoured box on each side of the superstructure. A 7.62mm general-purpose macine gun (GPMG) was installed in the turret front, between the missile launchers. Only 50 vehicles were produced before the Alvis 'Striker' was nominated as the successor to the anti-tank 'Ferret'.

Modifications to basic 'mark' variations

Where the suffix 'M' is appended to the mark designation (eg, Mk 1/2M), it indicates that the vehicle was modified to minimise damage and injury to the crew in the event of running over a mine. These modifications included a fixed fire-fighting system and a reduction in the number of bolt attachments for the suspension components.

Workshop modifications

Amphibious role

The earliest amphibious experiments with the 'Ferret' employed a rubberised, collapsible flotation screen like those fitted to WW2 DD tanks during the D-Day landings. These screens were fitted to some half-dozen Mk 1/3 vehicles, and when erected, provided a limited amphibious capability on calm inland waters, with the minimum of preparation. Unfortunately, the screens proved rather vulnerable to damage and for this reason, the vehicle crews were supplied with a puncture outfit!

The experiments took a slightly different turn when at least one Mk 2/3 vehicle was fitted with three rubberised-fabric flotation bags, designed to be inflated by a small on-board compressor or by engine exhaust gas; the bags were manufactured by RFD Limited of Godalming. A metal screen was erected around the engine compartment covers to prevent the engine being drowned by backwash during amphibious operations.

In 1958, a number of Mk 1 vehicles were modified to provide amphibious capability by building out the hull with blocks of rigid grp-skinned polyurethane foam.

Each of these variations, and particularly the versions using flotation bags and with foam buoyancy blocks, allowed the vehicle to float, but there was no means of forward propulsion other than the wheels and, for the amphibious capability to be effective, a towing vehicle

FV703 Mk 2/6 'Ferret' with BAC 'Vigilant' ATGW (TMB)

FV704 Mk 1/2 'Ferret' with fixed turret (IWM)

FV711 Mk 4 'big-wheeled Ferret' (BTMC)

CHAPTER 3.1: DAIMLER FERRET

FV711 Mk 4 'Ferret' with flotation screen erected (BTMC)

FV712 Mk 5 'Ferret' with 'Swingfire' ATGW (BTMC)

FV702 Mk 2 'Ferret' with rubberised flotation bags (TMB)

was required. These experiments were thus only seen as a stepping stone to the development of the truly amphibious Mk 4.

The Mk 4 achieved greater buoyancy by combining the flotation screen with the use of larger-section tyres, which were also used to provide propulsion in the water at a speed of about 3-5km/h.

Radar role
In the early 70's, a number of Mk 2/3 vehicles were adapted to carry the Elliott Automation ZB 298 ground surveillance radar system. This radar system was intended to locate motor transport and AFV's over long distances.

The scanning equipment was mounted on the turret top and the vehicle did not carry the normal turret machine gun. The radar could be stowed under the armour if necessary, and operated either from inside the vehicle, or dismounted, and operated from the ground.

Recovery role
In 1962, a Mk 2 'Ferret' was converted by the REME LAD (Light Aid Detachment) of the Royal Horse Guards to provide a light armoured recovery vehicle. The roof plates and turret were removed, and an adjustable 'A'-frame jib fitted to the rear; lifting power was provided by the use of a small hand winch located on the hull front, rigged to the jib.

The vehicle was put into service in this form, and trials were conducted to evaluate its usefulness. At some later date, the turret was refitted and the vehicle continued to be used for light recovery work in this form. A second vehicle was converted, this time with a fixed jib, but as with the first experiment, no series production was entered.

A replica of the first vehicle resides at the REME museum at Bordon in Hampshire.

Mine destroyer role
A number of Mk 2/3 vehicles were converted to mine detector/destroyer configuration in Cyprus by the addition of twin-wheel rollers on outriggers, running ahead of the front wheels.

Uprating
During the 1960's, Alvis, who had become the design authority for the 'Ferret', attempted to improve the vehicle's firepower. Prototype vehicles were demonstrated to foreign customers, firstly with a conical turret mounting a 20mm Hispano cannon; and secondly with a ring mount installed on the hull of a Mk 1 vehicle, designed to mount a 20mm Oerlikon cannon. Neither was successful.

In 1988, a further development program was undertaken

THE ROLLS-ROYCE 'B SERIES' ENGINE

CHAPTER 3.1: DAIMLER FERRET

to try and bring the vehicle up-to-date. Known as 'Ferret 80', this version used an all-welded aluminium-armour hull, together with the suspension and running gear of the Mk 4 version. The package included a Perkins 'Phaser' turbo-charged diesel engine, together with Chrysler A727 automatic transmission connected to the original drive line. Armaments included a 7.62mm machine gun, 25mm Hughes chain gun, or TOW anti-tank guided missile. This programme was not pursued beyond the development stage, and no production vehicles were manufactured.

GKN Defence, in a consortium with CKL International of Singapore, also exhibited a refurbishment package for the 'Ferret' at BAEE '86, and at the 1986 Asian Defence Show at Kuala Lumpur. Known as 'Harimau', the vehicle was equipped with a Deutz engine and a completely new turret design.

DESCRIPTION

Engine
Rolls-Royce B60, No 1, Mk 3A (first 20 vehicles only), or Mk 6A; dry sump.
Capacity: 4260cc.
Bore and stroke: 3.50 x 4.50 in.
Power output: Mk 3A engine, 120bhp (gross), 96bhp (net) at 3300rpm; Mk 6A engine, 129bhp (gross), 109bhp (net) at 3750rpm.
Maximum torque: 207 lbs/ft (gross); 195 lbs/ft (net) at 2000rpm.

Detail variations
Distributor limiter set at 3750rpm (crankshaft speed); oil cooler installed above engine; oil filter mounted remotely, in engine compartment; Ki-gass nozzles fitted to Mk 6A version; special rear support plate; rear-facing radiator; no clutch casing; horizontal centre outlet exhaust manifold; inlet manifold with horizontal carburettor-mounting flange.

Transmission
Driver-controlled, clutchless (fluid coupling) Wilson pre-selective epicyclic transmission; separate transfer box giving five speeds forward and reverse, with a separate forward-reverse control.

The pre-selector gearbox is best understood as a form of automatic transmission, where gear selection is carried out by the driver rather than by a combination of speed and fluid pressure. There is no conventional clutch or clutch pedal; this is replaced by a fluid coupling or torque convertor, together with a gear change pedal. The gears are operated by means of a small lever together with the gear change pedal: the gear is pre-selected by the lever (hence the name) and then actuated by the

FV701 Mk 1 'Ferret' with polyurethane/grp superstructure (BTMC)

FV701 Mk 2 'Ferret' fitted with ZB 298 radar (TMB)

FV701 Mk 2 'Ferret' with recovery jib and winch (REME)

pedal when required. Brake bands in the gearbox are lifted off to effect operation of the selected gear.

The differential was centrally placed, with separate H-layout drive shafts to bevel boxes at each wheel station; there were hub-mounted reduction gears at each wheel, intended to improve torque (ratios were 2.4:1 on Mk 1 and 2 vehicles, 3.5:1 on Mks 3, 4 and 5). The drive shafts were fitted with Tracta type constant-velocity joints at the outer ends.

Suspension

Fully-independent suspension was provided by means of a coil spring and wishbone assembly at each wheel station; each coil spring enclosed a single double-acting telescopic hydraulic damper bracket-mounted to the hull.

The suspension fitted to Mk 4 and 5 vehicles was of an uprated and strengthened design with fewer attachment points, giving increased mobility across country, combined with greater resistance to mine damage.

Steering gear

The steering was by recirculating-ball system on the front wheels only. The steering wheel was reversed, ie angled away from, rather than towards, the driver, and moved through 3.675 turns from lock to lock.

Braking system

Lockheed hydraulic braking system; drum size 330x65mm; dual leading shoes; servo assistance on Mk 2 and all subsequent vehicles, retro-fitted servo on some Mk 1 and Mk 1/2 vehicles. Mk 3, 4 and 5 vehicles had disc brakes.

On the Mk 1 and 2 vehicles, the parking brake operated mechanically on the transmission via twin externally-contracting shoes; on Mks 3, 4 and 5, there was a separate brake drum inboard of the front bevel boxes.

Road wheels

Standard WD pattern 6.50 x 16in light-alloy two-piece rims, mounting 9.00x16 run-flat (RF) tubed tyres; Mk 3, 4 and 5 vehicles were fitted with 11.00x20 RF tyres, or 12.00x20 RF for use in soft sand.

A single spare wheel was carried on Mk 1 and 2 vehicles (not Mk 2/6), on the left-hand side of the hull.

Hull and turret

The 'Ferret' was of monocoque construction, consisting of a welded, box-like hull of armoured steel, to which the suspension components were attached directly.

Hull
The hull was of welded armoured steel, either of open-topped design, with a removable canvas cover (Mk 1 vehicles), or mounting a fixed (Mk 1/2), or rotating turret (Mks 2-5).

A centrally-placed armoured hatch (about 300x450mm), together with two smaller side hatches, provided forward vision. Two small rear-facing hatches permitted visibility to the rear. All hatches were hinged, and could be closed-down for maximum protection, the three forward hatches having No 17, Mk 1 (x 1 magnification) periscopes fitted (the fixed turret of the Mk 1/2 version carried two additional forward-facing periscopes). The central hatch was provided with a removable glass windscreen (complete with a tiny 125mm long wiper blade!) which, when fitted, considerably reduced driver visibility.

The Mk 1 and 2 vehicles were also provided with vision slits, with removable splinter-proof glass block protection, in the hull and turret sides.

The driver was placed centrally at the front of the hull, sitting low down in a small seat, with his feet up against the well-sloped glacis plate. The remaining crew members were located behind the driver, squeezed into the relatively small space beneath the hull opening, or beneath and/or within the turret (according to version).

The front hatch doubled as an escape hatch for the driver, and there was an additional crew escape hatch on the left and right-hand sides of the hull, which also formed part of the spare wheel and stowage bin mountings.

Although the hull was provided with both lifting and lashing rings, no towing pintle was fitted.

Hull thickness, at the front varied, from 12mm at 50 degrees, to 16mm at 35 degrees; while at the sides, the thickness varied from 12mm at 20 degrees and 15 degrees, to 16mm at 15 degrees. Rear armour was 12mm and 6mm at 45 degrees. Under the driving compartment, the floor thickness was 10mm, with the thickness reduced to 6mm under the engine compartment. Ballistically, the 'Ferret' hull was superior to that of the 'Dingo'.

Hull stowage
Large external stowage bins (watertight on Mks 3 (Mk 1/1), 4 and 5), with hinged lids, were provided forward of the rear wheels and behind the front wheels on either side of the hull, and centrally on the right side.

Turret
The fixed turret on the Mk 1/2 version had a single, centre-hinged two-part top hatch.

Mk 2/2 vehicles were fitted with a three-door rotating turret, all other Mk 2 vehicles had a two-door rotating turret, with the rear door forming a useful commander's seat, and the front door providing a map table. The turret on the Mk 2 (except Mk 2/6 and Mk 2/7) and Mk 4 versions was manually traversed, while the turret on Mk 2/6 and Mk 2/7 vehicles had a Roballo ring with rack-and-pinion traversing gear. On the early Mk 2 models, the turret was identical to that fitted to the Mk 1 'Saracen' armoured personnel carrier, mounting a .30 calibre Browning machine cannon, and giving 360 degree rotation, combined with 15 degree depression and 45 degree elevation. On later Mk 2 and all Mk 4 models, the turret was increased in size to give an inside ring diameter of 760mm.

The turret thickness was 16mm at 15 degrees, with the turret roof being 8mm at 75 and 90 degrees.

The turret used on Mk 5 vehicles was of a completely different design, manufactured from aluminium, and intended to mount 'Swingfire' anti-tank missiles. The missiles were housed in armoured launch boxes which may be adjusted for up to 40 degree elevation. The turret also had 360 degree rotation and the front machine gun mount provided 15 degree depression and 70 degree elevation.

Electrical equipment
The vehicle was wired with a 24V electrical system, with negative to earth; the ignition system was fully screened and waterproofed.

The generator was a two-speed belt-driven machine with a maximum output of 25A at 600rpm; various versions were installed, either No 2, Mk 1, Mk 2, or, Mk 2/1. All versions had integral automatic centrifugal gear-change facility to maintain high output at low engine speeds. Later vehicles were equipped with an alternator and this modification was also applied retrospectively to vehicles in service.

Two 12V, 60Ah batteries were housed inside the crew compartment.

Fire-fighting equipment
All Mk 4 and Mk 5 vehicles, and all variations suffixed 'M' had a fixed carbon-dioxide fire-fighting system. In addition, all vehicles were provided with a number of portable BCF extinguishers mounted inside the crew compartment, inside the engine compartment, and outside the vehicle.

ARMAMENTS

With the exception of those versions designed to mount anti-tank missiles, the 'Ferret' was lightly armed, and was not generally intended to engage the enemy.

Smoke dischargers
All versions were fitted with two triple-barrelled smoke dischargers, one installed on either side of the hull at the front. These were designed for use with standard smoke grenades, fired electrically from a push-button control inside the hull, on the left-hand side within reach of any crew member.

Canvas or rubber covers were supplied to protect the dischargers when not in use.

Six additional smoke grenades were normally carried inside the vehicle.

Machine gun mountings
The Mk 1 and Mk 1/2 versions had no additional armaments but were fitted with a spigot mounting for a gun pintle: on the Mk 1, this was installed in front of the hull opening on the roof plate; on the Mk 1/2, it was on the fixed turret.

Originally this pintle was intended to accept the .303 Bren gun but this was replaced in service by the standard Light Machine Gun (LMG), requiring a slightly different design of spigot and pintle.

The turret fitted to Mk 2 versions normally mounted a .30 calibre Browning machine cannon. The Mk 5 turret mounted a 7.62mm general-purpose machine gun (GPMG).

Anti-tank missiles
The Mk 2/6 version mounted two BAC 'Vigilant' first-generation anti-tank missiles, similar to the later 'Swingfire' (see below) but with less-sophisticated features. The missiles could be fired either from inside the vehicle, or remotely, from up to 50m distant.

The Mk 5 version mounted two BAC 'Swingfire' anti-tank, wire-guided missiles. The 'Swingfire' was driven by a solid-propellant rocket motor and guided via a joystick control, which was connected to the missile in flight by a multi-core cable. The sighting/control module was fitted inside the vehicle turret, and again, launch control could be effected from inside the vehicle, or remotely.

RADIO EQUIPMENT

As a tactical vehicle, any 'Ferret' would be fitted with radio equipment appropriate to its role. In the early 1950's, a 'Ferret' would have been fitted with a No 19 or No 22 wireless set, both originally of WW2 vintage, but for most of their service lives, 'Ferrets' were contemporary with the 'Larkspur' range of tactical communications equipment.

The basic radio was installed on a suitable carrier mounted above the gearbox and behind the commander's seat, where it proved rather vulnerable to damage from crew members' feet as they entered and left the vehicle. The connecting and control boxes were fitted around the inside of the hull in positions accessible to the various crew members. The aerial tuner unit was normally installed inside the vehicle, except on Mk 2/6 vehicles where, because of the additional missile fire-control equipment, there was insufficient space. In these situations, the unit was mounted on the offside rear wheel arch. There was provision for antennae stowage across the front of the hull.

Larkspur

A typical standard 'Larkspur' station installed in a 'Ferret' might have comprised two radio sets together with the control harness, aerial tuner, junction boxes, and any ancillary equipment necessary to allow switching between the sets.

'Larkspur' radio stations in 'Ferrets' might have included HF/VHF combinations such as C12/C31, C12/B47, C12/B48 and C13/B47; or the C42/B47 VHF/VHF sets.

Clansman

'Larkspur' radios have been replaced by the British Army's 'Clansman' range and these have been around since the mid-1980's, certainly long enough to have been installed in 'Ferrets'.

For a while, it was not unusual to install a hybrid system. The 'Clansman Larch' adaptor box and 'B' cable harness allowed 'Larkspur' radios (eg, the C12 or C42 sets) to be used alongside 'Clansman' with no loss of operating features.

ANCILLARY EQUIPMENT

In common with any tactical vehicle where the crew might be expected to survive, perhaps behind enemy lines, on their own resources for days at a time. For this reason, a 'Ferret' carried a lot of ancillary equipment.

The following items appeared on the on the Ministry of Defence complete equipment schedule (CES) for Mk 1 and Mk 2 vehicles published in the 1969 edition of the User handbook (this list does not include items of personal kit for the crew or their weapons):

Mechanics tools
Adjustable spanner
Grease gun
Hammer
Keys for engine cover, flywheel plug and drain plugs
Oil cans, 1/2 pint and 1 quart capacities
Oil injector
Open ended spanners (7)
Pliers
Screwdriver
Spark plug spanner
Tommy bar
Tool bag
Wheel nut spanner
4-ton hydraulic jack and handle

Pioneer tools
Matchet
Matchet sheath
Pickaxe head
Pickaxe helve (carried separately)
Shovel
Wire cutters

Drivers and crew equipment
Anti-dim compound
Glass screens for observation ports
Inspection lamp
Periscopes
Removable windshield and windshield wiper assembly

Other equipment
Canvas bucket
Cleaning brushes (2)
Cooking pots
Foot pump
Funnel for fuel filler
Padlocks (for stowage bins, engine covers and turret hatch)
Plastic water container
Portable cooker
Sand channels/trench-crossing channels (2)
Starting handle
Strap (for pots and cooker)
Tow rope/recovery chain
Tyre pressure gauge

Weapons equipment
Case for signal pistol
Signal (Very) pistol
Tools and spares for .30 calibre Browning

Additional items
MoD 'Stowage sketches', dated 1961, include the following additional items:

First aid kits (2)
Camouflage net
CTC, BCF or water type fire extinguishers (at least 5)
Kettle (rather technically described as 'Vessel, boiling, electric')
Map case
Radio antenna case
Vacuum (Thermos) flasks (2)

Most of this equipment was carried inside the crew compartment or in the various stowage bins. 'Recovery chain chic' seemed to dictate that this item be carried attached to the front lifting rings and wrapped around the rear of the hull.

Additional stowage, in the form of a large open tray, was also often provided, hinge-mounted over the engine compartment on short legs. This would normally have been used to carry bulky items such as ammunition, fuel cans, rations, bedding and items of personal equipment for the crew. These stowage bins were evident during the Gulf war, which was probably the last time the 'Ferret' saw active service.

DOCUMENTATION
Technical publications
Technical handbooks
Data summary: scout car, Ferret, Mks 1-5. EMER V620.
Technical description: scout car, Ferret, Mks 1-5. EMER V622.
Waterproofing instruction no 1: scout car, Ferret, Mks 1-5. EMER V625-WPF.

User handbooks
Provisional user handbook: scout car, recce, Ferret, Mk 2. WO code 17830.
User handbook: scout car, Ferret, all marks. Army code 12174.

Servicing details
Servicing guide: Ferret, Mks 1 and 2. Army code 70423.
Servicing guide: Ferret, all marks. (code not known).
Servicing schedule: Ferret, Mks 1 and 2. Army code 14000.
Servicing schedule: Ferret, Mks 4 and 5. Army code 60402.

Parts lists
Illustrated spare parts list: scout car, Ferret, Mks 1 and 2. Army code 14992.
Illustrated spare parts list for instructors driving pamphlet. Army code 70514.

Repair manuals
Unit repairs: Ferret, Mks 1 and 2. EMER V623.
Field repairs: Ferret, Mks 1 and 2. EMER V624.

Radio installation
Stations, radio, in Ferret Mk 1 and 2. EMER K654, K655 instruction 1.
Wireless stations in Ferret Mks 1 and 2, conversion in stages to wireless station C13/B47. EMER K630, K632.

Bibliography
Armour of the West. Adshead, Ronald & Noel Aycliffe-Jones. London, Ian Allen, 1978. ISBN 0-711006-81-4.

British Army fighting vehicles and equipment: 1945 to the present. Tanks Illustrated 12. Dunstan, Simon. London, Arms and Armour Press, 1984. ISBN 0-853686-69-6.

British Army vehicles and equipment; part 1, armour. Smith, R E. Shepperton, Ian Allen, 1964.

Ferret: a pictorial round-up. ISO File 4. Paster, John. London, ISO Publications. ISBN 0-946784-26-4.

Ferrets and Fox. AFV Weapons Profile 44. Ogorkiewicz, R M. Windsor, Profile Publications, 1972.

Jane's AFV recognition handbook. Foss, Christopher. Coulsdon, Jane's Information Group, 1992. ISBN 0-710610-43-2.

Military Vehicles Fotofax. British armoured cars since 1945. Dunstan, Simon. London, Arms and Armour Press, 1989. ISBN 0-853689-94-6.

Modern British tanks and fighting equipment. Chamberlain, Peter & Chris Ellis. London, Arms and Armour Press, 1970. ISBN 0-853680-26-4.

NATO Armour. Perrett, Bryan. London, Ian Allen, 1971.

Wheeled armoured fighting vehicles in service. White, B T. Poole, Blandford Press, 1983. ISBN 0-713710-22-5.

CHAPTER 3.2

HUMBER 1 TON TRUCK
FV1600, FV1601, FV1604, FV1621

The standard British small cargo vehicle of WW2 was the 15cwt truck, and these vehicles were produced in large quantities by Bedford, Ford and Morris Commercial throughout the war years. Similarly, in its final incarnation, the ubiquitous American Dodge WC series, used by all of the Allies, was also rated at 15cwt.

The nominal payload rating for these vehicles tended to be rather conservative and most of them could take, and indeed received, a fair degree of abuse without complaint. At the end of the war, the Ministry of Supply disposed of large numbers of these trucks as being surplus to requirements, but those that remained were officially uprated, or perhaps re-named would be a better description, since no engineering changes were made, to 1 ton capacity. This was to become the standard post-war payload figure for small cargo trucks.

The post-war plan for a range of standardised vehicles covered 5cwt, 1 ton, 3 ton, and 10 ton capacities, in CT, GS and CL categories (see Chapter 1.1). The contract for the design and production of the 1 ton CT vehicle was awarded to the Rootes Group, working together with FVRDE at Chertsey. The project was designated FV1600.

Rootes set up a 'military vehicle department' where the design work was carried out. Once the design phase had been successfully completed, the manufacture, machining and assembly operations were shared between the company's Maidstone and Coventry factories.

Despite some initial teething problems, the FV1600 was a superb truck, constructed to a very high standard in every respect. The Rolls-Royce B60 engine provided ample power together with a high degree of reliability, and the Humber exhibited excellent highway performance, with an impressive off-road capability. Normally unheard of in military vehicles, the cab was fully-insulated and trimmed, and the truck was fitted with independent suspension, and power-assisted vacuum-hydraulic brakes. In common with all of the post-war CT range, it also incorporated built-in waterproofing which facilitated deep-water wading with the minimum of preparation. In fact, the FV1600 series was the only one of the CT vehicles which the services found fully acceptable.

Alongside the basic cargo vehicle, FFW/FFR variants were also produced as well as a small number of specialised vehicles designed to supply and support the armoured 'Hornet' air portable launcher for the 'Malkara' anti-tank guided missile. The armoured 'Hornet' launch vehicles themselves were also constructed on a Humber chassis.

Unfortunately, vehicle policy changes combined with the operational requirements of the time meant that few of the vehicles were issued and large numbers of new cargo trucks were put into store direct from the manufacturer. The trucks were subsequently withdrawn from store, often in small numbers, for conversion to other roles; for example, more than half the total production was subsequently to be converted to armoured vehicles to meet a short term need for APC's in Northern Ireland.

Ironically, although the cargo trucks and the other soft-skin variants were withdrawn and disposed of in little more than 15 years, many of the armoured vehicles continued to serve for the best part of another decade or more.

The armoured variants are dealt with separately in Chapter 3.3.

OVERVIEW

The FV1600 series was a purpose-designed CT class, 1 ton truck with optional four-wheel drive, intended for use over improved and unimproved roads, where it offered a high cross-country performance. It was designed as a general-purpose load carrier, for example for ammunition, mortar equipment, and general low- and medium-density stores, and as troop transport for up to eight men. A two-ton capacity winch was fitted to certain of the variations.

The fully-enclosed cab was intended for a crew of two, and on the passenger side, the cab roof was reinforced for a machine-gun mounting.

The cargo vehicle was also adapted to the radio role, intended to provide mobile wireless facilities in forward areas. The radio version was available with either a modified cargo body, or a lightweight house-type body complete with removable tent designed to provide office accommodation. The FFW/FFR vehicle also differed from the cargo version in being fitted with a two-speed generator, extra batteries and associated wiring for use with wireless sets.

Specialised versions included the FV1621 missile supply truck, and the FV1622 missile test truck, both designed for use with the Australian-built 'Malkara' anti-tank missile; and a variation of the FV1604 radio vehicle for use as a mobile command post for the US 'Corporal' surface-to-surface missile.

VEHICLE OUTLINES

FV1601/2

FV1604

SCALE 1:75

CHAPTER 3.2: HUMBER TRUCK

SPECIFICATION

Dimensions and weight

	FV1601/02	FV1604	FV1621	FV1622
Dimensions (mm):				
Length	5054	4928	5140	5054
Width	2083	2083	2140	2083
Height:				
to top of vehicle	2362	2711	2270	2362
to top of cab	2114	2114	2114	2114
Wheelbase	2743	2743	2743	2743
Track	1727	1727	1727	1727
Ground clearance	305	305	305	305
Weight (kg):				
Gross laden weight	5206	5206	5080	4725
Unladen weight	3819	4051	-	3819

Bridge classification: 5.

Performance

Maximum speed: on road (solo), 88km/h; on road with trailer, 72km/h; cross country (solo), 40km/h.
Fuel consumption: 0.31 litre/km, on road.
Maximum range: 483km on road.

Approach angle: 42 deg.
Departure angle: 36 deg.

Turning circle: 15.24m.
Maximum gradient: 30%.
Fording: unprepared, 762mm; prepared, 1981mm.

Capacity

Maximum load: 1000kg.
Maximum towed load: 1000kg.

A standard NATO-pattern tow hitch was provided (front and rear) to enable the vehicle to tow a 5 or 10cwt, or 1 ton trailer, mobile generator set, or field artillery pieces such as the 17 or 25 lb field gun, or 105mm Pack howitzer.

DEVELOPMENT

The original intention was to produce a British truck that offered all of the features of the WW2 Dodge 3/4 ton WC series. Work actually began in 1944 with prototypes being produced by the Austin Motor Company, but this phase of the project was terminated with the cessation of hostilities, and the Austin vehicle never made it into production.

It was not until 1947 that a new design brief was drawn up by FVRDE, calling for a sophisticated vehicle that would be able to maintain high average road speeds as well as providing good off-road performance and all-round agility. With suitable preparation, the truck was also required to undertake deep-water wading to a depth of 1981mm.

The specification included all-independent torsion-bar suspension, five-speed and reverse gearbox, separate transfer case giving optional two- or four-wheel drive, servo-assisted hydraulic brakes, resiliently-mounted front and rear axles, and 24V waterproofed and tropicalised electrical components. A number of vehicles were also provided with a mechanical winch for self-recovery.

The development contract was placed in 1947, and the design work, which was managed by Rootes Group's chief designer, RJ Murray, began in 1948. Although the basic specification for the vehicle was laid down by FVRDE, all of the detail design work was carried out by Rootes Engineering Department where a military vehicle section had been established especially for this purpose.

In 1949, the design was cleared, and an order placed for six prototypes, including two staff car versions. The staff car requirement was subsequently dropped, but prototypes of the basic cargo vehicle were submitted for testing in 1950, with one of the prototypes being sent to Canada for experience in cold climates.

There must have been a good deal of what these days we could call 'value engineering' going on between the development and production phases. In March 1953, during a House of Commons debate on military spending, Sir Antony Head, then Secretary of State for War, stated that his expenditure committee had examined the 'one-ton (CT) vehicle... to see what reductions could be made without sacrificing essential performance and strength'; the committee also considered whether there could be any reduction in body types. Apparently these deliberations resulted in a saving of £250 per vehicle, a considerable sum of money 40 years ago.

Rootes were given £1.1 million as capital assistance, and production began in 1952 at a price of about £2900 each. Early versions of the vehicle were fitted with the Rolls-Royce B60, Mk 2A engine but this was later to be replaced by the UNF-modified version, designated B60, Mk 5A.

Although pilot vehicles had been produced with a soft-top cab rather like their WW2 counterparts, the production truck was provided with a completely-enclosed cab which included roof-mounted observation hatches. The cab was of insulated double-skin construction providing protection to the occupants against exposure to extremes of both heat and cold. Military vehicles tended to be rather basic in the 1950's but the Humber cab was specified to a very-high standard and the vehicle must have been something of a revelation for the crew.

Unfortunately, the vehicles were not entirely satisfactory as delivered, and the War Office prepared a list of some 72 defects. The most serious of these defects, which had become apparent during troop trials, was a persistent oil leak from the rear axle. For a while, vehicles were frozen in depots while the defects were remedied, adding a cost of £47 per vehicle.

Once the problems were resolved, the final result was a superb vehicle which was well-liked by the user arms, but for which unfortunately, there were few uses. Various kits and modifications produced to adapt the vehicle for specialised roles, but no further development work was undertaken on the basic truck. However, Rootes remained the design parent for the vehicle until the project was effectively handed back to FVRDE in the mid 1960's.

Production
In 1951, the production contract was put out to tender, but as it happened, the work remained with the Rootes Group. Volume production of the basic FV1601 cargo vehicle began in 1952 and some 3700 vehicles were made before the contract was complete the following year. Certainly, all of the vehicles had been delivered by 1954.

Transmission and suspension components were manufactured at Rootes' Maidstone plant, with the engines being supplied fully-assembled from Rolls-Royce at Crewe. Chassis frames were manufactured by Rubery Owen, and the cab and front-end sheet metal pressings were produced by Fisher & Ludlow to designs produced in-house by Rootes. Final assembly work was carried out at Rootes' Ryton-on-Dunsmore facility near Coventry.

FV1600 prototype cargo truck (IWM)

FV1601 production cargo truck (TMB)

FV1604 wireless, light vehicle (TMB)

CHAPTER 3.2: HUMBER TRUCK

FV1604 wireless, light vehicle with penthouse erected (TMB)

FV1621 missile supply truck (TMB)

FV1622 missile test truck (TMB)

Many of the vehicles were not issued immediately, but were delivered to the Royal Army Ordnance Corps (RAOC) and put into store at the various Central Vehicle Depots. New vehicles were subsequently called-off from storage, either for issue to one or other of the services, or for conversion to other, more specialised roles.

The first conversion was to the FFW/FFR role, where the vehicle was fitted with a radio table, operators' seats and additional battery housings in the rear compartment; in addition, the engine was provided with a two-speed generator. These vehicles, which were outwardly little changed from the cargo version, were designated FV1602. A purpose-designed wireless truck was also specified, with a fully-enclosed, insulated house-type body produced by Marshalls of Cambridge, and designated FV1604.

Subsequent conversions were for small numbers of vehicles to provide support facilities for the 'Malkara' missile launch system (FV1621/1622). This work was carried out in about 1960.

Replacement and disposal
Despite a high degree of engineering excellence, in its basic cargo form, the Humber did not remain in service long. Rather like the Austin 'Champ', once the War Office had taken delivery of this particular new toy they realised that perhaps they didn't need it after all. Most had been disposed of by 1969 and there was really no direct replacement. Interestingly, a number of the vehicles sold at auction had civilian registration numbers which suggests that the Humbers were also used by other Government departments.

The specialised vehicles designed to support the 'Malkara' weapons system (FV1621/1622) may have enjoyed a slightly longer life, but became obsolete when the 'Malkara' itself was replaced by the BAC 'Vigilant' and 'Swingfire' missiles mounted on the Mk 5 'Ferret' (see Chapter 3.1) and later the Alvis 'Striker'.

By the late 1960's, the CT truck concept had been largely discredited anyway, and the all-conquering Land Rover was becoming available in additional versions designed to accept increasingly-higher payloads. Within less than two years, the forward-control 1 ton Land Rover 101 was beginning to be issued.

However, the Humber was an exceptionally-fine truck and a few demobbed vehicles did find application in civilian life, converted to fire tenders or light recovery vehicles. For example, during the late 60's, L W Vass, a Bedfordshire-based dealer in ex-Ministry vehicles was offering FV1601 cargo vehicles for use as light wreckers, fitted with a 3 ton capacity Harvey Frost crane

CHAPTER 3.2: HUMBER TRUCK

NOMENCLATURE and VARIATIONS

All of the FV1600 series trucks were manufactured under a single contract which covered only the basic cargo vehicle. Once the contract was complete, a large number of vehicles was recalled from storage, and either factory- or workshop-modified for various other roles (including conversion to armoured trucks and APC's, dealt with separately in Chapter 3.3).

In 1954/55, all versions were regraded from CT to GS classification when the CT concept was virtually abandoned.

The Humber name
The choice of the Humber name seems a little odd since the Rootes Group owned both the Karrier and Commer companies, both of which were more usually associated with commercial vehicles (and both of which supplied vehicles to the military during the 1950's). However, Humber had supplied a large number of staff cars, heavy utilities and armoured scout cars during WW2 and perhaps it was felt that this provided a more 'historic' link with the military.

Variations

FV1600. Truck, 1 ton, CT, cargo, 4x4, Humber
Prototype and pre-production vehicles, some with open cab, narrower rear body with external wheel arches, and different tailgate arrangements.

FV1601(A). Truck, 1 ton, CT, cargo, 4x4, Humber, Mk 1
Basic cargo vehicle, with open rear bodywork having hinged tailgate; 2 ton winch fitted. In the troop-carrying role, the vehicle could accommodate up to eight men seated on cushions on the side lockers.

FV1602(A). Truck, 1 ton, CT, cargo/FFW, (with winch), 4x4, Humber, Mk 1
Basic cargo vehicle modified for wireless/radio (FFW/FFR) role by the inclusion of additional batteries, a two-speed generator and matching control panel (designed to prevent the vehicle batteries from being discharged by the radio equipment), and radio connection box. A radio table and two operators' seats were provided in the rear, together with aerial mounts on the body sides. The vehicle was screened against both HF and VHF interference.

Some vehicles were fitted with a winch.

FV1604(A). Truck, 1 ton, CT, wireless light, 4x4, Humber, Mk 1
Purpose-built, fully-enclosed lightweight house-type body installed on cargo chassis; the winch was removed to allow the overall height of the body to be reduced to the minimum. The body, which was constructed by Marshall Motor Bodies of Cambridge, was provided with fittings

FV1601 truck modified to give open cab (IWM)

FV1601 same truck, alternative hood and unmodified doors (IWM)

FV1601 modified vehicle showing reduced height (IWM)

FV1601 cargo truck entering the FVRDE wading pit (IWM)

FV1601 cargo truck rigged for air dropping (IWM)

FV1601 same vehicle from rear (IWM)

to allow a tent to be attached to it, and erected to one side of the vehicle for use as an office.

Like the basic FFW/FFR version, the vehicle was modified for the wireless role with additional batteries, two-speed generator and matching control panel, and radio connection box. The ignition system was screened against both HF and VHF interference, and a separate battery-charging engine was sometimes installed in the rear of the body.

Some versions of this vehicle had a SCAM 21 metre high telescopic mast, installed on the rear of the body. Manufactured by Clark Masts Limited, these air-hydraulic masts were used to provide radio-relay station facilities.

FV1621. Truck, 1 ton, GS, missile supply, 4x4, Humber, Mk 1
Standard cargo vehicle modified for missile supply. Fitted with special aluminium rear body which included racking for nine 'Malkara' missiles, and high-pressure air bottle; radio equipment was installed in the cab. The open-type rear body, which was constructed by Marshall Motor Bodies of Cambridge, had drop sides, a detachable superstructure, tilt cover and hinged rear doors.

FV1622. Truck, 1 ton, GS, missile test, 4x4, Humber, Mk 1
Standard cargo truck modified as 'Malkara' missile test vehicle. A high-pressure air compressor and alternator were mounted in the rear body, intended to provide power for the FV2308(R) trailer-mounted functional test unit.

Factory modifications
At least one FV1601 cargo truck was modified to provide a low-profile vehicle with folding windscreen, cut-down cab and doors, and soft top, possibly intended to be air portable.

Workshop modifications
A number of FV1604 vehicles were converted to act as a command centre for the US-built Firestone 'Corporal' missile system. In this role, the standard house-type radio body was modified to allow the installation of equipment designed to receive target instructions and missile data, to conduct and control the countdown, and to issue firing instructions.

Vehicle variations FV1621 and FV1622 were intended for use with the 'Malkara' guided missile system, being described as 'missile supply' and 'missile test' trucks respectively. The FV1622 vehicle was always used in conjunction with the FV2308(R) 10 cwt trailer-mounted functional test unit. There are references in period documentation to suggest that two other variations existed for use with this weapons system: these were described as 'missile repair, Malkara' and 'power supply, electrical and pneumatic, truck-mounted, Malkara'. No

FV numbers or other information are available. However there is evidence to suggest that at least the latter is an alternative description for the FV1622 vehicle.

COMMERCIAL VARIATIONS

A few commercial specification Humbers were produced, some of which may have used a Commer engine, and some 30 or so were exported to the Middle East and to British colonies such as Australia where road conditions were not ideal. However, it would be fair to say that the poor old Humber didn't find much favour in civvy street either, being considered far too heavy, thirsty and complex for its relatively-small payload.

DESCRIPTION

Engine
Rolls-Royce B60, No 1, Mk 2A, Mk 5A or Mk 5K; wet sump.
Capacity: 4256cc.
Bore and stroke: 3.50 x 4.50in.
Power output: 130bhp (gross); 109bhp (net) at 3750rpm.
Maximum torque: 209 lbs/ft (gross); 197 lbs/ft (net) at 2050rpm.

Detail variations
Distributor limiter set at 3750rpm (crankshaft speed); standard wet sump with well at rear; oil filter mounted remotely, on inner wing; Ki-gass pipework and nozzles fitted (Mk 5A engines only); oil cooler fitted; dual exhaust manifold, with horizontal centre outlets; inlet manifold with horizontal flange for carburettor mounting; intake air horn positioned at 22.5 or 45 deg to offside; special rear support plate and bell housing adaptor.

Transmission
Driving through a 275mm Borg and Beck single dry-plate clutch, power was taken through a five-speed and reverse gearbox to the unit-construction back axle and single-speed transfer gear assembly. First and reverse were engaged by a sliding gear, whilst the other four speeds were of the constant-mesh helical type.

From the transfer case, an open prop shaft ran the length of the vehicle to drive the front axle, with a second, shorter shaft driving the winch on those vehicles so equipped. Engagement and disengagement of the front axle was effected by a simple dog clutch, with the mechanism installed within the axle casing, and controlled manually by a lever in the cab.

The transfer box ratios were 1.33:1 for the axle drive, and 1:1 for the winch. The gearbox contained no low ratios and first gear was not normally used for road work, being retained for steep gradients or tricky off-road terrain. Front-wheel drive was automatically selected as first gear was engaged, but had to be manually de-selected.

The axles, which were very similar in design, front and rear, featured spiral bevel crown wheel and pinion, with bevel type differentials. The differentials were offset to the right on both axles. Drive to the wheels was transmitted through halfshafts, each with two Tracta type constant-velocity joints, interchangeable front-to-rear and side-to-side. The hubs incorporated lifting flanges.

Both front and rear axles were resiliently-mounted on rubber sleeves, intended to reduce the transmission of road noise and vibration into the cab. Extensive use was made of magnesium alloys in the gearbox and axle casings.

Suspension
If four-wheel independent suspension was unusual in 1952 on relatively-small vehicles such as the 'Champ', it was unheard of on 1 ton trucks. Nevertheless, the Humber was provided with independent suspension at all four wheels by means of longitudinal torsion bars. The suspension movement at each wheel station was handled by transverse upper and lower wishbone links running in large surface oil-bath bearings.

Bump and rebound rubbers were provided for each wheel, together with large, double-acting telescopic hydraulic shock absorbers installed vertically between the axle and chassis member. Alternative types of shock absorber were used.

The front and rear torsion bars were of equal length, running along the outside of the main chassis members, one above the other. The bars were pre-stressed to extend their service life and thus were not interchangeable. All other suspension components were similar in design front-to-rear, and side-to-side, with the upper wishbone links being interchangeable.

Steering gear
Steering was controlled through a recirculating-ball type steering box.

The drop arm from the box was connected by a short drag link to one arm of a bell crank lever on a vertical pivot attached to the frame. Also connected to the bell crank was a steering rod, which acted on the offside wheel, and a track rod; the track rod was connected to an idler lever on the opposite frame member and this had a second steering rod which acts on the nearside wheel.

The steering system included a total of ten separate ball joints, and the smallest amount of wear must have resulted in considerable lost motion which would have been magnified by the size of the steering wheel.

A 450mm diameter steering wheel provided 3.75 turns from lock to lock, with a steering ratio of 21:1 measured at the drop arm.

Braking system
Lockheed vacuum servo-assisted hydraulic brakes were fitted at all four wheels, with twin-leading shoes in both the forward and reverse directions. The 'Hydravac' servo unit was mounted on the engine front support cross member. The brake drums were of cast-iron, 330mm diameter x 63.5mm width, giving a total braking area of 0.15sq m.

The brakes were not waterproofed but the master cylinder was of the sealed integral tank type, and the supplementary fluid reservoir was installed in the cab above the unprepared wading line.

The hand (parking) brake operated mechanically on all wheels through rods and cables; the handbrake linkage was compensated between the left- and right-hand wheels on each axle, but not from front to rear.

Road wheels
Wheels were 7.00B x 20in divided-disc steel type, each weighing close to 200 lbs with tyre. Standard tyres were 9.00x20 run-flat (RF), complete with tubes and bead spacers. Larger section sand tyres were used where the vehicle was expected to run on loose material.

One spare wheel was carried inside the cab.

A power take-off on the side of the gearbox drove a small mechanical piston-type compressor intended for tyre inflation.

Chassis
The massive chassis frame was of conventional design, consisting of channel-section main members, which incorporated mountings for the torsion bars, and braced by a welded central cruciform. Channel-section stiffeners were provided to form box-section cross members at the front and rear, outside the cruciform. Pilot vehicles were fitted with skid plates to protect the steering linkage, sump, and axle differentials.

The frame was upswept at the front to form a bumper mounting.

The same chassis basic frame was used for all of the (soft skin) variations, with differences in the mounting brackets according to the body type. Vehicles which were fitted with a winch had an extension bolted to the rear of the frame.

Lashing eyes were provided in strategic positions for securing the vehicle to the deck of a ship.

Cab and bodywork
Cab
The steel cab was of all-welded, double-skin construction with 'Isoflex' insulation incorporated between the inner and outer skins. The cab consisted of a floor, back panel, two side panels, wing valance and front panel, scuttle and roof assembly.

The bonnet, wings, and radiator grille were separate. The bonnet consisted of a fixed centre section attached to the scuttle and front panel, together with two side-hinged opening panels. The pressed-steel wings had wire-beaded edges, and were bolted to the wing valance, scuttle and front panels; there were mud flaps on the lower rear edges of the wings. The radiator grille was bolted to the front panel, and there were small wire-mesh inlets either side of the grille.

The cab doors were hung on adjustable knuckle-type hinges mounted on the 'A' posts, and the right-hand door could be locked with a key. Both doors were provided with a fixed light and a dropping light, of toughened glass.

The cab was designed to accommodate a crew of two, on adjustable, upholstered bucket seats with hinged backrests; the driver's seat was adjustable for height and reach, the passenger's seat could be placed in one of three vertical positions.

A removable, hinged two-part hatch was provided above each seat, with the hatch halves hinged to the front and rear, and with each half able to be opened separately. There was provision for mounting a light-machine gun over the left-hand hatch, where the roof was specially strengthened.

The windscreen consisted of two, separate bottom-hinged lights which could be retained in any position by adjustable stays; on the prototype vehicles, the screens were top-hinged. The cab also included a small glazed, sliding rear screen behind the driver.

The metal floor was covered with bituminised felt over plywood floorboards. Moulded felt or millboard trim was used to cover much of the exposed metalwork, and leathercloth and sponge rubber hip rings were used to protect the edges of the roof hatch openings.

Provision was made for mounting heating and air-conditioning equipment with ducts for de-misting and de-frosting the screens.

Cab stowage
The spare wheel was stowed inside the cab, behind the crew seats, with access provided by means of a bottom-hinged hatch fitted to the nearside of the cab behind the passenger door. When opened, the access hatch rested

on the ground, doubling as a ramp and runway for the wheel.

The batteries were also housed inside the cab, on a sliding tray. Access was obtained from outside the vehicle, via a small hinged door, low down in the cab on the offside.

Cargo bodywork
The standard cargo body was constructed from steel with floorboards of tongued-and-grooved hardwood; at the rear, there was a one-piece hinged tailgate. A removable canvas cover, supported on four steel hoops fitted into sockets in the body sides, covered the cargo area; the end curtains were sewn-in, with a roll-up section at the rear.

Separate rear wheel arches were screwed to the body side panels.

Internal stowage lockers were provided along the sides of the body, designed to double as troop seats. A small lockable stowage compartment was provided on each side behind the rear wheels.

The FFW/FFR version of the basic cargo vehicle (FV1602) was provided with two aerial mounting brackets, one each side of the vehicle forward of the rear wheel arches. Inside the rear body there were two folding operators' seats, additional battery housings, and a wireless table. The rear of the body was covered by the same type of tarpaulin as the basic cargo vehicle and conditions for the occupants cannot have been too comfortable in winter.

'Malkara' supply vehicles
The FV1621 'Malkara' missile supply vehicle had a lightweight aluminium body, similar to that fitted to the cargo vehicle, but with enclosed rear wheels. The body was fitted with drop-down sides and hinged rear doors; a canvas cover appears to have been used to disguise the shape of the body so that it appeared like the standard cargo vehicle.

FV1622, the 'Malkara' missile test truck, utilised the standard steel cargo truck body but some vehicles were certainly fitted with a steel roof over the canvas cover.

Wireless house-type bodywork
The lightweight house-type body fitted to the FV1604 vehicle had internal dimensions of 5182x2210x2667mm. The body consisted of aluminium-alloy panels on a riveted and welded framing of mild steel; the panels were riveted to the framing and electrically-bonded together by copper braid. The floor was of hardwood boards covered in steel sheet and linoleum.

The body was fully lined internally using hardboard panels, and the cavity between the inner and outer skins was filled with 'Isoflex' insulation. The rear access door had a drop-down window, protected by a fine wire mesh mosquito net, and was provided with a ventilator and black-out shutter. A Yale-type lock was fitted. Four sliding windows were fitted to the body, two to each side; these were also provided with a mosquito net and black-out shutter.

Inside the body were radio tables, and two stowage lockers, each accessible from both inside and outside the vehicle. The interior also included a reversible Vent-Axia fan, installed in a cowl on the roof, lighting equipment, and two sockets for connecting wander lights for the tent. A black-out switch ensured that the interior lights were extinguished as the door opened.

The exterior was provided with racks to house aerial mast sections when not in use, a canvas waterproofing flap and attachment fittings for a tent, cable drum brackets, and a pair of portable steps. There was also a small stowage compartment providing access to the under-floor space, on either side, forward of and behind the rear wheels; these compartments were used for stowing folding chairs.

The canvas or Rexine tent was erected on a tubular steel framework, and attached to the framing members by hooks and eyes. The frame was stored on the roof when not in use.

A very similar, but larger, body was also used on the contemporary 1 ton Austin GS radio vehicle (FV16003).

Electrical equipment
The Humber was wired on a 24V negative-earth electrical system. Both the cargo and FFW/FFR versions had two 12V 60Ah batteries in series, installed in the cab behind the seats, with additional batteries, (four 6V, 180Ah batteries) provided in the rear compartment on vehicles intended for the radio role. The main batteries were originally installed in waterproof containers, but the specification was changed during later production.

On the cargo version, a generator No 1, Mk 2 or Mk 2/1 was used, producing 12A at 28.5V maximum, under the control of a vibrating contact regulator. The generator installed on FFW/FFR vehicles was of the automatic two-speed type, either No 2, Mk 1 or Mk 2, with a maximum output of 25A, and designed to produce higher outputs at idle, and at low engine speeds. The control panel, which was of the current-limiting voltage control type, allowed charging of both the radio batteries and the main vehicle batteries at the same time.

All electrical components were waterproofed and radio-screened, and much of the equipment was common to other British military vehicles of the 1950's and 60's.

Winch

Where a winch was fitted, this was a mechanical two-ton, horizontal drum type, manufactured by Turner, and driven from a power take-off on the transfer case. Average rope speed, at an engine speed of 3750rpm, was 16.75m/min, with three layers of rope on the drum.

Engagement of the winch was effected by means of a sliding dog in the transfer case, controlled by a lever in the cab which selected either axle drive or winch drive. Rope fairleads were provided to both the front and rear of the vehicle, with guide bollards mounted on the chassis to permit winching from the front or rear.

An electrical cut-out circuit, wired through the ignition, was provided to protect the winch against overload.

Wading

Like the 'Champ', the design specification for the Humber required that the truck be able to undertake shallow wading with the minimum of preparation, in this case to a depth of 762mm.

All of the standard FVRDE-designed electrical equipment was waterproofed, and the engine breather and fuel tank vent lines were connected into the air intake system well above the 762mm water line.

A separate snorkel, similar to but larger than that used for the 'Champ', was available to replace the standard air intake on the right-hand scuttle side. With the snorkel in place, and with suitable preparation, the vehicle could be used for deep-water wading to a depth of 1981mm. Again as for the 'Champ', with the axle vents sealed and additional treatment of, for example dipstick openings, carburettor and other apertures, the truck could travel almost completely submerged. In these situations, the driver would kneel on the seat with the roof hatch open, and control the vehicle by means of the hand throttle.

ARMAMENTS

The area of the cab roof immediately above the passenger seat was reinforced to accept a light machine gun, for example the .303 Bren or LMG.

Clips were provided in various positions in the cab and rear bodywork to accept the standard Lee Enfield, SMLE No 4 .303 rifles which were in use at the time.

ANCILLARY EQUIPMENT

The following equipment was typically carried on the vehicle:

Mechanics tools
Ballpein hammer
Box spanners, AF (3) and tommy bar
Hardwood block
Open-ended spanners, AF (6)
Open-ended spanners, BA (3)
Open-ended spanners, BSW (5)
Pliers, sidecutting
Ring spanner
Screwdriver
Starting handle
Wheel brace
200mm adjustable spanner
4 ton jack

Pioneer tools
Matchet
Pickaxe head
Pickaxe helve (carried separately)
Shovel

Drivers and crew equipment
Camouflage net, woodland, Mk 3, 4270x4270mm
Rifles, no 4 Lee Enfield (2)

Other equipment
CTC fire extinguisher
First aid kit, large
Grease gun
Inspection lamp
Jerry can, gasoline
Jerry can, water (plastic on later vehicles)
Non-skid chains (4)
Oil and petrol injector
Oil can, 1 quart
Pressure oiler
Tow rope
Tyre pressure gauge
7.33m air hose

This equipment was either attached to the outside of the vehicle using various clips and brackets provided for that purpose, or stowed in the cab, or in the lockers in each rear wheel arch.

RADIO EQUIPMENT

Those vehicles intended for the wireless role (designated FFW) were supplied suppressed against electrical interference, with aerial base mountings ready for the user to install a specific radio kit; also installed in the rear of the vehicle were a radio junction box, 'B' type radio control harness, radio table, operators' seats, battery carriers, and lights. The FV1604 vehicle also included a ventilating fan, cable conduit, and stowage lockers.

FFW vehicles could be converted to the radio (FFR) role by the addition of a specialist installation kit.

The radio sets, control boxes etc, were installed on the

folding tables, with the batteries in the carriers on the floor beneath. The aerial tuner unit was installed on wall or on the framework for the canvas tilt, with the aerial bases and the aerials themselves mounted on the body sides, or roof, in the latter case, with one at each corner. External brackets were also provided on the FV1604 vehicle for an 11m fixed mast, or 21m air-hydraulic telescopic mast, and a battery charging unit was normally stowed in one of the interior lockers.

The radio equipment was installed in the cab of the 'Malkara' missile supply truck (FV1621).

A typical standard 'Larkspur' station installed in the FFW/FFR vehicles comprised a single HF or VHF set, or a combination of two or three radio sets together with the control harness, aerial tuner, junction boxes, and any ancillary equipment necessary to allow switching between the sets.

Commonly-encountered 'Larkspur' radio stations included a pair of C11-R210 sets, C11-R210/C42, C13/C42, C13/C45/B48, C42/B47, C45/B48, C42/C45/B48, or C45/C45/R209.

DOCUMENTATION
Technical publications
User handbooks
Provisional user handbook: truck, 1 ton, CT, cargo, 4x4, Humber, Mk 1, with winch. WO code 17765.
Provisional user handbook: truck, 1 ton, CT, FFW, 4x4, Humber, Mk 1. WO code 18363.
User handbook: truck, 1 ton, GS, cargo, 4x4, Humber, Mk 1, with winch; FFW; FFW, with winch. WO code 12515.
User handbook: truck, 1 ton, CT, 4x4, Humber, wireless light. WO code 12247.

Technical handbooks
Data summary: truck, 1 ton, GS, cargo, 4x4, Humber, Mk 1. EMER N250.
Technical description: truck, 1 ton, GS, cargo, 4x4, Humber, Mk 1, with winch; FFW; FFW, with winch; wireless light; armoured; armoured, with winch; armoured FFW. EMER N252.

Servicing details
Servicing schedule: truck, 1 ton, GS, cargo, 4x4, Humber, Mk 1. Army codes 10359, 13068.

Repair manuals
Unit repairs: truck, 1 ton, CT, 4x4, Humber, with winch. EMER N253.
Field repairs: truck, 1 ton, CT, 4x4, Humber, with winch. EMER N254 Part 1.
Base repairs: truck, 1 ton, CT, 4x4, Humber, with winch. EMER N254 Part 2.

Modification instructions
Truck, 1 ton, GS and armoured, 4x4, Humber. EMER N257, instructions 1-71.

Miscellaneous instructions
Truck 1 ton, Humber, all types. EMER N259, instructions 1-10.

Radio installation
User handbook: radio installation in FFR 'B' Vehicles. WO code 12798.

Bibliography
Humber FV1600 series. A unique British family of combat range trucks. London, Wheels & Tracks, no 6, 1984. ISSN 0263-7081.

CHAPTER 3.3

HUMBER 1 TON ARMOURED TRUCK
FV1609, FV1611, FV1612, FV1613, FV1622

During WW2 the Canadian GM-built 15cwt armoured truck had proved itself a useful device for delivering men and equipment to forward areas, at the same time providing protection against small-arms fire and shell splinters. When, in the 1950's, the British Army found itself embroiled in a number of minor uprisings and skirmishes, for example in Malaya and Kenya, there seemed to be a requirement for just such a machine. Since there were not sufficient quantities of 'Saracen' armoured personnel carriers (APC's) on hand, the War Office began to investigate the possibility of producing a small armoured truck which might also be able to double as an APC.

The Ministry of Supply felt that the Humber 1 ton FV1600 chassis would make an ideal basis for such a vehicle. Large numbers of these vehicles were already in storage, surplus to requirements, and were thus readily available for conversion. A number of complete trucks were taken out of store and returned to Rootes where they were stripped to the chassis, modified and rebuilt with armoured hulls.

The result was the FV1609 Humber 1 ton armoured truck.

The truck proved its value in service but its uses were somewhat restricted by the relatively lightweight armour and by the lack of a roof to the rear cargo area, so in the early 1960's, a large number of vehicles were modified and up-armoured to produce the FV1611, Mk 2 armoured personnel carrier, universally known as the 'Pig'. It's hard to say whether the nickname was a tribute to the vehicle's recalcitrant driving characteristics, or was more a recognition of the rather pig-like frontal profile.

Further development work led to the production of radio and ambulance versions, and the vehicle was also modified to operate and tow the 'Green Archer' battlefield mortar-locating radar system. There was also a more seriously reworked version, usually called 'Hornet', and intended to launch the Australian-designed 'Malkara' wire-guided anti-tank missile which was being produced under licence by the British Aircraft Corporation.

OVERVIEW

The vehicle was a small armoured truck/APC based on the standard FV1600 series Humber 1 ton chassis. It was designed for use on improved and unimproved roads,

THE ROLLS-ROYCE 'B SERIES' ENGINE

CHAPTER 3.3: HUMBER PIG

and was intended to provide armoured protection to personnel and equipment in forward areas.

The hull was constructed in the form of a simple welded-steel box which totally enclosed the driver and occupants; although, rather in the style of the US half-tracks of WW2, on early FV1609 vehicles, the rear cargo area was not fully enclosed.

Hydraulically-operated armoured visors, or hatches provided visibility and protection when closed down, and on the Mk 1 vehicles, there were observation and escape hatches above the driver's and passenger's seats. The louvred radiator grille, bonnet and scuttle were also of armoured steel.

The vehicle employed a B60 engine, and was normally driven by the rear axle; optional four-wheel drive was available for cross-country terrain.

The basic vehicle was developed in armoured truck, radio, armoured personnel carrier, ambulance and missile launcher variations.

DEVELOPMENT

The story of the FV1600 family is outlined in Chapter 3.2 but to briefly summarise, the project began in 1947 when a specification was drawn up by the Ministry of Supply, with prototypes and pilot models being produced in 1949/50. The manufacturing contract was placed with the Rootes Group in 1951, and the vehicles were manufactured and delivered between 1952 and 1954. There were more trucks delivered than were immediately required, and a large number was immediately placed in storage.

Work on the armoured variation began in the mid-1950's. Complete FV1601 vehicles were taken out of store and returned to the manufacturers for modification and rebuilding.

The basic design specification was laid down by FVRDE, and the design and development work was carried out by Rootes, possibly at their Manchester works, with the armoured hulls being constructed by J Sankey & Sons, later to become better known as GKN-Sankey, manufacturers of the FV432.

The pilot models were similar to the production FV1609 but the overall appearance was rather less 'box-like'. The armour was intended to provide protection against frontal attack from .300 SAAP rounds, and side and rear attack by .303 rounds; the floor was not armoured and there was no protection from mines. The sides of the cargo area were lower, with a more conventional canvas cover, and there was a single side-hinged rear door. As one might expect, there were small variations in the various

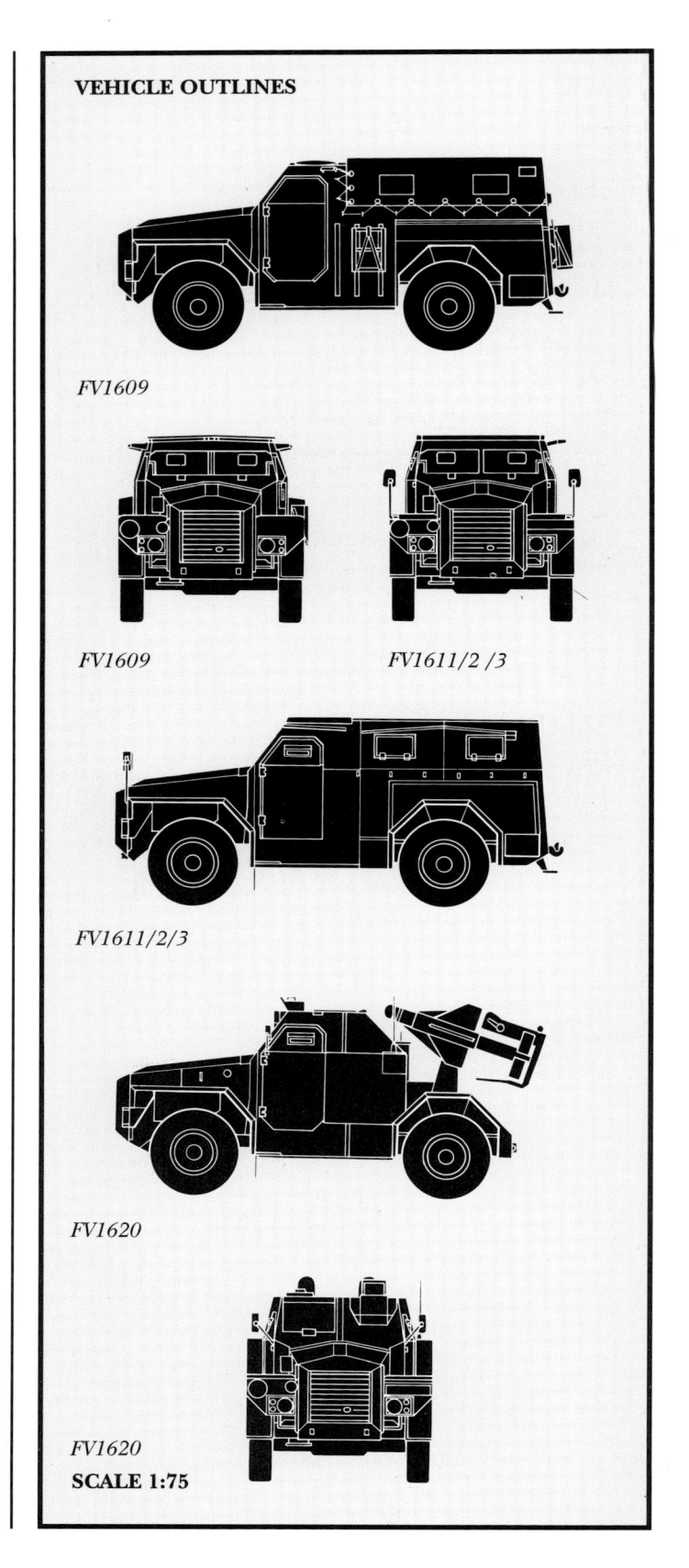

VEHICLE OUTLINES

FV1609

FV1609   *FV1611/2/3*

FV1611/2/3

FV1620

FV1620

SCALE 1:75

SPECIFICATION

Dimensions and weight

	FV1609	FV1611/2/3	FV1620
Dimensions (mm):			
Length	4928	4928	5050
Width	2045	2045	2220
Height	2121	2121	2340
Wheelbase	2743	2743	2743
Track	1715	1715	1727
Ground clearance	305	305	305
Weight (kg):			
Gross laden weight	5640	5790	5706
Unladen weight	4200	4770	5217

Bridge classification: 6.

Performance
Maximum speed: on road (solo), 90km/h; on road with trailer, 72km/h; cross country (solo), 40km/h.
Fuel consumption: 0.33 litre/km, on road.
Maximum range: 492km on road.

Approach angle: 46 deg.
Departure angle: 40 deg.

Turning circle: 15.24m.
Maximum gradient: 45%.
Side slope: 35%.
Fording: unprepared, 762mm; prepared, 1981mm.

Capacity
Maximum load: 1000kg.

---

pilot vehicles produced, one to another.

In 1956, a contract was placed for 20 vehicles, and the first FV1609 production armoured trucks appeared. For some reason, although the sides to the rear compartment were raised when compared to the pilot vehicles, the canvas tilt was unchanged which meant that the armoured sides were also covered by canvas. These FV1609 production models first saw service during the insurrections in Malaya and Cyprus.

The up-armoured Mk 2 version was produced in about 1960, designated FV1611; this version was also developed into ambulance and FFW/FFR versions. Aside from the increased thickness of armour, the major difference between the Mk 1 and Mk 2 models was the addition of a fully-armoured roof extending across the cab and cargo area, and the use of armoured floor plates. The cab roof escape hatches were covered by the additional armour. Armour-proving and anti-tank trials were conducted by FVRDE during 1961/62.

It was in Northern Ireland that the 'Pigs' really came into their own, serving as armoured personnel carriers, riot control vehicles, and general logistic support for the troops patrolling the streets. However, when the IRA acquired armour-piercing ammunition, it was found that there was insufficient protective armour, and all of the FV1611 vehicles remaining in service, some 500 in all, were returned to REME base workshops on the mainland to have the thickness of armour increased.

Production
All of the Humber armoured trucks were produced on chassis which had originally been manufactured as part of soft-skin cargo vehicles and subsequently put into storage; examination of photographs of production vehicles of both soft-skin and armoured variant will show that all were numbered in the same WD series (00 BK 00). The cabs and cargo bodies were removed and either put into store or disposed of as surplus to requirements, the chassis and running gear were modified to suit the new role, and armoured hulls were constructed.

Engineering modifications were made to the gearbox and transfer box ratios, and the rear drive-shaft joints were replaced with FVRDE-designed components which were better suited to accept the greater loads imposed by the heavier armoured body.

The pilot and early FV1609 production models were produced by Rootes working with Joseph Sankey; the hulls for the later FV1611 vehicles and variants were produced by the Royal Ordnance Factory at Woolwich. In all, a total of 1700 FV1600 vehicles were converted to the armoured role; close to 50% of the total FV1600 production.

CHAPTER 3.3: HUMBER PIG

The FV1620 'Malkara' launchers were based on extensively-modified FV1609 vehicles. The bodies and hulls were produced by Wharton Engineers of Elstree, working with the Royal Ordnance Factory; the missile launch system was supplied by the British Aircraft Corporation. The number of FV1620 vehicles produced cannot have been more than 10.

Replacement and disposal
The basic 'Pig' APC's enjoyed a rather longer service life than was at first anticipated. By the mid-1960's, the vehicle, which remember was only an expedient measure anyway, was beginning to show its age and was considered to be obsolete.

Many of them had been disposed of, and others had been withdrawn and put into store when, in 1969, the Irish 'troubles' flared up again and the vehicles were pressed back into service.

Disposal had begun in around 1967 when vehicles were auctioned through the usual channels. It doesn't take much imagination to see that there is no significant demand in civvy street for armoured trucks, so sales must have been disappointing. However, it is rumoured that when it was decided that 'Pigs' should be used to patrol the streets of Belfast and Derry, the Ministry was forced to repurchase vehicles which had already been sold to dealers, and perhaps even to private customers.

There was really no direct replacement for the 'Pig' in any of its roles. As an APC in Northern Ireland it was replaced in part by the various applique-armoured Land Rovers (sometimes called 'Piglets'), and elsewhere by the GKN-Sankey FV432, the GKN 'Saxon', and the Alvis CVR(T) 'Spartan'.

The 'Hornet' missile launcher was only deployed with the Parachute Squadron of the Royal Armoured Corps where it remained in service until it was replaced in the 1970's by the Ferret Mk 5, and ultimately by more-sophisticated ATGW launchers such as the Alvis 'Striker'.

NOMENCLATURE and VARIATIONS

The armoured variations of the FV1600 series were produced in two basic marks; early Mk 1 vehicles had an open rear compartment with low sides, later production Mk 1 vehicles had full-height sides but still without a roof over the rear compartment. The up-armoured Mk 2 vehicles (aside from the specialised 'Malkara' missile launcher) had full-height sides and were fully enclosed.

Various kits were available to adapt the vehicle to a variety of roles, and an enormous number of detail changes were made to vehicles in Northern Ireland.

Mock-up of FV1609 Mk 1 'Pig' (IWM)

Prototype of FV1609 Mk 1 'Pig' with low sides (TMB)

Prototype of FV1609 Mk 1 'Pig' with low sides (IWM)

FV1609 Mk 1 production 'Pig' (TMB)

FV1609 Mk 1 production 'Pig' (IWM)

FV1609 Mk 1 'Pig' FFW/FFR with WW2 1 ton trailer (IWM)

FV1609(A). Truck, armoured, 1 ton, 4x4, cargo, Humber, Mk 1

The original 1 ton armoured truck or personnel carrier based on the equivalent soft-skin FV1601 vehicle. Fully-enclosed armoured cab with roof hatches; open-topped rear cargo area with canvas tilt supported on tubular steel frame. The rear compartment had hinged double doors at the rear, each with a firing port, and there were two small firing or vision ports on each side of the body.

Early development vehicles had low sides to the open-topped cargo area, with a single side-hinged tailgate. The canvas tilt had vision panels let into the sides.

FV1611(A). Truck, armoured, 1 ton, 4x4, APC, Humber, Mk 2

Modified and up-armoured version of FV1609 intended for use as a small armoured personnel carrier for six fully-equipped personnel plus a crew of two. Similar body to the basic armoured truck but with an armoured-steel roof instead of the canvas tilt, and armoured floor. The external stowage boxes were removed from over the front and rear wheels, and at the rear were replaced by simple fabricated wheel arches; occasionally the rear face of the stowage box remained in place and was used as a registration plate mounting.

This was the most numerous of the FV1600 armoured variants. The vehicle was additionally up-armoured several times in the light of experience gained in Northern Ireland, most notably to withstand attack from armour-piercing 7.62mm rounds.

FV1612(A). Truck, armoured, 1 ton, 4x4, APC, FFW, Humber, Mk 2

As FV1611 but modified for the FFW/FFR role by the inclusion of additional batteries, two-speed generator designed to maintain a high output with the engine idling, radio connecting box, and radio operator's table and seating in the rear compartment. Intended for use as a command and reconnaissance vehicle in forward areas.

FV1613(A). Truck, armoured, 1 ton, 4x4, ambulance, Humber, Mk 2

As FV1611 but modified for use as a field ambulance with accommodation for three stretchers, eight seated patients, or one stretcher and four seated patients.

FV1620(A). Truck, 1 ton, air portable launcher, Phase 1, 4x4, Humber

Highly-modified version of basic FV1609 vehicle, known as 'Hornet'. Most of rear bodywork was removed and the cab redesigned. A hydraulic launcher arm was mounted on the rear chassis for two 'Malkara' wire-guided anti-tank missiles; two additional missiles were stored on the vehicle.

During transit, the launch arm was lowered to the rear deck of the truck, but when deployed for action, the arm was raised to allow the missiles to be launched over the vehicle cab. An optical sight was fitted to the vehicle roof and the missile was guided by a joystick control installed in the cab.

Workshop modifications
Most 'Pigs' were deployed in Northern Ireland where all kinds of modifications were made in an attempt to counter the effects of terrorist and riot attack. These modifications were made to suit whatever need arose at the time, and often the numbers of vehicles involved were not large.

Many vehicles had the upper portion of the rear doors cut away and replaced with an armoured flap, hinged from the roof to provide safer entry to and exit from the vehicle; sometimes a vision block was installed in this upper panel. Some of the vehicles up-armoured in the 1970's were later fitted with applique panels on the sides to deflect rocks and petrol bombs.

Typical simple modifications include the provision of armoured hinged side and rear skirts to reduce the chance of troops sheltering behind the vehicle from being shot in the legs; front 'cow catchers' for pushing road blocks and burning vehicles aside; installation of wire cage screens over lights, windscreen, vision ports, etc; vision blocks were installed in the armoured hatches; and some vehicles were fitted with tear gas launchers. Powered 'Vent-Axia' armour-protected extract ventilators were sometimes fitted to the rear body vision ports.

One vehicle was fitted with a roof-mounted searchlight together with a polycarbonate observation cupola. 'Pigs' have also been fitted with water cannon and fire extinguishing equipment for riot control, as well as being equipped as command centres for 'wheelbarrow' remote-control explosive ordnance disposal devices (EOD). At least one 'Pig' was fitted with the turret from a 'Ferret' or 'Saracen' installed on an armoured box on the roof.

The most intriguing variant was the so-called 'flying Pig'. These were fitted with hinged extending wire cages on the sides and roof which could be opened out to form a screen for the troops against rocks and other missiles, as well as being able to quickly provide a simple road block.

A number of basic FV1611 vehicles were converted to act as control and operations centres for radio-controlled 'drone' surveillance aircraft. The conversion involved the installation of additional electronics to suit the application. FV1611 vehicles were also developed for use as towing and electronics centres for the 'Green Archer' mortar-locating radar.

FV1611 Mk 2 'Pig' with 'cow catcher' (IWM)

FV1611 Mk 2 'Pig' (TMB)

FV1620 'Hornet' ATGW launcher (TMB)

CHAPTER 3.3: HUMBER PIG

FV1611 Mk 2 'Pig' heavily-modified for riot control (TMB)

FV1611 Mk 2 'flying Pig' with screens folded (IWM)

FV1611 Mk 2 'flying Pig' on the wing (IWM)

DESCRIPTION

Engine
Rolls-Royce B60, No 1, Mk 2A, Mk 5A or Mk 5F (FV1620 only); wet sump.
Capacity: 4256cc.
Bore and stroke: 3.50 x 4.50in.
Power output: 130bhp (gross); 109bhp (net) at 3750rpm.
Maximum torque: 209 lbs/ft (gross); 197 lbs/ft (net) at 2050rpm.

Detail variations
Distributor limiter set at 3750rpm (crankshaft speed); standard wet sump with well at rear; oil filter mounted remotely, on inner wing; Ki-gass pipework and nozzles fitted (Mk 5A engines only); oil cooler fitted; hydraulic power take-off (Mk 5F engines only); dual exhaust manifold, with horizontal centre outlets; inlet manifold with horizontal flange for carburettor mounting; intake air horn positioned at 22.5 or 45 deg to offside; special rear support plate and bell housing adaptor.

Transmission
The transmission was virtually identical to that employed on the unarmoured vehicles, with a 275mm Borg and Beck single dry-plate clutch, five-speed and reverse gearbox, and unit-construction back axle and single-speed transfer gear assembly. First and reverse were engaged by a sliding gear, the other speeds were of the constant-mesh helical type; the ratios were not the same as those used on the soft-skin variants.

From the transfer case, an open propeller shaft ran the length of the vehicle to the front axle, with a second, shorter shaft driving the winch. Engagement and disengagement of the front axle was by a simple dog clutch, with the mechanism installed in the axle casing, and controlled manually by a lever in the cab.

The transfer box ratios were 1.41:1 for the axle drive, compared to 1.33:1 on the unarmoured version, and 1:1 for the winch. The gearbox contained no low ratios, and first gear was not normally used for road work. Front-wheel drive was automatically selected as first gear was engaged, but had to be manually de-selected.

The front axle was identical to that used on the unarmoured version, with a spiral bevel crown wheel and pinion, and bevel type differential. Drive to the wheels was transmitted through halfshafts, each with two Tracta type constant-velocity joints.

The rear axle was similar, but in place of the Tracta joints, drive was transmitted through an FVRDE-designed constant-velocity coupling described as a 'Chobham' joint. This was developed to withstand the increased axle loadings imposed by the heavier armoured vehicles.

THE ROLLS-ROYCE 'B SERIES' ENGINE

The differentials were offset to the right on both axles, and the hubs incorporated lifting flanges.

Although this was really a hang-over from the soft-skin version, the front and rear axles were resiliently-mounted on rubber sleeves, intended to reduce the transmission of road noise and vibration into the cab. Extensive use was made of magnesium alloys in the gearbox and axle casings.

Suspension
Independent suspension was provided at all four wheels by means of longitudinal torsion bars; it appears that the same torsion bars were used as on the soft-skin versions, even though the 'Pig' was ultimately to weigh close to 7000kg (compared to around 4000kg). The suspension movement at each wheel station was handled by transverse upper and lower wishbone links running in large surface oil-bath bearings.

Bump and rebound rubbers were provided for each wheel, with large, double-acting telescopic hydraulic shock absorbers installed vertically between the axle and chassis member.

The front and rear torsion bars were of equal length, running along the outside of the main chassis members, one above the other. The bars were pre-stressed to extend their service life and thus were not interchangeable. All other suspension components were similar in design front-to-rear, and side-to-side, with the upper wishbone links being interchangeable.

Steering gear
Like the soft-skin versions, the steering gear consisted of a recirculating-ball type steering box, acting through an extraordinarily-complex system of joints and levers.

The drop arm from the box was connected by a short drag link to one arm of a bell crank lever on a vertical pivot attached to the frame. Also connected to the bell crank was a steering rod, which acted on the offside wheel, and a track rod; the track rod was connected to an idler lever on the opposite frame member and this had a second steering rod which acted on the nearside wheel.

Despite the increased weight, at 21:1 measured at the drop arm, the steering ratio was the same as that used on the unarmoured vehicles which must have called for considerable effort at the wheel at low speeds; perhaps this explains the name 'Pig'. A 450mm diameter steering wheel moved through 3.75 turns from lock to lock.

Braking system
Lockheed vacuum servo-assisted hydraulic brakes were fitted at all four wheels, with twin-leading shoes configured for both the forward and reverse directions.

The 'Hydravac' servo unit was mounted on the engine front support cross member. Cast-iron brake drums, 330mm diameter x 63.5mm width, provided a total of 0.15sq m of braking area for each wheel.

The brakes were not waterproofed but the master cylinder was sealed, and the supplementary fluid reservoir was installed in the cab above the unprepared wading line.

The hand (parking) brake was operated mechanically on all wheels through rods and cables; the handbrake linkage was compensated between the left- and right-hand wheels on each axle, but not from front to rear.

Road wheels
Wheels were 7.00B x 20in divided-disc steel type. Standard tyres were 11.00x20 run-flat (RF), complete with tubes and bead spacers. As the vehicle was up-armoured over the years, the resultant increase in weight made it necessary to use 'reinforced' and then 'extra-reinforced' tyres.

A power take-off on the side of the gearbox was provided to drive a small mechanical piston-type compressor intended for tyre inflation.

Chassis
The chassis frame was of conventional design, similar to that employed on the unarmoured vehicles, but with certain modifications to suit the armoured body.

The chassis itself consisted of channel-section main members which incorporated mountings for the torsion bars, and which were braced by a welded central cruciform. Channel-section stiffeners were provided to form box-section cross members at the front and rear, outside the cruciform. Body mounting brackets were welded to the top of the main members, and welded skid plates protected the steering linkage, sump, and axle differentials.

There were no bumper brackets but a short upswept extension was bolted to the rear end of each side member.

Lashing eyes were provided in strategic positions for securing the vehicle to the deck of a ship.

Hull
The armoured hull consisted of a combined cab and cargo compartment, constructed from LT100 armoured steel. The floor was at a common level across the cab and rear compartment, installed on a detachable subframe designed to provide minimal intrusion from the wheel arches. On the original FV1609 vehicle, the floor plates were of light alloy and were not armoured. A removable 610mm high partition was installed between the cab and rear compartment, simply to prevent the load from intruding into the driving area.

Cab

The scuttle and bonnet, and the louvred radiator air intake were also armoured, giving maximum protection to the crew and engine compartment. The air intake, front skid plate and engine side panels could be detached as a complete assembly to improve access to the engine; lifting eyes were fitted on the air-intake assembly for this purpose. The bonnet consisted of a fixed centre section attached to the scuttle and front louvre unit, together with two, lockable side-hinged opening panels.

On the pilot FV1609 vehicles, the cab roof was of 18swg steel sheet; the armour was extended across the roof of the cab on FV1611 and other Mk 2 vehicles.

The pressed-steel front wings were of a simple flat panel construction, bolted to the engine side panels and the scuttle. Mud flaps were fitted to the lower rear edges of the wings.

The armoured cab doors were hung on fixed knuckle-type hinges mounted on the 'A' posts; most vehicles were fitted with door stays which allowed the doors to be used as a screen for troops whilst the vehicle advanced forward. Early vehicles had the bottom corners of the doors cut away at an angle, while on the later production FV1611, the doors were square-cornered, possibly because of the increased thickness of armour. Both doors were fitted with a bottom-hinged armoured flap, lockable in the open or closed position. On FV1609 vehicles, the flap was provided with a vision slit with a rotating cover installed in the flap; on the later FV1611 vehicles, a glass vision block was fitted.

The cab was designed to accommodate a crew of two on upholstered bucket seats with hinged backrests; the driver's seat was adjustable for height and reach, the passenger's seat was fixed. An occasional seat could be fitted between the passenger and driver, and a canvas screen could be rolled down to the partition panel to separate the front and rear compartments.

On Mk 1 vehicles, a removable, forward-hinged escape hatch was provided above each seat.

A detachable windscreen was fitted to the front plate panel; when not in use, the screen panels were stowed on the cab doors, or behind the driver's seat. Hinged armoured flaps were fitted externally to the openings in front of both the driver and passenger; these flaps were hydraulically-controlled and could be locked in both the open and closed positions.

Rear compartment

On the early FV1609 vehicles, the armoured protection in the cargo compartment extended only to a height of 500mm from the floor. On later FV1609 vehicles, the armour was extended to the full height of the cargo area, and subsequently was further extended across the roof and floor on FV1611 and other Mk 2 vehicles.

It was not originally envisaged that the FV1609 vehicle would be used exclusively as an APC and the passengers were provided only with simple bench seats along each side. Removable plates in the floor could be lifted to provide foot wells but these wells had no armoured protection when the plates were raised.

Early FV1609 vehicles had a single side-hung rear door. Although later vehicles had double doors, many vehicles were subsequently modified to a three-door configuration; the existing doors were cut down, and a spring-assisted top-hinged flap fitted above.

Sheet-metal stowage bins were originally fitted over, and below the rear wheel arches, and in the forward edges of the front wings; the rear bins, and occasionally those at the front, were later removed. Some vehicles retained a small part of the rear stowage boxes, closed-off to form a mounting box for the rear lights. On FV1609 vehicles, there were additional stowage racks and support brackets installed on the body sides and on the rear doors.

The FFW/FFR version of the basic cargo vehicle (FV1612) was provided with two aerial mounting brackets, one each side of the vehicle forward of the rear wheel arches. Inside the rear body there are two folding operators' seats, additional battery housings, and a wireless table.

'Hornet' missile launch vehicles

The FV1620 'Hornet' missile launch vehicle consisted of an extended armoured cab designed for a crew of three. The rear bodywork was removed from behind the cab and the back of the cab was closed off with an armoured partition. An optical sight was mounted on the cab roof.

A hydraulically-operated launch arm was mounted on the chassis, designed to hold and launch two missiles; two further missiles were stored in armoured boxes attached to the cab sides. The arm could be elevated and traversed to allow the missiles to be launched over the cab.

Electrical equipment

Like its unarmoured counterpart, the armoured truck was wired on a 24V negative-earth electrical system. Both the truck/APC and FFW/FFR versions had two 12V, 60Ah batteries in series installed in the cab behind the seats, with additional batteries, (four 6V, 180Ah) provided in the rear compartment on vehicles intended for the radio role.

On the truck/APC versions, a generator No 1, Mk 2 or Mk 2/1 was employed, producing 12A at 28.5V maximum, under the control of a vibrating contact regulator. The generator installed on FFW/FFR vehicles was of the automatic two-speed type, either No 2, Mk 1 or Mk 2, with a maximum output of 25A, and designed to produce higher outputs at idle, and at low engine speeds. The control panel, which was of the current-limiting voltage control type, allowed charging of both the radio batteries and the main vehicle batteries at the same time.

All electrical components were waterproofed and radio-screened and much of the equipment was common to other British military vehicles of the 1950's and 60's.

Winch
Where a winch was fitted, this was a mechanical two-ton, horizontal drum type, manufactured by Turner, and driven from a power take-off on the transfer case. Average rope speed, at an engine speed of 3750rpm, was 16.75m/min, with three layers of rope on the drum.

Engagement of the winch was effected by means of a sliding dog in the transfer case, controlled by a lever in the cab which selected either axle drive or winch drive. Rope fairleads were provided to both the front and rear of the vehicle, with guide bollards mounted on the chassis to permit winching from the front or rear.

An electrical cut-out circuit, wired through the ignition, was provided to protect the winch against overload.

Wading
The design specification for the unarmoured Humber required that the truck be able to undertake shallow wading to a depth of 762mm with the minimum of preparation, and this requirement was carried through to the armoured versions.

All of the standard FVRDE-designed electrical equipment was waterproofed and the engine breather and fuel tank vent lines were connected into the air intake system well above the 762mm water line.

For the unarmoured versions, a separate snorkel was available to fit to the standard air intake on the right-hand scuttle side. Although the intake arrangements for the armoured trucks were different, the wading requirement was the same, so presumably a suitable snorkel was available.

With the snorkel in place, and with suitable preparation, the vehicle could be used for deep-water wading to a depth of 1981mm. With the axle vents sealed and additional treatment of, for example dipstick openings, carburettor and other apertures, the truck could travel almost completely submerged. In these situations, the driver would kneel on the seat with the roof escape hatch open, and control the vehicle by means of the hand throttle.

ARMAMENTS
Unusually for an armoured vehicle, with perhaps one solitary exception, none of the 'Pig' truck/APC variants were armed. Clips were provided in various positions in the cab and rear bodywork to accept the standard Lee Enfield, SMLE No 4 .303 rifles which were in use at the time.

Some vehicles were fitted with electrically-controlled smoke grenade launchers, installed either on the roof or on the top of the engine compartment cover.

'Hornet' missile launch vehicles
The 'Malkara' missile was originally developed in Australia to provide a long-range anti-tank capability. The missile was wire-guided by an operator using a joystick control; an optical sight (10x magnification) mounted in the vehicle roof allowed the missile to be tracked whilst in flight. The missile could also be launched by the operator up to 80m away from the vehicle using a separation sight and remote controller, connected to the vehicle by means of an umbilical.

Maximum range was 10,000m and this distance could be reached in 28 seconds. The high explosive anti-tank (HEAT) warhead weighed 27kg and was capable of knocking out any tank in service at that time. The vehicle carried four missiles, two ready to fire, and two for reload.

The complete vehicle and missile system was designed for air-dropping and, after landing, could be made ready for use in about 10 minutes.

ANCILLARY EQUIPMENT
The following equipment was typically carried on the vehicle:

Mechanics tools
Ballpein hammer
Box spanners, AF (3) and tommy bar
Hardwood block
Open-ended spanners, AF (6)
Open-ended spanners, BA (3)
Open-ended spanners, BSW (5)
Pliers, sidecutting
Ring spanner
Screwdriver
Starting handle
Wheel brace
200mm adjustable spanner
4 ton jack

Pioneer tools
Matchet
Pickaxe head

Pickaxe helve (carried separately)
Shovel

Drivers and crew equipment
Periscope, no 13 (3)
Rifles, no 4 Lee Enfield (2)

Other equipment
CTC fire extinguisher
First aid kit, large
Grease gun
Inspection lamp
Jerry can, gasoline
Jerry can, water (plastic on later vehicles)
Non-skid chains (4)
Oil and petrol injector
Oil can, 1 quart
Pressure oiler
Tow rope
Tyre pressure gauge
7.33m air hose

This equipment was either attached to the outside of the vehicle using various clips and brackets provided for that purpose, or stowed in the cab, or in the lockers in each rear wheel arch.

RADIO EQUIPMENT

Those vehicles intended for the wireless role (designated FFW) were supplied suppressed against electrical interference, and with three aerial base mountings ready for the user to install a specific radio kit; also installed in the rear of the vehicle were a radio junction box, 'B' type radio control harness, radio tables, operators' seats, battery carriers, and lights. The FV1604 vehicle also included two 'Vent-Axia' ventilating fans, fixing brackets welded to inside of the hull, cable conduit, and stowage lockers.

FFW vehicles could be converted to the radio (FFR) role by the addition of a specialist installation kit. The following radio versions of the truck were listed in EMER N253, dated 1966: Truck, armoured FFR; Truck, armoured, radio, special, unfitted; Truck, armoured, radio; Truck, armoured, radio, type G; Truck, armoured, radio, type H; Radio station, truck mounted.

The radio sets, control boxes etc, were installed on the tables, with the batteries in the carriers on the floor beneath. The aerial tuner unit was installed on the wall, with the aerial bases and aerials mounted on the hull sides, one at each corner.

The radio equipment and launch-control electronics were installed in the cab of the 'Malkara' launch vehicle (FV1620).

A typical 'Larkspur' station installed in the FFW/FFR vehicles comprised a single HF or VHF set, or a combination of two or three radio sets together with the control harness, aerial tuner, junction boxes, and any equipment necessary to allow switching between sets.

Commonly-encountered 'Larkspur' radio stations included a pair of C13 sets, C12/C42, C11-R210/C42, C13/C42, C13/C45/B48, C42/B47, C45/B48, C42/C45/B48, or C45/C45/R209.

DOCUMENTATION

Technical publications
Technical handbooks
Data summary: truck, armoured, 1 ton, 4x4, APC, Humber, Mk 2. EMER N250/2.
Technical description: truck, 1 ton, GS, cargo, 4x4, Humber, Mk 1, with winch; FFW; FFW, with winch; wireless light; armoured; armoured, with winch; armoured FFW. EMER N252.

User handbooks
User handbook: truck, 1 ton, armoured, 4x4, Humber; with winch; FFW. WO codes 18365, 12246.

Servicing details
Servicing schedule: truck, 1 ton, GS and armoured, 4x4, Humber, Mks 1 and 2. Army codes 10359, 11315, 13068.

Parts list
Illustrated parts catalogue: truck, armoured, 1 ton, Humber, Mks 1 and 2. Army code 12815.

Repair manuals
Field repairs: truck, 1 ton, armoured, 4x4, Humber (with winch), Mk 2. EMER N252/2.
Unit repairs: truck, 1 ton, armoured, 4x4, Humber, with winch, Mk 2. EMER N253/2.
Base repairs: truck, 1 ton, armoured, 4x4, Humber, with winch, Mk 2. EMER N254/2.

Modification instructions
Truck, 1 ton, GS and armoured, 4x4, Humber. EMER N257, instructions 1-71.

Miscellaneous instructions
Truck 1 ton, Humber, all types. EMER N259, instructions 1-10.

Radio installation
User handbook: radio installation in FFR 'B' Vehicles. WO code 12798.

Bibliography
Humber FV1600 series. A unique British family of combat range trucks. London, Wheels & Tracks, no 6, 1984. ISSN 0263-7081.

CHAPTER 3.3: HUMBER PIG

CHAPTER 4

THE B80/81 ENGINES
B80 Mks 1-3, Mks 5-6; B81 Mk 3, Mks 7-8

CONTENTS

4.1	Alvis 'Saladin'	115
4.2	Alvis 'Saracen'	125
4.3	Alvis 'Stalwart'	137
4.4	GKN 'Trojan' & Vickers 'Abbot'	157
4.5	Leyland 'Martian'	163
4.6	Thornycroft light mobile digger	175
4.7	Airfield vehicles:	179

Alvis runway friction test vehicle
Alvis 'Salamander'
Douglas 10 ton fire tender
Douglas/BROS 'Sno-Flyr'
Douglas/Sentinel aircraft tug
Thornycroft 'Nubian' 3 and 5 ton fire tender

4.8	Minor applications and prototypes:	189

Albion 5 ton truck
BOC/Tasker 15 ton oxygen plant
'Cambridge' tracked carrier
'Centurion' ARV
Thornycroft 'Nubian' 3 and 5 ton truck
Vauxhall/Albion 3 ton truck

DATA SUMMARY

Dimensions and weight
Overall installed dimensions
Length: 1282mm.
Width: 669mm.
Height: 945mm.

Dry weight: B80, 454kg; B81, 458kg.

Performance	B80	B81
Bore	88.9mm, 3.50in	95.25mm, 3.75in
Stroke	114.3mm, 4.50in	114.3mm, 4.50in
Swept volume (cc)	5675	6516
Compression ratio	6.4:1	6.4:1
Firing order	16258374	16258374

Gross output (bhp at 3750rpm):
uninstalled	165	195-220

Gross torque (lbs/ft):
uninstalled	280	330-335

Fuel consumption (max demand, litres/hr):
at 3000rpm	52	62-64
at 3750rpm	61	74-82

PRODUCTION SUMMARY

Mark	Qty	Vehicle and FV number	
B80, Mk 1 engines:			
Mk 1B	-	'Oxford' CT24/CT25 tracked carrier	-
Mk 1C	1	Marine application	-
Mk 1D	67	Albion 6x6, 5 ton truck	FV14001 FV14004
		Leyland 'Hippo' Mk 2	-
		Vauxhall 3 ton truck	FV1301 FV1313
		Thornycroft 4x4, 'Nubian'	FV13403
		Thornycroft 6x6, 'Nubian'	FV14101 FV14103
B80, Mk 2 engines:			
Mk 2A	69	Leyland 'Martian'	FV1100
Mk 2C	2	-	-
Mk 2D	297	Thornycroft 4x4, 'Nubian'	FV13403
		Thornycroft 6x6, 'Nubian'	FV14101 FV14103
Mk 2F	11	'Cambridge' tracked carrier	FV401
Mk 2H	25	Leyland 'Martian'	FV1103
Mk 2K	-	Douglas/BROS 'Sno-Flyr'	-
Mk 2P	100	'Centurion' ARV winch	FV4006
B80, Mk 3 engines:			
Mk 3A	275	Alvis 'Saladin'	FV601
		Alvis 'Saracen'	FV603 FV604
B80, Mk 5 engines:			
Mk 5C	145	Douglas/Sentinel aircraft tug	FV2241
		Aldous Mk VII harbour tug	-
Mk 5D	108	Thornycroft 4x4, 'Nubian'	FV13403
		Thornycroft 6x6, 'Nubian'	FV14101 FV14103
Mk 5F	16	'Cambridge' tracked carrier	FV401 FV402
		Thornycroft 4x4, 'Nubian'	FV13403
		Thornycroft 6x6, 'Nubian'	FV14101 FV14103
Mk 5H	237	Thornycroft 'Nubian'	-
Mk 5L	259	Heavy ferry pontoon raft	-
Mk 5N	137	Douglas/Sentinel aircraft tug	FV2241
Mk 5P	282	'Centurion' ARV winch	FV4006
Mk 5Q	22	Thornycroft 4x4, 'Nubian'	FV13403
		Thornycroft 6x6, 'Nubian'	FV14101 FV14103
B80, Mk 6 engines:			
Mk 6A	1518	Alvis 'Saladin'	FV601
		Alvis 'Saracen'	FV603 FV604 FV610 FV611
Mk 6D/L	1131	Alvis 'Saladin'	FV601
Total	**4702**		

Mark	Qty	Vehicle and FV number	
B81, Mk 5 engines:			
Mk 5A	8	City Electric airfield power unit	-
Mk 5G	105	Vernon 50kVA generator set Petbow generator set	- -
Mk 5H	1010	Leyland 'Martian'	FV1103 FV1110 FV1119 FV1121 FV1122
Mk 5K	386	Leyland 'Martian'	FV1119
Mk 5M	8	BOC/Tasker oxygen plant	FV3523
Mk 5Q	143	Thornycroft 4x4, 'Nubian'	FV13403
		Thornycroft 6x6, 'Nubian'	FV14101 FV14103
Mk 5R	26	Thornycroft 6x6, 'Nubian'	FV14161
B81, Mk 7 engines:			
Mk 7D	5	Thornycroft light mobile digger	-
Mk 7F	5	Tracked carrier	FV421
Mk 7H	2	Douglas 10 ton fire tender	FV11501
Mk 7K	141	Thornycroft 6x6, 'Nubian'	FV14161
Mk 7P	15	Thornycroft 6x6, 'Nubian'	FV14151
B81, Mk 8 engines:			
Mk 8A	221	Alvis 'Salamander'	FV651 FV652
		Alvis runway friction test vehicle	FV651
Mk 8B	1082	Alvis 'Stalwart'	FV620 FV622 FV623 FV624
Mk 8F	812	GKN 'Trojan' Mk 1	FV432
Mk 8G	9	Vickers 'Abbot' SPG	FV433
Total	**3978**		

CHAPTER 4.1

ALVIS SALADIN
FV601

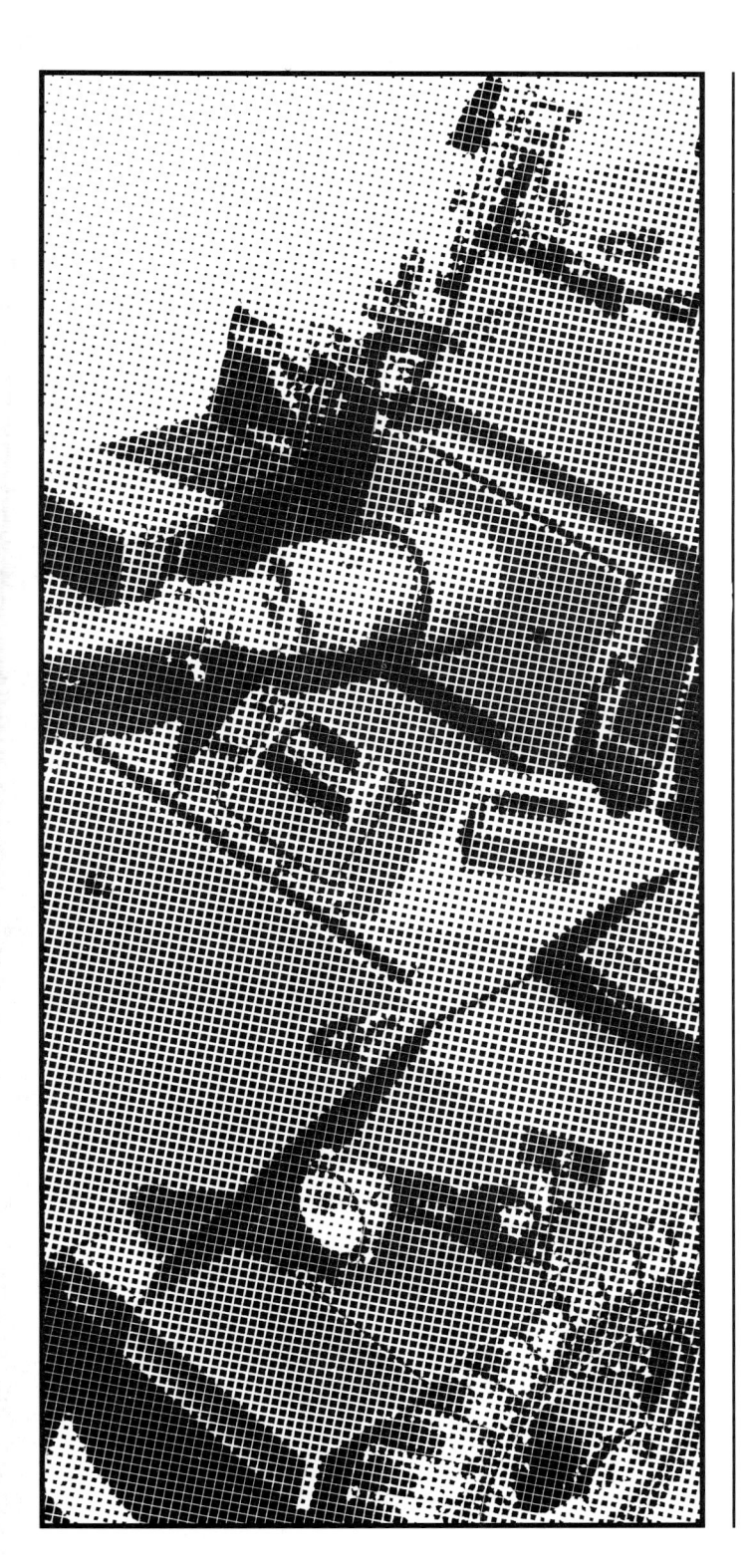

In 1946 the War Office General Staff issued an outline specification for a heavy armoured car which was intended to replace the wartime Daimler Mk 2, and the larger AEC, as well as American vehicles such as the 'Greyhound', 'Staghound', and 'Boarhound'. The document defined an armoured car as an 'armoured wheeled reconnaissance vehicle', and stated that such a vehicle was intended to 'harass and pursue a retreating enemy... and to engage comparable enemy vehicles, infantry and unarmoured vehicles, and enemy armoured vehicles at short range'.

By 1947, FVRDE had prepared a detailed design brief, but despite the appearance of working prototypes in 1952/53, it was not until 1958 that the first vehicle was accepted into service. The reason for this apparently-protracted development cycle was that no sooner had the specification for the FV601 'Saladin' been agreed, than the insurrection in Malaya decreed that priority be given to the 'Saracen' APC (see Chapter 4.2). Thus, the 'Saladin' found itself in a queue for production.

In fact, Alvis, who were to build the 'Saladin' were so busy with the 'Saracen' project that the contract for the pre-production vehicles was given to Crossley Motors, only reverting to Alvis when the Crossley factory was subsequently closed down.

Based on the same six-wheel chassis and running gear as its APC counterpart, the 'Saladin' employed a rear-mounted B80 engine, together with a fluid flywheel and pre-selector transmission. With its specially-developed 76mm gun, together with coaxial and anti-aircraft machine guns, the six-wheeled 'Saladin' packed a considerable punch for a wheeled reconnaissance vehicle.

The 'Saladin' enjoyed considerable export success, and has been described as one of the most successful British armoured fighting vehicles of the post-war period.

OVERVIEW

The 'Saladin' was a six-wheeled heavy armoured car designed to mount a 76mm gun and two general-purpose machine guns, one installed co-axially with the main armament, the other, for anti-aircraft defence, mounted on the turret roof.

The vehicle was designed for a crew of three, consisting of commander, gunner and driver. There was stowage within the hull for 43 rounds (42 on Mk 1) for the main

CHAPTER 4.1: ALVIS SALADIN

gun, together with 2750 rounds (3000 on Mk 1) for the machine guns.

The armoured turret and hull, 8-32mm thick, provided all-round protection from light anti-tank and field artillery fire, light and medium machine guns, and rifle fire, as well as from close detonation of anti-tank mines. The rotating turret was designed to turn through a full 360 degrees, with power traverse and manual back-up.

Power was supplied by a B80 eight-cylinder engine, mounted in the rear of the hull, and arranged to drive all six wheels through a pre-selector gearbox and single-speed transfer case. Steering was provided by the two forward axles, and excellent on- and off-road performance was provided by means of torsion-bar suspension, with all six wheels being independently-sprung. This gave the 'Saladin' a very high level of mobility: off-road it offered performance equal to any comparable vehicle, and was able to reach places previously accessible only to tracked vehicles.

'Saladin' was designed to be air portable: one vehicle to an AW660 aircraft, two in a Beverley.

The vehicle was produced in Mk 1 and Mk 2 form and there were no significant variants.

DEVELOPMENT

In June 1947, 'General Staff Policy Statement 2' (GSPS 2) laid down the basic specification for armoured cars, defining the broad role of the vehicle and setting out the main characteristics. Among other features, it was proposed that the post-war armoured car should be immune to near misses from projectiles equivalent to medium artillery, including air bursts from proximity fuses. The vehicle should be able to move silently; a 'high-speed' reverse gear was required, and a winch was to be fitted for self-recovery. It was proposed that the vehicle should accommodate a crew of four, and that it should be able to operate fully closed-down.

When the detailed specification for what was to become the FV601 'Saladin', was drawn-up by FVRDE later that same year many of these features were abandoned. Nevertheless, the specification called for a vehicle of similar external dimensions to the WW2 Daimler, but offering higher levels of protection, improved hitting power, and better all-round performance.

GSPS 2 had already recognised that it was 'impossible to mount a weapon, either orthodox or unorthodox in an armoured car... which would fulfil the requirements... and yet be small and light enough for air portability', and the first mock-up of the vehicle was produced using a two-pounder gun, similar to that fitted to the Daimler.

VEHICLE OUTLINES

SCALE 1:75

CHAPTER 4.1: ALVIS SALADIN

SPECIFICATION

Dimensions and weight

	FV601, Mk 1	FV601, Mk 2
Dimensions (mm):		
Length:		
gun forward	5277	5284
hull only	4910	4930
Width	2516	2540
Height:		
to gunner's periscope	-	2930
to top of turret	2257	2190
Wheelbase:		
front/centre	1524	1524
centre/rear	1524	1524
Track	2032	2032
Ground clearance	426	426
Weight:		
Gross laden weight	10,690	11,278
Unladen weight	-	9144

Bridge classification: 11.
Ground pressure: 11,200kg/sq m.

Performance

Maximum speed, on road, 73km/h; average speed, off road, 32km/h.
Approach angle: 60 deg.
Departure angle: 50 deg.

Fuel consumption: 0.60 litre/km, on road; 1.08 litre/km, off road.
Maximum range: 400km.

Turning circle: 14.63m.
Vertical obstacle: 460mm.
Ditch crossing (trench) without channels: 1520mm.
Maximum gradient: 46%.
Maximum gradient for stop and restart: 30%.
Maximum side slope: 30%.

Fording: unprepared, 1066mm; prepared, with deep-water wading kit, 2135mm.

The gun was designed to fire armour-piercing discarding sabot (APDS) rounds. It was no surprise therefore that in the event, it was felt that this lacked the necessary power to be really effective against hard targets, and a new quick-firing 76mm gun, the L3A1 and L5A1, was designed by the Royal Armaments Research and Development Establishment (RARDE) especially for the 'Saladin'.

Two prototypes were produced by Alvis, appearing in late 1952 and early 1953. These vehicles were submitted, without turrets, to FVRDE for assessment. Early photographs show the vehicle on test with concrete blocks to simulate the weight of the turret, and encircling rubber tracks fitted to the wheels on the centre and rear axles, as had been tried on Scammells during WW2. The tracks were quickly discarded, both by the steering action of the wheels and by the FVRDE designers.

However, after extensive trials, the vehicles were generally felt to be suitable for, at least limited production, but by this time Alvis were committed to producing the 'Saracen' APC. The first production contract, for six Mk 1 vehicles, was awarded to Crossley Motors. Although the company was originally a motor car manufacturer, there was some logic to the move since Crossley had also constructed armoured cars during WW1 and between the wars, and in 1948, had been taken over by AEC who had been producing armoured cars during WW2.

The six pre-production 'Saladins' had appeared by 1954, and it was originally intended that Crossley should be nominated as design parent for the vehicle. Unfortunately, this was not to be: Crossley built their last vehicle in 1956, and in 1958 the factory was closed and production reverted to Alvis.

During 1957, the pre-production vehicles underwent trials for gun range and accuracy, as well as armour-proving and anti-tank mine capabilities.

Production

The production vehicles, designated Mk 2, differed from the Mk 1 models in only minor detail: the engine was changed from a B80, Mk 3A to a Mk 6A (and subsequently to a Mk 6D); the shape of the turret rear was changed; the drum brakes were replaced by discs, as on the 'Stalwart'; the gun sights were modified; and changes were made to the engine covers. There were also small changes to the stowage arrangements for ammunition for the main gun.

Production took place between 1958 and 1972, and a total of 1177 'Saladins' was produced. Further small changes took place during the production run when the gun barrel counterweight was omitted, and the machine gun ring mount was simplified. Changes were also made to the armour.

CHAPTER 4.1: ALVIS SALADIN

In addition to the British Army, 'Saladins' served with Australia, Abu Dhabi, Bahrain, Ghana, Honduras, Hong Kong, Indonesia, Jordan, Kenya, Lebanon, Libya, Muscat, Nigeria, Oman, Portugal, Qatar, Sierra Leone, South Yemen, Sri Lanka, Sudan, Tunisia, Uganda, and United Arab Emirates. Vehicles were also used by the West German border police.

Technical problems

Like the 'Saracen and 'Stalwart', the 'Saladin' had a built-in technical restriction which reduced its reliability when run on hard surfaces.

The drive train transmitted power to each of the wheels via the centre axle, which in turn, was connected to the gearbox and transfer case through a single differential.

Although the differential was able to handle variations in the speed of rotation of the wheels on the vehicle from one side to the other, the three wheels on each side were driven as a single unit. If there was any significant difference in the diameter of the tyres on these wheels, perhaps due to uneven wear or the use of different makes and types of tyre, stresses would begin to build-up in the drive line which could not be dispersed when the vehicle was travelling on hard surfaces because the wheels were not able to slip.

For this reason, prolonged running on macadam or concrete inevitably caused severe tyre wear due to scrubbing, or actual bevel-box breakage or drive shaft damage. This damage would not have been immediately apparent to the user since the vehicle was able to drive equally well on, say two powered axles, as on the normal complement of three.

To avoid this type of damage, these vehicles were only driven on hard-surfaced roads when absolutely necessary. Although, by the nature of the vehicle, this was less of a problem with the 'Saracen' than say the 'Stalwart', there were situations when use on hard surfaces could not be avoided. It was then normal practice to put one set of wheels up the kerb, or off the edge of the road from time to time to allow the drive line stresses to unwind.

Replacement and disposal

As military thinking changed during the 1960's and 70's, there was increased emphasis being placed on NBC protection as well as on sophisticated battlefield electronics. Work on a replacement for the FV600 range began in 1960 and a contract was placed in 1967.

The need for an old-fashioned heavy armoured car had simply disappeared, and by about 1980, the 'Saladin' had been largely replaced in front line service by the much-lighter and more nimble FV721 'Fox', and the tracked FV701 'Scorpion'.

Prototype 'Saladin' at FVRDE, without turret (IWM)

Prototype 'Saladin' with ballast weights and rear wheel tracks (IWM)

Mk 1 'Saladin' showing longer rear to turret (IWM)

Mk 2 production 'Saladin' (BTMC)

Mk 2 'Saladin' with BAC 'Swingfire' (BTMC)

Mk 2 'Saladin' with flotation screen erected (TMB)

A few soldiered on in Cyprus until the mid-1980's but any remaining 'Saladins' are destined to see out the rest of their lives as gate guardians.

NOMENCLATURE and VARIATIONS

FV601. Armoured car, 6x6, Saladin

FV601(A). Mock-up and prototype vehicles were produced by Alvis, and originally equipped with the 'Pipsqueak' two-pounder gun. This was never intended as a long-term measure, and was replaced by the 76mm RARDE-designed weapon. Two prototypes were produced, initially without turret and gun.

FV601. Armoured car, 6x6, Saladin, Mk 1

FV601(B), Mk 1. Pre-production vehicles, in more-or-less definitive form, produced by Crossley Motors. Armed with 76mm RARDE gun. Total of six vehicles produced.

FV601. Armoured car, 6x6, Saladin, Mk 2

FV601(C), Mk 2. Production version of 'Saladin' produced by Alvis, and armed with the 76mm gun. Detail changes only, particularly to the turret design, when compared to the Mk 1 vehicle.

FV601(D), Mk 2. Variant produced exclusively for use by the West German border police; detail changes included no co-axial machine gun, German driving lamps, German smoke dischargers, etc.

Factory modifications

The 'Saladin' always had a clearly defined role to which it was extremely well-suited, and it did not really lend itself to modification for other roles.

Anti-tank role

There was just one factory variation, produced by Alvis as a private venture in about 1970, and designed to provide an anti-tank capability.

Pilot versions of the 'Saladin' were produced equipped with the BAC 'Swingfire' wire-guided, anti-tank missile. The launch boxes were installed either side of the turret, which was otherwise unaltered, and reload missiles were stored in armoured boxes fitted to the rear wheel arch tops. The missiles could be fired from within the vehicle, or remotely at 50m distance, using a separation sight.

At least one vehicle was supplied to the British Army for troop trials, but there was no production contract.

Uprating

Towards the natural end of the service life of the vehicle, Alvis attempted to uprate and up-gun it, perhaps hoping to secure export orders from overseas customers already deploying 'Saladins'. Demonstration vehicles were produced equipped with a Perkins 'Phaser' turbo-charged diesel engine, and with an uprated 90mm gun.

CHAPTER 4.1: ALVIS SALADIN

Uprated 'Saladins' were also produced by A F Budge (Military).

Workshop modifications
In the late 1960's, a 'Saladin' was equipped with the GEC-Elliott Automation ZB 298 ground surveillance radar. The scanner was mounted on top of the turret, which retained the 76mm gun, and the electronic equipment was installed in boxes attached to the turret sides.

Surprisingly for such an aggressive-looking vehicle, 'Saladins' were used in Northern Ireland for a short period in the early 1970's. For these duties, the vehicles were fitted with the usual complement of Makrolon screens and wire mesh guards over everything breakable or vulnerable; some vehicles were also fitted with angle iron wire cutters rather in the style of WW2 Jeeps.

Experiments were also conducted with the use of flotation screens to improve wading performance but there was no series production of vehicles so equipped.

DESCRIPTION

Engine
Rolls-Royce B80, No 1, Mk 3A (Mk 1 vehicles only), Mk 6A (most production vehicles), or Mk 6D/L; dry sump.
Capacity: 5670cc.
Bore and stroke: 3.50 x 4.50in.
Power output: 165bhp (gross), 136bhp (net) at 3750rpm.
Maximum torque: 280 lbs/ft (gross); 257 lbs/ft (net) at 1750rpm.

Detail variations
Distributor limiter set at 3750rpm (crankshaft speed); no air horn on Mk 3A version; short water jacket to inlet manifold; oil filter mounted remotely in engine compartment; oil cooler installed horizontally in engine compartment; Ki-gass nozzles, pipework and non-return valve fitted; engine installed on special four-point mounting; twin cooling fans with idler pulley for belt tensioning; horizontal centre outlet exhaust manifold; inlet manifold with horizontal flange for carburettor mounting; no clutch casing; belt-driven hydraulic pump for braking and steering system, combined with small compressor for tyre inflation.

Transmission
Power from the engine was delivered to a five-speed pre-selective epicyclic gearbox through a fluid coupling, with a separate transfer box giving five speeds forward and reverse. There was a separate forward-reverse control.

The pre-selector gearbox is fully described in Chapter 3.1 but it can be considered as a form of automatic transmission where gear selection is carried out by the

Mk 2 'Saladin' disembarking from landing craft (REME)

Definitive Mk 2 'Saladin' on manoeuvres (TMB)

Mk 2 'Saladin' production line (BTMC)

driver by means of a small manual lever, but with the actual gear changes handled automatically by brake bands in the gearbox. The driver selects the next gear he requires and uses the gearchange pedal to make the change when the gear is needed.

The transfer box was bolted directly to the gearbox, which in turn was mounted directly to the engine. The transfer box also incorporated the forward/reverse control, which was engaged by means of a sliding dog clutch, together with the differential. Early transfer cases were of cast iron, on later vehicles the construction was changed to aluminium-alloy. All five gears were available in reverse, and the transfer box ratio was 2.43:1.

From the differential, power was taken to the centre bevel box which drove the centre axle, and then via lateral drive shafts, running inside the hull, to front and rear bevel boxes and to the other axles. Final drive to the wheels was transmitted by articulating axle shafts to an epicyclic hub reduction gear, with a ratio of 4.125:1. Each drive shaft had two Tracta constant-velocity joints.

Suspension

All six wheels were independently sprung by means of pre-set, adjustable torsion bars running longitudinally on the outside of the hull. The actual suspension movement was handled by unequal length, parallel wishbone links attached to brackets on the hull.

Two double-acting hydraulic shock absorbers were provided above each of the front and rear wheels, and one above each centre wheel. Each wheel was also equipped with two telescopic rubber bump and rebound dampers, installed in tubular metal housings.

Steering gear

Steering was effected on the front four wheels by means of a hydraulically-assisted recirculating ball mechanism.

The steering wheel was mounted to a column, which in turn was connected via two bevel boxes to a transverse cross shaft. The shaft was connected by ball joints to a system of rocking beams, or levers, on either side of the vehicle, together with shafts which projected forwards to the outside of the hull. Hydraulic steering rams provided assistance to the steering shafts. Drop arms on either end of the shafts were connected to the road wheels by means of ball joints and drag links. There were no less than 14 lubrication points in the steering system.

Power assistance was provided automatically as soon as the wheel was moved from straight-ahead. Operation of the steering wheel opened the hydraulic steering control valve, directing oil under pressure to the steering rams. The hydraulic pressure was generated by a belt-driven pump, together with piston type accumulators.

Five turns of the steering wheel were required from lock-to-lock, giving a 14.63m turning circle.

Braking system

Each of the six road wheels was provided with a hydraulically-operated servo-assisted disc-brake system. The brakes were applied by means of externally-generated pressure via the brake pedal, which was connected to power valves in the hydraulic system. The discs were 413mm diameter.

The Mk 1 vehicles were fitted with drum brakes, with 75mm wide brake shoes operating in drums of 394mm diameter, giving a total braking area of 0.31sq m.

Hydraulic pressure for braking was generated by the same pump that provided steering assistance; twin warning lights on the driver's control board indicated when there was sufficient pressure in the braking system.

The emergency brake operated on all six wheels by a ratchet and mechanical linkage system.

Road wheels

Wheels were 8.00B x 20in two-piece alloy rims, mounting 12.00x20 run-flat (RF) tubed tyres with bead spacers.

No spare wheel was carried; the vehicle was able to travel with only slightly reduced performance on a punctured or damaged run-flat tyre, and anyway the suspension and drive line design allowed continued mobility with up to two wheel stations completely disabled.

Hull and turret

The 'Saladin' was of monocoque construction, consisting of a welded box-like hull of armoured steel, to which the suspension and drive line components were attached.

Hull

The hull was of welded armoured-steel plates, divided into two compartments by an armoured bulkhead.

The forward, or fighting compartment, was hexagonal in shape, and intended to be occupied by the three-man crew, who were forced to share this space with the carbon dioxide cylinders for the fire-fighting system, and the drinking water tank. The rear compartment housed the engine and auxiliaries. The transmission and drive shafts were mounted between the rear compartment floor and the hull bottom plate. Drainage and access points in the bottom plate were protected by screwed cover plates.

Air was admitted to the engine compartment through the six louvred access doors, and expelled through the grille at the top of the rear compartment.

The driver was placed centrally in the hull, positioned low down in an adjustable seat, with his feet up against the glacis plate; the steering wheel angle was reversed to save space. There was provision for the two additional crew members behind him: the commander/loader sat up in the turret, while the gunner/operator's seat was on the turret basket floor.

Vision for the driver was provided by means of a centrally-placed, bottom-hinged armoured hatch which could be closed down for maximum protection; in this situation, three No 17 periscopes were used to provide forward visibility. A removable glass windscreen, complete with electric wiper could be installed in the hatch.

The driver's forward hatch also doubled as an escape route, and there were additional escape hatches on either side of the hull.

Hull thickness at the glacis plate and nose was 12mm at 45 degrees, and 14mm at 42 degrees respectively; hull sides were 16mm thick at 20 degrees; rear plate was 16mm; hull roof was 10-12mm; floor, 8-12mm.

Hull stowage
There were triangular stowage boxes located between the wheels on either side, with additional lockable stowage boxes attached to the wheel arch tops.

Turret
The turret was of welded-steel construction, with a maximum thickness of 32mm at 15 degrees on the front, 16mm on the sides and rear, and 10mm on the roof.

The turret was mounted on a ball race on top of the hull giving a full 360 degree traverse. The turret turntable, or basket floor, was suspended by struts from the turret and accommodated seats for the crew, fittings for stowage, and a rotary base junction for the electrical connections between turret and hull.

Traversing was by power-assisted manual operation through a torque amplifier and gearbox unit. A separate manual control was provided for the commander. The turret sealing ring could be inflated for deep water wading, and there was a Schrader safety valve which prevented excess pressure being generated in the ring and allowed rapid deflation once wading was over.

The gun mantlet was supported in trunnion blocks which provided 10 degree depression and 20 degree elevation by means of a hand wheel. A friction lock held the turret in any position.

Hinged hatches were provided on the turret roof for the commander and gunner, and there were five No 18 periscopes mounted in the turret itself. On early vehicles, a machine gun ring was attached to the hull roof; this was later superseded by a simple traversing mount.

The turret was ventilated when closed down by means of a ventilator in the rear turret plate through which some of the engine cooling air was diverted. A ventilating fan to extract gun fume was located behind the armoured cowl at the front of the turret. In 1957, there were experiments with alternative extract fans in an effort to improve the hull ventilation.

Electrical equipment
The 'Saladin' was wired with a 24V electrical system, negative to earth. The ignition system was both screened against radio interference and waterproofed.

On early vehicles, the generator was a No 2, Mk 1 or No 2, Mk 2 machine with a maximum output of 25A; on later vehicles, this was replaced by a No 4, Mk 1 machine, with a maximum output of 75A at a minimum 750rpm (engine speed). All three types were provided with an automatic two-speed facility, designed to maintain maximum generator output at low engine speeds.

Two 12V 60Ah batteries were housed inside the crew compartment.

Fire-fighting equipment
The 'Saladin' was fitted with automatic flame detector equipment, in conjunction with a fixed, manually-operated carbon-dioxide fire extinguishing system covering the engine bay. Manual carbon tetrachloride and methyl bromide extinguishers were available in the fighting compartment.

ARMAMENTS

The 'Saladin' normally mounted three weapons: a 76mm main gun, and two .30 calibre or 7.62mm machine guns; in addition, there were smoke dischargers on the turret sides. A 9mm Sten gun would normally have been carried inside the fighting compartment, as well as the personal weapons of the crew.

Main gun
The main gun, designated L3A1 or L5A1, was designed especially for the 'Saladin' by the Royal Armaments Research and Development Establishment (RARDE).

It was a 76mm calibre quick-firing weapon with a rifled barrel, suitable for use with high explosive (HE), high explosive squash head (HESH), smoke, or canister (scatter rounds for use against infantry). Muzzle velocity with HESH rounds was 533m/sec, giving an effective range of around 5500m.

Sighting was by a 6x magnification optical sight in the turret roof.

Stowage within the hull was provided for 42 (Mk 1 vehicles) or 43 (Mk 2 vehicles) rounds.

Smoke dischargers

The 'Saladin' was provided with two six-barrelled smoke dischargers, mounted either side of the turret. These were designed for use with standard smoke grenades, fired electrically from a push-button control inside the hull, on the right-hand side.

Eighteen additional smoke grenades were normally carried inside the vehicle.

Machine gun mountings

Early vehicles were fitted with a ring mount for an anti-aircraft machine gun on the turret roof; on later vehicles the ring mount was replaced by a simple traversing mount (No 8, Mk 1).

Originally a .30 calibre Browning machine cannon (L3A3 or L3A4) would have been employed, but this was subsequently replaced in service by the 7.62mm standard Light Machine Gun (LMG).

There was stowage for up to 2750 machine gun rounds (3000 on Mk 1 vehicles).

RADIO EQUIPMENT

As a tactical vehicle, a 'Saladin' would have been fitted with radio equipment to enable it to remain in contact with its regiment or squadron net. At the time the Mk 1 vehicles were issued, this would have been by means of radio sets which were essentially of WW2 vintage, but later in the vehicle's life, radio stations from the 'Larkspur' range were used.

The basic radio sets were installed in the rear turret overhang, behind the commander. The connecting and control boxes were fitted around the inside of the hull in convenient positions. The aerial tuner unit was normally installed inside the vehicle.

Early 'Saladins' were fitted with No 19 and No 12 sets; on the later vehicles, once the 'Larkspur' equipment was in use, the radio station might have comprised a C12/B47, C42/B47 or C13/B47 combination, or No 31 AFV set.

The radio installation would comprise the two radio sets together with the 'B' control harness, aerial tuner, junction boxes, and any ancillary equipment necessary to allow switching between the sets.

ANCILLARY EQUIPMENT

As a tactical fighting vehicle, the 'Saladin' crew might have been expected to survive, perhaps behind enemy lines, on their own resources for days at a time. The vehicle carried a considerable amount of kit in order to make this possible.

The following items appeared in the 'Complete equipment schedules' and stowage diagrams of 1972 and 1974:

Mechanics tools and equipment
Adjustable spanner
Brake adjustment tool
Fan pulley adjustment spanner
Grease gun
Hammer
Keys for engine cover, flywheel plug and drain plugs
Oil cans, 1/2 pint and 1 quart capacities
Open ended spanners (7 x AF, 5 x BSW/BSF)
Oil injector
Pliers
Screwdriver
Spark plug spanner
Spark plug
Tommy bars
Tool bag
Tubular box spanners (3)
Wheel nut spanner
4-ton hydraulic jack and handle

Pioneer tools
Crowbar
Matchet
Matchet sheath
Pickaxe head
Pickaxe helve (carried separately)
Shovel
Wire cutters

Drivers and crew equipment
Anti-dim compound
Anti-gas respirators (3)
Bedding rolls (3) with blankets and ground sheet
Binoculars
Binocular mounting assembly
Greatcoats (3)
Haversacks (3)
Heavy-duty gloves
Inspection lamp
Periscopes (3 x No 17, 5 x No 18)
Removable windshield and windshield wiper assembly
Spotlight
Torch and batteries

Other equipment
Bulbs
Camouflage net, 7200x7200mm
Canvas bucket
Carbon dioxide cylinder head and piercing equipment (2)
Cleaning brushes (3)
Compressor hose

Cooker and pots
Drinking water tank
First aid kit
Fire extinguishers, CTC or BCF type
Funnel for fuel filler
Inter-vehicle starting lead
Map case
Padlocks (for stowage bins, engine covers and turret hatch)
Ration boxes
Shaped tarpaulin for use as bivouac, tent pegs, poles etc
Starting handle
Tarpaulin for use as engine cover
Tow rope/recovery chain
Tyre pressure gauge
Vacuum (Thermos) flasks (2)
Water boiling vessel
Water bottle
Water container (5 gal)

Weapons equipment
Bag and chute for spent cartridges
Case for signal pistol
Clinometer, AFV sight No 4
Machine gun tripod
Mounting for machine gun
Muzzle and breech cover for 76mm gun
Sight, periscope No 17
Signal (Very) pistol
Smoke discharger covers
Tools and spares for 76mm gun
Tools and spares for .30 calibre Browning

Radio equipment
Antenna carrying case
Antenna rods
Microphones and headsets
Spare parts for (appropriate) radio set

This equipment was carried inside the crew compartment, in the various stowage bins, or strapped to the exterior of the vehicle.

DOCUMENTATION

Technical publications
Technical handbooks
Data summary: armoured car, Saladin, Mk 2. EMER V630.
Technical description: armoured car, Saladin, Mk 2. EMER V632.
Waterproofing (deep) instructions: armoured car, Saladin, Mk 2. EMER V635 WPF, instruction 1.

User handbook
Armoured car, Saladin, Mk 2. WO code 12232.

Servicing schedule
Armoured car, Saladin, Mk 2. WO codes 12692 and 14963.

Parts list
Illustrated parts list: armoured car, Saladin, Mk 2. Army code not known.

Repair manuals
Unit repairs: armoured car, Saladin, Mk 2. EMER V633.
Field repairs: armoured car, Saladin, Mk 2. EMER V634 Part 1.
Base repairs: armoured car, Saladin, Mk 2. EMER V634 Part 2.

Stowage diagrams
Armoured car, Saladin, Mk 2. Army code 12856.

Complete equipment schedule
Simple equipment: armoured car, Saladin, Mk 2. Army code 33008.
Complex equipment: armoured car, Saladin, Mk 2. Army code 30188.

Bibliography
Armour of the West. Adshead, Ronald & Noel Aycliffe-Jones. London, Ian Allen, 1978. ISBN 0-711006-81-4.

British armoured cars since 1945. Dunstan, Simon. London, Arms and Armour Press, 1989. ISBN 0-853689-94-6.

Jane's AFV recognition handbook. Foss, Christopher. Coulsdon, Jane's Information Group, 1992. ISBN 0-710610-43-2.

Modern British tanks and fighting equipment. Chamberlain, Peter & Chris Ellis. London, Arms and Armour Press, 1970. ISBN 0-853680-26-4.

NATO Armour. Perrett, Bryan. London, Ian Allen, 1971.

Saracen. ISO File 2. Howard, Peter. London, ISO Publications. ISBN 0-946784-06-X.

Wheeled armoured fighting vehicles in service. White, B T. Poole, Blandford Press, 1983. ISBN 0-713710-22-5.

CHAPTER 4.2

ALVIS SARACEN
FV603, FV604, FV610, FV611

In the late 1940's, FVRDE had begun design work on a six-wheel drive heavy armoured car to replace the vehicles that had been used during WW2.

The intention was that the same six-wheeled chassis, designated FV600, would also be used as the basis for an armoured personnel carrier (APC), and a command vehicle (ACoP/ACV). In the event, the command vehicle project (FV602) was not developed, but in time the basic APC itself was converted into both an armoured command vehicle, and an armoured command post. Finally, although it was initially a private venture and did not form part of the official FV600 project, a further chapter was added to the story in the late 1950's when Alvis developed what was essentially the same chassis into the highly-successful 'Stalwart' high-mobility load carrier (see Chapter 4.3).

The basic requirements for the APC variant were laid down in 'General Staff Policy Statement 66' (GSPS 66) produced in 1947. The plan called for the design work to be undertaken immediately, but for production to be deferred: it was suggested that a prototype should be ready by 1952, with vehicles being issued for troop trials in 1957. This was to allow manufacturing resources to be concentrated on the armoured car variant.

Although prototypes of what was to become the FV601 'Saladin' armoured car had been commissioned by the Ministry of Supply from Alvis, before production could begin, the situation which had developed in Malaya in 1948, demonstrated that there was a more pressing need for the APC variant, and the project priorities were changed. It was arranged that the pre-production 'Saladins' would be produced by Crossley Motors, while Alvis, who were design parents for the whole FV600 family, concentrated on the FV603 'Saracen' armoured personnel carrier.

A version of the existing 'Saladin' chassis was employed, effectively turned around the other way, with the engine at the front. No time was wasted in getting to work; pilot models were produced for appraisal, and working prototypes were delivered in 1951. Such was the urgency of the project, that the prototype vehicles, designated Mk 1, were still being put through field trials at the same time as production of the Mk 2, definitive APC version began.

Production vehicles started coming off the line at the Alvis Coventry works in December of 1951.

CHAPTER 4.2: ALVIS SARACEN

Despite all this urgency, 'Saracens' were not delivered fast enough anyway, and the Ministry began to look around for a stop-gap measure, commissioning the Humber 'Pig' APC's (see Chapter 3.3), and then the tracked FV432 (see Chapter 4.4). So, from having no APC's at all in 1950, by the mid-1960's, the British Army had no less than three to choose from: the 10-man six-wheeled 'Saracen', the six-man four-wheeled 'Pig', and the 10-man tracked FV432, which was ultimately intended to replace the 'Saracen'. However, even after the delivery of large numbers of the tracked FV432 APC, 'Saracens' remained in service, being used mainly for internal security purposes in Northern Ireland.

For a while, the 'Saracen' was extremely successful, becoming the standard APC of the British Army during the 1950's and 60's. Although it was taken out of front line service towards the end of the 60's, the vehicle remained in use in certain restricted roles well into the 1980's. If there was any criticism to be made, it was perhaps that the vehicle lacked the speed and mobility necessary to maintain battle station with the NATO tanks of the period which were becoming increasingly agile and powerful.

OVERVIEW

The 'Saracen' was a six-wheeled armoured personnel carrier which was also developed into command vehicle, command post and ambulance variants. Modification kits were available to convert the basic APC to internal security, and ambulance roles; and to convert the ACoP to mount the FACE field artillery computer.

Designed for a crew of two, driver and commander, the APC could carry up to ten men, 2000-2500kg of cargo, or a mixed load. The vehicle was produced in two basic hull designs, and in six different marks.

An armoured hull, up to 16mm thick, gave all-round protection against rifle fire from any direction, .50 calibre weapons, and close detonation of anti-tank mines. A small turret was fitted to most APC and some ACoP/ACV vehicles, mounting a .30 calibre Browning or 7.62mm machine gun, and there was a ring for a 7.62mm anti-aircraft machine gun.

Power was provided by a B80 eight-cylinder engine, mounted at the front of the chassis, driving all six wheels through a pre-selector gearbox and single-speed transfer case. Both the front and centre axles were steered, and excellent on- and off-road performance was provided by means of all-wheel independent suspension using lateral torsion bars.

The vehicle was of monocoque chassis-less construction, and the hull consisted simply of an enclosed, armoured

VEHICLE OUTLINES

FV603/4

FV610

SCALE 1:75

SPECIFICATION

Dimensions and weight

	FV603	FV604	FV610	FV611
Dimensions (mm):				
Length	4979	4979	5235	5235
Width	2514	2514	2514	2514
Height:				
overall	2438	2438	1879	2336
to top of hull	2000	2000	-	-
Wheelbase:				
front/centre	1524	1524	1524	1524
centre/rear	1524	1524	1524	1524
Track	2032	2032	2032	2032
Ground clearance	406	406	406	406
Weight (kg):				
Combat weight:	10,161	10,161	11,176	11,176
(Mks 5 and 6)	-	-	11,214	11,214
Unladen weight:	8637	8637	9602	9602
(Mks 5 and 6)	-	-	10,237	10,237
Bridge classification	11	11	12	12

Ground pressure: 9800 kg/sq m.

Performance
Maximum speed, on road, 70km/h; average speed, off-road, 32km/h.
Approach angle: 53 deg.
Departure angle: 53 deg.
Side overturn angle: 45 deg.

Fuel consumption: 0.59 litre/km, on road; 0.95 litre/km, off road.
Maximum range: 400km, on road; 209km, off road.

Turning circle: 13.70m.
Vertical obstacle: 460mm.
Ditch crossing (trench) without channels: 1520mm.
Maximum gradient: 42%.
Maximum gradient for stop and restart: 30%.
Fording: unprepared, 787mm; prepared, with fording plate, 1066mm; prepared, with deep-water wading kit, 1981mm.

---

steel box in which the engine and drive line components were mounted. The driver was placed centrally in the hull, behind the engine, with three seats behind for the section commander, radio operator and one passenger. The rear compartment was equipped with seating for eight, and had double doors for rapid entry and exit; three firing ports were provided along either side, with one in each rear door.

No NBC filtration system was fitted, and the vehicle was not normally provided with night vision equipment.

The 'Saracen' was always designed to be air portable: one vehicle per Hercules aircraft, three vehicles in a Belfast.

DEVELOPMENT

GSPS 66, dated July 1947, set out the basic design parameters for what was described as a 'heavy armoured personnel carrier'. It was proposed that the vehicle should offer a comparable level of protection to the then-current universal tank, and should provide seating for a total of 16 personnel including a crew of three. Hatches and exits were to be arranged so that 'the whole section... be able to leave the vehicle at the same time', and considerable emphasis was placed on comfort, ventilation, temperature control, and dust and rain exclusion. There was a requirement for one vehicle-mounted machine gun with 180 degrees traverse.

By the time that FVRDE drew up the detailed specification for what was to become the 'Saracen' wheeled APC in 1948, some of these requirements had already been reduced.

However, the FVRDE design brief called for the highest possible standards of off-road performance without compromising crew and passenger safety, combined with a sufficient level of armoured protection to withstand small arms and rifle fire, and mine damage. The vehicle was to be fully-enclosed with accommodation for a crew of two, together with seating for ten passengers. As a pure load carrier, the 'Saracen' was to be capable of carrying 2500kg on the road or 2000kg across country; alternatively, it could accommodate a mixed load consisting of seven men and up to 450kg of, for example RE stores.

Motive power was provided by a Rolls-Royce B80 engine, and the vehicle featured clutchless pre-selector transmission driving through a fluid flywheel, independent torsion-bar suspension, and hydraulic power-assisted steering and braking systems.

In common with all of the armoured fighting vehicles of this period, the 'Saracen' specification required that the vehicle be able to wade to a depth of more than one metre with no special preparation other than the fitting of a wading plate to the radiator air intake, and to a greater depth with a wading kit fitted. FVRDE experimented with several types of wading kit for the 'Saracen', using a variety of intake arrangements for the engine and crew air supply, and employing canvas screens for the engine compartment covers.

The drive line configuration and hull design provided the optimum internal space and headroom, and allowed rapid entry and exit through large double doors at the rear. Initially, the roof-mounted turret was identical to that fitted to early Mk 2 'Ferrets', with the rear of the turret opening to either side; there was also a machine-gun ring mounted on the rear of the hull roof.

Particular attention was paid to leg room, seating and ventilation inside the hull. Interior ventilation ducts were installed along each side of the hull, and each occupant had an aircraft-style adjustable nozzle outlet. Although an excellent idea in principle, the ventilation arrangements were not so clever in practice, particularly where the vehicle was used in very hot conditions. The air required to ventilate the interior was admitted through dome-shaped inlets on the hull side; because of the engine cooling arrangements, the air drawn into the interior tended to be mixed with hot air expelled from the engine compartment. Conditions inside the vehicle could quickly become intolerable.

Once the pilot models had been assessed, fully-working prototypes of the FV601 Mk 1 vehicle were built and delivered to FVRDE for trials in 1951. There were few differences between the prototype and production versions, which were to be designated Mk 2. The vehicle was further developed into Mk 3, 4, 5 and 6 versions; the Mk 4 was not used by the British Army.

The rigid hull and independent suspension allowed the vehicle to maintain high cross-country speeds, while the power-assisted controls reduced the physical strength required to drive the vehicle for extended periods. Alvis claimed that during the trials phase, vehicles were able to maintain an average speed of 33km/h over rough terrain without undue driver or crew fatigue.

The first and second prototype vehicles were put through extensive trials at Chertsey and elsewhere, completing more than 45,000km of testing between them, with only minor failures and replacements. Perhaps this was just as well bearing in mind that the production contract had already been allocated, and work on the production vehicles had begun. Problems were experienced with the suspension and with the cooling and interior ventilation system. In fact, the cooling and ventilation

Prototype of FV610 'Saracen' ACoP (IWM)

FV603(A) Mk 1 'Saracen' APC (RS)

FV603(C) Mk3 'Saracen' APC with reverse flow cooling (IWM)

CHAPTER 4.2: ALVIS SARACEN

FV604(A) Mk 1 'Saracen' ACoP (IWM)

FV610 'Saracen' ACoP (TMB)

FV610 'Saracen' ACoP with penthouse erected (BTMC)

system problems were to recur whenever the vehicle was operated in hot climates, and were not satisfactorily resolved until the 'reverse flow cooling' system was installed in the FV603(C) variant.

Tropical condition trials were also undertaken in Australia during the period 1955/56.

Eventually, the 'Saracen' was developed into two basic hull designs. The smaller APC hull was also used as a basis for the field ambulance conversion; while the larger hull of the armoured command post and armoured command vehicles was also used for the FV611 purpose-built ambulance. The increased height of the larger hull allowed occupants to stand inside the vehicle.

Various modification kits allowed the vehicle to be adapted to a variety of other roles. There were also versions of the vehicle developed solely for export markets, for example an open-topped version of the APC was supplied to Kuwait in the 60's, but these were not in service with the British Army.

Production
The manufacturing contract was placed with Alvis almost as soon as the prototype vehicles began trials and a total of 1838 'Saracens' was manufactured, the majority being delivered to the British Army.

In addition to the British Army, 'Saracens' saw service with the armies of Indonesia, Jordan, Kuwait, Lebanon, Libya, Nigeria, Qatar, South Africa, Sudan, Thailand, and the United Arab Emirates; the vehicle was also deployed with the Hong Kong police.

Production of vehicles for export continued until 1972.

Technical problems
Like all of the Alvis six-wheelers, the 'Saracen' had a built-in technical restriction which could reduce its reliability when run on hard surfaces.

The drive train transmitted power to each of the wheels via the centre axle, which in turn, was connected to the gearbox and transfer case through a single differential.

Although the differential was able to handle variations in the speed of rotation of the wheels on the vehicle from one side to the other, the three wheels on each side were driven as a single unit. If there was any significant difference in the diameter of the tyres on these wheels, perhaps due to uneven wear or the use of different makes and types of tyre, stresses would begin to build-up in the drive line which could not be dispersed when the vehicle was travelling on hard surfaces because the wheels were not able to slip.

For this reason, prolonged running on macadam or concrete inevitably led to severe tyre wear due to

CHAPTER 4.2: ALVIS SARACEN

scrubbing, or actual bevel-box breakage or drive shaft damage. This damage was not immediately apparent to the user since the vehicle was able to drive equally well on, say two powered axles, as on the normal complement of three.

To avoid this type of damage, these vehicles were only driven on hard-surfaced roads when absolutely necessary. Although, by the nature of the vehicle, this was less of a problem with the 'Saracen' than say the 'Stalwart', there were situations when use on hard surfaces could not be avoided. It was then normal practice to put one set of wheels up the kerb, or off the edge of the road from time to time to allow the drive line stresses to unwind.

Replacement and disposal

The 'Saracen' offered excellent performance for its day, but the relatively-low maximum cross-country speed, the lack of NBC equipment, and the restricted amphibious capability tended to limit the situations for which the vehicle was suitable. By the end of the 1950's these limitations were becoming something of a drawback and the War Office had already planned a replacement.

In its armoured personnel carrier role, it was originally intended that the tracked FV432 would replace the 'Saracen' in front line service and this was generally the case. However, the 'Pig' had already been used as a partial-replacement in internal security situations, for example in Northern Ireland.

In the command post role, the 'Saracen' was replaced by the FV432 command variant, and partly by the Alvis 'Sultan'.

Inevitably a few 'Saracens' remained in service in specialised roles until well into the 1980's.

NOMENCLATURE and VARIATIONS

The vehicle was produced in six marks, although Mk 4 vehicles were never used in the UK. There were two hull configurations, and four basic variants, of which the FV603 APC was the most numerous.

Variations

FV603. Carrier, personnel, wheeled, Saracen
FV603(A), Mk 1. Original 'Saracen' basic armoured personnel carrier designed for a crew of two, with seating for eight in the rear compartment, plus two additional seats behind the crew. Fitted with a three-door rotating turret identical to that installed on the Mk 2 'Ferret', and mounting a .30 calibre Browning machine gun.

FV603(A), Mk 1/5. As above, but with frontal applique armour, and vision blocks for driver. Used for training purposes only.

FV603(B) 'Saracen' ambulance conversion (IWM)

FV603 'Saracen' APC 'Kremlin' conversion for Ulster (REME)

FV610 'Saracen' fitted with 'Robert' (No 9, Mk 1) radar (TMB)

FV604(A) 'Saracen' ACoP in service in W Germany (IWM)

FV603(A) Mk 1 'Saracen', flexible trunking for wading trials (TMB)

FV603(A) Mk 1 'Saracen', rigid trunking for wading trials (REME)

FV603(B), Mk 2. Similar vehicle to the Mk 1 'Saracen' but with slightly larger, redesigned two-door turret (as the later Mk 2 'Ferret'), intended to mount a 7.62mm machine gun. The other major change was that whilst Mk 1 vehicles were fitted with air-bag type hydraulic accumulators, the Mk 2 vehicle employed a piston-type accumulator; all vehicles were subsequently converted to this configuration. Some versions were turretless.

FV603(B), Mk 2/5. As Mk 1/5 APC but based on Mk 2 vehicle.

FV603(B), Mk 5. As basic Mk 2 vehicle but with full applique armour and up-armoured turret designed to mount a 7.62mm machine gun; new seating and vision blocks for driver; smoke dischargers on turret (where fitted). No machine gun ring.

FV603(C), Mk 3. As standard Mk 2 vehicle, but with 'reverse flow cooling' system (RFC) installed during production. In this variation, air was drawn through raised louvres at the rear of the engine compartment and passed across the engine before being expelled through the radiator and front louvres; a steel baffle was placed in front of the radiator to prevent a conflict of air flow. Sometimes referred to as FV603(C), Mk 2.

FV603(C), Mk 6. As Mk 3 vehicle with reverse flow cooling, but provided with full applique armour and up-armoured turret, new seating and vision blocks for driver.

FV604. Armoured command vehicle, wheeled, Saracen
FV604(A), Mk 1. Modified version of the FV603(A) vehicle converted to the command role with hull fittings for two canvas penthouses, rearranged internal seating and addition of roof windows. Some versions without turret. The conversion work was detailed in EMER V617 'Modification instruction no 50'.

FV604(A), Mk 2. As above but based on the FV603(B), Mk 2 vehicle.

FV604(B), Mk 5. As above but based on the FV603(B), Mk 5 vehicle.

FV610. Armoured command post, RA, wheeled, Saracen
High-sided hull version of basic turretless APC designed to provide greater height for the occupants. The interior was intended for a crew of six, and was provided with map boards, seating, and horizontal working surfaces. Early versions retained the turret, and although this was subsequently omitted, the roof window and machine-gun ring mount were retained. Also provided with extra batteries and a separate charging engine mounted externally. The interior space could be extended by the use of two penthouse tents which attached to the rear.

FV611(A). Ambulance, wheeled, Saracen
Armoured ambulance conversion of FV610 ACoP. Includes accommodation for two stretcher patients, and four seated. The work, which was estimated to require a total of 140 man-hours, was detailed in EMER V619 'Miscellaneous instruction no 30', dated April 1975.

Factory modifications
In the 1960's, a number of RFC-equipped 'Saracens' were delivered to Kuwait without the roof; none of these vehicles was used by the British Army.

Anti-tank role
As a private venture, Alvis produced a version of the FV603(B) 'Saracen' in 1970 which was fitted with BAC 'Swingfire' anti-tank missiles, mounted in launch boxes either side of the hull. Provision was made inside the vehicle, which was designed for a crew of three, to stow an additional six missiles. The missiles themselves were able to be fired from within the vehicle, or remotely. A 1m high retractable sight was mounted on the hull roof.

Uprating
Towards the end of the service life of the 'Saracen', Alvis attempted to update the vehicle by the installation of a Perkins 'Phaser' turbo-charged diesel engine, and by making various detail modifications. Again, none of these vehicles entered British Army service.

Uprated 'Saracens' were also offered by A F Budge (Military).

Workshop modifications
The reverse flow cooling system (RFC) was retro-fitted to a number of FV603, Mk 1 and Mk 2 vehicles, as well as to FV611 command posts. The work was detailed in EMER V617 'Modification instruction no 64'.

Internal security role
Vehicles which were used in Northern Ireland for internal security duties were modified in various ways to protect them from riot and terrorist activities.

These vehicles, which were known as 'Kremlin 1' and 'Kremlin 2', were converted from Mk 2 to Mk 5 configuration, and Mk 3 to Mk 6. In addition to the up-armouring and other conversion work, typical modifications included wire screens to protect against RPG-7 rockets; up-armouring around the firing ports; provision of wire screens to observation ports and periscope positions; and the fitting of frontal rams, rather like those used on the Humber 'Pig', for pushing barricades and burning vehicles aside.

Radar role
Some time around 1962, a 'Saracen' FV610 ACoP was experimentally fitted with surveillance radar (radar system, No 9, Mk 1, also known as 'Robert') and issued for troop assessment. The radar scanning equipment was mounted on the hull roof, and electrical power was provided by a separate generator trailer.

Other roles
A number of FV603 vehicles were converted to the ambulance role prior to delivery of the FV611 version. Other roles for the 'Saracen' include sonic deception vehicle; field artillery computer equipment (FACE) carrier; battlefield surveillance radar (ZB 298) vehicle; and specialised riot control/crowd dispersing vehicle, with foam gun and water cannon mounted in a special turret.

DESCRIPTION

Engine
Rolls-Royce B80, No 1, Mk 3A (Mk 1 vehicles only), or Mk 6A; dry sump.
Capacity: 5670cc.
Bore and stroke: 3.50 x 4.50in.
Power output: 165bhp (gross), 136bhp (net) at 3750rpm.
Maximum torque: 280 lbs/ft (gross); 257 lbs/ft (net) at 1750rpm.

Detail variations
Distributor limiter set at 3750rpm (crankshaft speed); no air horn on Mk 3A version; short water jacket to inlet manifold; oil filter mounted remotely in engine compartment; oil cooler installed horizontally in engine compartment; Ki-gass nozzles, pipework and non-return valve fitted; engine installed on a special support plate; twin cooling fans with idler pulley for belt tensioning; horizontal centre outlet exhaust manifold; inlet manifold with horizontal flange for carburettor mounting; no clutch casing; belt-driven hydraulic pump for braking and steering system, combined with small compressor for tyre inflation.

Transmission
Power from the engine was delivered to a five-speed pre-selective epicyclic gearbox through a fluid coupling, with a separate transfer box giving five speeds forward and reverse.

The pre-selector gearbox is described in Chapter 3.1 but it can be compared to automatic transmission where gear selection is carried out by the driver by a small lever, but with the actual gear changes handled automatically by the gearbox. The driver selects the next gear he requires and uses the gearchange pedal to make the change when the gear is needed.

The transfer box was bolted directly to the gearbox to form a single unit, which in turn was mounted directly to the engine. The transfer box also incorporated the differential and the forward/reverse control, which was engaged by means of a sliding dog clutch. Early transfer cases were of cast iron, on later vehicles the construction was changed to aluminium-alloy. All five gears were available in reverse, and the transfer box ratio is 2.43:1.

The 'Saracen', 'Ferret', and 'Saladin' were all equipped with essentially the same transmission. The 'Saracen' had its engine installed at the front of the chassis, on the other two vehicles, the engine was at the rear. This meant that although the shift patterns were the same, the 'Saracen' had the control quadrant installed on the driver's left, where the other two vehicles had the change on the right; similarly, the forward-reverse control moved one way on the 'Saracen', and the opposite way on the 'Ferret' and 'Saladin'.

From the differential, power was taken to the centre bevel box which drove the centre axle, and then via lateral drive shafts, running inside the hull, to front and rear bevel boxes and to the other axles. Final drive to the wheels was transmitted by articulating axle shafts to an epicyclic hub reduction gear, with a ratio of 4.125:1. Each drive shaft was fitted with two Tracta constant-velocity joints.

Suspension

All six wheels were independently sprung by means of pre-set, adjustable torsion bars running longitudinally on the outside of the hull. The actual suspension movement was handled by unequal length, parallel wishbone links attached to brackets on the hull.

Two double-acting hydraulic shock absorbers were provided above each of the front and rear wheels, and one above each centre wheel. Each wheel was also equipped with two telescopic rubber bump and rebound dampers, installed in tubular metal housings. These dampers were very similar in size and general appearance to the shock absorbers and it could appear that the vehicle was fitted with four shock absorbers to the front and rear wheels.

The suspension was very supple, with a total movement of 255mm; 90mm from static position to bump, and 165mm from static to rebound.

Steering gear

Steering was effected by means of the front four wheels using a hydraulically-assisted recirculating ball mechanism.

The steering wheel angle was reversed to save space, and was mounted to a column which, in turn was connected via two bevel boxes to a transverse cross shaft. This cross shaft was connected by ball joints to a system of rocking beams, or levers, on either side of the vehicle, together with shafts which project forwards to the outside of the hull. Hydraulic steering rams provided direct assistance to the steering shafts. Drop arms on either end of the shafts were connected to the road wheels by means of ball joints and drag links. There were no less than 14 lubrication points in the steering system.

Power assistance was provided automatically as soon as the wheel was moved from the straight-ahead position. Operation of the steering wheel opened the hydraulic steering control valve, directing oil under pressure to the steering rams. The hydraulic pressure was generated by a belt-driven pump, together with bag or piston type accumulators.

Five turns of the steering wheel were required from lock-to-lock, giving a 13.7m turning circle.

Braking system

Each of the six road wheels was provided with a hydraulically-operated twin leading shoe braking system. The brakes were applied by means of externally-generated pressure via the brake pedal, which was connected to power valves in the hydraulic system.

The brake shoes were 75mm wide, with drums of 394mm diameter, giving a total braking area of 0.31sq m.

Hydraulic pressure was generated by the same pump that provided steering assistance, and twin warning lights on the driver's control board indicated when there was sufficient pressure in the braking system.

The emergency brake operated on all six wheels by a ratchet and mechanical linkage system.

Road wheels

Early vehicles were fitted with 7.00B x 20in two-piece steel rims, mounting 11.00x20 run-flat (RF) tubed tyres with bead spacers; on later vehicles, the wheels were 8.00B x 20in, and some vehicles were fitted with alloy rims like those used on the 'Saladin' and 'Stalwart'.

In August 1976, EMER V619 'Miscellaneous instruction no 33' required all remaining 7.00B x 20in steel wheels to be replaced by 8.00B x 20in steel or aluminium wheels. At the same time, tyres for the 8.00B rim were stated to be 12.00x20 RF HS2.

No spare wheel was carried; the vehicle was able to travel with only slightly reduced performance on a punctured or damaged run-flat tyre, and anyway the suspension and drive line design allowed continued mobility with up to two wheel stations completely disabled.

A small tyre compressor was fitted, belt-driven from the engine.

Hull and turret

The 'Saracen' was of monocoque construction, consisting of a welded box-like hull of armoured steel, to which the suspension and drive line components were attached directly.

Hull

The hull was of welded armoured-steel plates, divided into two compartments by an armoured bulkhead.

The forward compartment housed the engine and auxiliaries, while the rear compartment was assigned to the crew and passengers. The transmission and drive shafts were mounted between the rear compartment floor and the hull bottom plate. Drainage and access points in the bottom plate were protected by screwed cover plates.

Air was admitted to the engine compartment through frontal louvres, and allowed to exit via a trunking system attached to the hull immediately behind the four hinged engine access covers.

The driver was placed centrally in the hull, with provision for three additional crew members behind him; in the APC role, there was seating for four troops along each side of the rear compartment. The simple driver's seat in Mk 1, 2 and 3 vehicles was adjustable for height and position; a full-length seat was installed in Mk 5 and 6 vehicles, complete with head restraint and three-point over-the-shoulder harness.

Flat working surfaces and bench seating were installed in the rear of vehicles intended for the ACoP and ACV roles, while ambulance vehicles were provided with accommodation for two stretchers on the left of the rear compartment, and four seats on the right. Large double doors allowed rapid access and entry to the rear, and there were drop-down hinged steps. ACoP and ACV vehicles were provided with fittings for two penthouse tents to be erected at the sides and rear.

Vision for the driver was provided by means of a centrally-placed armoured hatch together with two smaller side hatches. The hatches were top hinged and could be closed down for maximum protection; in this situation, No 17 periscopes were used to provide forward visibility. A removable glass windscreen, available in alternative types, complete with vacuum or electric wiper could be installed in the front-facing hatch. Three bottom-hinged firing ports were installed along each side, with one additional port in each of the rear doors.

The driver's forward hatch also doubled as an escape route, and there were additional escape hatches on either side of the hull.

The turreted vehicles were provided with two apertures in the hull roof, one for mounting a turret ring, the other, which was protected by a sliding steel plate and transparent window panel, was intended for operating an anti-aircraft machine gun on a rotating ring. Vehicles without turret were fitted only with the machine gun ring; the ambulance version had no machine gun ring, and the roof aperture was covered by armoured plate.

A towing pintle was mounted at the rear suitable for a 1 ton trailer.

Hull thickness at the front varied between 10 and 12mm at 40 degrees; while at the sides, the thickness was 12mm at 20 degrees. The hull top was 8mm thick, and the bottom plate 12mm.

Hull stowage

There were triangular stowage boxes located between the wheels on either side, two on the right-hand side, and one on the left.

The ACoP and ACV variants had additional stowage on the hull roof for the tent and supporting framework; on some versions, a cable reel was attached to the upper left rear of the hull, and there were box containers installed on the wheel arch tops for radio batteries. A supporting framework was provided on the right-hand side of the vehicle for a charging set.

Turret

Mk 1 vehicles had a three-door rotating turret designed to mount a .30 calibre Browning machine cannon; Mk 2 and later vehicles had a two-door rotating turret designed for a 7.62mm machine gun, with the rear door forming a useful commander's seat, and the front door providing a map table. Turrets on Mk 5 and 6 vehicles had additional applique armour.

The turret was installed to run on a roller race ring, and was manually traversed, giving a full 360 degree rotation, combined with 15 degree depression and 45 degree elevation. A friction lock was used to hold the turret in the 12 o'clock position (gun forward).

The turret thickness, without applique armour, was 16mm at 15 degrees, with the turret roof being 8mm at 75 and 90 degrees.

Electrical equipment

The 'Saracen' was wired with a 24V electrical system, negative to earth, and the ignition system was both screened against radio interference and waterproofed.

The early vehicles (first 250) were fitted with a single-speed CAV Type G7A247X generator with a maximum output of 40A. On later vehicles, an automatic two-speed generator was used, either a No 2, Mk 1 machine, or a No 2, Mk 2; maximum output was 25A at 600rpm (engine speed). The two-speed facility was designed to maintain generator output at low engine speeds.

Two 12V 60Ah or 64Ah batteries were housed inside the crew compartment; additional radio batteries, where fitted, were installed in a box on the wheel arch.

Fire-fighting equipment
The 'Saracen' had no fixed fire-fighting system; portable extinguishers were located both inside and outside the vehicle.

ARMAMENTS

The 'Saracen' was not intended as an offensive vehicle and was only lightly armed.

Smoke dischargers
All APC versions were fitted with two triple-barrelled smoke dischargers, one installed on either front wheel arch; additional smoke dischargers were also occasionally mounted either side of the turret. These were designed for use with standard smoke grenades, fired electrically from a push-button control inside the hull.

Canvas or rubber covers were used to protect the discharger barrels.

Twelve additional smoke grenades were normally carried inside the vehicle.

Machine gun mountings
All variants, except the ambulance, were fitted with a ring mount for an anti-aircraft machine gun on the hull roof. Originally the .303 Bren gun would have been employed, but this was subsequently replaced in service by the 7.62mm standard Light Machine Gun (LMG).

The turreted versions mounted either a .30 calibre Browning machine gun or 7.62mm general-purpose machine gun (GPMG).

Ammunition stowage was provided for up to 33 machine gun magazines, seven boxes of .30 calibre rounds, and 12 x 2in mortar bombs (and launcher).

RADIO EQUIPMENT

As a tactical vehicle, a 'Saracen' would have been fitted with whatever radio equipment was appropriate to its role; this might have included wireless sets which were essentially of WW2 vintage, or the radio stations from the 'Larkspur' range which started to come into service in the mid-1950's.

The basic radio sets were installed on suitable carriers mounted behind the driver and either side of the commander's seat. The connecting and control boxes were fitted around the inside of the hull in convenient positions. The aerial tuner unit was normally installed inside the vehicle.

Early radios
Suitable early radio stations might include No 19, No 31, No 68 or No 88 sets, or a Canadian No 52 set.

Larkspur
A typical standard 'Larkspur' station installed in a 'Saracen' might have comprised two radio sets together with either the 'A' or 'B' control harness, aerial tuner, junction boxes, and any ancillary equipment necessary to allow switching between the sets.

Suitable 'Larkspur' sets included HF/VHF combinations such as C11/C31, C12/C31, C12/C45, C12/B47, C12/B48 and C13/B47; R209 and R210; or the C42/B47 VHF/VHF sets.

ANCILLARY EQUIPMENT

The 'Saracen' crew and occupants might have been expected to survive, perhaps behind enemy lines, on their own resources for many days. The vehicle carried a considerable amount of kit to make this possible.

The following items appeared in the 'Tools, spares and stowage' section of the 1959 issue of the User handbook:

Mechanics tools and equipment
Adjustable spanner
Brake adjustment tool
Fan pulley adjustment spanner
Grease gun
Hammer
Keys for engine cover, flywheel plug and drain plugs
Oil cans, 1/2 pint and 1 quart capacities
Oil injector
Open ended spanners (7 x AF, 5 x BSW/BSF)
Pliers
Screwdriver
Spark plug spanner
Spark plug
Tommy bar
Tool bag
Tubular box spanners (5)
Wheel nut spanner
4-ton hydraulic jack and handle

Pioneer tools
Crowbar
Matchet
Matchet sheath
Pickaxe head
Pickaxe helve (carried separately)
Shovel
Wire cutters

Drivers and crew equipment
Anti-dim compound
Glass screens for observation ports
Heavy-duty gloves
Inspection lamp
Key to rear doors
Periscopes
Ration boxes
Removable windshield and windshield wiper assembly
Spotlight

Other equipment
Bulbs
Camouflage net
Canvas bucket
Cleaning brushes (4)
Compressor hose
CTC, fire extinguishers, BCF or water type (at least 5)
First aid kits (2)
Funnel for fuel filler
Inter-vehicle starting lead
Map case
Padlocks (for stowage bins, engine covers and turret hatch)
Sand channels/trench-crossing channels (2)
Starting handle
Tyre pressure gauge
Water container (2 gal)

Weapons equipment
Tools and spares for .30 calibre Browning
Tripod assembly

Radio equipment
Antenna rods
Antenna carrying case
Microphones and headsets
Spare parts for (appropriate) radio set

Most of this equipment was carried inside the crew compartment or in the various stowage bins.

DOCUMENTATION

Technical publications

Technical handbooks
Data summary: carrier, personnel, wheeled, Saracen. EMER V610.
Technical description: APC, wheeled, Saracen, Mks 1 and 2. EMER V612.

User handbooks
APC, wheeled, Saracen, Mks 1 and 2, and armoured command post, RA. WO code 12363.
Saracen, Mks 1-6. Army code 61335.

Servicing schedule
APC, wheeled, Saracen, Mks 1 and 2. Army codes 11926, 11928, 14250/1.

Parts list
Illustrated parts list: APC, wheeled, Saracen, Mks 1 and 2. Army code 12259.

Repair manuals
Unit repairs: carrier, personnel, wheeled, Saracen, Mks 1 and 2, APC and ACoP. EMER V613.
Field repairs: carrier, personnel, wheeled, Saracen, Mks 1 and 2, APC and ACoP. EMER V614 Part 1.
Base repairs: carrier, personnel, wheeled, Saracen, Mks 1 and 2, APC and ACoP. EMER V614 Part 2.

Modification instructions
Saracen, all marks, all derivatives. EMER V617, instructions 1-119.

Miscellaneous instructions
Saracen, all marks, all derivatives. EMER V619, instructions 1-35.

Bibliography

Armour of the West. Adshead, Ronald & Noel Aycliffe-Jones. London, Ian Allen, 1978. ISBN 0-711006-81-4.

British army vehicles and equipment. Smith, R E. London, Ian Allen, 1968.

Fighting vehicles and weapons of the modern British Army. Pugh, Stevenson. London, Macdonald, 1962.

Jane's AFV recognition handbook. Foss, Christopher. Coulsdon, Jane's Information Group, 1992. ISBN 0-710610-43-2.

Jane's armoured personnel carriers. Foss, Christopher. London, Jane's Publishing Company, 1985. ISBN 0-710603-54-1.

Making tracks: British carrier story, 1914-1972. Chamberlain, P & C Ellis. Windsor, Profile Publications, 1973. ISBN 0-853830-88-6.

Modern British tanks and fighting equipment. Chamberlain, Peter & Chris Ellis. London, Arms and Armour Press, 1970. ISBN 0-853680-26-4.

NATO Armour. Perrett, Bryan. London, Ian Allen, 1971.

Saracen. ISO File 2. Howard, Peter. London, ISO Publications. ISBN 0-946784-06-X.

Wheeled armoured fighting vehicles in service. White, B T. Poole, Blandford Press, 1983. ISBN 0-713710-22-5.

CHAPTER 4.3

ALVIS STALWART
FV620, FV622, FV623, FV624

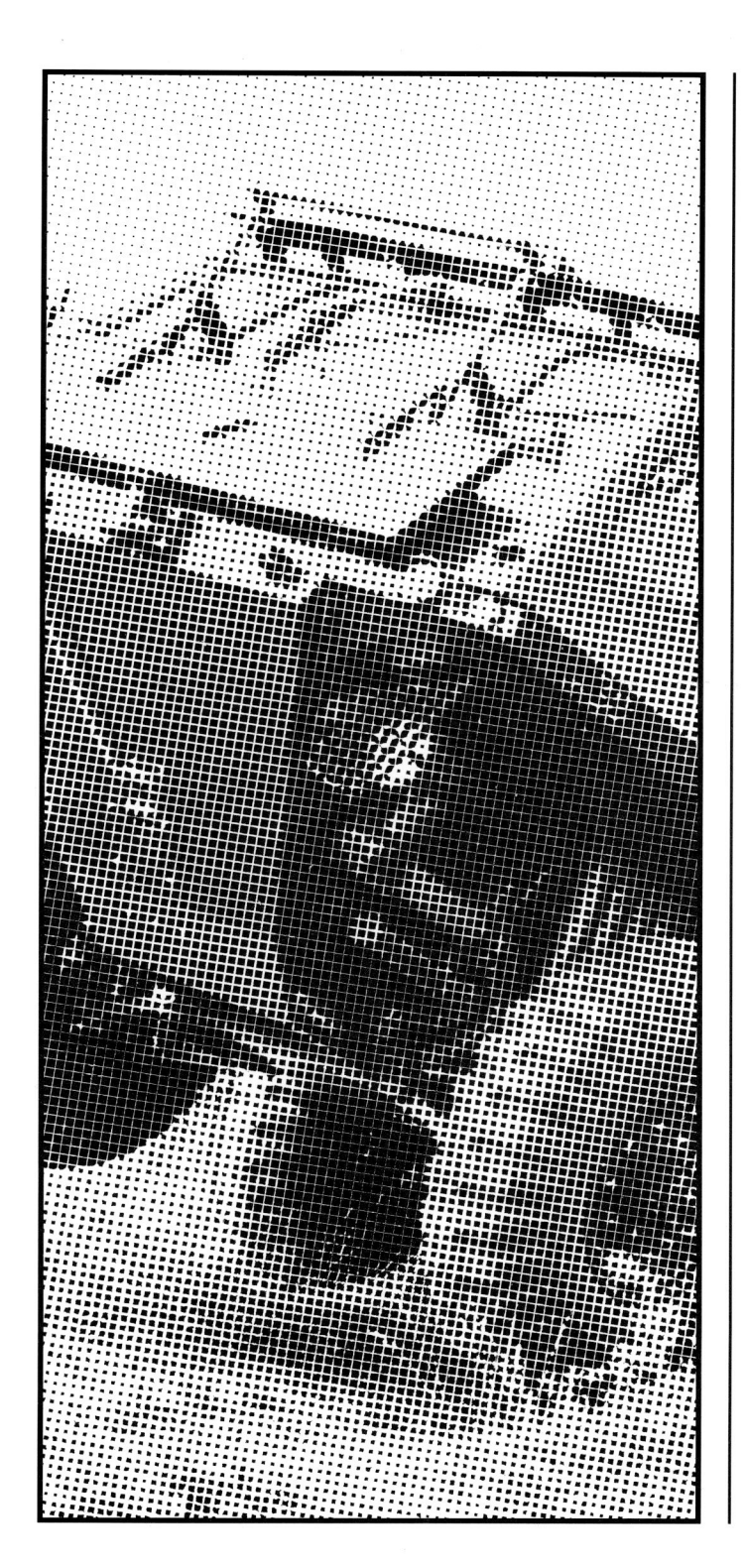

In the years which followed the end of WW2, and throughout the 1950's, the British Army relied on American GMC DUKW vehicles wherever there was a requirement for amphibious operations. Unlike the US Army, who had further developed the amphibious concept during the post-war years, producing vehicles such as the 'Super Duck' and LARC amphibians, the War Office had not commissioned any such work.

However, during those years of uneasy post-war peace, military thinking regarding the use of amphibious vehicles had changed. During WW2, the major role played by DUKWs was in plying from ship to shore, where port unloading facilities were not available. Following the Soviet blockade of Berlin in 1948 and the ensuing cold war, the received wisdom was that WW3, should it ever break out, would be fought on the German plains and that the viability of river crossings would be of enormous strategic importance. It became NATO policy that amphibious vehicles should be made available to reduce this dependency on existing bridges.

In developing the 'Stalwart', initially as a private venture, Alvis recognised that the British Army had a need for a modern, high-mobility multi-purpose amphibious vehicle - a need which it did not appear to be addressing. Alvis believed that the extreme mobility and versatility of the 'Stalwart' would allow it to reach forward troops under all conditions, and to maintain battle station with the normally-more mobile tanks and tracked vehicles.

Although there had been a War Office plan to produce a cargo-carrying tracked vehicle (FV431) as a high-mobility load carrier, only prototypes were produced and there was no quantity production. Documents produced at the time suggest that the 'Stalwart' was able to replace the FV431, offering comparable performance at lower cost.

In terms of its mobility, at the time of its introduction the 'Stalwart' was virtually a new concept in military transport. By any measure it was a most impressive machine. Its independent suspension and six-wheel drive ensured a level of mobility which fell little short of that of a tracked vehicle, without the attendant costs and maintenance problems. At the same time, the Hydrojet propulsion system provided real amphibious capability.

The cross-country performance of the 'Stalwart' became something of a benchmark and throughout its service life, it was often used as a comparison in trials with other vehicles. In 1967 for example, 'Stalwarts' were involved in the so-called Mud Lark mobility trials in Thailand. Here, the 'Stalwart' had performed very creditably when tested against the American M561 6x6 'Gama Goat', which was rather prone to breaking drive shafts, and the tracked FV432, which, in its original form, had not acquitted itself well in trials in the Australian bush.

The 'Stalwart' was enormously successful, replacing the aging DUKWs, and going on to become the mainstay of the British Army's amphibious fleet throughout the 1960's, 70's and 80's. In fact, the vehicle was only superseded from service when NATO doctrine no longer decreed that amphibious transport was required, preferring instead to rely on the advances being made in heavy-lift helicopter technology and modern bridging equipment.

OVERVIEW

Described by the military authorities as a 'high-mobility load carrier', usually abbreviated to HMLC, the Alvis 'Stalwart' was a six-wheel drive amphibious cargo-carrying vehicle possessing exceptional off-road abilities. It is worth noting that the 'Stalwart' was the only wheeled vehicle in the Army's 1970's fleet to be described as 'high mobility'.

Typical uses included the transport of troops, where it could accommodate up to 38 fully-equipped men, and the delivery of medium-density cargo such as jerry can or bulk fuel, ammunition, and stores from supply heads to forward areas over hard surfaces and rough terrain. The height of the cargo bed, in relation to all NATO tanks, made the transfer of supplies particularly easy. The 'Stalwart' also had a true amphibious capability which allowed river and waterway crossing without time-consuming preparation.

The vehicle had a modern appearance which belied its age, and was an extremely rugged and good-looking truck. With its six large, equally-spaced wheels, huge tyres, and boat-like shape, the 'Stalwart' was very distinctive. The deeper flanking windscreens of the Mk 2 version, particularly, conspired to present a rather insect-like appearance from the front.

The vehicle was of monocoque construction, with a frameless light-alloy body consisting of a cab and cargo bed, with drop sides and a hinged tailgate. The body was designed in the form of an enclosed, watertight hull, and was of all-welded construction. The cab, which had no doors, and was entered by means of hinged roof hatches, was intended for a normal crew of two to three men, according to version, with the driving position located in the centre.

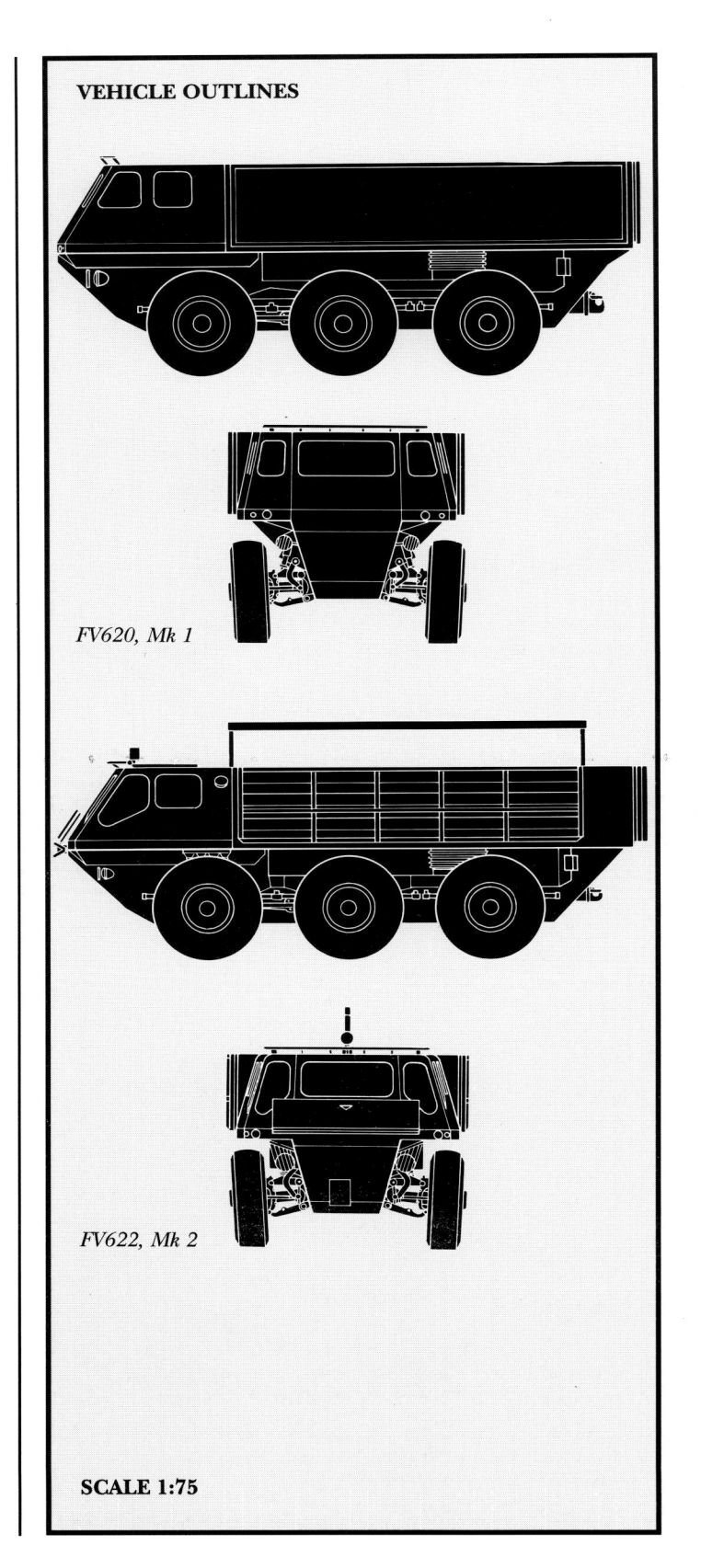

VEHICLE OUTLINES

FV620, Mk 1

FV622, Mk 2

SCALE 1:75

CHAPTER 4.3: ALVIS STALWART

SPECIFICATION

Dimensions and weight

	Mk 1 FV620	Mk 2: FV622	FV623	FV624
Dimensions (mm):				
Length	6400	6400	6400	6400
Width:				
overall	2600	2600	2600	2600
over tyres	2400	2400	2400	2400
crane slewed 90 deg	-	-	3300	3300
Height:				
to top of cab	2400	2400	2400	2400
to top of tarpaulin	2640	2640	-	-
over crane	-	-	3000	3000
load platform	1530	1530	1530	1530
Wheelbase:				
front/centre	1524	1524	1524	1524
centre/rear	1524	1524	1524	1524
Track	2060	2060	2060	2060
Ground clearance, laden	400	400	362	362
Weight (kg):				
Laden:	13,683	14,429	15,554	15,554
for flotation	-	-	14,586	14,586
Unladen	8443	8890	9938	9938
Bridge classification	14	14	18	18
Crane dimensions:				
Minimum reach (mm)	-	-	1850	1850
Maximum reach (mm)	-	-	1850	5400
Max slew, right (deg)	-	-	180	180
left (deg)	-	-	350	350
Max lift height (mm)	-	-	6900	6900
Max load (kg)	-	-	3039	3039
Load at max reach (kg)	-	-	1452	1452

Performance

	Mk 1 FV620	Mk 2: FV622	FV623	FV624
Speed (km/h):				
Maximum, on road	50	63	63	63
Average, off road	32	32	32	32
Maximum, in water	6.5	9.5	9.5	9.5
Static thrust (kgf)	998	998	998	998

Fuel consumption: 0.71 litre/km, on road.
Maximum range: 515-483km, on road.
Turning circle: 16.76m.
Vertical obstacle: 450mm.
Ditch crossing (trench): 1520mm.
Gradient: maximum, 60%; stop and restart, 33%.
Maximum side overturn gradient: 40%.
Approach angle: 42.30 deg, laden; 38.30 deg, unladen.
Departure angle: 29 deg, laden; 36 deg, unladen.

Capacity
Maximum load: 5000kg or 24 cubic metres.
Maximum towed load: 10,000kg.

The 'Stalwart' featured a centrally-mounted B81 engine, located low down in the hull and beneath the cargo deck, facing towards the rear. The transmission components were also installed beneath the deck, and the engine was arranged to drive through a conventional clutch and five-speed gearbox/transfer case. The power was conveyed via the transfer gears to a single limited-slip differential, and then to the central pair of wheels. From here, distribution was by open transmission shafts running inside the hull, via bevel boxes to the other four wheel stations.

All vital fluids, including fuel, engine oil, hydraulic fluid and coolant could be replenished from outside the vehicle without disturbing the cargo. Access also remained available whilst the vehicle was afloat.

Twin Dowty Hydrojet propulsion units were driven by power take-off from the gearbox, with separate controls to vector the jet thrust. The vehicle was able to travel in water at a maximum speed of 6.5km/h (Mk 1 vehicles), or 9.5km/h (Mk 2 vehicles). A hinged trim board was erected at the front of the vehicle to counter the effects of the bow wave, during amphibious operation.

Unlike the WW2 DUKW, the 'Stalwart' had no rudder or propellers, and thus the vehicle's amphibious abilities were not easily compromised during rough off-road use. However, should the Hydrojet system have become inoperative for any reason, the vehicle could also be manoeuvred, at a reduced speed, and steered in the water by means of its wheels.

DEVELOPMENT

During the 1950's, Alvis had enjoyed considerable success with sales to the British Army of their six-wheel drive 'Saracen' and 'Saladin' vehicles, as well as with the military/commercial 'Salamander' fire and crash tender chassis. Towards the end of the decade sales of these vehicles were slowing, and Alvis began to explore ways of maintaining production levels.

An amphibious version of the FV652 6x6 'Salamander' chassis had already been supplied to a South American customer for transporting cattle carcasses across difficult terrain and it seemed to Alvis that this might form the basis of a high-mobility military cargo vehicle. So, in 1959, Willy Dunn, Chief Engineer at Alvis appointed a design team headed by Andrew Kemp to begin development work on what was to become the 'Stalwart' using the existing 'Salamander' chassis as a basis.

Possibly unbeknown to Alvis, War Office Policy Statement 26 had already described a high-mobility load carrier of 5 to 8 tons capacity, but this was envisaged as a tracked vehicle. Designated FV431, and forming part of the

CHAPTER 4.3: ALVIS STALWART

FV430 family, a number of prototypes had been constructed and submitted for troop trials, albeit, due to the weight of the cab armour, with a reduced capacity of 3.5 tons. As a private venture, Alvis offered the first prototype 'Stalwart' to the War Office, where it was considered that it might form a viable alternative to this vehicle. In February 1960, the offer was accepted.

Initially, the plan was to produce three prototype vehicles. The first, known as PV1, was delivered in 1960, while the second, PV2, was available by June 1961. Alvis held back on the third until any basic problems which were apparent with the first two had been resolved, and it was finally delivered to FVRDE for assessment in November 1961, by then looking very much like a production 'Stalwart'.

The first prototype vehicle was not amphibious, but was simply a high-mobility 5 ton cargo vehicle sharing many drive line and suspension components with the existing FV600 series 'Saracen' and 'Saladin' range, already in service in substantial numbers. Like the 'Salamander' on which it was most-closely based, the 'Stalwart' was rear-engined, with a B81 unit installed beneath the rear cargo floor. Prototype PV2 which did feature amphibious capability, was fitted with Dowty propulsion units and underwent swimming trials at FVRDE in 1961. Prototype PV3 was also amphibious, and employed Saro-Gill Hydrojet propulsion units. However, these units were not satisfactory, and the Dowty equipment was chosen for the production versions.

There was generally a degree of resistance within both the War Office and FVRDE to the 'Stalwart', but it did have some support in the services themselves. Despite the progress with the FV431 project, the Royal Armoured Corps had become extremely interested in the 'Stalwart', and during 1960 had subjected the first prototype to a 5000 mile trial. By April 1961, pressure was being put on the War Office to drop the FV431 and adopt the 'Stalwart', and at a meeting of some 41 high-ranking personnel held at FVRDE, it was agreed that both FV431 and 'Stalwart' vehicles would be submitted for troop trials.

The 'Stalwart' possessed excellent mobility across even the most difficult terrain. It was extremely well designed and constructed, and easily resisted damage due to mechanical vibration from poor surfaces, and from projecting rocks, tree stumps etc. On trials, it showed itself able to cross a 1750mm wide ditch, to surmount a 450mm vertical obstacle, and to climb a gradient exceeding 45 degrees. It also exhibited excellent resistance to mine damage and was perfectly able to travel with one, or even two, wheels missing.

By now, the writing was clearly on the wall for the FV431 project. Towards the end of 1961, General Staff

Prototype 'Stalwart' PV1 at the Alvis factory (BTMC)

Prototype 'Stalwart' PV1 on trials at FVRDE (BTMC)

FV620 Mk 1 'Stalwart' (with air-brushed details) (TMB)

FV620 Mk 1 'Stalwart' on trials (TMB)

FV620 Mk 1 'Stalwart' in service in Aden (IWM)

Definitive FV622 Mk 2 'Stalwart' (TMB)

Operational Requirement (GSOR) 1061 laid down the basic characteristics of the production 'Stalwart', stating that the vehicles were required in service no later than 1965.

In April 1962, it was stated that the 'Stalwart' was largely able to meet the operational requirements of GSOR 1061 and that Alvis should finalise the development as a private venture which meant that there would be no development contract. It was planned that the specification would be finalised and contracts placed by the end of July 1962.

Production

With detail modifications, prototype PV3 led to the production of the FV620, Mk 1 'Stalwart'. The first orders were submitted to Alvis in August 1962 and a total of 250 Mk 1 units was produced.

In 1966, the Mk 1 was replaced by the FV622, Mk 2 vehicle, and followed by the FV623 and FV624 variants. When compared to the Mk 1, the later vehicle offered increased power and mobility, particularly in the water, together with simplified maintenance procedures and increased reliability. The total production of all Mk 2 vehicles was 1322 at a unit price of around £15,000 each; the production total can be broken down into 1085 examples of the FV622, 117 of the FV623, and 120 FV624 units. The Mk 2 remained in production until 1971.

At the time of the vehicle's introduction in 1961, it was proposed that the B81 engine eventually be replaced with the multi-fuel Rolls-Royce K60 unit which had a similar dimensional profile. Although it was suggested that the work could feasibly be carried out in base workshops, the change was never made. Interestingly, a similar swap was made for the FV432 armoured personnel carrier.

Most of the production total went to the British Army, but vehicles also saw service in Austria, Sweden, and Switzerland. A production Mk 1 vehicle was sent across to Aberdeen Proving Ground for trials, but whether this was on behalf of the British Army, or whether Alvis were looking for US sales is not recorded. The vehicle was also demonstrated to West Germany in May 1962.

In 1964, Alvis had entered into a collaborative venture with the French heavy truck manufacturer Berliet, and when the French Army were planning to replace their fleet of WW2 DUKW's, Berliet presented its own version of the Mk 1 'Stalwart' under the name 'Auroch'. The intention was that Berliet would build 'Stalwarts' under licence in France. However, despite the obvious success of the vehicle in Britain, sadly, orders were not forthcoming.

CHAPTER 4.3: ALVIS STALWART

Technical problems

Despite its rugged appearance and superb off-road capabilities, the 'Stalwart' had a built-in technical limitation which reduced its useful application on hard surfaces.

The drive train was designed to transmit the power to each of the wheels via the centre axle. This in turn, was connected to the gearbox and transfer case through a single limited-slip differential.

Although the differential was able to handle variations in the speed of rotation of the wheels on the vehicle from one side to the other, the three wheels on each side were driven as a single unit. If there was any significant difference in the diameter of the tyres on these wheels, perhaps due to uneven wear or the use of different makes and types of tyre, stresses would begin to build-up in the drive line which could not be dispersed when the vehicle was travelling on hard surfaces because the wheels were not able to slip.

For this reason, prolonged running on macadam or concrete inevitably led to severe tyre wear due to scrubbing, or actual bevel-box or drive shaft damage.

The damage would not be immediately apparent to the user since the vehicle would drive equally well on, say two powered axles, as on the normal complement of three. It was for this reason that white bars were often painted on the hubs. As long as the bars remained in line, all was well in the transmission department; if one or more bars was out of line with the others, that drive train was damaged.

To avoid this type of damage, standing orders decreed that 'Stalwarts' should only be driven on hard-surfaced roads when absolutely necessary. When this situation could not be avoided, it was normal practice to put one set of wheels up the kerb, or off the edge of the road from time to time to allow the drive line stresses to unwind.

Replacement and disposal

It is no longer part of NATO strategy to employ amphibious vehicles and the 'Stalwart' has no direct replacement.

In June 1985, REME issued a modification instruction ordering the removal of the Dowty Hydrojet units, and for a period, 'Stalwarts' remained in service being used simply as high-mobility trucks. However, with nearly 7 litres of Rolls-Royce petrol power the 'Stalwart' carried a considerable overhead in fuel consumption terms and it wasn't long before the vehicle was replaced by more-or-less equally-capable if less impressive machinery, albeit without amphibious ability.

FV623 Mk 2 'Stalwart' artillery limber (BTMC)

FV624 Mk 2 'Stalwart' REME fitters' vehicle on trials (REME)

Swimming FV622 Mk 2 'Stalwart' (TMB)

CHAPTER 4.3: ALVIS STALWART

FV622 Mk 2 'Stalwart' on mobility trials (BTMC)

FV622 Mk 2 'Stalwart' under heavy braking (TMB)

'Stalwarts' under production at Alvis (BTMC)

The British Army started disposing of 'Stalwarts' in quantity in the early 1990's. At the time of writing, large stockpiles of surplus vehicles exist at various dealers around the UK, and despite the obvious technical competence of the specification, there are few immediate commercial applications for a vehicle of this type. In an effort to render the vehicle more attractive to commercial concerns, A F Budge (Military), who at one time were rumoured to have more than 400 of the beasts, have been installing Perkins 'Phaser' turbo-charged diesel engines. A few have found buyers in this form.

The 'Stalwart' was very much a product of its time, the like of which will probably never be seen again.

NOMENCLATURE and VARIATIONS

The vehicle existed in three major variations: cargo vehicle, artillery limber, and engineering fitters' vehicle.

The original 5 ton cargo vehicle was produced in both Mk 1 and Mk 2 form. The artillery limber and REME fitters' vehicles were based on the Mk 2 version, and were fitted with an Atlas or Swedish HIAB hydraulic crane unit installed between the cab and cargo bed, to produce what these days is known as a CALM (crane, lorry-mounted). The crane, which was driven from the gearbox power take-off, had a maximum 3035kg lifting capacity.

All variations of the Mk 2 vehicle were equipped with a hydraulic winch, also driven from the power take-off, giving a maximum pull of 6000kg for self-recovery.

Variations

FV620. Truck, high mobility load carrier, 5-ton, 6x6, Stalwart, Mk 1
Original HMLC, 5 ton amphibious cargo vehicle. Capable of 6.5km/h in water.

FV622. Truck, high mobility load carrier, 5-ton, 6x6, Stalwart, Mk 2
Improved version of Mk 1 vehicle, capable of 9.5km/h in water. Fitted with winch for self-recovery. Changes made to cab layout, and to front and side windows to improve visibility on roads; technical changes also made to chassis and running gear to reduce maintenance and improve reliability.

FV623. Truck, high mobility load carrier, 5-ton, 6x6, Stalwart, limber
Artillery limber. As Mk 2 vehicle but with Atlas 3001 or HIAB hydraulic crane installed in the cargo bed. A partitioned area in the cargo bed was provided to accommodate an additional four crew members, two either side of the crane column. Intended primarily for handling palletted loads for the FV433 'Abbot' self-propelled gun.

FV624. Truck, high mobility load carrier, 5-ton, 6x6, Stalwart, REME fitters

Purpose-designed REME fitters' vehicle based on standard FV622 unit, sometimes with a Gloster-Saro UBRE (unit bulk replenishment equipment) refuelling pack installed in the cargo bed. Also fitted with the Atlas or HIAB crane, intended for changing truck and light AFV power packs in the field, and for similar medium to heavy maintenance and repair tasks.

Radio role

All vehicles were fitted with a radio junction box and connecting cable; special FFW/FFR versions exist of both the Mk 1 and Mk 2 vehicles, with a radio mounting tray and battery tray located in the cab.

Factory modifications

In 1967, Alvis proposed and demonstrated a version of the 'Stalwart' equipped to launch the BAC 'Swingfire' first-generation, wire-guided anti-tank missile.

The conversion kit consisted of lightweight 'pin-up' armour designed to protect the cab, power-operated missile launcher boxes installed in the cargo area, and launcher control equipment which could be operated from the vehicle or deployed remotely. The vehicle carried a total of 16 missiles in four protected trays.

Workshop modifications

A number of Mk 1 vehicles were retro-fitted with a hydraulic winch.

The EMI 'Ranger' anti-personnel mine-laying system was also mounted in the cargo bed of 'Stalwarts' deployed in Germany. The 'Ranger' system consisted of 1296 mines loaded into a multiple launch array capable of ejection at up to 140m to form an instant minefield.

Basic FV620 and FV622 cargo-carrying 'Stalwarts' were also modified to fulfil the UBRE role, with bulk fuel tanks and Gloster-Saro pumping equipment installed in the cargo bed. This equipment replaced the old jerry-can system, improving both safety and efficiency.

Although the 'Stalwart' was able to cope with river bank exit conditions which would have defeated DUKW's or LARC's, experiments were also apparently made with rockets mounted on the vehicle to assist exit in particularly difficult circumstances.

DESCRIPTION

Engine

Rolls-Royce B81, No 1, Mk 8B, Mk 8B/1, or Mk 8B/2; dry sump.
Capacity: 6516cc.
Bore and stroke: 3.75 x 4.50in.
Power output: 220bhp (gross), 195bhp (net) at 3750rpm.
Maximum torque: 330 lbs/ft (gross); 315 lbs/ft (net) at 2250rpm.

Detail variations

Distributor limiter set at 3750rpm (crankshaft speed); oil filter mounted remotely in engine compartment; engine was installed 'back-to-front' on a special four-point mounting, with radiator and separate header tank at rear; twin cooling fans with idler pulley for belt tensioning; horizontal front outlet exhaust manifold; inlet manifold with horizontal flange for carburettor mounting; long water jacket to inlet manifold; power take-off for brake compressor and power steering pump; hour meter records total time ignition was switched on.

Accelerator and choke controls were hydraulically operated.

Transmission

Power from the engine was delivered to the gearbox through a 305mm twin-plate dry clutch; the clutch control was hydraulic. In February 1972 all vehicles were fitted with a visual clutch-wear indicator.

The gearbox, manufactured by Meadows on Mk 1 vehicles and by Alvis on the Mk 2, was of the helical, constant-mesh type, giving five forward speeds; double declutching was required for downward changes. Engagement was effected manually by a remote linkage system, although early vehicles were provided with air assistance, achieved by connecting the gearchange mechanism to the braking system compressor. This feature was subsequently removed and the mechanism converted to manual operation. The transmission was provided with a separate oil pump and filter assembly.

The transfer box and power take-off were connected to the gearbox to form a single unit. The transfer box also incorporated the forward/reverse control, which was engaged by means of a sliding dog clutch, together with a limited slip 'No-spin' type differential. All five gears were available in reverse, and the transfer box ratio was 3.13:1. The power take-off, which provided power for the propulsion system, winch and crane (when fitted), was driven by a separate idler gear from the primary shaft.

From the differential, power was taken to the centre bevel box which drove the centre axle, and then via lateral drive shafts, running inside the hull, to front and rear bevel boxes and to the other axles. Final drive to the wheels was transmitted by articulating axle shafts to an epicyclic hub reduction gear, with a ratio of 4.125:1. Each drive shaft was fitted with two Tracta constant-velocity joints.

Late production FV622 versions, and all FV623 and FV624 vehicles, had a centralised, gravity-feed lubrication system for the front and rear bevel boxes (and speedometer drive), utilising the hull central cross member as an oil reservoir.

Propulsion system
Propulsion in the water was provided by two Dowty Hydrojet single-stage axial-flow marine units, installed either side of the engine and transmission assembly and mounted integral with the hull. The units were driven by propeller shafts from a power take-off mounted on the gearbox, and controlled by means of two levers in the cab.

The units operated by taking in water through intake apertures in the side of the vehicle, passing it through a 255mm diameter, nine-bladed vane propeller and discharging it at high pressure at the rear.

Changes of direction whilst wading were achieved by means of rotating 'scoops' on the Hydrojet outlets which were used to vector the thrust. The 'scoops' were controlled by twin levers in the cab, and could also be rotated through 180 degrees to provide reverse thrust, while retaining full directional control.

Suspension
All six wheels were independently sprung by means of individual pre-set torsion bars installed longitudinally along the outside of the hull. The suspension movement was handled by unequal length, parallel wishbone links attached to brackets on the hull.

Two double-acting hydraulic shock absorbers were provided at each of the front and rear wheels, with one to each of the centre wheels. Two rubber bump and rebound dampers, mounted in telescopic housings, were also provided at each wheel. These dampers were very similar in size and general appearance to the shock absorbers, making it seem that there were four shock absorbers at the front and rear wheels.

The total suspension movement was 255mm; 90mm from static to bump, and 165mm to rebound.

Steering gear
The steering system operated on the front and centre axles and was controlled through a recirculating-ball cross-shaft box. The two axles were connected together by a system of drop arms and drag links, with the wheels on the centre axle operating through a smaller degree of angular movement when compared to those of the front axle.

The steering box was provided with hydraulic power-assistance from an engine-driven pump, and incorporated a hydraulic cylinder and piston assembly, together with a control valve. The valve directed hydraulic fluid, under pressure, to the appropriate side of the piston as determined by the steering wheel position. The hydraulic circuit included a separate fluid filter.

The steering gear included a road-wheel position indicator which helped position the vehicle when leaving water.

Braking system
The braking system operated twin-pot calliper disc brakes on all six wheels, by means of dual air-over-hydraulic circuits; disc diameter, 406mm.

Two 'Airpaks', with pressure maintained from a compressor driven by the engine power take-off, provided servo air assistance. The compressor, which supplied 0.56 cubic metres of air per minute at 1250rpm, could also be used for tyre inflation. An alcohol evaporator unit was fitted to draw vapourised alcohol into the air-brake system, thus preventing any moisture in the circuit from freezing during operation at sub-zero temperatures.

When correctly adjusted, the brakes were enormously powerful and the vehicle could almost be stood on its nose during emergency braking.

The twin emergency brake was ratchet operated, acting through Bowden-type cables to contracting bands on drums mounted on the front bevel boxes.

A separate hand control was provided on the steering column to operate the trailer brakes when the vehicle was towing.

Road wheels
10.00 x 20in light-alloy two piece rims, mounting 14-ply 14.00x20 NDCC tubed tyres, with bead spacers; early Mk 1 vehicles were fitted with run-flat (RF) tyres. Non-skid chains could be fitted to the tyres to improve traction.

Even without run-flat tyres, the vehicle was able to continue running with up to two wheels disabled, and for this reason, no spare was carried.

Hull
The aluminium-alloy hull was of all-welded construction, consisting of a cab and separate cargo area; the nose and belly plates were of increased thickness (6mm) to reduce the possibility of damage during embarkation or wading.

The hull was completely watertight, with all mechanical components housed beneath the cargo deck. A removable cover plate provided access to the fuel tank drain plug from below, and drain plugs were also provided for the bilges, front and rear.

Tow hooks were provided at both front and rear. Eight lashing eyes along the lower edges of the hull allowed the vehicle to be secured to a ship's deck.

Cab

The cab had no doors but was provided with two circular, roof hatches, which were hinged and lockable. A small air deflector on the cab roof pushed air up and over the cargo area.

The three windscreen panels, and the side windows were of armoured glass; the forward windscreens were fixed, the rear side windows could be opened, both for ventilation and to provide an escape hatch. The Mk 2 had deeper corner windows than the original version, giving improved sightliness to the sides. EMER 'Modification instruction no 64' called for the installation of windscreen washers.

The cab had a centrally-placed driver's seat, with a single passenger seat to its left (FV620/622), or with a passenger seat either side (FV623/624). Inertia-reel seat belts were provided for both driver and passenger(s). The seat backs, which folded forwards, incorporated metal tread plates designed to assist in gaining access to the vehicle through the roof hatches.

A full-width hot-water heater installed behind the seats provided comfort conditions for the crew, as well as providing windscreen demisting facilities.

Cargo area

The cargo area had drop-down sides and a hinged tailgate, opening through 180 degrees; the side panels and tailgate were sealed to prevent water entering the cargo area during amphibious operation.

A bulkhead partition close to the rear tailgate provided a plenum to allow cooling air from the engine compartment to escape; this bulkhead could be removed for loading the vehicle from the rear. The limber and REME fitters' versions were provided with a second partitioned area enclosing four small folding seats, two each side of the crane, set aside for the additional crew members; the bulkhead used to separate this area was removable for stowage.

Access to the engine and transmission was gained through removable floor panels. These panels were obviously a source of difficulty with certain types of cargo, and in June 1972, a modification instruction called for the fitting of liquid-proof cargo floor panels and drip rails to prevent spilt fuel from dripping onto the (normally hot!) engine.

Weather equipment

A central rail ran the full length of the cargo compartment to support a PVC/nylon cover, reinforced with leather at stress points. The limber and REME fitters' versions had an additional cover, provided with small vision panels which, together with a tubular metal frame, was designed to protect the ancillary crew compartment.

Electrical equipment

24V electrical system, negative ground; fully screened and waterproofed. A belt-driven No 10, Mk A alternator, with integral rectifier system to convert the ac output to dc, provided electrical power for the various vehicle systems. Maximum alternator output was 90A, 24V over the speed range 1900-9250rpm (pulley speed).

Three thermal-trip circuit breakers provided protection against excess current and fault conditions.

Two 12V, 100Ah batteries were housed inside the cab.

Bilge pumps

A fully-submersible electric bilge pump was installed at the rear of the hull, adjacent to the engine driving belt pulley; the capacity of the pump was 100-135 litres per minute.

Alternative types of manual bilge pump were also installed to provide a back-up should the electric pump fail. On early vehicles, the pump was a semi-rotary type, installed on the cab bulkhead behind the driver's seat. Late production vehicles employed a diaphragm pump, mounted on the cab floor

An electrical bilge level warning system was installed.

Fire-fighting equipment

The vehicle was fitted with a 'Firewire' automatic fire alarm system which was designed to give warning of overheating or fire in the engine compartment by means of warning lights and an audible Klaxon horn.

A manually-operated fire-fighting system was installed, operated by means of two red, T-shaped handles attached to the cab roof in front of the crew, each discharging one bottle of gaseous extinguishing medium. In addition, there were four portable hand-operated extinguishers, two inside the cab, and two outside.

Crane

FV623 and FV624 variations were fitted with a hydraulic crane, supplied either by Atlas (type 3100/66) or HIAB, and driven from the gearbox power take-off. The crane was of the double-acting ram type, and the levers and hydraulic control block were installed on the top of the engine air intake, immediately behind the cab roof. The crane was controlled with the operator in a standing position, from the right-hand roof hatch.

Maximum capacity was 3035kg with the jib fully retracted, and there were five manual extension settings, from 1800mm to 4050mm; maximum lift was 6900mm with the jib fully extended. The jib could be slewed through 350 degrees from right to left, and 180 degrees from left to right; an anti-slew pin secured the jib centrally, in the transit position, over the cargo area while the vehicle was travelling.

Winch
All Mk 2 'Stalwarts' were fitted with a 6000kg hydraulic drum winch, manufactured by either Boughton (up to vehicle number 352) or Herbert Morris, and intended for self-recovery; winches were also fitted to a number of Mk 1 vehicles. The winch was installed at the front of the vehicle, below the cab floor, with fairlead rollers in a casing welded to the hull front skid plate. A bell-shaped rubber gaiter on the winch yoke-shaft housing provided a seal for the winch compartment, allowing complete immersion during amphibious operations.

The winch pump was of the gear type, driven from the gearbox power take-off, and installed on the same hydraulic circuit as the power assistance for the steering. The winch controls were installed in the driver's cab, where a rope-layer indicator was also provided, protruding through the cab floor plates.

RADIO EQUIPMENT

All 'Stalwarts' were fitted with a radio junction box and radio battery connecting cable in the cab, for use with 'Larkspur' equipment. Vehicles intended for the FFW/FFR role were also provided with trays for the radio and for mounting additional batteries.

Typical 'Larkspur' wireless stations included HF/VHF combinations such as C12/C31, C12/C47, C12/B48 and C13/B47; or the C42/B47 VHF/VHF sets.

Two aerial bases were mounted on the cab roof, together with a mounting plate for the aerial tuner unit.

ANCILLARY EQUIPMENT

The MoD 'Complete equipment schedule' (34188) dated March 1975, listed the following on-board equipment for the 'Stalwart':

Mechanics tools
Adjustable spanner
Battery filler spout
Combination spanner
Grease gun
Hammer
Hand oiler
Key socket wrenches (2)
Lubrication gun
Pliers
Non-adjustable spanner
Oil can
Screwdriver
Starting handle
Tyre inflator
Tyre inflator hose
Tyre pressure gauge
Wood block (510x75x200-300mm)
4 ton hydraulic jack

Pioneer tools
Pickaxe head
Pickaxe helve (carried separately)
Shovel

Drivers and crew equipment
Bulkhead light
Cooking pot
Extension lamp
Portable cooker
Spotlight

Other equipment
BCF fire extinguishers (4)
Inter-vehicle starting cable
Lashing straps (8)
Plastic water container
Wire tow ropes (2)

The wire tow ropes were carried, one attached to each eye on the front bottom corners of the hull, and stowed around the front corners of the cab and attached to the rear grab handles by rings and lanyards.

DOCUMENTATION

Technical publications
Technical handbooks
Data summary: truck, high mobility load carrier, 5 ton, 6x6, Stalwart, Mks 1 and 2; Stalwart, limber; Stalwart, REME fitters. EMER V640.
Technical description: truck, high mobility load carrier, 5 ton, 6x6, Alvis/Stalwart, Mks 1 and 2. EMER V642.
Technical description: truck, cargo, HMLC, 5 ton, 6x6, Alvis/Stalwart, Mk 2; truck, cargo, HMLC, with winch and crane, 5 ton, 6x6, Alvis/Stalwart. EMER V642/2.

User handbook
Truck, high mobility load carrier, 5 ton, 6x6, Alvis Stalwart, Mks 1 and 2. Army codes 20817, 22156.

Complete equipment schedule
Truck, high mobility load carrier, 5 ton, 6x6, Stalwart, Mks 1 and 2. Army codes 33749, 34153.

Servicing schedule
Truck, high mobility load carrier, 5 ton, 6x6, Stalwart, Mks 1 and 2. Army codes 14959, 60281.

Parts lists
Provisional spare parts list: truck, high mobility load carrier, 5 ton, 6x6, Alvis Stalwart. Army code 13894.

Spare parts list: truck, high mobility load carrier, 5 ton, 6x6, Alvis Stalwart. Army code 14226.

Repair manuals
Unit repairs: truck, high mobility load carrier, 5 ton, 6x6, Alvis/Stalwart. EMER V643.
Unit repairs: truck, cargo, HMLC, 5 ton, 6x6, Alvis/Stalwart (FV622); truck, cargo, HMLC, with winch and crane, 5 ton, 6x6, Alvis/Stalwart (FV623). EMER V643/2.
Field repairs: truck, high mobility load carrier, 5 ton, 6x6, Stalwart, Mks 1 and 2; Stalwart, limber; Stalwart, REME fitters. EMER V644/1, V644/2 Part 1.
Base repairs: truck, high mobility load carrier, 5 ton, 6x6, Stalwart, Mks 1 and 2; Stalwart, limber; Stalwart, REME fitters. EMER V644/1, V644/2 Part 2.

Modification instructions
Truck, high mobility load carrier, 5 ton, 6x6, Alvis Stalwart. EMER V647, instructions 1-103.

Miscellaneous instructions
Truck, cargo, HMLC, 5 ton, 6x6, Alvis Stalwart. EMER V649, instructions 1-66.

An FV601 Alvis 'Saladin' stands sentry duty as a TA gate guardian. Since the end of their service careers, these vehicles are not commonly encountered, and are not popular with collectors. This one is unusual in serving out its retirement with its original owners.

Nearside of the same 'Saladin', giving an excellent view of the 76mm L5A1 gun and the co-axially mounted .30 calibre Browning machine cannon; a 7.62mm light machine gun would also have been mounted on the turret. Six smoke-grenade dischargers are installed either side of the turret alongside the main gun. Note how the size of the rear-view mirrors has tended to increase over the years.

Left. **Part of a batch of some 50 or so 'Saracens', including both APC and ACoP variants, awaiting disposal in a dealer's yard.**

Below left. **Close-up view of one of the cooling-air intake towers installed as part of the reverse flow cooling system, fitted to the FV603(C) Mk 3 'Saracen'. A similar tower is also fitted in place of the second of the two left-hand engine compartment covers.**

Above. **This photograph clearly shows the source of the 'Saracen' interior cooling problems. To the bottom right of the picture is the square outlet from the engine compartment cooling trunking, while at the top left is one of the intake fans for the rear compartment ventilation system.** It does not require much imagination to see how the hot air from the engine is introduced into the crew area. This was only solved with the introduction of the reverse flow cooling system.

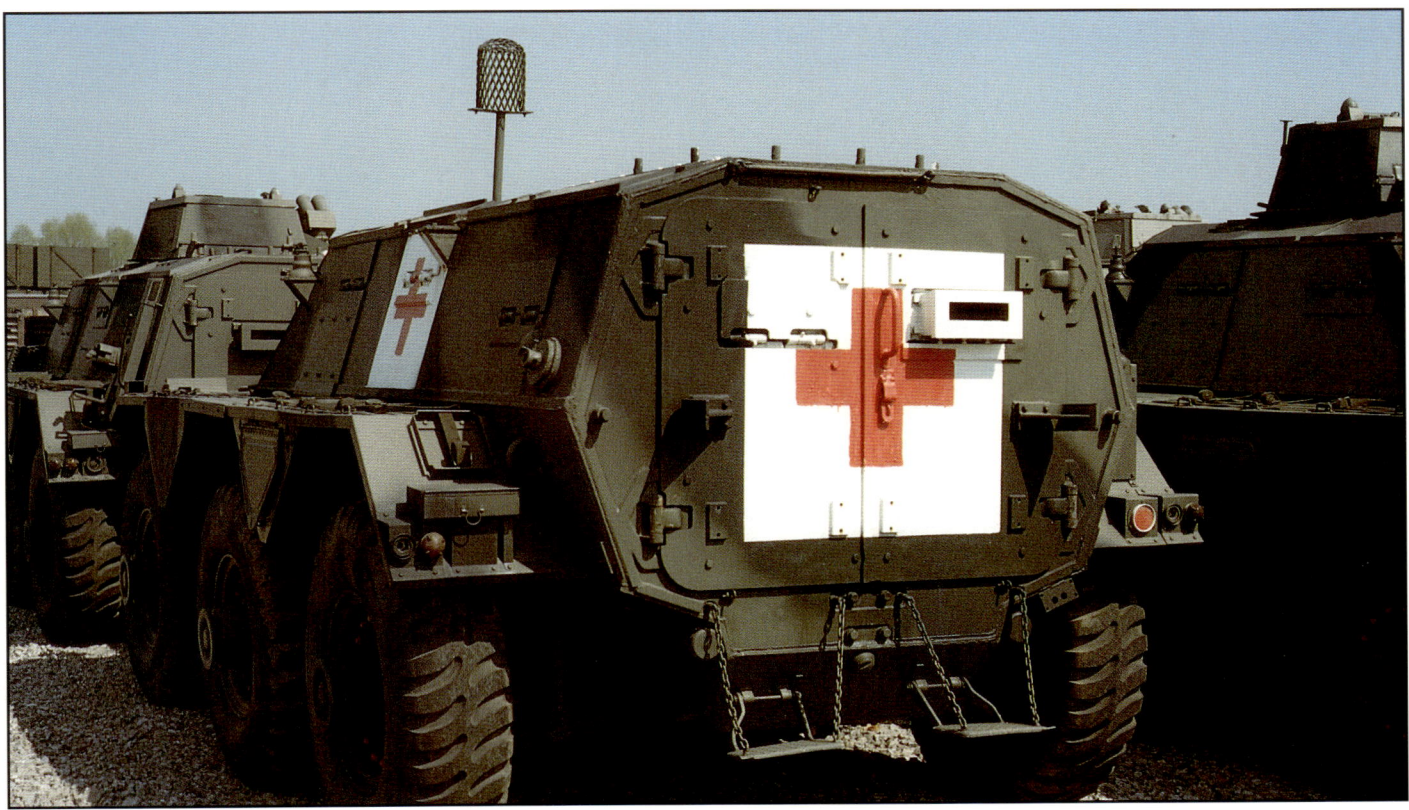

Top left. **An FV604 'Saracen' APC** awaits its fate in a surplus yard. There is little interest among collectors for these vehicles. The picture shows clearly the four square hatches provided for access to the engine compartment.

Top right. **An FV604 'Saracen'** still owned by the Ministry of Defence and used as a gate guardian. The anti-aircraft machine-gun ring mount can clearly be seen towards the rear of the roof.

Above. **An FV603(B) 'Saracen'** ambulance conversion. The 'lobster pot' apparently mounted above the roof is actually a wire cage used to protect the warning beacon. The offside rear door clearly shows the vision block.

THE ROLLS-ROYCE 'B SERIES' ENGINE

Left. An **FV622 Mk 2 'Stalwart'** lies rotting in a dealer's yard. This is how the Ministry of Defence treats £15,000 of high-tech equipment once it's served its purpose. The photograph shows well the deeper flanking windscreens of the Mk 2 version. The opened hatch is the only means of access for the crew.

Below left. A crane-equipped **FV623** or **FV624 Mk 2 'Stalwart'** shows the hydraulic crane at full reach, giving a 6.9m lift from the ground. The photograph also shows the aerodynamic spoiler mounted on the cab roof.

Below. Detail view of **FV622 Mk 2 'Stalwart'** showing clearly one of the outlets of the Dowty Hydrojet propulsion system. The mechanical linkage, which is used to control the rotating scoops, can be seen above the outlet; the vanes of the scoop itself can just be seen to the left of the outlet.

Right. An **FV1119 'Martian'** recovery vehicle shows the bumper-mounted vice and air-brake connections to one side of the radiator. The anti-aircraft gunners' hatch can just be seen above the nearside windshield.

Far right. The same vehicle displays its 15,000kg capacity hydraulic crane and the rear-mounted A-frame towing equipment. The rear stabiliser jacks are also in evidence, as well as the spade-type earth anchor.

Right. **The archetypal FV622 Mk 2 'Stalwart'** *clearly showing the plywood surfshield. Note the recovery cable neatly stowed around the lower edge of the cab, and passing through the winch fairlead rollers in the hull front skid plate.*

Below right. **FV1119 'Martian'** *recovery vehicle showing the operating position for the recovery equipment. The winch fairlead rollers can clearly be seen below the nearside headlamp, arranged for front pulls.*

THE ROLLS-ROYCE 'B SERIES' ENGINE

Left. FV432 armoured personnel carrier. Only the Mk 1 vehicles were fitted with the 'B Series' engine; later vehicles used the multi-fuel K60. A handful of the early 'Abbot' self-propelled guns, which employed a similar chassis, were also fitted with the B81.

Far left. Close-up view of the FV432 APC showing the circular roof hatch which provided access for the commander, and formed part of the roof-mounted cupola, and the square driver's hatch. Also apparent are the smoke-grenade dischargers and the front escape hatch. The flotation screen and associated equipment have been removed.

Left. Close-up view of the digging equipment of the Thornycroft light mobile digger. The photograph shows the reversible spoil conveyor and the clawed digging heads, which are mounted on a hydraulically-driven chain.

Left. Thornycroft light mobile digger with the digging equipment raised into the travelling position. Note how the three-stage rams (see opposite) have lifted and tilted the digging equipment to lay back along the booms. The hydraulic fluid tanks are located aft of the oil-cooling radiators.

THE ROLLS-ROYCE 'B SERIES' ENGINE

Above. **Thornycroft light mobile digger.** Front three-quarter view with the digging equipment ready to work. Note the half-cab and the massive fabricated-steel booms carrying the digging equipment. This vehicle has the double-reduction geared hubs. The radiator which can be seen behind the cab is used to cool the hydraulic fluid.

Right. **Thornycroft light mobile digger,** this time seen from the rear, with the digging equipment lowered. Note the enormous number of hydraulic pipes and the double-acting three-stage rams used to elevate the digging equipment. The exhaust silencer can just be seen to one side of the cab.

FV2241 Douglas 'Tugmaster' heavy aircraft tractor. The two-piece windscreen has long gone, emphasising the simple lines of the body. The engine-driven compressor can just be seen behind the radiator grille, and the cable which can be seen coming from the engine compartment towards the camera is the remains of the hand throttle control. Despite its appearance, the vehicle is still in use at the Museum of Army Transport, Beverley, where it has been used to manoeuvre their 'Beverley' transport aircraft.

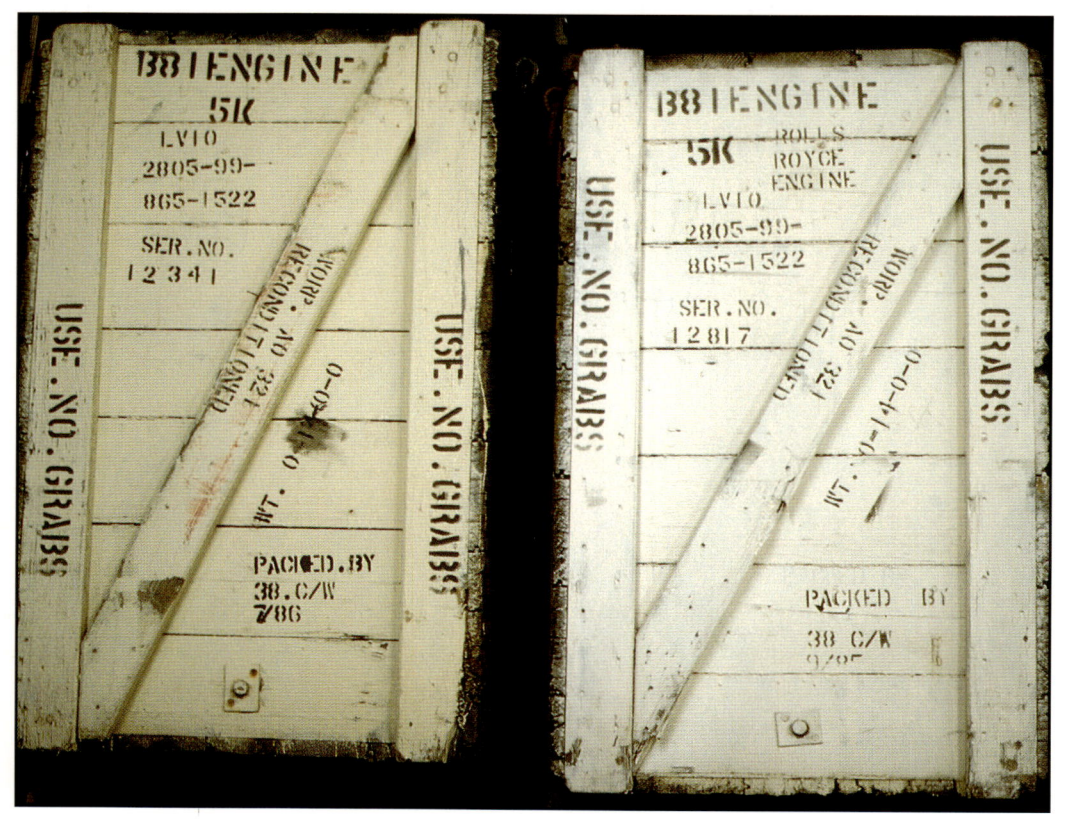

…They can still be found. These reconditioned and crated B81 Mk 5K engines, intended for the 10 ton Leyland 'Martian', were carefully stored in a surplus dealer's warehouse. It is unlikely that they will ever be used.

CHAPTER 4.4

GKN TROJAN & VICKERS ABBOT
FV431, FV432, FV433

Although it was essentially an open vehicle, and thus provided only restricted armoured protection, the WW2 'universal' bren gun carrier proved to be an extremely useful device for delivering men and materiel to the front line. However, it could not really be classified as an armoured personnel carrier (APC), and for the duration of WW2, the British Army had no purpose-designed APC's of its own, relying instead on the US White and International Harvester half-tracks.

It was not until the Malayan crisis that the War Office finally realised that perhaps such a vehicle might be useful and in 1952, began to take delivery of Alvis 'Saracen' wheeled APC's (see Chapter 4.1). Although these vehicles were to go on to give 20 or more years service, within a few years of their introduction it had become obvious that they suffered a number of disadvantages, and that a more versatile and mobile replacement was required.

Inevitably, the authorities looked to the other side of the Atlantic to see if anything could be learned from American practice. In the early 1950's, the US Army had abandoned half-tracks and had specified fully-tracked APC's with the successful aluminium-armoured M59 and M113 carriers, produced by the Food Machinery & Chemical Corporation (FMC).

The Ministry of Supply believed that there was already considerable expertise available at FVRDE arising from the design and use of tracked carriers during WW2. The American experience provided confirmation that this was the right route, and the Ministry began to look at the possibility of designing a tracked APC to replace the 'Saracen', following similar lines to the FMC machines.

After several false starts, the resulting FV430 series provided a compact APC suitable for providing mobility during conventional or nuclear war, as well as lending itself to conversion to a variety of other roles. With its armoured-steel hull construction and full NBC filtration pack, the FV432 was able to provide protection against small-arms fire and shell fragments, as well as against chemical attack, nuclear radiation and flash burn.

Initially dubbed 'Trojan', the FV430 series remained in service from 1962 until the early 90's. Although most of the production vehicles were powered by the Rolls-Royce multi-fuel K60 engine, as a stop-gap measure while development of the K60 was completed, the Mk 1 versions of the basic FV432, as well as a handful of the

CHAPTER 4.4: FV432

related FV433 'Abbot' self-propelled guns, were equipped with the trusty B81 engine.

OVERVIEW

The FV432, Mk 1 'Trojan' was a fully-enclosed, air-portable tracked APC, providing accommodation for a crew of two, together with seating for 10 fully-equipped men. The driver sat at the front, on the right-hand side, with the commander behind him, under the cupola. The vehicle was not armed, but a ring mount was provided on the cupola for a general-purpose machine gun.

The 'Trojan' was of all-steel monocoque construction, with the engine mounted at the front left of the hull. The running gear comprised five rubber-tyred roadwheels per side, suspended on torsion bars, and running on composite steel/rubber tracks. Motive power was provided by a Rolls-Royce B81 engine, driving through a GM-Allison TX200 six-speed semi-automatic transmission. The transmission was located to one side of the engine on the same subframe, forming a complete compact power pack.

Forced ventilation facilities were provided, together with NBC filtration, to ensure safe comfortable conditions when closed down. Unlike the comparable American APC's, the vehicle was not truly amphibious, but a rubberised-fabric flotation screen could be erected to allow deep-water wading, with the tracks providing propulsion and steering in the water.

Although not strictly speaking a 'variant', the FV433 'Abbot' self-propelled gun was constructed on a similar chassis, albeit with a lower-profile hull. Produced by Vickers Defence Systems at Elswick, and equipped with a Royal Ordnance Factory (ROF) 105mm rifled gun, the 'Abbot' shared many components with the FV432.

DEVELOPMENT

Immediately following WW2, the War Office made several attempts to replace the universal carrier with a similar machine. The first 'improved' version was the CT20 series 'Oxford' tracked carrier family, and at least two examples of this series, the CT24 and CT25, employed B80, Mk 1 engines. However, few of these were constructed before the project was abandoned, and work began on the similarly-abortive FV401/402 'Cambridge' carrier (see Chapter 4.8).

The 'Cambridge' project too, eventually came to nothing, but during the mid-1950's, FVRDE also designed the largely-experimental FV420 and FV500 families. A number of variants were planned, and prototypes of the FV421 were constructed and issued for troop trials in North Africa. In the end, this project too was cancelled

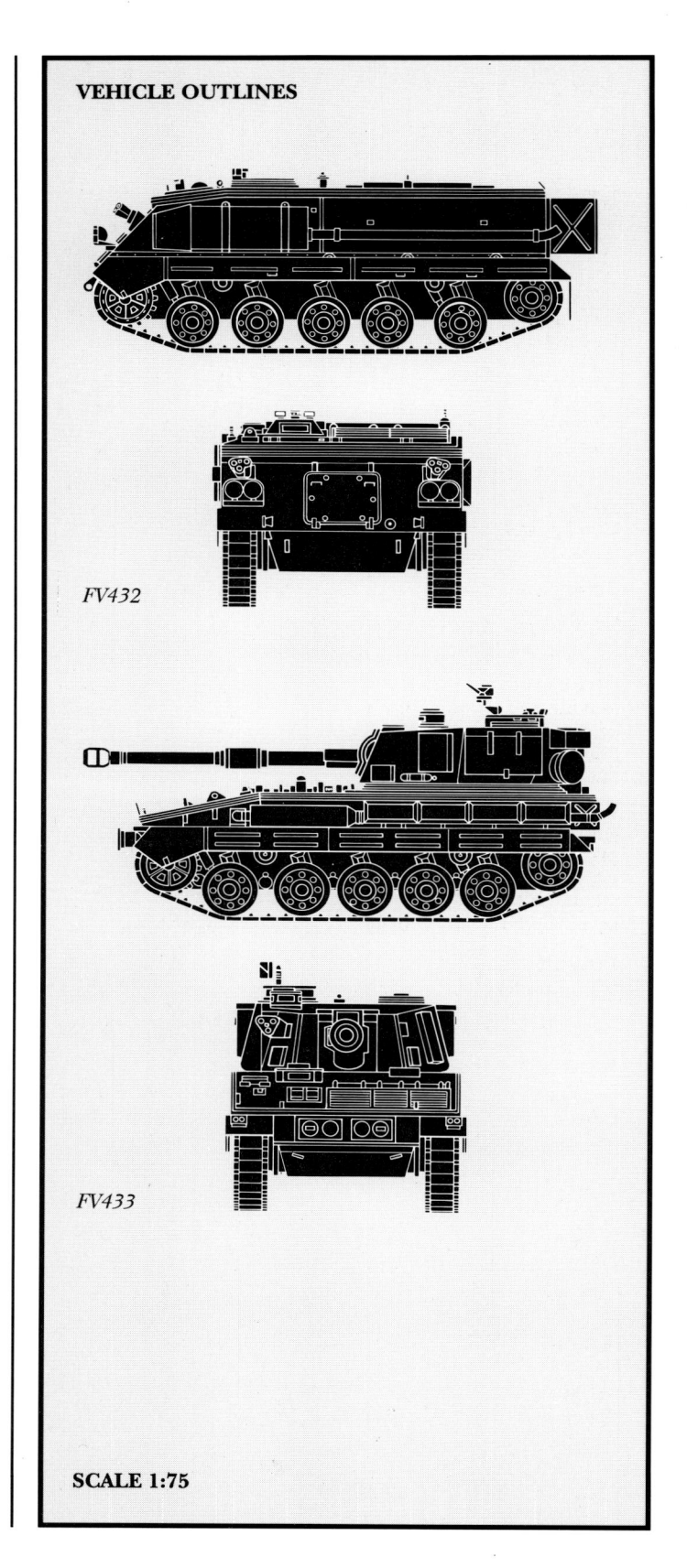

VEHICLE OUTLINES

FV432

FV433

SCALE 1:75

SPECIFICATION

Dimensions and weight

	FV432	FV433
Dimensions (mm):		
Length	5110	5830
Width	2641	2640
Height:		
to top of hull	1880	2650
to top of machine gun	2286	-
Ground clearance	407	407
Track dimensions:		
width	350	350
length on ground	2819	2819
pitch	117	117
centres	2184	2184
Weight (kg):		
Combat weight	14,967	17,500
Unladen weight	12,700	15,454
Bridge classification	16	18
Ground pressure (kg/sq m)	740	858

Performance
Maximum speed: 56km/h (FV433, 48km/h), on road; 6.5km/h (FV433, 5km/h), in water.
Fuel consumption: 1.19 litre/km, on road.
Maximum range: 570km.

Vertical obstacle: 609mm.
Ditch crossing: 2050mm.
Maximum gradient: 60%.
Side slope: 30%.
Fording: unprepared, 1066mm (1219mm, FV433); amphibious, with appropriate preparation.

Capacity
Maximum capacity: 10 men or 3670kg cargo.

---

and none of the vehicles made it into full production.

However, none of this work was wasted, and in 1958 a new proposal was made for a tracked APC, drawing on the experience gained during the FV420 project. Once again, the vehicle was designed at FVRDE, and during the development phase, similar vehicles produced by other nations were examined; an American M59 and an Anglo-German HS 30 were purchased for study.

The Australian Army was also considering the purchase of tracked APC's at around the same time and was asked to comment on the relevant War Office Policy Statement (WOPS 26 'Common user tracked vehicles'), and to help finalise the specification.

In August 1959, the War Office published the design specification for the FV432, and the first examples were delivered for troop trials in Germany in 1961. Extensive trials were also undertaken at Chertsey and the vehicle went through considerable detail modification before being approved for production in July 1962.

In September 1962, two prototypes were delivered to Australia for joint trials in hot/wet, hot/dry and road conditions. The outcome of these field trials, which resulted in the Australians purchasing the competing M113, confirmed many of the shortcomings of the prototype vehicles which had already been highlighted by FVRDE during the Chertsey trials.

It was always planned that the FV432 would form part of a family of vehicles based on the same chassis, and of these, the FV431 load carrier, and (early) FV433 self-propelled gun versions were also powered by Rolls-Royce 'B Series' engines.

Load carrier variant
In October 1960, a specification was issued for an armoured load-carrier variant, designated FV431. Prototypes were constructed in 1962 and delivered for troop trials but the weight of the armour severely restricted the load-carrying capacity.

It was at about the same time that Alvis had put forward the PV1 'Stalwart' prototype as a possible high-mobility load carrier, and this was preferred by some of the user arms who pressed for comparative trials. A prototype FV420 was ballasted to simulate the weight of the FV431, and put through its paces against the 'Stalwart'. It was suggested that an armoured version of the 'Stalwart' might be more appropriate, but in the end, the basic FV620 HMLC, which, of course was not armoured, acquitted itself extremely well, and was selected for production.

The FV431 quietly died.

CHAPTER 4.4: FV432

Self-propelled gun variant

Work on the design of the FV433 'Abbot', which was intended to replace the venerable 25 lb field gun with a more powerful and mobile weapon, had begun as a separate project at FVRDE in the late 1950's. The first prototype appeared in 1961, and the vehicle began troop trials in 1962.

The two projects were later brought together and the FV433 shared many of the transmission components and design features of the FV432.

Like the FV432, the definitive production version of the 'Abbot' was powered by the multi-fuel K60 engine, but early examples of the vehicle employed a B81 unit.

Production

The FV432 production contract was awarded to J Sankey & Sons (now GKN-Sankey) and the first production vehicles were manufactured at Smethwick in the West Midlands, and delivered in 1963 under the name 'Trojan'. Although the name was particularly apt, and indicated that someone in the specifying chain at least had both a sense of humour and a classical education, it was later to be dropped to avoid possible confusion with the motor car manufacturer of the same name.

The basic FV432, in its Mk 2 guise, was developed into a very large number of variants and, at one time, was in use with practically every unit of the British Army. Major variants included the 'Abbot' 105mm self-propelled gun, a command vehicle, mortar carrier, maintenance carrier, mine layer, radar and recovery vehicles.

A total of 3000 FV432's of all marks were constructed but only the Mk 1, and a handful of early FV433 'Abbots' (less than 10 vehicles) were powered by the Rolls-Royce B81 engine. Rolls-Royce production records show that 812 B81, Mk 8F and Mk 8F/2 engines were produced for the Mk 1 variant, and this would seem to suggest somewhere around 500 vehicles.

Subsequent production employed the multi-fuel K60 which had a similar dimensional profile.

Replacement and disposal

The FV432, Mk 1 vehicles were quickly disposed of once the Mk 2, with its multi-fuel engine, became available. Some were used as development or experimental vehicles, but most probably ended up as hard targets.

By the end of the 1980's, the whole FV432 family had begun to be superseded. The smaller Alvis CVR(T) 'Spartan' vehicles had capacity for four men only and thus were only a partial replacement for the larger FV432, but these had started to enter service in 1978. A more complete replacement came from the GKN 'Saxon' wheeled APC, and the GKN 'Warrior' mechanised

FV432 Mk 1 'Trojan' APC (IWM)

FV433 'Abbot' 105mm self-propelled gun (TMB)

Power pack of FV432 Mk 1 showing engine and transmission (RR)

combat vehicle (formerly known as MCV-80) which the MoD began to accept in 1986.

NOMENCLATURE

FV432. Armoured personnel (infantry) carrier, Trojan, Mk 1.
FV433. 105mm field artillery, self-propelled, Abbot, Mk 1.

DESCRIPTION

Engine
Rolls-Royce B81, No 1, Mk 8F or 8F/2 (FV432); B81, Mk 8G (FV433); dry sump.
Capacity: 6516cc.
Bore and stroke: 3.75 x 4.50in.
Power output: 240bhp (gross); 195bhp (net) at 2700rpm.
Maximum torque: 330 lbs/ft (gross); 315 lbs/ft (net) at 2250rpm.

Detail variations
Distributor limiter set at 3750rpm (crankshaft speed); engine and transmission mounted on subframe which could be removed and run outside the vehicle on flying leads for test purposes; oil filter mounted remotely, on engine subframe; inlet manifold with horizontal carburettor-mounting flange; single exhaust manifold with vertical outlet facing forward; transmission installed to one side of engine; radiator mounted above engine with forced cooling via two thermatic fans.

Transmission
Located to one side of the engine on the same subframe, and driven via a 1:1 geared transfer case attached to the back of the engine, the transmission was a GMC Allison TX-200 unit built in the UK by Rolls-Royce under a licence agreement. Shifting was semi-automatic, with six forward speeds and one reverse available. The driver selected the speed range required using a shift lever, either 1-2, 3-4, 3-5, and 3-6, or reverse and neutral; gear changes within the selected range were automatic.

Drive to the tracks was via sprockets attached to the final drives at the front of the vehicle.

The transmission had with three power take-offs.

Suspension
Independent suspension was provided by horizontal torsion bar at each of the five wheel stations. A hydraulic shock absorber was fitted above the front and rear wheels; this was changed to a friction-type shock absorber on later vehicles.

Steering gear
The steering unit was mounted at the front of the engine compartment, connected to the transmission by a short propeller shaft, and coupled by hydraulic linkage to the driver's steering levers. Operating the steering levers applied flexible friction bands on the steering unit brake drums thus slowing or stopping the track on one side of the vehicle, and allowing a skid turn to be made.

Braking system
The braking system shared the same components as the steering gear, with brake bands acting directly onto brake drums. There was no secondary braking system and in the event of a drive-train failure or brake-drum collapse, the vehicle would be left without steering or braking control.

Wheels and tracks
There were five rubber-tyred road wheels each side, running on 350mm wide steel tracks. Two track-return idler rollers were provided above the road wheels.

The tracks consisted of 91 steel links either side, each link fitted with a removable rubber road pad; rubber-bushed steel pins were used to connect each track link to its neighbour. Track tension was maintained by hydraulic adjustment of the rear idler wheel.

Track life was stated to be in excess of 5000 kilometres.

Hull
The flat-sided box-like hull of the FV432 was of all-welded construction, fabricated from (maximum) 16mm thick armoured steel. The glacis plate sloped at 60 degrees, with a horizontal roof extending to the rear. Some vehicles were fitted with a short, full-length skirt covering the track-return idlers.

Two jettisonable fuel tanks, mounted on the upper rear hull, either side of the door, held 190 litres of fuel each.

Access for the driver and commander respectively was provided by two hinged roof hatches, one square, one circular. The circular hatch formed part of a roof-mounted cupola, capable of rotation through 360 degrees; three periscopes in the cupola were provided for observation when closed down. A single, wide-angle periscope was provided for the driver.

A side-hinged rear door, approximately 1000mm wide, provided access to the rear compartment where fold-up seating was provided along each side for a total of 10 men. A large, four-part hinged circular roof hatch was provided for escape purposes.

The interior of the hull was well padded to reduce the possibility of injury to the occupants during cross-country operations.

Electrical equipment
The vehicle was wired with a 24V electrical system, with

negative to earth; the ignition system was fully screened and waterproofed.

A high-output ac alternator, with built-in rectifier, provided power for the vehicle systems. Six 12V, 60Ah batteries were housed inside the crew compartment.

Ventilation equipment
A positive-pressure forced ventilation system with external NBC filter provided fresh-air ventilation for the crew and passengers. The air was pumped through a duct located along the top of the hull, with individual diffusers located at each occupant's position. The paper air filter was located in a steel housing on the right-hand side of the hull.

When closed down, the interior could be completely sealed against unfiltered external air, and if necessary, could be operated in this condition for up to four days.

There was provision for incorporating heating and cooling equipment into the ventilation system for use in excessively hot or cold climates.

Amphibious equipment
A rubberised-fabric flotation screen was erected on 10 metal stays to provide the vehicle with sufficient buoyancy for amphibious operations. It was also necessary to inflate a rubberised bladder and attach it to the glacis plate to prevent the nose from being swamped.

Propulsion and directional control in the water was provided by the tracks, and the maximum speed in the water was 6.5km/h. Visibility in the water was severely restricted by the flotation screen.

Later in their service careers, most FV432's had the amphibious equipment removed.

ARMAMENTS

FV432 'Trojan'
The 'Trojan' was provided with a ring mount on the roof cupola, intended for use with a 7.62mm GPMG; 2750 rounds were carried. Triple-barrelled electric smoke-grenade dischargers were mounted on the hull front at either side.

FV433 'Abbot'
The 'Abbot' mounted a 105mm ROF rifled gun. The gun turret, which was fully-traversable, could be elevated from -5 to +70 degrees. The maximum range of the gun was 17,000m; at high angle, the range reduced to 2500m. The barrel had both a fume extractor and a large, double-baffle muzzle brake.

The vehicle carried 40 rounds and could fire high explosive (HE), high-explosive squash head (HESH), smoke and illuminating projectiles. The maximum rate of fire was 12 rounds a minute; a mechanical rammer was used to load the projectile, but the cartridge case was loaded by hand. Gun barrel life was anticipated to be approximately 10,000 rounds.

Triple-barrelled smoke dischargers were mounted either side of the turret.

RADIO EQUIPMENT

Basic 'Larkspur' radio installations in the FV432 included B47, B48, C13, C42, C45 and C48 sets, together with intercom facilities for the driver and commander. Radio antenna were mounted on the flat roof.

DOCUMENTATION

Technical publications
Technical description: APC, tracked, FV432, Mk 1. EMER E102/2.

User handbook: armoured personnel carrier (tracked) (FV432), Mk 1. WO code 14168.

Illustrated spare parts list: carrier, personnel, full-tracked, FV432, Mks 1 and 1/1. WO code 14660.

Unit repairs: APC, tracked, FV432, Mk 1. EMER E103/2.

Complete equipment schedule: carrier, personnel, full-tracked, FV432, Mks 1 and 1/1. WO code 33061.

Radio installation: user handbook for radio installation C42/C42/B47 in armoured personnel carrier, FV432. Air Ministry publication ATP 25, no ES 10223.

Bibliography
Armour of the West. Adshead, Robin and Noel Aycliffe-Jones. London, Ian Allen, 1978. ISBN 0-711006-81-4.

British vehicles and army equipment. Smith, R E. London, Ian Allen, 1968. ISBN 0-711000-20-4.

Fighting vehicles and weapons of the modern British Army. Pugh, Stevenson. London, McDonald, 1962.

Jane's AFV recognition handbook. Foss, Christopher. Couldsdon, Jane's Information Group, 1992. ISBN 0-710610-43-2.

Jane's armoured personnel carriers. Foss, Christopher. London, Jane's Information Group, 1985. ISBN 0-710603-54-1.

Making tracks: British carrier story, 1914 to 1972. Chamberlain, P and Chris Ellis. Windsor, Profile Publications, 1973. ISBN 0-853830-88-6.

NATO armour. Perrett, Bryan. London, Ian Allen, 1971. ISBN 0-711002-09-9.

CHAPTER 4.5

LEYLAND MARTIAN
FV1103, FV1110, FV1119, FV1121, FV1122

The largest vehicle in the post-war CT family was the massive Leyland 30 ton heavy-artillery tractor, designated FV1200. Design work was carried out by Dennis Brothers of Guildford, and several prototypes were produced by Leyland Motors. Although these were submitted for testing in 1954, the vehicle was never put into quantity production.

However, it was intended that the FV1200 would be equipped with the 18 litre Rolls-Royce 'Meteorite' 80 petrol engine, and so the largest of the CT vehicles to be fitted with a 'B Series' engine was the Leyland 'Martian' FV1100 family.

FVRDE had defined the 10 ton FV1100 range as part of the specification for post-war vehicles originally set out in a War Office paper in 1944. The first prototypes, produced in 1951, were of the cargo variant, and there is some evidence to suggest that these were produced by Thornycroft rather than Leyland. These 10 ton cargo trucks were probably intended to replace the ageing WW2 AEC 'Matadors', and Leyland 'Hippos', and in one of those little twists of fate that conspire to make life interesting, it's worth noting that 'Hippos' had already been used as mobile test-beds for the B80 prototype engine.

The first production examples however, were not of the cargo vehicle, but were the medium artillery tractor. Like all the production 'Martians', these vehicles were built by Leyland Motors of Lancashire. Alongside the medium artillery tractor, the vehicle was developed into long- and short-wheelbase cargo variants, a heavy recovery vehicle, and a special artillery tractor for the 8in howitzer. It was also planned that the same chassis would be used as a tractor unit for semi-trailers (FV1101), a 2500 gallon fuel tanker (FV1111), a 5 ton crane truck (FV1114), a workshop and machinery truck (FV1118), and an armoured command vehicle and signals office (FV1113); none of these latter proceeded beyond the design or prototype stage.

The cargo variant was the most numerous but the recovery vehicle, of which some 280 examples were constructed, was probably the most interesting since it was among the last of the 'old-fashioned' heavy recovery tractors.

Despite an initial problem with unreliability, the 'Martian' eventually proved itself to be a well-built and impressive truck. It was very much in the same mould as the classic Scammells, with three-point suspension, incorporating

CHAPTER 4.5: LEYLAND MARTIAN

a centrally-pivoted front axle and a walking beam at the rear. The Rolls-Royce engine provided enormous reserves of low-down power.

The recovery vehicles, which were the last of the family to be supplied, remained in service for the longest period, some not being demobbed until the mid-1980's.

OVERVIEW

The Leyland 'Martian' was a heavy 6x6 load-carrying chassis designed to mount, what were described at the time as 'low-profile' bodies, for the cargo, artillery tractor and recovery roles.

The prototypes and the first 25 vehicles produced were powered by a front-mounted Rolls-Royce B80 engine, normally driving the rear wheels, but with optional six-wheel drive available. The B80 was replaced in production by the more-powerful B81, and the earlier vehicles were subsequently upgraded. Power was transmitted to the wheels through a four-speed and reverse gearbox, and three-speed transfer case.

The truck was intended for heavy and severe cross-country conditions, with excellent off-road performance. The front axle was centrally-pivoted and suspended on a transverse semi-elliptical spring. Drive to the front wheels, when required, was transmitted vertically through the king pins, a system previously employed on the WW2 Mack trucks. The rear suspension and drive train arrangements broadly followed the Scammell design, employing a gear-driven, centrally-pivoted walking beam suspended on longitudinal semi-elliptic springs.

Steering effort was reduced by the use of hydraulic assistance, and the brakes were operated by compressed air.

Available in long- and short-wheelbase versions, there was a choice of body to suit the specific role, with some vehicles being provided with a mechanical or hydraulic winch, installed beneath the floor. The bodies were constructed by Mann-Egerton, Marshalls of Cambridge, Park Royal Vehicles, and EDBRO-B&E Tippers, according to the version; the recovery equipment was built by Royal Ordnance Factories.

All versions had a fully-insulated, enclosed steel cab with front seating for a crew of two or three, with a 12-man crew cab installed on the artillery tractor version; an additional gunner's platform was positioned beneath a roof-mounted machine gun hip ring, behind the front seats. The cab was designed to be split at the waistline to reduce the overall height to 2540mm for shipping.

Both of the cargo vehicles, and the howitzer tractor were fitted with an open steel body with detachable sides and

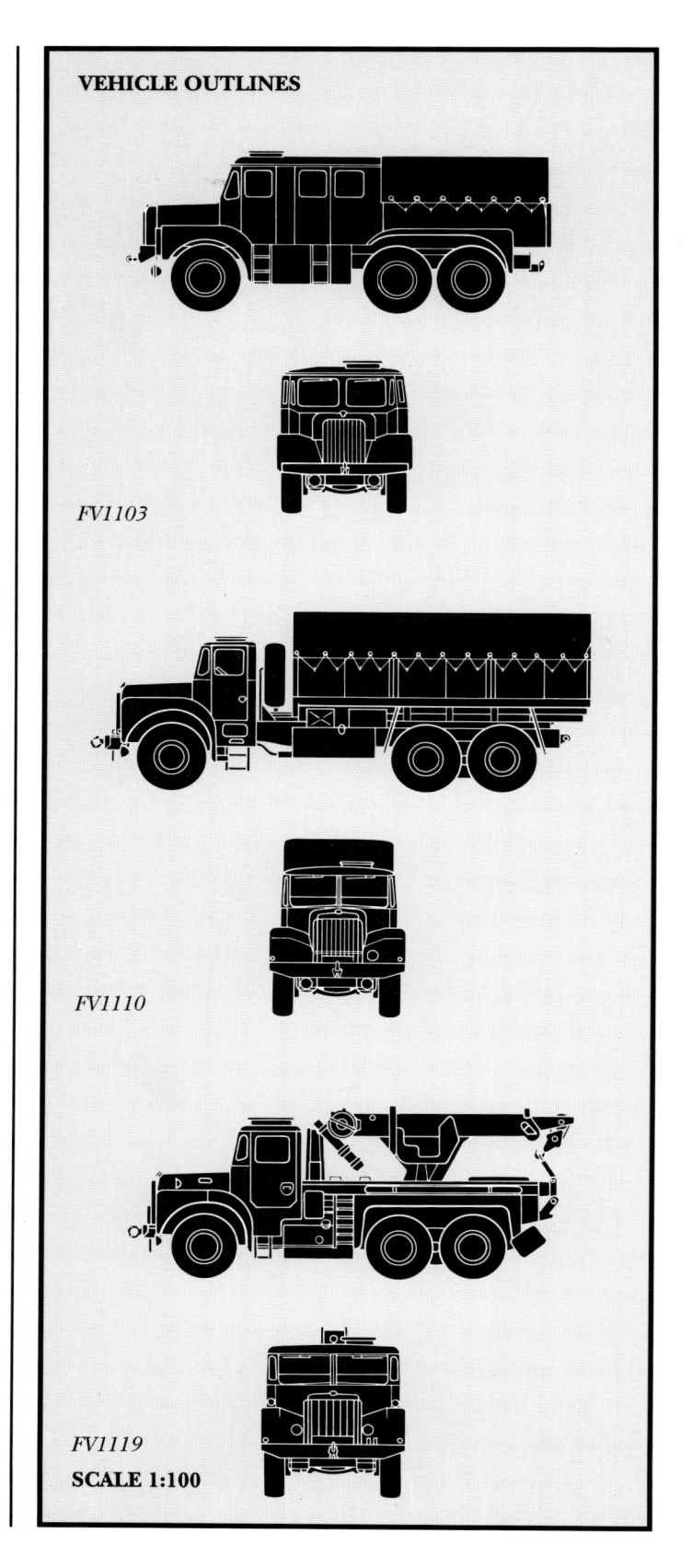

VEHICLE OUTLINES

FV1103

FV1110

FV1119

SCALE 1:100

SPECIFICATION
Dimensions and weight

	FV1103	FV1110	FV1119	FV1121/2
Dimensions (mm):				
Length	8185	9068	8890	8230/8380
Width overall	2591	2591	2591	2591
Height:				
to top of cab	3073	3010	2990	3073
to top of tarpaulin	-	3607	-	3190/3580
over crane	-	-	3200	-
load platform	1384	1711	-	1711
Wheelbase	4420	5410	4420	4420
Track:				
front	2089	2089	2100	2089
rear	2096	2096	2100	2096
Ground clearance	465	465	465	465
Weight (kg):				
Laden	18,660	23,610	-	24,600
Unladen	14,310	13,440	21,630	14,310
Bridge classification	24	22	22	23
Crane dimensions:				
Min reach (mm)	-	-	3050	-
Max reach (mm)	-	-	5490	-
Max slew:				
right (deg)	-	-	120	-
left (deg)	-	-	120	-
Max lift height (mm)	-	-	8235	-
Max load (kg)	-	-	15,000	-
Load at max reach (kg)	-	-	1500	-

Performance

	FV1103	FV1110	FV1119	FV1121/2
Speed (km/h):				
Maximum, on road	42	42	56	42
Average, off road	25	25	25	25

Fuel consumption: 0.81 litre/km, on road.
Maximum range: 485-560km, on road.
Turning circle: 21.34m.
Maximum gradient: 33%.
Maximum gradient for stop and restart: 26%.
Approach angle: 40 deg.
Departure angle: 36 deg (all versions except FV1119); 42 deg (FV1119).
Fording: unprepared, 760mm; prepared, 1980mm.

Capacity
Maximum load: 10,000kg.
Maximum towed load: 7500-8000kg.

---

tailgate; a fabric tilt and tubular framework was used to cover the cargo area. The body on the (FV1103) artillery tractor consisted of a crew cab, with a smaller wooden, open cargo compartment to the rear.

The recovery tractor was fitted with a 15 ton hydraulic crane unit on a steel platform body. In design, the crane resembled the Austin Western units fitted to US military vehicles during WW2. A 15 ton hydraulic winch was installed beneath the rear body.

DEVELOPMENT

FVRDE specification numbers were allocated in chronological sequence, and these tell us that, regardless of the manufacturing sequence, the long wheelbase cargo truck was designed first, followed by the FV1103 artillery tractor, and then the recovery vehicle. At a later date, specifications were prepared for the two short wheelbase vehicles which were converted from the FV1103 artillery tractor: the FV1121 cargo truck, and the FV1122 artillery tractor.

Cargo vehicles
The first variant to be prototyped was the cargo vehicle, and at least one example (tested by FVRDE as project FVPE 4071) was produced in 1951, costing the Ministry £8550. One source, writing close to the time suggests that Thornycroft were responsible, but it seems more likely that it was Leyland. Whoever produced it had no cause to be pleased with their efforts for the vehicle was described in a War Office paper of 1955 as being subject to so many failures that it had to be returned to the makers for reworking.

A commercial cab design was used, originally intended to have built-in front wheel arches. In the prototype military application, the wheel arches took the form of simple cycle wing mudguards attached to, and moving with the front wheels, rather in the style of the Scammells of the period. This conspired to give the cab and wheel arch area a curious cut-off, unfinished look.

In the early 1950's, a prototype short wheelbase wooden-bodied flat-bed truck was also produced and tested by FVRDE as project FVPE 4290. Whether the flat-bed body was simply a convenient way of ballasting the truck to simulate the weight of specialised bodies, or whether it was intended to be produced in this form is not known. Certainly a flat-bed truck was not among the variants listed in the War Office 'Comparative schedule of post-war vehicles' produced in 1951.

At a later date, a second version of the cargo truck was produced, using the short wheelbase chassis. Designated FV1121, this appears to have been a subsequent conversion of the FV1103 artillery tractor.

CHAPTER 4.5: LEYLAND MARTIAN

Artillery tractor
The second documented prototype was for the FV1103 artillery tractor, intended to replace the AEC 'Matadors', and designed for towing 5.5, 7.5 and 8in howitzers, as well as 40mm anti-aircraft guns, and other field pieces. This was passed to FVRDE for trials, and apart from some minor problems with the steering was considered satisfactory.

During the 1960's, a second version of the artillery tractor (FV1122) was produced, designed to tow the American-designed 8in howitzer (or 'atomic cannon' as it had become known). Evidence suggests that, like the FV1121 cargo vehicle, this might also have been a conversion of the FV1103 vehicle. In this role, the 'Martian' replaced the ageing WW2 Mack tractors.

By 1954, production of the artillery tractor had begun, and the plan was that the cargo vehicle would follow. At this time, the average price per vehicle was contracted at £7850.

The first 25 vehicles were fitted with a B80 engine, this was then replaced in production by the more-powerful B81 and the intention was that the earlier vehicles would be upgraded. However, the problems were far from over and in 1955, it was reported that all the tractors so far produced were 'frozen' in MoS depots with design defects, sufficiently serious to prevent their issue to units.

Recovery vehicle
Development of the recovery vehicle arose out of the serious shortage of heavy recovery vehicles. This shortage remained until well into the 1960's in spite of the delivery of the Scammell GS range 'Explorer' FV11301 recovery vehicles in 1950. The recovery version of the 'Martian' family was an attempt to address the shortage whilst also providing a CT-type vehicle with enhanced cross-country capability.

Work on the FV1119 recovery version began in the mid 1950's, with production vehicles being issued to units, at a cost of £22,500 each, during 1962/63.

Bearing in mind the ultimate fate of the 'B Series', it is slightly ironic that the earlier Scammell FV11301 was diesel-engined whilst the later Leyland used the Rolls-Royce petrol engine.

Production
All of the production chassis were constructed by Leyland Motors with production taking place over a roughly 15 year period spanning the early 1950's through to the mid 1960's. No bodies were produced by Leyland, and the completed, running cab-and-chassis assemblies were delivered to the bodybuilder to be equipped with the appropriate body. There is evidence to suggest that at

Prototype FV1110 'Martian' cargo truck (IWM)

Prototype FV1110 'Martian' variant with flat bed body (IWM)

Prototype FV1119 'Martian' heavy recovery tractor (REME)

FV1103 'Martian' artillery tractor (TMB)

FV1103 'Martian' artillery tractor with 5.5in howitzer (MP)

FV1110 'Martian' (18ft) cargo truck (IWM)

least some of the recovery vehicles were converted from cargo vehicle or artillery tractor chassis, and it is possible that some un-bodied, but otherwise completed chassis were put into store.

The bodies for the FV1103 artillery tractor were coach-built either by Park Royal Vehicles at their North London works, or by Mann-Egerton at Norwich. Cargo bodies were constructed by EDBRO-B&E Tippers at Leyland, by Park Royal Vehicles, or by Marshall's of Cambridge.

The recovery equipment was designed and built by Royal Ordnance Factories working with Leyland Motors.

According to the contract records held at Beverley, the total number of vehicles produced was 1380. This includes slightly less than 60 of the FV1103 artillery tractor, and 280 recovery vehicles. Although this leaves around 500 cargo vehicles, it must be remembered that a number of FV1103 tractors were apparently converted to cargo and howitzer tractor configurations.

Replacement and disposal
The cargo vehicles and the FV1122 artillery tractor remained in service until the mid 1970's, the cargo vehicles being replaced by the Foden medium-mobility, and improved medium mobility range.

The recovery vehicles and FV1103 artillery tractors remained in service longer. The recovery vehicles were certainly still in use in some numbers in 1985, but were eventually replaced by more modern AEC 'Militant' designs, and subsequently by the Eka-equipped Foden and Scammell vehicles with their sophisticated hydraulic lifting and towing equipment.

The artillery tractors were not replaced since there was no longer a requirement for heavy artillery pieces generally; the 8in howitzer, particularly, had certainly been replaced by more modern guided weapons.

As far as having 'second careers' goes, whilst demobbed recovery vehicles might have appealed to those garage operators called upon to recover heavy vehicles, albeit at a considerable fuel cost, the cargo and artillery variants found little use outside of military life.

NOMENCLATURE and VARIATIONS

The 'Martian' name
Rather like the hapless Austin 'Champ' which only acquired its name by association with the equivalent commercial vehicle, the 'Martian' was never officially named by the military authorities. It was only when Leyland started to market a commercial version under that name that the FV1100 series found itself being described as 'Martian'. The name was never officially sanctioned.

CHAPTER 4.5: LEYLAND MARTIAN

Variations

FV1103(A). Tractor, 10 ton, CT, medium artillery, 6x6, Leyland, Mk 1
Short-wheelbase chassis equipped as a towing and supply vehicle for medium artillery (up to 8 ton gross weight). Fitted with insulated crew cab for 12; a small timber-sided cargo body allowed up to 5000kg of ammunition to be carried behind the cab. Fitted with a 10 ton mechanical winch.

FV1110(A). Truck, 10 ton, CT, cargo (18ft), 6x6, Leyland, Mk 1.
Long-wheelbase cargo truck with steel drop-side body and canvas tilt; body sides and pillars could be removed to provide a flat platform, of 5500x2210mm. Some vehicles were fitted with an 8 ton mechanical winch.

FV1119(A). Tractor, 10 ton, CT, recovery, heavy, 6x6, Leyland, Mk 1
Short-wheelbase chassis fitted with hydraulic recovery crane having an extending and slewing jib, with a 15 ton two-speed hydraulic winch installed under the cab, configured for front and rear pulls. Intended for recovery and suspended tow of wheeled and tracked vehicles up to 10 ton weight; also designed for use with the FV3221 10 ton heavy recovery trailer.

FV1121(A). Truck, 10 ton, CT, cargo (16ft), dropside, 6x6, Leyland, Mk 1
Short-wheelbase cargo truck with 4880x2440mm steel drop-side body and canvas tilt; body sides and pillars can be removed to provide a flat platform. Fitted with 10 ton mechanical winch, and particularly suitable for bridging operations.

Possibly converted from FV1103 artillery tractor.

FV1122. Tractor, wheeled, 10 ton, GS (8in howitzer), 6x6, Leyland, Mk 1
Modified version of FV1121, intended as a towing and supply vehicle for the heavy artillery 8in howitzer, either with or without the appropriate limber; body and cab designed to accommodate an 11-man crew. A chain hoist was incorporated to enable the gun trail to be lifted to the towing position.

Possibly converted from FV1103 artillery tractor.

Field modifications

In 1957, MEXE adapted an FV1110 cargo truck especially for carrying bow pontoons for bridging. Although there were some reservations about the suitability of the attachments, the vehicle was generally considered to be suitable .for the role and this possibly led to the production of the FV1121 vehicle which was described as being suitable for use by bridging units.

FV1119 'Martian' heavy recovery tractor (TMB)

FV1119 'Martian' showing recovery equipment (IWM)

FV1119 'Martian' heavy recovery tractor, rear view (IWM)

CHAPTER 4.5: LEYLAND MARTIAN

FV1122 'Martian' tractor for 8in 'atomic' howitzer (TMB)

Chassis and cab of FV1103 after conversion, without new body (TMB)

FV1121 'Martian' (16ft) cargo truck (TMB)

DESCRIPTION

Engine
Rolls-Royce B80, No 1, Mk 2H (first 25 vehicles only); B81 Mk 2H; B81 Mk 5H (most production vehicles); B81 Mk 5K (some FV1119 recovery vehicles only); wet sump.
Capacity: B80, 5675cc; B81, 6516cc.
Bore and stroke: B80, 3.50 x 4.50in; B81, 3.75 x 4.50in.
Power output: B80, 165bhp (gross), 136bhp (net) at 3750rpm; B81, 220bhp (gross), 195bhp (net) at 3750rpm.
Maximum torque: B80, 280 lbs/ft (gross); 257 lbs/ft (net) at 2250rpm; B81, 330 lbs/ft (gross); 315 lbs/ft (net) at 2250rpm.

Detail variations
Distributor limiter set at 3750rpm (crankshaft speed); Mk 5K engine also fitted with 'Iso-Speedic' governor; oil filter mounted on engine block; oil cooler installed between radiator and cooling fan; horizontal rear outlet exhaust manifold; inlet manifold with horizontal flange for carburettor mounting; long water jacket to inlet manifold; power take-off for brake compressor and power steering pump.

Transmission
Driving through a 280mm Borg and Beck twin dry-plate clutch, power was transmitted through a four-speed and reverse gearbox, to a three-speed transfer gear assembly housed in a unit-constructed auxiliary gearbox. First and reverse were engaged by a sliding gear, whilst the other four speeds were of the constant-mesh helical type. The auxiliary gearbox also provided drive for the winch, or winch hydraulic motor.

From the auxiliary gearbox, open propeller shafts ran the length of the vehicle to drive the front and rear axles; the rear prop shaft was split on the long wheelbase versions and fitted with a centre pillow block. A third, shorter shaft was used to drive the winch or winch pump where applicable. Engagement and disengagement of the front axle was effected by a sliding coupling sleeve, with the mechanism installed within the auxiliary gearbox casing, and controlled manually by a lever in the cab. The auxiliary gearbox also included sliding dog speed change and winch control facilities, operated by means of a third centrally-located lever in the cab.

The transfer box ratios were 1.055:1, 1.360:1 and 2.690:1 for the axle and (mechanical) winch drives, and 1:1 for the winch hydraulic pump power take-off on recovery vehicles. Low auxiliary gear was interlocked through the all-wheel drive system, and could not be engaged unless the front-axle drive was also selected.

Drive to the single rear axle casing was transmitted to a bevel-gear type differential and then through axle shafts and spur-type reduction gears to the four road wheels.

THE ROLLS-ROYCE 'B SERIES' ENGINE

The reduction gears were housed in walking-beam gear cases located on either side of the chassis; the cases being designed to articulate on central pivots attached to the chassis members.

The solid front axle casing incorporated a bevel-gear type differential from which power was transmitted, via axle shafts and bevel gears, to the road wheels. In order to gain maximum ground clearance at the front, the drive was passed vertically through the swivel (king) pins, with the top bevel gears transmitting drive from the axle to the vertical pin, and the bottom gears transferring the power to the hub and road wheel. The axle and bevel-gear housings were mounted in a torque frame which had its rear end attached to the main chassis members by means of ball ends located in spherical bearings.

It was originally intended that a central tyre inflation system would be used, allowing the tyre pressures to be altered while the vehicle was moving, and although the valve housings were installed on the hub, the system was never completed.

Suspension
Suspension was provided at three points by means of semi-elliptical springs. No shock absorbers were fitted.

A single spring with 14 leaves, installed across the chassis at the front axle, was pivoted centrally in a rubber-mounted swivel housing, designed to handle movement of the road wheels. The right-hand end of the spring was attached to the torque frame by a shackle spring, the other end resting on a pivoted rocker.

The rear suspension consisted of two longitudinal main springs, each with 10 leaves, together with additional helper springs on the recovery vehicle, installed on each side of the chassis. The axle shaft casing was attached to the springs by U bolts, with the walking-beam gear casings designed to pivot on the axle casing. A mechanical locking device was provided on the rear suspension of the recovery vehicle to assist in lifting operations. Torque-reaction arms were installed in 'Metalastik' bushes on the axle and chassis frame.

Bump movement of both the front and rear axles was limited by rubber stops on the chassis frame. Total suspension movement from bump to rebound was 305mm at the front, and 255mm at the rear.

Steering gear
Steering was controlled through a hydraulically-assisted cam-and-roller type steering box.

Steering action from the wheel was transmitted through the steering column, via bevel gears at its base and through a short prop shaft to a relay box which incorporated a cam-and-roller mechanism. A drop arm from the relay box was connected by a short drag link to a triple-armed relay lever pivoted on the front torque frame; steering rods were used to connect the relay lever to the front wheel swivels. A third arm was used to connect the relay lever to a hydraulic ram designed to provide power assistance.

There were two designs for the hydraulic system according to the type of air/hydraulic accumulator used. In the 'Series 1' design, fitted to the first 286 vehicles, either a single air-bag or a single piston-type accumulator was fitted, while the 'Series 2' employed two piston-type accumulators.

Both systems operated in broadly the same way. The action of turning the wheels from the straight-ahead position opened a steering control valve in the hydraulic circuit; this allowed hydraulic fluid to be pumped under pressure to the hydraulic ram which imparted the appropriate movement to the steering relay lever, either pushing or pulling according to which way the steering wheel was turned. As soon as the wheel was turned in the opposite direction, the action of the ram was reversed and assistance was provided to return the wheels to the straight-ahead position.

A massive 560mm diameter steering wheel was fitted, giving 6.33 turns from lock to lock.

Braking system
All six wheels were provided with twin-leading shoe air-operated brakes, actuated by a conventional foot pedal. In addition, there was a hand-operated trailer braking system and a separate hand-operated 'hill-holder' system designed to apply all of the brakes.

Air pressure was generated by a twin-cylinder compressor, gear-driven from the engine power take-off, maintained in two chassis-mounted reservoirs. The braking system air was drawn through a combined air cleaner and anti-freeze device, designed to prevent the braking system from icing up. A gauge on the dash indicated braking system air pressure to the driver.

The cast-iron brake drums were 394mm diameter x 118mm width on the rear wheels, and 108mm width on the front, giving a total braking area of 0.74 sq m.

The hand (parking) brake operated via a cross shaft acting mechanically on two friction pads bearing on a disc fitted to the rear of the auxiliary gearbox. Alternative designs were employed according to the vehicle role. A conventional ratchet-operated lever was provided in the cab.

Road wheels
Wheels were 10.00 x 20in four-piece disc type, with a

separate locking rim, mounting 15.00x 20 bar-grip type cross-country tyres and tubes. Non-skid chains could be fitted to the front wheels, and overall chains to the rear.

Cargo and recovery vehicles carried a single spare wheel: on cargo vehicles, the wheel was mounted on a crane-type carrier located behind the cab; on recovery vehicles, it was carried flat, on the rear deck beneath the crane jib. The FV1103 artillery tractor carried two spare wheels, one each inside stowage compartments at the rear of the body on either side; a detachable jib could be mounted to the tilt framework for handling the spare wheel, and a hinged compartment door doubled as a runway in the open position.

The braking system compressor could also be used for tyre inflation.

Chassis
There were two basic chassis designs according to wheelbase. The shorter was used for the FV1103 and FV1122 artillery tractors, and the FV1121 cargo vehicle; the recovery vehicle employed a variation of the short chassis. The longer chassis was used only for the FV1110 cargo vehicle.

Deep channel-section side members formed the main chassis rails, with six or seven channel-section or fabricated cross members, according to the length of the chassis, and two tubular cross members. Located behind the front-spring cross member on both chassis types was a fabricated cruciform bracket designed to support the ball end of the front axle torque frame. Cast-steel brackets at the rear, with pressed-in bronze bushes, supported the rear spring eyes. On the long wheelbase version, the additional cross member was used to provide a mount for the prop shaft pillow block.

A towing pintle was attached to the rear cross member. The front bumper was bolted directly to the underside of the main channels, and was also used to mount a towing hitch.

The chassis frame used on the recovery vehicle was a 'composite' version of the tractor and truck frames. The rear cross member and tie channels were omitted, and the frame members modified to accept the subframe for the recovery equipment. The front bumper included a vice mounting, while the rear crossmember was modified to mount hydraulic outrigger jacks.

Cab and bodywork
Although the basic cab and front-end sheet metal was essentially the same on the five variants, there were actually three distinct cab designs. A short, deep cab was used on the FV1110 cargo and FV1119 recovery vehicles; a longer, crew cab was fitted to the FV1103 artillery tractor; and a slightly-extended version of the short cab was used on the FV1120 and FV1121 vehicles which had been converted from artillery tractors.

In addition, each vehicle had a unique rear body according to its designated role.

Cab
The steel cab consisted of a welded-steel frame with steel outer panels riveted to it; the outer panels, which were of double-skin construction, had 'Isoflex' insulation incorporated between the inner and outer skins. The cab consisted of upper and lower assemblies, bolted together in such a way that they could easily be dismounted to reduce the overall height for shipping.

A removable, hinged two-part hatch was provided in the cab roof above the passenger's seat, with the hatch halves hinged to the sides, and with each half able to be opened separately. There was provision for mounting a light-machine gun over the hatch, where the roof was specially strengthened.

The FV1103 artillery tractor was fitted with four hinged doors, two each side; all other versions had just one door each side. Steel ladder type steps were provided beneath each door. The front doors in each case were key-lockable. All doors were fitted with drop-down windows, with a fixed quarterlight installed between the door and windscreen pillar. The crew cabs were also fitted with sliding windows behind the rear doors. The split windscreen consisted of two fixed lower lights, together with two top-hinged upper lights. The original short cab, used on the FV1110 and FV1119 vehicles, also included two small glazed, sliding rear screens behind the driver and passenger.

The short cab used on the FV1110 and FV1119 vehicles extended some 300-400mm below the doors and was provided with stowage lockers in this space, whilst the crew cab had open racking below the doors.

Those cabs used on the converted FV1120 and FV1121 vehicles were a hybrid of the two types. The original crew cab was cut just ahead of the D post (the post on which the second door would have been hung) and a new rear closure panel was made up and fitted, giving a slightly increased length when compared to the short cab. The shape of the doors was different to the short cabs, and the grab handles were of a different design. Having started life a crew cabs they did not extend below the doors, but the open racking was omitted.

At the front, the cab was bolted to a steel dash plate and bonnet support assembly, and attached to the chassis. The support assembly also provided a mounting for the wooden cab floorboards.

The bonnet, wings, and radiator grille were separate. The bonnet consisted of a fixed centre section, incorporating a hinged centre inspection panel; this was attached to the bonnet support and radiator. Two double-hinged opening panels provided access to the engine at each side.

Massive pressed-steel wings were bolted to the bonnet support panel and chassis side members, with treadgrip strips attached to the tops of the wings. The radiator was provided with side panels and a steel front guard assembly.

The smaller cabs were designed to accommodate a crew of two or three. The driver was provided with an upholstered bucket seat, adjustable for height and reach; there was a fixed bench seat with separate back rests for up to two passengers. A platform was provided beneath the hip ring for use by an anti-aircraft gunner. The crew cab included two additional rows of bench seating for nine passengers.

Armour plates were incorporated below the floor and toeboards, and behind the rear seats on the FV1103 artillery vehicle.

Cargo bodywork
Constructed from a welded-steel framework, with hinged, detachable steel panels and a hardwood floor, the cargo body was produced in two lengths to suit the alternative wheel bases. The side panels and tailgate could be removed, together with the intermediate posts, to provide a flat loading area. Simple rear mudguards were attached to the underside of the body, in front of, and behind the rear wheels.

A removable canvas cover, supported on four steel hoops fitted into sockets in the intermediate posts to cover the cargo area.

Additional bench seating was incorporated in the rear bodywork of the FV1122 artillery tractor.

FV1103 artillery tractor bodywork
The rear bodywork of the artillery tractor was constructed from wooden sections on a steel framework. Although the tailgate was hinged, the sides were fixed. A pressed-steel mudguard assembly covered both rear wheels.

Like the cargo versions, a removable canvas cover was supported on four steel hoops to cover the cargo area.

Recovery vehicle equipment
The recovery equipment was mounted on a subframe of supporting channels, to which was mounted a simple steel platform body. Stowage lockers in the platform were provided for the various items of loose equipment. Stabiliser brackets and outrigger jacks were attached to the subframe at strategic points to assist in recovery operations, and a jib stay and 'A' frame bracket was bolted to the rear support channels; the 'A' frame could be fitted in one of two positions. A hinged spade-type earth anchor at the rear of the vehicle allowed pulls up to 30 tons.

A dual-section extensible jib, mounted on a vertically-pivoted post, was bolted to the recovery equipment subframe. Jib extension, luffing and slewing actions were provided by means of hydraulic rams. Hoisting was effected by a hydraulic winch mounted at the end of the jib, with a disc brake to hold the load. Provision was made for single- or twin-fall reeving of the winch rope by twin pulleys on the jib; a twin sheave block was carried for 4-fall reeving.

Jib control was carried out from a cab on the right-hand side of the outer column; a protective cage was fitted to the cab on prototype vehicles only.

Electrical equipment
The 'Martian' was wired on a 24V negative ground electrical system, with two 12V 60Ah batteries in series, installed in metal containers in the cab.

Generator No 1, Mk 2 or Mk 2/1 was fitted, producing 12A at 28.5V maximum, under the control of a vibrating contact regulator.

All electrical components were waterproofed and radio-screened, with much of the equipment common to other British military vehicles of the 1950's and 60's.

Winch
Two types of winch were employed according to role: a mechanical winch was fitted to some cargo vehicles, and to the FV1103 artillery tractor; a hydraulic winch was installed on recovery vehicles.

Mechanical winch
Cargo vehicles, and some artillery tractors, were fitted with a mechanical 8 or 10 ton, vertical drum winch, manufactured by Wilde, and driven from a power take-off on the auxiliary gearbox. The winch frame was bolted to the rear end of the chassis, with fairleads at front and rear and cable rollers installed along the chassis. Average rope speed, at an engine speed of 1000rpm, was 4.57, 7.62 and 3.66m/min, in first, second and reverse gears respectively.

Engagement of the winch was effected by means of a sliding dog in the auxiliary gearbox, controlled by a lever in the cab. An electrical cut-out circuit, wired through the ignition, was provided to protect the winch against overload.

Hydraulic winch
Recovery vehicles were fitted with a two-speed, 15 ton,

horizontal-drum hydraulic winch installed under the rear of the cab. Rope fairleads were provided at front and rear, and cable rollers were installed along the chassis. Average rope speed, for a 15 ton pull, in low gear, was 4.57m/min, and for a 5 ton pull, in high gear, 13.73m/min.

The winch was driven by a reversible hydraulic motor, through a two-speed epicyclic gearbox; the motor itself was driven from a power take-off on the auxiliary gearbox. A pneumatic rope tensioner was provided. Engagement of the drive for the winch motor was effected by means of a sliding dog in the auxiliary gearbox, controlled by a lever in the cab. The winch was protected against overloading by a pressure-relief valve in the hydraulic circuit.

Wading

Like all of the post-war CT type vehicles, the 'Martian' was expected to be able to wade, with the minimum of preparation, to a depth of 762mm.

All of the standard FVRDE-designed electrical equipment was waterproofed, and the engine breather and fuel tank vent lines were connected into the air-intake system well above the 762mm water line.

A separate intake snorkel, often carried on the right-hand front wing, could be fitted. With this in place, and with other suitable preparation, the vehicle could be used for deep-water wading to a depth of 1981mm.

ARMAMENTS

The area of the cab roof immediately above the passenger seat was reinforced to accept a light machine gun, for example the .303 Bren or LMG.

Clips were provided in various positions in the cab and rear bodywork to accept the standard rifles in use at the time.

ANCILLARY EQUIPMENT

The following equipment is typically carried on the vehicle, but obviously not every item is carried on every variant:

Mechanics tools
Adjustable spanner, 200mm
Box spanner, AF and tommy bar
D ring shackle, 3 ton SWL
Pliers, sidecutting
Screwdriver
Starting handle
8 ton jack

Crew equipment
First aid outfit
Gloves, light duty (3 pairs)
Ration boxes
Tent and poles

Other equipment
Air hose, 10m long
Calculator, recovery load
Cooker
Cooking pot
Extension lamp
Fire extinguishers
Inter-vehicle starting cable
Jerry can
Non-skid chains (6)
Padlocks
Triple chain hoist
Tyre pressure gauge
Vehicle loading ramp
Water container

Pioneer tools
Axe
Pickaxe head
Pickaxe handle
Shovel

Recovery equipment
'A' frame assembly
Adaptor link for snatch block
Chain, 130mm long
Chain sling
Crowbar, 2135mm long
Emergency airbrake hose, adaptor and coupling
Extension light board
Floodlight
Folding saw
Gas bottles, oxygen and acetylene
Ground roller
Hacksaws (2)
Jib support
Jib warning light
Lamps
Pulley blocks (4)
Ramp for moving guns
Rope slings (4)
Rope, 37m and 18m length
Scotch blocks (2)
Searchlights (3)
Shackles (14)
Skid blocks (2)
Sledge hammer
Spreader bar
Towbar, 2285mm long

Vice
Warning light
Winch rope cover
Wire cutters
Wire rope, 10m long
Wire rope slings (2)
Wrecking bars (2)
20 ton jack

This equipment was either attached to the outside of the vehicle using clips and brackets provided for that purpose, stowed in the cab, or in the various lockers and compartments.

DOCUMENTATION

Technical publications
User handbooks
User handbook: tractor, 10 ton, CT, med arty, 6x6, Leyland, Mk 1. Army code 12239.
User handbook: recovery vehicle, heavy, 6x6, Leyland. Army code 13621.

Technical handbooks
Data summary: truck, 10 ton, GS, cargo, 6x6, Leyland Mk 1; tractor 10 ton, GS med arty, 6x6, Leyland, Mk 1. EMER N620.
Data summary: recovery vehicle, heavy, 6x6, Leyland. EMER N620/1.
Technical description: truck, 10 ton, GS, cargo, 6x6, Leyland Mk 1; tractor 10 ton, GS med arty, 6x6, Leyland, Mk 1. EMER N622.
Technical description: recovery vehicle, heavy, 6x6, Leyland. EMER N622/1.

Servicing details
Servicing schedule: tractor, 10 ton, CT, med arty, 6x6, Leyland, Mk 1. Army code 13615.
Servicing schedule: recovery vehicle, heavy, 6x6, Leyland. Army code 13608.

Parts lists
Illustrated spare parts list: recovery vehicle, wheeled, 6x6, Leyland. WO code 13837.
Illustrated spare parts list: truck, cargo, 10 ton, 6x6, Leyland; tractor, wheeled, GS, 10 ton, 6x6, Leyland. Army code 14886.

Repair manuals
Unit repairs: tractor, 16 ton, med arty, 6x6, Mk 1, Leyland. EMER N623.
Unit repairs: recovery vehicle, heavy, 6x6, Leyland. EMER N623/1.
Field repairs: tractor, 16 ton, med arty, 6x6, Mk 1, Leyland. EMER N624.
Field repairs: recovery vehicle, heavy, 6x6, Leyland. EMER N624/1.
Base repairs: tractor, 16 ton, med arty, 6x6, Mk 1, Leyland. EMER N624 Part 2.
Base repairs: recovery vehicle, heavy, 6x6, Leyland. EMER N624/1 Part 2.

Complete equipment schedules
Simple equipment: truck, cargo, with winch, 10 ton, 6x6, Leyland. Army code 33754.
Simple equipment: tractor, wheeled, GS, medium artillery, 10 ton, 6x6, Leyland. Army code 33832.
Simple equipment: recovery vehicle, heavy, 6x6, Leyland. Army codes 30552/1, 33833.

Bibliography
Breakdown. A history of recovery vehicles in the British Army. Baxter, Brian S. London, HMSO, 1989. ISBN 0-112904-56-4.

The Leyland Martian. Profile of the British Army's FV1100-series 10 ton 6x6 range. London, Wheels & Tracks, no 23, 1988. ISSN 0263-7081.

CHAPTER 4.6

THORNYCROFT LIGHT MOBILE DIGGER
NSN 3805-99-893-5335

For the common footsoldier, WW1 was a very static affair, with army pitched against army in a complex trench system spreading for miles across the Franco-Belgian border. The armies dug themselves in and stayed that way. Battles were fought and won, and men sacrificed in their tens of thousands, for literally just yards of ground.

By the time WW2 came, the armies were mechanised and mobility brought fluidity to the battlefield. Certainly the infantryman still needed to dig foxholes and latrines, and to conceal weapons, but there was not the same need for mile after mile of trench. The strategists must still have wondered if trench warfare was really a thing of the past, for in 1943, the Experimental Tunnelling Establishment, which had responsibility for investigating trenching techniques, commissioned a Bedford QLD designed for digging trenches.

In the event, nothing was to come of this project but some 20 years later, the Military Engineering Experimental Establishment (MEXE) at Christchurch, in Hampshire, came up with a sophisticated wheeled trenching machine based on a Thornycroft 'Nubian' chassis. This machine was able to dig a 610mm wide trench at a rate of 3.5m a minute. The vehicle's digging heads were hydraulically-driven by means of chains, and the transmission incorporated a 'creep' facility which allowed the vehicle to automatically move forward whilst digging was in progress.

The answer to a soldiers' prayer!

OVERVIEW

The Thornycroft light mobile digger was intended for the rapid excavation of slit and continuous trenches, and holes and pits for field defences in all kinds of soil. It was intended to be used by relatively unskilled operatives and, although special training was required, it certainly did not require the degree of skill called for when using, for example, a hydraulic excavator.

The vehicle was provided with four-wheel drive to ensure that, regardless of terrain, it remained fully mobile between operations, and was constructed on a 'Nubian' 3 ton, 4x4 forward-control chassis.

The digging equipment, consisting of a hydraulically-operated digging head, with chains and a spoil conveyor, was mounted at the rear end of two parallel boom arms. These booms could be slewed to either side to allow

CHAPTER 4.6: THORNYCROFT LMD

digging outside of the vehicle centreline.

The engine was coupled to the rear wheels for normal road use via a gearbox and two-speed transfer case, with optional front wheel drive for off-road operation. The digging equipment and 'creep' transmission were hydraulically-driven from the engine power take-off.

DEVELOPMENT

Work on the air-portable trenching machine, or 'light mobile digger' as it was officially described, began at MEXE in 1961.

A Thornycroft 'Nubian' 3 ton, 4x4, with a B81, Mk 5 engine, was chosen as a basis, employing a version of the chassis similar to that used in 1960 for a 13 ton commercial dump truck. The digging machinery and spoil conveyor were based on contemporary coal-cutting equipment, and the National Coal Board were said to have provided some assistance in the design.

The Thornycroft team included A W Pollitt who was Chief Engineer, E W Brown, Chief Designer, and Don Pearson who was the designer in charge of the 'Nubian' range. Reg Spencer from Rolls-Royce was also closely involved with the work.

The initial prototype was constructed in 12 weeks, and a fully-operational chassis was delivered to FVRDE for trials in February 1962. During these trials, the vehicle was used to remove more than 8000 cubic metres of soil, and was tested in a range of soil types including non-cohesive gravel, sand, chalk/flint, chalk, cohesive sand, clay/sand, and wet clay.

Initially, considerable difficulties were encountered with the rate of wear of the digging heads in anything other than soft soils.

In 1970, MEXE was merged with FVRDE to form the Military Vehicles Engineering Establishment (MVEE). Progress had apparently been slow, for the unfinished project now fell under control of the new MVEE organisation. In 1971, the vehicle appeared at the British Military Vehicles Exhibition at Chertsey, where it was still described as 'under development'. By this time, the vehicle was fitted with a B81, Mk 7 engine. The Rolls-Royce records show that just five of these engines were produced, which would suggest that there were no more than three development vehicles.

Production

Production work was carried out both at the Thornycroft works at Basingstoke, and by Leyland Motors at the Scammell plant at Watford. The actual number of vehicles constructed exceeded 100.

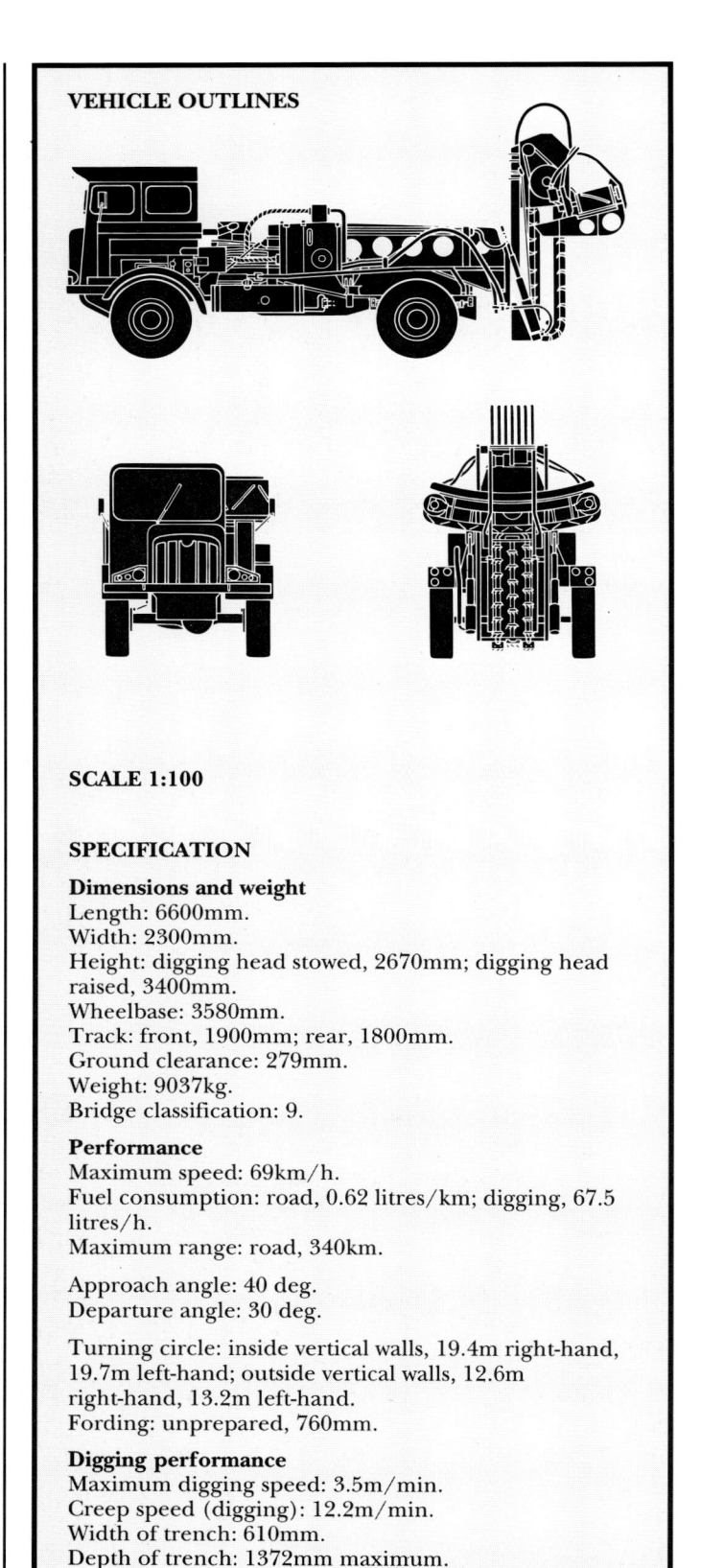

VEHICLE OUTLINES

SCALE 1:100

SPECIFICATION

Dimensions and weight
Length: 6600mm.
Width: 2300mm.
Height: digging head stowed, 2670mm; digging head raised, 3400mm.
Wheelbase: 3580mm.
Track: front, 1900mm; rear, 1800mm.
Ground clearance: 279mm.
Weight: 9037kg.
Bridge classification: 9.

Performance
Maximum speed: 69km/h.
Fuel consumption: road, 0.62 litres/km; digging, 67.5 litres/h.
Maximum range: road, 340km.

Approach angle: 40 deg.
Departure angle: 30 deg.

Turning circle: inside vertical walls, 19.4m right-hand, 19.7m left-hand; outside vertical walls, 12.6m right-hand, 13.2m left-hand.
Fording: unprepared, 760mm.

Digging performance
Maximum digging speed: 3.5m/min.
Creep speed (digging): 12.2m/min.
Width of trench: 610mm.
Depth of trench: 1372mm maximum.

CHAPTER 4.6: THORNYCROFT LMD

Prototype LMD undergoing digging trials (RS)

Production LMD showing digging equipment (RS)

LMD in action (RR)

'Issue 1' of the associated EMER was dated May 1976, so it would be reasonable to assume that the vehicle did not enter service significantly before that date. No FV number was allocated but the vehicle was assigned a NATO stock number (NSN 3805-99-893-5335)

Replacement and disposal
There was no direct replacement for this vehicle and all of the production total had been disposed of by 1990. At least three machines are known to exist in preservation, including the prototype.

In the army of the 1990's, this role is now filled by modified commercial back-acting excavators, usually with four-wheel drive.

NOMENCLATURE

NSN 3805-99-893-5335. Trenching machine, wheeled, 4x4, Thornycroft.

The machine was categorised as a 'Class C' vehicle.

DESCRIPTION

Engine
Rolls-Royce B81, No 1, Mk 5 (prototype vehicle), Mk 7D or 7D/2; wet sump.
Capacity: 6516cc.
Bore and stroke: 3.75 x 4.50in.
Power output: 210bhp (gross) at 3200rpm.
Maximum torque: 330 lbs/ft (gross) at 2500rpm.

Detail variations
Engine governor set at 3200rpm; compression ratio 7.25:1; oil filter mounted on crankcase; five-bladed cooling fan mounted on water pump; standard well-type sump; conventional clutch housing; twin exhaust manifolds with centre horizontal outlets; inlet manifold with horizontal flange for carburettor mounting; crankcase breather connected to carburettor inlet; distributor mounted lower on crankcase to give reduced height.

The engine suspension system incorporated additional rubber torque-reaction mountings at the clutch housing.

Transmission
The engine was arranged to drive through a twin dry-plate 275mm diameter clutch to a four-speed and reverse syncromesh gearbox. A short high-level propeller shaft ran from the gearbox to a two-speed transfer box, with two, long low-level shafts taking the power from the transfer box to the front and rear axles. The transfer box ratios were 1:1 in the high-gear range, and 2.26:1 in the lower range.

Axles on early vehicles were manufactured by

Thornycroft, and were both of the double-reduction driven type, with epicyclic spur gears at the wheel hubs providing an overall reduction ratio of 7.48:1. The later vehicles, which were produced by Scammell, did not have the hub reduction gears and the axles were possibly made by AWD of Camberley.

A power take-off on the transfer case, running at the high-ratio speeds was used to drive the hydraulic pumps.

Suspension
Live axles were fitted front and rear, suspended on semi-elliptic springs, with double-acting piston-type shock absorbers.

Steering gear
Marles cam and double-roller steering gear was used, with the drop arm connected to the offside wheel by means of a short drag link. The steering action was transferred to the nearside wheel by a conventional tie rod fitted behind the axle.

The vehicle was of the forward-control type (cab-over), with the steering box mounted close to the forward end of the offside chassis rail.

Braking system
Vacuum-assisted hydraulic brakes were fitted acting on all four wheels. The drums were 420mm diameter with 76mm wide linings; total braking area, 0.1 sq m per wheel.

The mechanical hand brake operated on the rear wheels only.

Road wheels
Standard WD 8.00B x 20in two-piece divided disc wheels, mounting 12.00x20, 14-ply run-flat (RF) tyres.

No spare wheel was carried.

A small 'David' mechanical compressor, driven by power take-off from the main gearbox, was provided for tyre inflation.

Chassis
Conventional ladder-type chassis consisting of deep channel-section side members, with eight welded cross members. The main chassis members were drilled for weight reduction beneath the cab.

The digging unit was mounted on a pair of deep boom arms, drilled for lightness, and mounted on the chassis by vertical pivots on the side members.

Cab and bodywork
An enclosed sheet-metal cab was fully glazed to the sides and rear, and designed to give protection to the operator, as well as providing all-round visibility during digging operations. The roll-up driver's door was of canvas.

Although production vehicles were fitted with an enclosed cab, the development versions consisted simply of a chassis on which the engine, transmission and digging equipment were mounted, and had no cab.

Electrical equipment
Standard 24V electrical system, wired negative earth; two 12V 50Ah batteries were fitted, together with a No 11, Mk 1 alternator.

Digging equipment
The digging equipment consisted of two channel-section boom arms, which normally lay parallel to, and along the chassis rails. The booms were vertically-pivoted on 'king' posts positioned approximately midway along the chassis. These arms projected to the rear of the chassis and, at their rear ends, carried a frame on which the digging head assembly was fitted. Components of the digging equipment were supplied by a number of manufacturers and assembly was probably carried out by the MEXE workshops.

The digging head, which could be raised and lowered to give a maximum trench depth of 1372mm, consisted of three hydraulically-driven chains, with an operating speed of 244m/min, fitted with digging claws at approximately 150mm centres. A transverse belt conveyor, running at 335m/min, removed the digging spoil to one side or the other of the vehicle.

The king post pivots allowed the boom arms to be slewed to either side of the chassis, some 10 degrees in either direction, allowing digging operations outside the centreline of the vehicle. In the stowed position, the digging head was pulled back to lay on the booms.

Whilst digging was in progress, the mechanical transmission was completely disconnected, and a secondary 'hydrastatic' transmission system allowed the vehicle to creep forward. The rear suspension was lockable to allow the digging head to start cutting.

DOCUMENTATION

Technical publications
Data summary: trenching machine, wheeled, 4x4. EMER Q080/1.

Technical folder: trenching machine, wheeled, 4x4. Army code 22469.

User handbook: trenching machine, wheeled, 4x4. Army code 60326.

Complete equipment schedule: trenching machine, wheeled, 4x4. Army code 31099.

CHAPTER 4.7

AIRFIELD VEHICLES
FV651/2, FV2241, FV6001, FV13402/3, FV14150/1, FV14161

It wasn't just the Army who were in love with the 'B Series' engines, the Royal Air Force seemed to think they were a pretty good idea too, using them wherever instant power, good old-fashioned low-down 'grunt', and long life were prime requirements. Examples included fire tenders and foam generators, aircraft tractors, and runway snow clearers. Of these, by far the majority were those engines used in fire-fighting applications.

Experience gained during the 1940's had shown that aqueous foam was an excellent medium for extinguishing all types of fire, as well as being able to help prevent accidental ignition of spilt fuel during the forced landing of an aircraft. With the added advantages of low-toxicity and cleanliness in use, foam quickly became established as the best extinguishing medium, and by the mid-1950's whenever new vehicles were procured, it was standard to specify fire-crash-foam tenders, which were designed to carry both water and foam compound.

During WW2, the RAF had used four types of fire tender, retrospectively designated Mks 1-4. The series continued into the 1950's with new designs, and 'B Series' engines were employed in Mk 5 and 7 fire tenders constructed on the Thornycroft 'Nubian' chassis, and Mk 6 machines based on the Alvis 'Salamander'. Although not forming part of this numbered series, it is also worth mentioning that in the 1970's, the RAF purchased just one example of the Alvis 'Stalwart', converting it for use as an amphibious fire and rescue tender (see Chapter 4.3).

The second largest application consists of those engines used in aircraft tugs. A total of 137 B80 engines were supplied to Douglas, and later to Sentinel, for heavy aircraft tractors.

Finally, there were a couple of oddballs: an experimental runway friction test vehicle on an Alvis 'Salamander' chassis, and a Douglas runway snow plough with snow-clearing equipment supplied by British Rotary Snow Ploughs. There was also a Pyrene foam-generator trailer employing a B81, Mk 7P engine; a dozen or so of these were produced for the Ministry of Aviation, but no further details are to hand.

ALVIS RUNWAY FRICTION TEST VEHICLE

There is an old aviator's expression which says 'a good landing is one you walk away from', and while there is a certain amount of truth in this, it can be argued that it is a rather simplistic view. The successful landing of an

CHAPTER 4.7: AIRFIELD VEHICLES

aircraft, as opposed to simply getting it down on the ground in one piece, depends on a more complex set of factors. These include, for example the speed and angle of approach, and the wind speed and direction. However, the braking effort available from the aircraft is also important, as are the tyre tread condition, and the coefficient of friction of the runway surface.

In the early 1960's, in conjunction with the then Road Research Laboratory (RRL) and the Ministry of Aviation, FVRDE modified an FV651 Alvis 'Salamander' chassis, fitting it with equipment to measure the coefficient of friction of the surface on which it was run. The RRL already had experience of such a vehicle, having modified a front-wheel drive Citroen 'Big 6' to take friction measurements from road surfaces.

The centre axle and wheel stations were removed from the 'Salamander' chassis, and the transmission modified to give a 4x4 configuration. A single test wheel, fitted with an aircraft tyre, was installed in the centre of the vehicle, together with dynamometer measuring equipment which was arranged to measure the forces at work between this wheel-and-tyre and the runway surface.

The vehicle was shown at the 1962 exhibition of British military vehicles at Chertsey, or to be more precise, it appeared in the printed exhibition guide. The only photograph which seems to exist is very heavily retouched which might suggest that, at least at the time the guide was produced, no vehicle actually existed. Certainly, there was no series production and no record of what became of this vehicle.

Description
Based on the 'Salamander' fire-crash-foam tender chassis, the runway friction test vehicle was modified to provide permanent four-wheel drive, together with a fifth non-powered wheel which could be progressively braked independent of the vehicle's main braking system.

The chassis was powered by a rear-mounted Rolls-Royce B81, Mk 8A engine driving through a fluid coupling to a pre-selective gearbox with five forward and five reverse gears, and a single-speed transfer case. The drive was taken from the transfer case to a central differential, and then by in-board drive shafts arranged in an H pattern, to bevel boxes at the front and rear axles, which incorporated dual epicyclic reduction gears.

Lateral torsion bars installed on the outside of the chassis, together with hydraulic telescopic shock absorbers, provided independent suspension for all four road wheels.

Hydraulic power-assistance was provided for the steering, which operated by recirculating-ball mechanism, acting

FV622 Alvis 'Stalwart' equipped as a fire/rescue vehicle (BTMC)

Alvis runway friction test vehicle based on FV651 'Salamander' (TMB)

FV6001 Prototype 'Salamander' fire-crash-foam tender (IWM)

CHAPTER 4.7: AIRFIELD VEHICLES

Prototype FV651 'Salamander' fire-crash-foam tender (BTMC)

FV651 'Salamander' tender with body and equipment by Pyrene (TMB)

Prototype FV2241 Douglas 'Tugmaster' heavy aircraft tractor (IWM)

on the front axle only. Hydraulic drum brakes, with 'Hydrovac' servo assistance, were designed to operate on all four wheels; the handbrake mechanism was mechanical, again designed to operate on all wheels.

The wheels were light-alloy WD divided disc type, 10.00B x 20in, mounting 14.00x20 cross-country tyres.

A fifth wheel was installed on a centrally-mounted swing axle which allowed it to be raised and lowered in relation to the runway surface, from inside the vehicle. A separate hydraulic braking system was connected to this wheel, together with dynamometer measuring equipment.

The braking system was arranged in such a way that a variable, but controlled load, of up to 5 tonnes, could be applied to the fifth wheel, and at the same time, the braking effect could be measured for various types of runway surface. The dynamometer would record the exact loading at which the wheel locked and the tyre broke traction with the surface.

Nomenclature
FV651 (modified). Runway surface friction test vehicle.

Dimensions and weight
Length: 5486mm.
Width: 2515mm.
Height: 3048mm.
Wheelbase: 3048mm.
Track: 2045mm.

Weight: 10,313kg, laden.

Performance
Maximum speed: 101km/h, on road.

ALVIS 'SALAMANDER'

In the early 1950's, the RAF took delivery of a new general-purpose fire tender, designated Mk 6. The vehicle was developed by FVRDE to meet an Air Ministry requirement for a high-performance, relatively high-speed, off-road fire-crash-foam truck, capable of reaching the site of a fire or aircraft crash with rescue equipment, and of delivering 40,000 litres of foam in two minutes.

The prototype, FV6001, appeared in 1953, based on the Alvis 'Saladin' chassis, and fitted with Pyrene foam fire-fighting equipment. Design improvements were introduced for the production vehicles, designated FV651 and FV652: the chassis was strengthened and reinforced, and the vehicles were fitted with fire-fighting equipment supplied by either Pyrene or Foamite. A total of 221 B81 engines was supplied to Alvis for this application, suggesting perhaps 120-150 vehicles.

And what better name for the Alvis fire appliance than 'Salamander', an elemental Greek spirit supposedly living in fire.

Description

Based on the 'Saladin' heavy armoured car chassis, the 'Salamander' was a high-mobility fire-crash-foam tender designed for fighting large aircraft fires. The vehicle featured permanent six-wheel drive, combined with independent suspension, and was capable of negotiating all types of terrain at relatively high speed. The specification was developed by FVRDE to make maximum use of tested suspension and transmission components from the FV600 range.

The vehicle was completely self-contained, carrying foam-generating equipment capable of producing 40,000 litres of foam in two minutes, and dispersing this from a roof-mounted monitor, or from side hoses. A 75 litre chlorobromomethane unit, supplied by the General Fire Appliance Company of Addington, was also installed, together with 30m hand lines for connection to the side outlets.

The 'Salamander' was powered by a Rolls-Royce B81, Mk 8A or Mk 8A/1 engine installed at the rear of the chassis, driving through a Daimler fluid 'flywheel' coupling to a Wilson pre-selective gearbox with five forward and five reverse gears, and a single-speed transfer case. A power take-off from the transfer case was used to drive the pumping equipment.

Power was transmitted from the transfer case to the centre axle and differential, and then by in-board drive shafts arranged in an H pattern, to bevel boxes at the front and rear axles, providing permanent six-wheel drive. The hubs incorporated dual epicyclic reduction gears. Lateral torsion bars installed on the outside of the chassis, together with hydraulic telescopic shock absorbers, provided independent suspension for all six wheels. Although the nature of the vehicle meant that it was unlikely to present operational problems, with its single central differential, the 'Salamander' would have suffered from the same technical deficiencies as the other six-wheeled Alvis chassis, exhibiting serious drive line wind-up when operating on hard surfaces.

Hydraulic power-assistance was provided for the steering, which operated by recirculating-ball mechanism, acting on the front and centre axles; the angle of operation for the centre axle was slightly reduced when compared to the front. Hydraulic drum brakes, with 'Hydrovac' servo assistance, were designed to operate on all six wheels; the handbrake mechanism was mechanical, again designed to operate on all wheels.

Later version of FV2241 Douglas 'Tugmaster' at FVRDE on test (IWM)

Sentinel-built FV2241 heavy aircraft tractor with enclosed cab (MP)

FV11501 Douglas 10 ton fire tender (TMB)

CHAPTER 4.7: AIRFIELD VEHICLES

Douglas/BROS 'Sno-Flyr' rotary snow plough

FV13402 3 ton 4x4 'Nubian' fire-crash-foam tender (IWM)

FV13402 3 ton 4x4 'Nubian' tender, Pyrene body/equipment (IWM)

The wheels were light-alloy WD divided disc type, 10.00B x 20in, mounting 14.00x20 cross-country tyres.

The body of the prototype vehicle (FV6001) consisted of a simple flat-panelled 'box', intended to house the crew and equipment, and to enclose the mechanical components. The cab, which was both insulated and heated, was designed to accommodate a crew of six including the driver, who was seated in a central position. Integral lockers and stowage facilities were provided for hose reels, power saws, ladders and other rescue equipment, and lighting equipment was installed for night operation.

The chassis of the prototype vehicle was very little changed from the Alvis 'Saladin' on which it was based, even retaining the distinctive wheel-arch lockers between the wheels. However, on the production vehicles, a number of modifications were introduced to provide additional torsional strength by the inclusion of box-section side and cross members.

Nomenclature and variations
FV6001. Truck, fire crash foam, 6x6
Prototype for FV650 series built by Alvis using a 'Saladin' heavy armoured car chassis. The vehicle was exhibited at the 1954 Chertsey exhibition of military vehicles.

FV651(A). Truck, 6x6, CT, fire crash foam, Mk 6, GP
First production version of FV650 series. Modified, reinforced version of Alvis 'Saladin' chassis, with foam equipment by Pyrene or Foamite, and bodywork by University Commercials and Coachworks.

FV652(A). Truck, fire crash foam, Mk 6A, 6x6
Second production version with foam equipment by Pyrene.

Dimensions and weight
Length: 5496mm.
Width: 2515mm.
Height: 3015mm.
Wheelbase: 1524/1524mm.
Track: 2045mm.

Weight: 13,717kg, laden (12,218kg for FV6001); 6249kg, unladen.

Performance
Maximum speed: 80km/h, on road; 40km/h, cross country.
Range: 160km.
Foam delivery: 20,000 litres/min for 2 minutes.

Capacity
Foam compound: 20,000 litres.
Chlorobromomethane extinguishant: 73 litres.

DOUGLAS 'TUGMASTER'

At the close of WW2, there was obviously no longer any need to maintain the same massive fleet of aircraft, and as the inventory returned to the reduced peacetime levels, the RAF found itself with a surplus of aircraft tractors. Although some of these tractors dated back to the 1930's, this surplus might have been all very well, but for the advent of larger aircraft, and specifically with the delivery of the 'V bomber' fleet. It quickly became apparent that many of these older tugs would no longer be sufficiently powerful, and new, heavier machines would clearly be required.

A number of the smaller David Brown tractors were retained, for example for towing smaller aircraft and air-conditioning and power-supply trailers, but in 1953 the RAF placed a pre-production contract for the supply of new standardised heavy aircraft tugs. The early machines, dubbed 'Tugmaster', were supplied by F L Douglas (Equipment) of Cheltenham, but an improved production version was subsequently produced by Sentinel.

Description

The 'Tugmaster' was a 6/8 ton, 4x4 heavy aircraft tug with a drawbar pulling power of 95 tonnes; it was also equipped with a winch and electrical generator.

A front-mounted B80, Mk 5N engine was mounted on a heavy-duty chassis, equipped with a 355mm Daimler fluid-flywheel coupling and four-speed Wilson epicyclic self-changing transmission, driving through a two-speed transfer case to either the rear wheels, or to all four wheels. The transmission configuration was selected to avoid potentially-damaging snatch effects during towing.

A Coventry 'Victor' horizontally-opposed four-cylinder air-cooled engine was installed forward of the rear axle, driving a 112V 10kW generator supplied by Vernon Industries, and intended to provide power for the aircraft's electrical equipment, and for the hydraulic braking and steering system. Contact was maintained with the towed aircraft by a cable intercom system.

Live axles were suspended on laminated semi-elliptical springs at each wheel station, without shock absorbers. The four-wheel servo-assisted brakes were air-pressure operated by means of a small compressor driven by an engine power take-off, and the handbrake operated mechanically on the rear wheels only.

The steering was hydraulic power-assisted, operating through a cam and double-roller mechanism. Wheels were 7.33 x 20in three-piece rims, shod with 11.00x20 cross-country 'bar-grip' pattern tyres; twin wheels were used on the rear axle.

FV14150 5 ton 6x6 'Nubian' tender, Pyrene body/equipment (BTMC)

FV14151 5 ton 6x6 'Nubian' tender, Sun body/equipment

FV14161 5 ton 6x6 'Nubian' RN tender, Sun body/equipment

A 7750kg capacity Darlington mechanical winch was fitted ahead of the rear axle for the recovery of damaged aircraft.

The mechanical equipment was enclosed by a simple open body with a fixed windscreen; bench seating was provided for a driver and engineer. There appears to have been more than one body style, and some Sentinel tugs particularly were fitted with an enclosed cab, possibly as a workshop modification at a later date.

Nomenclature
T/AH; RAF stores reference 16A/2239; FV2241. Tractor, 6/8 ton, heavy aircraft.

Dimensions and weight
Length: 6405mm.
Width: 2440mm.
Height: 2135mm (2185mm for Sentinel).
Wheelbase: 2794mm.
Track: front, 1880mm; rear, 1854mm.
Ground clearance: 311mm.

Weight: 13,745kg, laden; 13,644kg, unladen (12,536kg for Sentinel).

Performance
Maximum speed: 16km/h, on road.
Turning circle: 15.86m.

Capacity
Maximum towed load: 95 tonnes.
Maximum winch load: 6/8 tons.

Documentation
Tractor, 6/8 ton, heavy, aircraft. Air publication AP4566A.

DOUGLAS 10 ton FIRE APPLIANCE

Produced in 1961, and first shown at the 1962 British military vehicles exhibition at Chertsey, the Douglas 10 ton fire-crash tender was developed by FVRDE for the Ministry of Aviation to provide a fast, highly-mobile fire-crash tender for use on civil aerodromes. With 4500 litres of water and nearly 700 litres of foam compound on board, the vehicle was capable of dealing with fires in the largest types of commercial aircraft in use at that time.

It seems that the unit was not enthusiastically welcomed by the civil aviation authorities who preferred the similarly-equipped, but less esoteric 'Nubian' 5 ton, 6x6 appliances from Thornycroft. The production records show that just two engines were supplied for this application. This would suggest that possibly only one prototype was produced, and the vehicle certainly did not make it into production.

Description
Powered by a Rolls-Royce B81, Mk 7H, and designated FV11501, the Douglas fire-crash tender was constructed on a heavy-duty 10 ton off-road chassis intended to provide good cross-country performance.

The front-mounted engine was arranged to drive through a 280mm diameter twin dry-plate clutch to a four-speed and reverse synchromesh gearbox and three-speed transfer box. Driven axles were provided at front and rear providing two-wheel, or optional six-wheel drive. Suspension was provided by semi-elliptical leaf springs, inverted at the rear, with shock absorbers installed on the front axle only.

High-pressure air-operated brakes were provided for all six wheels, operating via a small compressor driven from the engine power take-off. A multi-pull ratchet-type handbrake operated mechanically on all of the rear wheels.

The steering was of the cam-and-roller type, with hydraulic power assistance. Wheels were of WD divided-disc type, size 15.00 x 20in, mounting 15.00x20 cross-country type tyres and tubes. Non-skid chains were available for the front wheels, with overall chains for the rear.

The pumping equipment could deliver a minimum of 3500 litres of foam per minute through two 65mm hose connections, drawing from water and foam compound tanks in the rear body: a monitor was installed on the cab roof. The enclosed body, with provision for a crew of six, was produced by Sun Engineering of Kingston-upon-Thames, Surrey.

Nomenclature
FV11501. Truck, 10 ton, fire tender (foam), 6x6, Douglas.

Dimensions and weight
Length: 8230mm.
Width: 2440mm.
Height: 3040mm.
Wheelbase: 4350mm.
Track: front, 1990mm; rear, 1910mm.

Weight: unladen, 11,820kg; laden, 17,180kg.

Performance
Maximum speed: 60km/h.
Range: 168km.
Foam delivery: minimum 3500 litres/min.

Capacity
Water: 4500 litres.
Foam compound: 680 litres.

DOUGLAS/BROS 'SNO-FLYR'

The 'Sno-Flyr' has proved something of an enigma.

A comprehensive technical description appeared in both the 1953 and 1956 editions of the Air Ministry 'Data book of RAF vehicles', together with photographs, which would seem to suggest that vehicles were actually in service. On the other hand, the only photographs which have come to light, and the only ones which have appeared in print elsewhere, are so heavily retouched that they might well be photo-composites, which would seem to suggest that no vehicles existed. The RAF Museum at Hendon have no details of the machine, and the Rolls-Royce production records, despite listing the vehicle, show that no engines were supplied for the application.

However, there is no doubt that the British Rotary Snow Plough Company (BROS) did supply some 'Sno-Flyr' vehicles to the Air Ministry, even though it is hard to say whether or not this particular vehicle actually existed.

Description
Designed for rapid removal and dispersal of either loose, or compacted and frozen snow from runways, aprons and access roads, the 'Sno-Flyr' consisted of a BROS rotary snow plough and casting system, Model M9A-270/360P, mounted on a Douglas heavy 4x4 truck chassis, with fully-enclosed bodywork.

Based on contemporary American designs, the BROS rotary snow plough used revolving blades to cut into frozen snow and break it up, with a chain-driven revolving feeding rake to deliver the loosened snow into a heavy-duty fan, or casting rotor. Adjustable casting chutes discharged the snow in a wide arc to either side of the unit, normally piling it alongside the runway.

The plough was fitted with gathering wings to either side, a revolving feeding rake, twin casting rotors, and two casting chutes. All of these components were mounted on a push frame extending under the front axle of the carrier vehicle, and hinged to the chassis. Raising and lowering actions for the ploughing equipment were controlled by Swift 'Hydromo' hydraulic rams. The rake was able to cut and undercut from 50mm to 2440mm, and the unit could clear a 4420mm wide path through light snow with the wings extended, or a 2794mm path through heavier snow with the wings folded.

The plough unit was driven by two Meadows 6PJ630 Mk 1/2 six-cylinder petrol engines, mounted in the rear body, and driving the casting rotors by means of Vulcan Sinclair 'Fluidrive' hydraulic couplings and propeller shafts.

A front-mounted Rolls-Royce B80, Mk 2K engine was used to power the chassis, driving through a twin dry-plate clutch of 280mm diameter, to a five speed and reverse gearbox, and a two-speed transfer case. Drive was transmitted to the rear wheels only, in either high or low ratio, or to all four wheels, using only the lower ratio; engagement of four-wheel drive was automatic when low ratio was selected.

Double reduction, bevel and double-helical gear axles were suspended on semi-elliptical leaf springs. Air-operated brakes were provided on all four wheels, operating via a small compressor driven from the engine power take-off. A multi-pull ratchet-type handbrake operated mechanically on the rear wheels only.

The steering was of the worm-and-nut design, with Lockheed hydraulic power assistance. Wheels were either of split-rim divided disc design, or were three- or four-piece types: size 14.00 x 20in, mounting 14.00x20 cross-country type tyres and tubes.

The bodywork consisted of a separate cab and rear body. The cab was of wood-and-metal construction, with separate seating for the driver and a plough operator. Bearing in mind the conditions under which the plough was likely to be used, the cab was very sensibly heated, and provided with powerful compressed-air operated windscreen wipers. The rear van-type body was of all-steel construction, fitted with three sliding doors on each side.

Nomenclature
RAF stores reference 16A/1758. BROS 'Sno-Flyr' rotary snow plough, model M9A-270/360P, type 35500 (Douglas).

Dimensions and weight
Length: 10,312mm.
Width: 2794mm, with gathering wings folded.
Height: 3355mm.
Wheelbase: 4423mm.
Track: front, 1930mm; rear, 1830mm.
Ground clearance: 200mm, with plough raised.

Weight: 15,527kg.
Bridge classification: 16.

Ploughing performance
Maximum speed, plough raised: 10-13km/h, according to conditions.
Ploughing speed: 0.4-24km/h, according to conditions.
Cutting width: 2794mm with wings folded; 4420mm with wings extended.
Cutting height from ground: 50-2440mm.

Turning circle: 26.23m.

Documentation
Data book of RAF vehicles: special-purpose vehicles, Douglas/BROS snow plough. Air publications AP2782A, AP2782C.

THORNYCROFT 'NUBIAN' FIRE TENDERS

The Basingstoke firm of Transport Equipment (Thornycroft) was one of the oldest established British commercial vehicle concerns, having started producing steam wagons in 1895. During the Great War, Thornycroft had supplied more than 5000 'J type' trucks to the War Office, and again between 1939 and 1945, the Ministry of Supply purchased some 5000 of the 1938-designed 3 ton, 4x4 'Nubian' chassis.

The 4x4 'Nubian' remained in production after the war, and in about 1952, prototypes of a 6x6, 5 ton version were produced using a modified version of the same chassis. Although essentially a commercial truck, the 'Nubian' was also available to both military and commercial customers with the option of a Rolls-Royce B80/81 engine in place of the Thornycroft diesel. With the addition of heavy-duty axles and wheels, the 'Nubian' was able to provide more than adequate cross-country performance, so when FVRDE started to look for suppliers for the new Mk 5 and Mk 7 RAF fire tenders in the mid-1950's, the proven Thornycroft chassis seemed the ideal solution.

The smaller Mk 5 machine was adopted to replace the 1944 wartime pattern tenders, many of which were still in use, while the larger, 6x6, Mk 7 was also intended for use on commercial airfields and Admiralty air bases.

Both versions of the chassis were equipped for fire-fighting and bodied by a variety of specialists including Gloster-Saro, Sun Engineering, Pyrene, and Foamite. Vehicles could be found in dual-purpose water/foam tender form as well as the more normal fire-crash-foam configuration. Versions of some of these appliances were also used by the Army.

Description
The 'Nubian' was a heavy-duty commercial truck supplied in chassis-cab form in 3 ton, 4x4 and 5 ton, 6x6 configurations. Alongside its general-service applications, the chassis was suitable for bodying as a fire-crash-foam tender to specifications laid down by the Ministries of Supply and Aviation.

A Rolls-Royce B80, Mk 1D, 2D or 5D engine was fitted in the 4x4 chassis; a B81, Mk 5Q or 5R was used in the 6x6. The engine was installed in a forward-control layout, driving through a 280mm twin dry-plate clutch to a unit-constructed four-speed and reverse gearbox, with two-speed transfer case: a power take-off on the main and/or transfer gearbox was provided to drive the pumping equipment. Drive was transmitted to the rear axle(s) only in high ratio, and to all axles in low ratio.

The axles were of the double reduction type, with spiral bevel gears, and hub-mounted epicyclic reduction gears. Suspension was provided by semi-elliptical springs, with double-acting piston type shock absorbers.

Steering was of the Marles cam-and-roller type. Wheels were 8.00B x 20in War Office divided-disc type, shod with 12.00x20 cross-country tyres.

The brakes were vacuum servo-assisted, or air-pressure assisted hydraulic, acting on all wheels; a mechanical handbrake operated on the rear wheels only, by means of rods and linkages or air pressure.

Specialist bodies were constructed by a number of firms and there were considerable detail variations, one vehicle to another. Most vehicles included a powerful roof-mounted foam monitor as well as hand lines.

Nomenclature and variations

TF/B80; FV13402. Truck, 3 ton, GS, fire crash foam, Mks 5/5A, Thornycroft
Basic Mk 5 RAF fire-crash-foam tender for airfield fire-fighting; carried water and foam compound sufficient for 10,000 litres of foam. 84 vehicles supplied.

TFB/B80; FV13403. Truck, 3 ton, GS, 4x4, fire tender, dual purpose, Thornycroft
Dual-purpose fire-crash and domestic water tender intended to supplement the FV651, Mk 6 fire tender; carried 3200 litres of water, with Coventry Climax pumping equipment capable of supplying 1350 litres per minute. 99 vehicles supplied.

TFA/B81; FV14150. Truck, 5 ton, 6x6, fire crash foam, GS, Mk 7, Thornycroft
Basic Mk 7 RAF fire-crash-foam tender able to produce up to 41,000 litres of foam, according to equipment fitted; had foam monitor and water/foam storage tanks.

FV14151. Truck, 5 ton, 6x6, fire crash foam, GS, Thornycroft
Fire-crash-foam tender developed for the Ministry of Transport and Civil Aviation for use on civilian airfields; carried 3500 litres of water and 450 gallons of foam compound, producing foam at a rate of 3150 gallons per minute from a centrifugal pump. Chassis was also available with plastic (GRP) cab.

FV14161. Truck, 5 ton, 6x6, fire crash, RN, Thornycroft
Dual-purpose water/foam tender intended for use on Royal Naval air stations; carried 4500 litres of water and 225 litres of foam. In addition to the B81 engine for motive power, a B60, Mk 5C unit was installed to drive the pumping equipment. 24 vehicles supplied.

CHAPTER 4.7: AIRFIELD VEHICLES

Dimensions and weight

	3 ton, 4x4	**5 ton, 6x6**
Typical dimensions (mm):		
Length	6020	6830
Width	2280	2270
Height	3015	3170
Wheelbase	3660	3730
Track:		
front	1860	1860
rear	1870	1960
Ground clearance, laden	330	330
Typical weight (kg):		
Laden	8890	12,254
Performance:		
Maximum speed (km/h)	89	96
Turning circle (mm)	1680	-

Documentation

User handbook: chassis, 3 ton, GS, 4x4, Thornycroft, Nubian, TF/B80. Air publication 4397A (UH).

General and technical information, and repair and reconditioning instructions: Thornycroft 'Nubian' TF/B80 FC, 3 ton, 4x4 chassis. Air publication 4397A, volumes 1 and 6.

CHAPTER 4.8

B80: MINOR APPLICATIONS & PROTOTYPES
FV401/2, FV1301/13, FV3523, FV4006, FV14001/4, FV14101/2/3

Although the quantities of B80/81 units produced did not match the number of B40 and B60 engines, the eight-cylinder engines were actually used in the greatest variety of vehicles. Examples ranged from the 'Saladin' and 'Saracen' AFV's, through the amphibious 'Stalwart', the Leyland 'Martian', and relatively low-volume machines such as the FV432 Mk 1, and the Thornycroft light mobile digger (LMD). All of these have been dealt with in the preceding chapters.

The Rolls-Royce production records show that a total of 4702 B80 and 3978 B81 engines were produced. By far the greatest proportion of the production went into the Alvis FV600 series. Of the vehicles not already described in preceding chapters, in total, some 400 were allocated to the 'Cambridge' tracked carrier project, which ultimately came to nothing; the 3/5 ton chassis produced by Albion, Thornycroft and Vauxhall; the 'Centurion' ARV winch; and a BOC/Tasker mobile oxygen plant. In this chapter, these applications are examined in a little more detail.

Other applications, not dealt with in this book include, for example: 67 B80, Mk 1D engines supplied for experimental use in WW2 Leyland 'Hippo' trucks; 11 B80, Mk 2 engines for the 'Oxford' CT24/25 tracked carrier project; 145 B80, Mk 5C engines for the Aldous Mk 7 harbour motor tug; 259 B80, Mk 5L engines used in the heavy ferry pontoon raft; and 113 B81, Mk 5A and Mk 5G units supplied to Vernon, City Electric and Petbow for use in generator sets and aircraft ground units. An unknown number of B80, Mk 1A engines was also supplied to India for military use, but no further details are available.

ALBION 5 ton CHASSIS

At the same time that Vauxhall declined further involvement in the FV1300, 3 ton CT chassis project (see the end of this chapter), it was decided that the payload would be uprated to 5 tons. A decision was also taken that the project would be continued under the design parentage of Albion Motors, who had already supplied some 6x6 FT15N chassis in the mid-1940's which were experimentally equipped with B80, Mk 1 engines.

It was also in about 1953/54 that the CT truck concept was discredited and the vehicle category was changed to GS.

Albion's approach was to use components from a fairly-conventional existing commercial chassis, designating the result WD66N. This produced a vehicle capable of carrying a 5 ton payload, and offering good performance both on and off the road.

The vehicle was produced in prototype form during 1955, and was shown at the 1956 exhibition of British military vehicles at Chertsey as a chassis-cab intended for use as a medium recovery vehicle, and as a complete vehicle with a steel cargo body by Strachans. The cost was stated to be £5650, close to the figure already agreed for the 3 ton FV1300 (see below).

The contract records show that somewhere between five and nine examples of FV14001 were produced, both with and without winch, and perhaps two examples of the FV14004. The project does not appear to have progressed any further and no series production was entered. One of the FV14001 cargo vehicles survived in commercial service as a wrecker with a Somerset garage for some years after demob, albeit with a Bedford engine in place of the Roll-Royce unit.

Description

The Albion was based on an existing commercial truck, and was supplied in chassis/cab form in 5 ton, 6x6 configuration. The chassis was intended to be bodied as a general service cargo vehicle or medium recovery tractor.

A Rolls-Royce B80, Mk 1D engine was installed, in a semi-forward-control layout, driving through a 280mm twin dry-plate clutch to a unit-constructed five-speed and reverse gearbox, with two-speed transfer case. Drive was transmitted to the rear axles only in high ratio, and to all axles in low ratio.

The axles were provided with worm gears to the rear, and spiral bevel gears to the front; the front axle was also equipped with hub-mounted spur reduction gears. Suspension was provided by semi-elliptical springs, with double-acting telescopic shock absorbers.

Steering was of the worm-and-roller type. Wheels were 8.00B x 20in War Office divided-disc type, shod with 12.00x20 cross-country tyres. Brakes were air-pressure assisted hydraulic, acting on all wheels; a mechanical handbrake operated on the rear wheels only, by means of rods and linkages or air pressure.

The cab was a strange angular affair with the engine installed under a square bonnet in a semi-forward control layout. In the practice of the time, a covered hip ring was installed in the cab roof above the passenger seat for an anti-aircraft gun.

FV14001 Albion 5 ton cargo vehicle (TMB)

FV14004 Albion 5 ton recovery vehicle chassis-cab (TMB)

FV3523 BOC/Tasker 15 ton oxygen plant semi-trailer (TMB)

FV401 'Cambridge' infantry carrier (prototype 4) (IWM)

FV402 'Cambridge' armoured observation post (prototype 1) (IWM)

FV4006 'Centurion' ARV from rear (TMB)

The cargo vehicle was fitted with a standard steel, drop-sided body constructed by Strachans (Successors) of Acton; the body was covered by a canvas tilt supported on steel hoops. The recovery vehicle was intended to be fitted with a mechanical winch, together with a hydraulically-operated recovery crane but no photographs appear to exist of the completed vehicle, if indeed there ever was a complete vehicle.

Nomenclature and variations
FV14001. Truck, 5 ton, GS, cargo, 6x6, Albion
Basic 5 ton, steel-bodied cargo vehicle: up to nine examples constructed in 1955.

FV14004. Truck, 5 ton, GS, medium recovery, 6x6, Albion
Chassis-cab supplied for use as a medium recovery vehicle, and intended to mount a 15 ton winch and 4 ton hydraulic crane; the prototype vehicle was fitted with a 10 ton winch but no recovery equipment.

Dimensions and weight
Length: 7163mm.
Width: 2438mm.
Height: 3277mm.
Wheelbase: 3180mm.
Track: front, 1899mm; rear, 1930mm.

Weight: laden, 12,710kg; unladen, 7220kg.

Performance
Maximum speed: on road, 56km/h; cross country, 25km/h.

BOC/TASKER 15 ton OXYGEN PLANT

After WW2 there was a widely-held view that Britain should become self-sufficient in the manufacture of all kinds of military equipment. There were two reasons for this. Firstly, the high rates of loss of equipment carried by the Atlantic convoys had demonstrated how vulnerable Britain was to naval blockade. The second reason was far more prosaic; the USA wanted hard currency and, in 1945, Britain had precious little of that left.

The Americans had produced trailer-mounted oxygen producing plant during WW2, and the FV3523 semi-trailer, with its British Oxygen (BOC) supplied equipment was an attempt to create a similar piece of kit.

The intention was that the plant would be used for producing oxygen in the field. The primary use would probably have been for oxy-acetylene welding plant (there was a similar trailer-mounted acetylene generator), but it is possible that the oxygen produced was of sufficient purity for medical uses. Oxygen may also have been in use at this time as a rocket fuel and perhaps the plant was intended for refuelling ATGW's which were becoming more widespread.

CHAPTER 4.8: B80 MINOR APPLICATIONS

Description

The FV3523 mobile oxygen plant consisted of a twin-axle 15 ton Tasker semi-trailer on which was mounted a thermally-insulated, enclosed steel body, housing equipment for the production of liquid oxygen. The equipment comprised a B81, Mk 5M engine driving a six-stage 15 ton capacity compressor, together with purifiers and storage plant.

Suspension was provided by centrally-pivoted semi-elliptic springs, and the trailer was fitted with pressure-operated air brakes and a ratchet type handbrake. The wheels were 8.00B x 15in, with 10.00x15 tyres; there were four wheels fitted to each axle.

The trailer chassis was supplied by Taskers of Andover; the body was constructed by Portsmouth Aviation; and the gas plant was supplied by British Oxygen Gases Company.

Rolls-Royce records show that eight engines were supplied to British Oxygen Company for use in 'oxygen and nitrogen generators'. There appears to be no further record of the latter but the Chilwell contract records show that just one oxygen generator was ordered, in 1957, so perhaps this is all there was. The trailer appeared at the 1962 Chertsey exhibition.

Bearing in mind the stated total weight of the trailer was more than 25,000kg laden, it's difficult to see what might have been available as a suitable prime mover. The AEC FV11001 'Militants', and the Thornycroft FV11401 'Big Ben' tractors were only rated at 10 tons, and while the Thornycroft 'Mighty Antar' tractors certainly had sufficient performance, being rated at 50/60 tons, it would appear that they were over-qualified for the job.

Nomenclature
FV3523(A). Semi-trailer, 15 ton plant, oxygen.

Dimensions and weight
Length: 9500mm.
Width: 2880mm.
Height: 3800mm.
Track: rear, 2240mm.

Weight: laden, 25,908kg.

'CAMBRIDGE' TRACKED CARRIER

It can be argued that the FV430 series (see Chapter 4.4) was the direct descendant of the ubiquitous WW2 'universal' or bren gun carriers, which had their origins in the 1930's. Both of these families of vehicle are well-known to most enthusiasts, but what is perhaps not quite so well-known, is that between them came two other types of tracked carrier, known as the 'Oxford' and 'Cambridge'.

FV4006 'Centurion' ARV on a No 6 'Centurion' bridge (IWM)

FV14101 'Nubian' 5 ton 6x6 cargo vehicle with early steel cab (IWM)

FV14101 'Nubian' 5 ton 6x6 cargo vehicle with later steel cab (IWM)

CHAPTER 4.8: B80 MINOR APPLICATIONS

FV14103 'Nubian' 5 ton 6x6 on a No 6 'Centurion' bridge (IWM)

FV14103 'Nubian' 5 ton 6x6 field artillery tractor (TMB)

FV1301 Vauxhall 3 ton 6x6 prototype, wooden ballast body (IWM)

The Cadillac V8-engined 'Oxford' CT20 tracked carrier was designed by the Wolseley division of the Nuffield Organisation at the end of WW2, and was intended as a direct replacement for the then-standard universal carrier. Although, in the event, the 'Oxford' was never produced in sufficient numbers, it did give rise to a number of prototype and experimental vehicles, which themselves were projected as possible replacements. Two of these, known as 'carrier, tracked CT24' and 'CT25', were designed and powered by Rolls-Royce. Eleven examples of the B80, Mk 2F engine were supplied for this application, and although these variants were not produced in quantity, in turn, they led directly to the post-war FV401 'Cambridge' tracked carrier and its derivatives.

The 'Cambridge' was first proposed in 1946 when 'War Office Policy Statement 26' set out the requirements for what was described as an 'Anglicised' version of the CT20 carrier. It was originally intended that the vehicle would be produced in eight variants including infantry carrier (FV401), OP team carrier (FV402), light artillery tractor (FV403), light GP carrier (FV405), command post (FV406), tentacle (FV407), ambulance (FV408), and command post (FV409).

It is often said that the army fights the next war with the strategies and technology of the last, and the 'Cambridge' carrier could certainly be used to demonstrate that there is at least some truth in that statement. The 'Cambridge' could be shown to have evolved directly from a pre-war design and must have seemed a curious anachronism one decade into the atomic age.

The vehicle was designed and built by Rolls-Royce, and although prototypes appeared in 1950, only the FV401 and FV402 versions were actually produced. Pilot models were issued for troop trials during the mid-1950's, but the number of vehicles involved cannot have been more than a dozen or so. The Rolls-Royce records show that 16 B80, Mk 5F engines were produced for this application and there was also an unknown number of Mk 2F engines.

It's a pity that there was no series production because the 'Cambridge' was the only post-war British military vehicle to be designed, built, and engined by Rolls-Royce.

Description
The 'Cambridge' was a simple light-armoured tracked carrier, produced in universal (infantry), and armoured observation post (OP) variants. The vehicle consisted essentially of little more than a mobile armoured box; the hull floor was double-skinned, with the outer plates arranged in a V formation to disperse mine blast.

CHAPTER 4.8: B80 MINOR APPLICATIONS

A Rolls-Royce B80, Mk 2F or Mk 5F engine was installed in the rear of the hull, driving the tracks through a five-speed Wilson pre-selective gearbox, or Hobbs semi-automatic clutchless transmission system, to a 'Cletrac' steering unit. Forward and reverse gears were controlled separately, and all five speeds were available in either direction.

The FV401 infantry carrier was designed to accommodate a crew of seven personnel including the driver; while the OP version was designed for a crew of five; both vehicles also included emergency seating for three on the padded transmission housing.

The hull of the basic FV401 was open-topped but torsion-bar assisted hinged flaps were provided at the sides, front and rear of the personnel compartment, arranged so that the compartment could be partially closed-down to protect against air blast. A grenade net was also provided for use when the blast shields were raised. The FV402 armoured OP carrier was fitted with a roof which enclosed the forward compartment. Hinged doors at the front and rear of the roof could be held open on stays to improve visibility. Both versions were fitted with a collapsible rubberised-fabric flotation screen.

Suspension was by four independently-sprung pairs of road wheels on each side, with hydraulic shock absorbers fitted between the front and rear wheels and the hull.

Unlike the FV430 series where the braking and steering system was combined, the 'Cambridge' used a 'Cletrac' unit to facilitate steering, with a separate main braking system controlled both by levers and a foot pedal. The main braking system could also be used for making skid turns.

The 460mm wide steel tracks were driven by sprockets at the front, with adjustable idler wheels at the rear; there were two upper track return rollers. The upper portion of the tracks was normally covered by sheet metal skirts.

Stowage bins were installed were provided at the sides and rear of the vehicle; the rear bins were hinged to allow them to be lifted clear of the hull perimeter in order that the rubberised-fabric flotation screen could be raised. The front plates of the side bins could be lowered to provide easier loading.

Nomenclature and variations
FV401. Carrier, universal, Cambridge, Mk 1
Open-topped universal tracked infantry carrier designed for seven personnel. Also known as 'Carrier, universal, No 4'. Modification instructions were also produced demonstrating conversion to the battalion anti-tank (BAT) role where the vehicle would tow a 120mm gun.

FV1301 Vauxhall 3 ton 6x6 with steel body (prototype 7) (IWM)

FV1313 Vauxhall 3 ton 6x6 artillery tractor, 25lb field gun (IWM)

FV1313 Vauxhall 3 ton 6x6 artillery tractor showing rear body (IWM)

FV402. Carrier, armoured, OP, Cambridge, Mk 1
Armoured observation post with a fully-enclosed, armoured forward compartment designed for a crew of five, and open area to the rear of the hull to accommodate the engine.

Dimensions and weight

	FV401	FV402
Dimensions (mm):		
Length:		
rear bins down	4674	4674
rear bins up	4362	4362
Width	3390	2553
Height:	-	2018
air blast shields down	1700	-
air blast shields up	1969	-
grenade net fitted	2033	-
Weight (kg):		
Unladen	7620	7620
Laden	9652	8890

Bridge classification: 12.
Ground pressure: 500kg/sq m.

Performance
Maximum speed: 56km/h.
Trench crossing: 1750mm.
Maximum gradient: 40%.
Maximum side slope: 30%.
Fording, unprepared: FV401, 1066mm; FV402, 1219mm.

Documentation
Provisional user handbook: carrier, universal, Cambridge, Mk 1, and carrier, armd, OP, Cambridge, Mk 1. WO codes 18362, 17767.

'CENTURION' ARV

In 1944, design work began on the 'Centurion' main battle tank.

Prototypes were first delivered in May 1945, and during a 15 year period, the 'Centurion' was produced in 13 marks, with production ending in 1961. With its 105mm L7A2 main armament, an all-up weight approaching 52,000kg, and Rolls-Royce V12 'Meteor' power plant, the 'Centurion' was an impressive and formidable machine.

Most of the production total was of the main battle tank, but other variants included an armoured recovery vehicle (ARV), beach armoured recovery vehicle (BARV), armoured vehicle Royal Engineers (AVRE), and two types of bridgelayer (see Chapter 2.3).

In its definitive Mk 2 form, the armoured recovery vehicle employed a B80 engine to provide electrical power for the main winch motor.

REME produced a Mk 1 prototype based on the existing 'Centurion' tug in 1951, with 10 production vehicles delivered that same year. These vehicles employed a Bedford engine to drive the winch, and it was not until the development of the Mk 2 that the Rolls-Royce engine was used.

Work on the much-modified 'official' FVRDE-designed Mk 2 ARV began in 1954 and, ironically, a certain amount of redesigning was necessary before production could begin. However, Vickers began manufacture, based on the Mk 3 tank chassis during 1956 at their Elswick factory, and the first batch of Mk 2 'Centurion' ARV's came into service the same year. Many remained in use well into the late 1980's, when they were replaced by Chieftain ARV's.

Description
Based firstly on the Mk 1 'Centurion' chassis and transmission, and later on the Mk 3, the 'Centurion' ARV consisted of an armoured box-like superstructure housing a recovery winch, with a hydraulic spade at the rear to provide an earth anchor for maximum pulling power. A hull-mounted 'A' frame jib, which was normally carried separately, could be installed on the front of the hull and raised to act as a crane for the removal or replacement of ARV power packs in the field, or for towing disabled vehicles.

The tank chassis was stripped of the turret and main armament to provide a basic chassis and power unit on which the ARV was constructed; the loss of the weight of a turret gave the vehicle a remarkable hill-climbing ability. The driver was seated at the front, on the right-hand side, with an armoured superstructure behind him designed to house the winch and to provide accommodation for the remaining three crew members. A roof-mounted commander's cupola provided facilities for a .303 Browning or 7.62mm pintle-mounted anti-aircraft machine gun. Stowage lockers were provided along the hull at each side.

The 31,000kg electric winch was powered by a B80, Mk 2P or Mk 5P engine; the capacity could be increased to 90,000kg by the use of snatch blocks. The winch generator and motor were rated at 400V, 160A at 3250rpm, with a maximum output of 275A. Designed to be able to provide maximum pull to the rear, the winch could also be rigged to provide a pull of 20,000kg to either side of the vehicle by the use of pulleys.

A large hydraulically-operated earth anchor was installed at the rear, and would have been normally raised for travelling. The crane jib provided a straight lift of 10,000kg using the winch.

Nomenclature
FV4006. Armoured recovery vehicle, Centurion, Mk 2.

Dimensions and weight
Length: 8966mm.
Width: 3390mm.
Height: 2895mm.

Weight: unladen, 47,247kg; laden, 50,295kg.
Bridge classification: 50.
Ground pressure: 9000kg/sq m.

Performance
Maximum speed: 35km/h.
Vertical obstacle: 915mm.
Trench crossing: 3352mm.
Maximum gradient: 60%.
Maximum side slope: 30%.
Fording: 1450mm.

Winching performance
Maximum straight pull: 31,000kg.
Maximum pull with snatch blocks: 90,000kg.
Maximum winching speed: 7625mm/min.
Jib: maximum lift, 10,000kg; towing capacity (folded), 5333kg.

Documentation
Illustrated spare parts list: tank, ARV, Centurion Mk 2. WO codes 17809, 12063.

Breakdown. A history of recovery vehicles in the British Army. Baxter, Brian S. London, HMSO, 1989. ISBN 0-112904-56-4.

THORNYCROFT 'NUBIAN' 3/5 ton CHASSIS

During the years 1939-45, the Basingstoke firm of Thornycroft had supplied some 5000 3 ton, 4x4 'Nubian' chassis to the War Office, mostly for use as general service cargo vehicles. Although the basic design dated back to 1938, with the addition of heavy-duty axles and wheels, the 'Nubian' had provided more than adequate cross-country performance, proving itself to be extremely reliable in service.

The model remained in production after the war, and in about 1952, the company also produced prototypes of a 6x6, 5 ton variant using a modified version of the same chassis. With the standard Thornycroft diesel replaced by a Rolls-Royce B80 or B81 engine, the two chassis types were included in the FVRDE inventory. Both the 3 and 5 ton vehicles were intended to be bodied as GS cargo vehicles, with the 5 ton vehicles also serving as field artillery tractors; documentation also exists which suggests that there was a 4x4, 3 ton artillery tractor version.

The total number of vehicles supplied, under three separate contracts, was perhaps 177; the 3 ton vehicles were produced between 1950 and 1953, while the 5 ton version was supplied from 1954 to 1957.

Description
The 'Nubian' was a heavy-duty commercial truck supplied in chassis/cab form in 3 ton, 4x4 and 5 ton, 6x6 configurations, and designed to be bodied as a general service cargo vehicle or artillery tractor. The 5 ton chassis was available in long and short versions.

A Rolls-Royce B80, Mk 1D, 2D or 5D engine was fitted in the 4x4 chassis; a B81, Mk 5Q or 5R was used in the 6x6. The engine was installed in a forward-control layout, driving through a 280mm twin dry-plate clutch to a unit-constructed four-speed and reverse gearbox, with two-speed transfer case; the two propeller shafts used to drive the front and rear axles were of equal length. Drive was transmitted to the rear axle(s) only in high ratio, and to all axles in low ratio. A mechanical compressor was driven from the main gearbox.

The axles were of the double reduction type, with spiral bevel gears, and hub-mounted epicyclic reduction gears; axle design was similar front and rear. Suspension was provided by semi-elliptical springs, with double-acting piston-type shock absorbers.

Steering was of the Marles cam-and-roller type. Wheels were 8.00B x 20in War Office divided-disc type, shod with 12.00x20 cross-country tyres. Brakes were vacuum servo-assisted, or air-pressure assisted hydraulic, acting on all wheels; a mechanical handbrake operated on the rear wheels only, by means of rods and linkages or air pressure.

12V electrical equipment was used on vehicles fitted with the Mk 1D engine; on other versions the electrical system was 24V.

The cargo vehicle cabs were supplied in two basic types: a traditional steel framed-and-panelled cab which was produced in two versions, and an alternative glass-fibre composite cab. The steel cargo and artillery tractor bodies were constructed by Strachans (Successors) of Acton, with the latter also being supplied by Park Royal Vehicles; early examples of the vehicle were fitted with wooden cargo bodies. Most versions had a canvas-covered hip ring in the cab roof above the passenger seat.

Artillery tractors were fitted with a 5 ton winch driven by a power take-off from the gearbox.

Nomenclature and variations

FV13402. Truck, 3 ton, GS, cargo, 4x4, Thornycroft
Basic wooden or steel-bodied 3 ton cargo vehicle. A total of 171 vehicles constructed during 1950/53.

FV14101. Truck, 5 ton, GS, cargo, 6x6, Thornycroft
Basic 5 ton cargo vehicle: three examples constructed in 1954/55. Chassis available in short and long versions, to suit 3813mm and 4270mm cargo bodies respectively.

FV14102. Truck, 5 ton, GS, cargo, 6x6, Thornycroft
Modified version of the basic 5 ton cargo vehicle, possibly a plastic-cabbed version of FV14101; one vehicle only constructed in 1955.

FV14103. Truck, 5 ton, GS, field artillery tractor, 6x6, Thornycroft
Medium artillery tractor with steel crew cab and rear cargo body.

Dimensions and weight

	3 ton, 4x4	5 ton, 6x6
Typical dimensions (mm):		
Length	6405	6786, 6325
Width	2337	2440
Height	3508	3278
Wheelbase	3660	3660
Track:		
front	1860	1860
rear	1870	1960
Ground clearance, laden	355	355
Typical weight (kg):		
Laden	8890	12,727
Unladen	4837	7227
Bridge classification	9	13
Performance:		
Maximum speed (km/h):		
on road	56	56
cross country	25	25
Turning circle (mm)	1680	-

Documentation
User handbook: chassis, 3 ton, GS, 4x4, Thornycroft, Nubian, TF/B80. WO code 17835.

VAUXHALL/ALBION 3 ton CHASSIS

It was always intended that the post-war CT family of vehicles would include a 3 ton, 6x6 chassis. The original FVRDE plan, produced in 1947, called for the vehicle to be produced in cargo, medium artillery tractor, signals, recovery tractor, telephone/radar repair and maintenance, and ambulance versions.

Even before any manufacturing work was begun, the range had been simplified and it was decided that only cargo, artillery tractor and recovery tractor versions would be produced, and twelve prototypes were commissioned by the Ministry of Supply from Vauxhall Motors in 1949. The first was to be delivered at the end of 1950, with the remaining examples to follow at monthly intervals. Unspecified 'difficulties' at Vauxhall delayed the delivery of the vehicles but nine had been delivered and were available for trials by early 1952.

The family was designated FV1300, and although FVRDE drew up specifications for all of the variants, the only versions which were prototyped were the single-cab cargo truck, with a 4270mm wheelbase, and the crew-cabbed medium artillery tractor, with a shorter 3660mm wheelbase. There was no series production and none of the other projected versions came to anything.

At an average cost of £5500 each, these vehicles were not cheap. Unfortunately they were also not particularly reliable either and problems were rife. In 1953 the trials were abandoned and the project cancelled, and although the Ministry did not publish a complete list of the problems encountered, the vehicle was described in War office reports as being 'inordinately complicated' and '...giving every indication of problems to come'. It was put on record that there were serious weaknesses in the frame design which led to an unacceptable rate of failure during cross-country trials.

Although no further work was carried out on the 3 ton chassis, the project struggled on for a couple more years with the chassis weight increased to 5 tons. However, before this happened, Vauxhall declined further involvement, or perhaps were not offered any further involvement, and the vehicle's design parentage passed to Albion (see above).

Description
The FV1300 series was a 3 ton, 6x6 medium chassis produced in prototype form as a long wheelbase cargo truck, and a short wheelbase artillery tractor.

A B80, Mk 1D engine was installed, driving through a Borg and Beck 280mm dry-plate clutch, to a three-speed forward and reverse gearbox, and two-speed transfer case; all speeds were available in forward and reverse.

Independent suspension was provided all round; there were lateral torsion bars at the front, with a complex arrangement of walking beams and torsion bars at the rear.

Two body styles were used: the artillery tractor was fitted with a four-door crew cab, with a small rear, wooden cargo body designed to carry ammunition; the cargo vehicle had a two-door cab, with a wooden-bodied drop-sided rear cargo bed. A roof hatch and hip ring were installed over the passenger seat for use by an anti-aircraft machine gunner.

Nomenclature
FV1301. Truck, 3 ton, CT, cargo, 6x6, Vauxhall
Prototype cross-country cargo truck with optional six-wheel drive.

FV1313. Truck, 3 ton, CT, medium arty tractor, 6x6, Vauxhall
Prototype medium artillery tractor designed for towing light/medium field artillery such as the 25 lb field gun. Fitted with four-door cab for a crew of six.

Dimensions and weight
Length: 6100mm.
Width: 2388mm.
Height: 2590mm.
Wheelbase: 4270mm, FV1301 cargo vehicle; 3660mm, FV1313 artillery tractor.

Capacity
Maximum load: 5090kg.

ALPHABETIC INDEX
Numeric entries in italic indicate photographs

A

Abbot 143, 157-163, *160 see also specific entries*
Aberdeen Proving Ground
    Champ 57
    Stalwart 141
AC, fuel pumps 32
Accessories, FVRDE-designed 8
ACoP's, Saracen 126, 131
ACV's
    Martian 163
    Saracen 126, 131
AC-Delco 17
Admiralty, Champ 61
AEC armoured cars 115
Air dropping
    Champ *62*
    Ferret 78
    Humber 1 ton 95
Airfield vehicles 179-188
Albion
    5 ton 24, 189, *190 see also specific entries*
    FT15N *12*, 17
    WD/HD/23 73
Aldous motor tug 189
Alternators 41
    Stalwart 146
    Thornycroft LMD 178
Aluminium engines 22
Alvis
    runway friction test vehicles 179, *180*
    Saladin *see Saladin*
    Salamander *see Salamander*
    Saracen *see Saracen*
    Stalwart *see Stalwart*
Ambulance
    Champ *59*, 60
    Pig 103
    Saracen 126, 129, 132
Amphibious capability
    Cambridge 194
    Ferret 82, *83*
    FV432 162
    Saladin 119, *119*
APC's
    FV432 157
    Pig 101
    Saracen 126
Applications, engines 20
Armaments
    Abbot 162
    Centurion ARV's 195
    Champ 65
    Ferret 86
    FV432 162
    Humber 1 ton 99
    Martian 173

Pig 110
Saladin 122
Saracen 135
Armoured command vehicles, *see ACV's*
Armoured personnel carriers, *see APC's*
Arnold, Wally 22
Artillery limbers, Stalwart *142*, 143
Artillery tractors
    Martian 166, *167*, 168
    Matador 166
    Nubian 196
    Vauxhall 3 ton *194*, 197, 198
ARV's, Centurion *191, 192*
Auroch 141
Austin
    3/4 ton prototype 91
    Austin Healey 3000 24
    Champ *see Champ*
    engine manufacture 20
    K5 17
Austin Western 165
Australian Army 79, 159
Auto Diesels 10kVA generator *72*, 74
AWD 178

B

B40 engines 12, *13*, 18, *30*
    carburettors 32, *34*
    clutch 38
    cooling fans 38
    distributors 40
    fuel pumps 32
    Ricardo diesel *14*, *15*, 23
B60 engines 12, *13*, 18, 23
    carburettors 32, *34*
    clutch 38
    commercial applications 24
    distributors 40
    fuel pumps 32
    lightweight version 22
    marine applications 23
    short stroke 22
B61 engines 11
    coolant flow 35
    water jacket 28
B61G engines 24
B61SV engines 11
B80 engines 12, *12*, 18, 23
    carburettors 32, *34*
    clutch 38
    commercial applications 24
    distributors 40
    fuel pumps 32
    inlet manifolds 32
    Ricardo diesel *16*, 23

INDEX

B81 engines 12, *13*, 23
   carburettors 32, *34*
   clutch 38
   commercial applications 24
   coolant flow 35
   distributors 40
   fuel pumps 32
   inlet manifolds 32
   water jacket 28
B81G engines 24
B81SV engines 11
   commercial applications 24
BAC Swingfire 93
   Ferret 82, 86
   Saladin 119, *119*
   Saracen 132
   Stalwart 144
BAC Vigilant 81, 93
   Ferret 86
Base overhauls, engines 43
Base standard, engines 43
Bentley
   4.25 litre engine 14
   Mk 'VI' 23
Berliet 141
Big-wheeled Ferret 81, *82*
Bilge pumps, Stalwart 146
Birkenshaw, Jack 14
BMC 57
BOC/Tasker, oxygen plant *190*, 191
Bodywork
   Albion 5 ton 191
   Champ 64
   Humber 1 ton 97
   Land Rover 70
   Martian 172
   Nubian 187, 196
   Salamander 183
   Sno-Flyr 186
   Thornycroft LMD 178
   Tugmaster 185
   Vauxhall 3 ton 197
Bore and stroke 16
Boughton winches 147
Braking system
   Abbot 161
   BOC/Tasker oxygen plant 192
   Cambridge 194
   Champ 63
   Douglas fire appliances 185
   Ferret 85
   FV432 161
   Humber 1 ton 97
   Land Rover 70
   Martian 170
   Nubian 187, 196
   Pig 108
   Saladin 121
   Saracen 133
   Sno-Flyr 186
   Thornycroft LMD 178
   Tugmaster 184
Breakage, piston ring 28
Brichrome wearing sleeves 28

Bridge, Centurion 72
Bridging
   Centurion 71
   Martian 168
Brightray exhaust valves 15
British Filters oil filters 34
British Rotary Snow Ploughs *see* Sno-Flyr
Brown, E W 176
BSF engines 27
BSF screw threads 16, 27
Budge (Military), A F 120, 132, 143
Bushell, John 22

C

Cab
   Albion 5 ton 190
   Humber 1 ton 97
   Martian 171
   Pig 109
   Sno-Flyr 186
   Stalwart 146
   Thornycroft LMD 178
Cable layer, Champ 60, *60*
Cambridge, observation posts *191*
Cambridge 158, *191*, *192*
see also specific entries
Camshafts 30
   bearings 31
   driving gears 31
Capital assistance
   Champ 58
   Humber 1 ton 92
Carburettors 15, 32, *35*
   Carter 33
   Solex 32, *35*
   Stromberg 24
Cargo vehicles
   Albion 5 ton 191
   Champ *58*, 60
   Humber 1 ton *92*, 94
   Martian *166*, *167*, *168*, *169*
   Nubian *192*, *193*, 196
   Pig *104-106*, 105
   Stalwart *140-142*, 143
   Vauxhall 3 ton *194*, 197, 198
Carriers
   Cambridge 158, *191*, 192
   CT24/CT25 11, 17, 158, 189, 193
   FV420 158
   FV500 158
   Oxford 11, 17, 158, 189, 192
   universal 11, 157, 192
Carter carburettors 33
Category 'B' vehicles, design 8
CAV 17
   alternators 41
   generators 41
   starter motors 41
Centurion, ARV's 71, *191*, *192*, *195 see also specific entries*
Centurion bridgelayer 71-73, *72 see also specific entries*

Champ 6, *8*, 9, *13*, 18, 55-66, *58-60 see also specific entries*
Chassis
   Champ 63
   Land Rover 70
   Martian 171
   Thornycroft LMD 178
Chieftain, ARV's 195
Chieftain 71
Chobham joint 108
Chobham magnetic compass, Champ *61*, 62
CKL International 84
CL vehicles, unsuitability 6
Clan Iron Foundry 15
Clansman, Ferret 87
Cletrac steering gear 194
Clutch 38
Coils, ignition *36*
Cold start equipment, Ki-gass 13, 33, *34*
Combat vehicles *see CT vehicles*
Combustion chambers, design 15
Commercial applications, engines 13, 23
Commercial variations
   Champ 62
   Humber 1 ton 96
   Martian 167
Commonality, engine components 12
Complexity, category 'B' vehicles 9
Component interchangeability, engines 42
Connecting rods 29
Cooling fans 38
Cooling system 35
Corporal missiles 90, 95
Coventry Victor engines 184
Cranes
   Atlas 143, 146
   Austin Western 165
   Centurion ARV's 196
   HIAB 143, 146
   Jones KL66 42, *72*, 73
   Martian 165, 172
   Stalwart 139, 146
Crankcases 28
Crankshafts 28
   bearings 29
   dampers 29
   seals 29
Crossley Motors 115, 117, 125
CT vehicles 6
   discontinuation 10
CT24/CT25 carriers 11, 158, 189, 193
Cylinder blocks 28
Cylinder heads 30

D

Daimler
   Dingo 78, 79, 85

   Ferret *see Ferret*
   Mk 2 armoured cars 115, 116
Darlington winches 185
David Brown 184
David Korrect, fuel pumps 32
Defects
   Champ 58
   Humber 1 ton 92
Dennis
   fire appliances 24
   FV1200 series *9*, 163
Derby Bentley 4.25 litre engine 14
Design, category 'B' vehicles 8
Design parents 8
Deutz diesel engines 84
Development
   Abbot 158
   Albion 5 ton 189
   B Series engines 11
   Cambridge 193
   Centurion ARV's 195
   Champ 56
   Ferret 78
   FV432 158
   Humber 1 ton 91
   Land Rover 68
   Martian 165
   Nubian 187, 196
   Pig 102
   Saladin 116
   Saracen 127
   Stalwart 139
   Thornycroft LMD 176
   Vauxhall 3 ton 197
Diesel engines 24
   Champ *14*, *15*, 23, 62
   Deutz 84
   K60 25, 141, 157, 160
   Perkins Phaser 84, 120, 132, 143
   Ricardo *14*, *15*, 23, 62
Dimensions
   Abbot 159
   Albion 5 ton 191
   Auto Diesels 10kVA generator 74
   BOC/Tasker oxygen plant 192
   Cambridge 195
   Centurion bridgelayer 72
   Champ 57
   Douglas fire appliances 185
   engines 16, 29
   Ferret 79
   FV432 159
   Humber 1 ton 91
   Jones KL66 crane 73
   Land Rover 68
   Martian 165
   Nubian 187, 197
   Pig 103
   Saladin 117
   Salamander 181, 183
   Saracen 127
   Sno-Flyr 186

INDEX

Stalwart 139
Thorncroft LMD 176
Tugmaster 185
Vauxhall 3 ton 198
Dingo 78, 79, 85
Disposal
   Champ 59
   Ferret 80
   FV432 160
   Land Rover 69
   Martian 167
   Pig 104
   Saladin 118
   Saracen 130
   Stalwart 142
   Thornycroft LMD 177
Distributors *36*, *40*
Documentation
   Auto Diesels 10kVA generator 74
   Cambridge 195
   Centurion ARV's 196
   Centurion bridgelayer 73
   Champ 65
   engines 44
   Ferret 88
   FV432 162
   Humber 1 ton 100
   Jones KL66 crane 73
   Martian 174
   Nubian 187
   Pig 111
   Saladin 124
   Saracen 136
   Sno-Flyr 187
   Stalwart 147
   Thornycroft LMD 178
   Tugmaster 185
Dodge WC Series 89, 91
Douglas
   aircraft tugs *see* Tugmaster
   fire appliances 24, 185 *see also specific entries*
Douglas/BROS, runway snow ploughs *see* Sno-Flyr
Dowty Hydrojet 137, 139, 140, 142, 145
Driveline wind-up
   Saladin 118
   Saracen 129
   Stalwart 142
DUKW's 137-139
Dunn, Willy 139

E

Earth anchors, Centurion ARV's 195
EDBRO-B&E Tippers 164
Electrical equipment
   Abbot 161
   Champ 64
   Ferret 86
   FV432 161
   Humber 1 ton 98
   Land Rover 70

Martian 172
Nubian 196
Pig 109
Saladin 122
Saracen 134
Stalwart 146
Thornycroft LMD 178
EMI Ranger 144
Engine life 43
Engine service record 43, *40*
Engines 11-44, *30-33 see also specific entries*
   Abbot 161
   aircraft ground units 189
   Albion 5 ton 190
   Aldous motor tug 189
   B40, B60/61, B80/81 *see specific entries*
   BOC/Tasker oxygen plant 192
   Cambridge 194
   Centurion ARV's 195
   Champ 62, 63
   Coventry Victor 184
   CT24/CT25 carriers 189
   Deutz diesel 84
   Douglas fire appliances 185
   Ferret 84
   FV432 *33*, 161
   heavy ferry 189
   Hippo 189
   Humber 1 ton 96
   K60 25, 141, 157, 160
   Land Rover 70
   Martian 169
   Meadows 186
   Meteor 71, 195
   Meteorite 163
   Nubian 187, 196
   Oxford carriers 189
   Perkins Phaser diesel 84, 120, 132, 143
   Petbow generator sets 189
   Pig 107
   Ricardo diesel *14-16*, 23, 62
   Saladin 120
   Salamander 180, 182
   Saracen 132
   Snippet 23
   Sno-Flyr 186
   Stalwart 144
   Thornycroft LMD 177
   Tugmaster 184
   Vauxhall 3 ton 197
ERF trucks 24
Executive Committee Army Council 6
Exhaust valves 31
Expenditure
   Champ 10
   Humber 1 ton 10, 91
Experimental development, engines 22
Experimental Tunnelling Establishment 175
Explorer, Scammell 166

Explosive ordnance disposal, Pig 106

F

F60 engines 23, 24
FACE field artillery computer equipment 126
Fans, cooling 38
FB60 engines 24
Ferret 11, 18, 39, 77-88, *80-84*, 104, 133 *see also specific entries*
Ferry, heavy 23
FFW/FFR
   Champ *59*, 60
   Humber 1 ton *93*, 95
   Pig 103
   Stalwart 144
Fieldmouse 78
Fighting Vehicles Research and Development Executive *see* FVRDE
Fire tenders
   Douglas 185
   Nubian 187
   RAF 179
   RN 187
   Salamander 182
Firewire 146
Fire-fighting equipment
   Douglas fire appliances 185
   Ferret 86
   Foamite 181, 187
   Gloster-Saro 187
   Pyrene 181, 187
   Saladin 122
   Salamander 183
   Saracen 135
   Stalwart 146
   Sun Engineering 185, 187
Fisher & Ludlow 64, 92
Floating Ferret 81, *81*
Flotation screens
   Cambridge 194
   Ferret 82, *83*
   FV432 158, 162
   Saladin 119, *119*
Fluid flywheels 38, 39
Flying Pig 106, *107*
Foamite, fire-fighting equipment 181, 187
Foden 167
Fording seals *39*, 42
Fox 25, 80, 119
French Army 79, 141
Fuel consumption, engines 29
Fuel pumps 32, *34*
Fuel system 31
FV numbers 6
FV1100 series *see* Martian
FV1101 *see* Martian
FV1103 *see* Martian
FV1110 *see* Martian
FV11103 *see* Jones KL66 crane
FV1111 *see* Martian
FV1113 *see* Martian

FV1114 *see* Martian
FV1118 *see* Martian
FV1119 *see* Martian
FV1121 *see* Martian
FV1122 *see* Martian
FV11301 166
FV1200 series *see* Leyland FV1200
FV1300 series *see* Vauxhall 3 ton
FV1301 *see* Vauxhall 3 ton
FV1313 *see* Vauxhall 3 ton
FV13402 *see* Nubian
FV13403 *see* Nubian
FV14000 series *see* Albion 5 ton
FV14001 *see* Albion 5 ton
FV14004 *see* Albion 5 ton
FV14101 *see* Nubian
FV14102 *see* Nubian
FV14103 *see* Nubian
FV14150 *see* Nubian
FV14151 *see* Nubian
FV14161 *see* Nubian
FV1600 series *see* Humber 1 ton
FV16003 98
FV1601 *see* Humber 1 ton
FV1604 *see* Humber 1 ton
FV1609 *see* Pig
FV1611 *see* Pig
FV1612 *see* Pig
FV1613 *see* Pig
FV1620 *see* Pig
FV1621 *see* Humber 1 ton
FV1622 *see* Humber 1 ton
FV1800 series *see* Champ
FV18001 *see* Land Rover
FV1801 *see* Champ
FV1802 *see* Champ
FV2241 *see* Tugmaster
FV2308 95
FV2401 *see* Centurion bridgelayer
FV3523 *see* BOC/Tasker
FV4002 *see* Auto Diesels
FV4006 *see* Centurion ARV
FV401 *see* Cambridge
FV402 *see* Cambridge
FV403 *see* Cambridge
FV405 *see* Cambridge
FV406 *see* Cambridge
FV407 *see* Cambridge
FV408 *see* Cambridge
FV409 *see* Cambridge
FV420 158
FV421 158
FV430 192
FV430 series *see* FV432
FV431 137, 140, 159
FV432 25, 102, 126, 130, 141, 157-163, *160 see also specific entries*
FV433 *see* Abbot
FV500 series 158
FV600 series *see* Saladin, Saracen, Stalwart
FV6001 *see* Salamander
FV601 *see* Saladin
FV603 *see* Saracen
FV604 *see* Saracen

THE ROLLS-ROYCE 'B SERIES' ENGINE

INDEX

FV610 see Saracen
FV620 see Stalwart
FV622 see Stalwart
FV623 see Stalwart
FV624 see Stalwart
FV651 see Salamander
FV652 see Salamander
FV701 see Ferret
FV703 see Ferret
FV711 see Ferret
FV712 see Ferret
FVRDE 6, 17
   design team 14
FVRDE specification '2051' 40

G

G60 engines 24
Gama Goat 138
Gas-burning engines 24
General Fire Appliance Co, 182
General service vehicles see GS vehicles
General Staff Operational Requirement '1061' 141
General Staff Policy Statements
   '2' 116
   '35' 6, 10
   '66' 125, 127
Generators 39, 41
   Centurion ARV's 195
   Champ 64
   Ferret 86
   Humber 1 ton 98
   Land Rover 70
   Martian 172
   Pig 110
   Saladin 122
   Saracen 135
   Tugmaster 184
   two-speed 34
   Vernon Industries 184
GKN 25 see also FV432
GKN Defence 84
GKN-Sankey 102, 160
Gloster-Saro
   fire-fighting equipment 187
   UBRE 144
GM-Allison TX200 transmission 158, 161
Governors, engine 42
Green Archer 101, 107
Griffiths, George 14
Grylls, Harry 16
GS vehicles 6, 9
GSOR '1061' 141
GSPS
   '2' 116
   '35' 6, 10
   '66' 125, 127
Gun platform, Champ 60, 61
Gutty 57, 58

H

Hanomag 23
Harimau 84
HCB-Angus, fire appliances 24
Head, Sir Antony 91
Heavy ferry 189
Henry, Freddie 56
Henschel 23
Herbert Morris winches 147
Hippo 12, 17, 189
Hobbs transmission, Cambridge 194
Hornet 90, 101, 105, 106, 109
Hotchkiss 23
Hoverlift trailer, B80 engines 18
Hudsons 69
Hull
   Abbot 161
   Cambridge 194
   Centurion ARV's 195
   Ferret 85
   FV432 161
   Pig 108
   Saladin 121
   Saracen 134
   Stalwart 145
Humber
   1 ton 6, 8, 9, 89-100, 92-95 see also specific entries
   Pig see Pig
Hydraulic power coupling 39
Hydraulic pumps, Centurion bridgelayer 38
Hydrojet 137, 139, 140, 142, 145

I

Ignition coils 36, 41
Ignition filters 38, 40
Ignition system 40
Inlet manifolds 32
Inlet valves 31
Iso-Speedic engine governors 31, 42
Issigonis, Alec 56

J

Jaguar XK engines 25
Jeep 55, 57, 59, 67, 70
Jenner, Charles (Jnr) 14
Jones KL66 crane 72, 73

K

K60 engines 25, 141, 157, 160
Kemp, Andrew 139
Ki-gass cold start equipment 13, 33, 34
Kremlin 130, 132
Kuwaiti Army 129
K&L Steel Founders and Engineers 73

L

L3A1/L5A1 gun 117, 122
L7A2 gun 195
Land Rover 56, 59, 67-70, 69, 93 see also specific entries
LARC amphibians 137
Larkspur
   Champ 56, 65
   Ferret 86
   FV432 162
   Humber 1 ton 100
   Pig 111
   Saladin 123
   Saracen 135
   Stalwart 147
Leaded fuels 32
Leyland
   FV1200 series 9, 163
   Hippo 12, 17
   Martian see Martian
Leyland Motors 18, 71, 176
LRDG, Champ 61
Lubrication systems 33
Lucas 17

M

Machine gun mountings
   Champ 65
   Ferret 86
   Saladin 123
   Saracen 135
Mack 164
Magnicon alternators 74
Maintenance, problems 5
Malkara 90, 93, 101, 110
   launcher 105, 106
   missile supply truck 93, 95, 98
   missile test truck 93, 95, 98
Mann-Egerton 164
Manufacturers, engines 18
Marine applications 23
Mark designations, engines 13
Marshalls of Cambridge 93, 95, 164
Martian 6, 9, 18, 163-174, 166-169 see also specific entries
McFarlane Engineering 74
Meadows
   engines 186
   gearboxes 144
Merlin engines 18
Meteor engines 71, 195
Meteorite engines 163
MEXE 168, 175, 176, 178
Military acceptance, engines 17
Military Engineering Experimental Establishment see MEXE
Military Vehicles Engineering Establishment see MVEE
Miller, Doug 14
Mine destroyer, Ferret 83
Mine proofing, Ferret 82
Mobat 56
Morris C8 18
Mosquito 57
Mudlark 57, 58, 68
   wading 40, 62
Murray, R J 91
MVEE 176

N

National Coal Board 176
NBC filtration 158
Nomenclature
   Abbot 161
   Albion 5 ton 191
   Auto Diesels 10kVA generator 74
   BOC/Tasker oxygen plant 192
   Cambridge 194
   Centurion ARV's 196
   Centurion bridgelayer 72
   Champ 59
   Douglas fire appliances 185
   engines 12
   Ferret 80
   FV432 161
   Humber 1 ton 94
   Jones KL66 crane 73
   Land Rover 69
   Martian 167
   Nubian 187, 197
   Pig 104
   Saladin 119
   Salamander 181, 183
   Saracen 130
   Sno-Flyr 186
   Stalwart 143
   Thornycroft LMD 177
   Tugmaster 185
   Vauxhall 3 ton 198
Nubian 175, 179, 192, 193, 196 see also specific entries
Nuffield Mechanisations 57

O

Observation posts, Cambridge 191
Octane rating 32
Oil coolers 34
Oil filters 34
Oil pressure relief valves 35
Oil pressure switches 42
Oil pumps 34
Oxford carriers 11, 158, 189, 192
Oxygen plant 191

P

Packaging, engines 18
Panhard AML 79
Park Royal Vehicles 164
Pearson, Don 176
Performance
   Abbot 159
   Albion 5 ton 191
   Auto Diesels 10kVA generator 74
   Cambridge 195
   Centurion ARV's 196
   Centurion bridgelayer 73
   Champ 57
   Douglas fire appliances 185
   engines 29
   Ferret 79
   FV432 159
   Humber 1 ton 91

INDEX

Jones KL66 crane 73
  Land Rover 68
  Martian 165
  Nubian 187, 197
  Pig 103
  Saladin 117
  Salamander 181, 183
  Saracen 127
  Sno-Flyr 186
  Stalwart 139
  Thornycroft LMD 176
  Tugmaster 185
Perkins Phaser diesel engines 132, 143
  Ferret 84
  Saladin 120
Phantom III 16
Phantom IV 24
Phillips, Jack 14
Pig *13, 31*, 101-112, *104, 105*, 126, 130 see also specific entries
Piglet 104
Pioneer, Scammell 17
Piston rings *28*, 30
Pistons 29
Pollitt, A W 176
Power couplings 38
Power take-offs, engines 42
Prices
  Albion 5 ton 190
  Champ 58
  Champ engines 15
  engines 15
  Humber 1 ton 92
  Land Rover 15
  Martian 165
  Stalwart 141
  Vauxhall 3 ton 197
Production
  Abbot 160
  Champ 57
  engines 18
  Ferret 79
  FV432 160
  Humber 1 ton 92
  Land Rover 68
  Martian 166
  Pig 103
  Saladin 117
  Salamander 181
  Stalwart 141
  Thornycroft LMD 176
Production data
  Abbot 160
  Albion 5 ton 190
  BOC/Tasker oxygen plant 192
  Cambridge 193
  Centurion ARV's 195
  Champ 59
  engines 22
  Ferret 79
  FV432 160
  Humber 1 ton 92
  Land Rover 69
  Martian 167

Nubian 187, 196
  Pig 104
  Saladin 117
  Salamander 181
  Stalwart 141
  Thornycroft LMD 176
Propulsion system, Stalwart 145
Prototypes, engines 17
Pyrene
  fire-fighting equipment 181, 187
  foam-generator trailer 179

R

Radar
  Ferret 83, *84*
  Green Archer 101, 107
  No 9 Mk 1, Robert 130, 132
  Saladin 120
  Saracen 130, 132
  ZB '298' 83, *84*, 120
Radio equipment
  Champ 65
  Ferret 86
  FV432 162
  Humber 1 ton 99
  Pig 111
  Saladin 123
  Saracen 135
  Stalwart 147
Radio screening 40
RAF fire tenders
  Mk '5' 179, *184*, 187
  Mk '6' 179, *180*, 181, *181*
  Mk '7' 179, *184*, 187
  Mks '1-4' 179
Ranger mine-laying 144
RARDE 117, 122
Rear axle, Champ 58
Recovery equipment
  Austin Western 165
  Eka 167
  Martian 172, 173
  ROF 172
Recovery vehicles
  Ferret 83, *84*
  Foden 167
  Martian 164, 166, *166*
  Scammell 167
  Vauxhall 3 ton 197
REME 59
  Centurion tugs 195
  engine repair policy 43
  fitters' vehicles, Stalwart *142*, 144
Replacement
  B Series engines 25
  Champ 59
  Ferret 80
  FV432 160
  Humber 1 ton 93
  Land Rover 69
  Martian 167
  Pig 104
  Saladin 118

Saracen 130
  Stalwart 142
  Thornycroft LMD 177
Reverse flow cooling, Saracen *128*, 129, 132
Ricardo diesel engines 14-16, 23
  Champ *14, 15*, 23, 62
Rings, piston *28*, 30
Riot control, Pig 106
RN
  Champ 61
  fire tenders 187
Road Research Laboratory 180
Road wheels, *see wheels*
Robinson, Les 14
Robotham, Roy 10, 11, 14
ROF
  105mm rifled gun 158, 162
  recovery equipment 164, 172
  Leeds 71
  Woolwich 103
Rootes Group 89
Royal Armaments Research and Development Establishment 117, 122
Royal Navy
  Champ 61
  fire tenders 187
Royal Ordnance Factories *see ROF*
Royce, Sir Henry 14, 16
Rubery Owen 92
Runway friction test vehicles 179

S

Saladin 11, *16, 18*, 115-124, *118-120*, 133, 139 see also specific entries
Salamander *13, 17*, 139, 179, 180, *180, 181* see also specific entries
Samaritan 25
Samson 25
Sankey, J 102, 160
Saracen 101, 115, 118, 125-136, *128-131*, 139, 157 see also specific entries
Saro-Gill Hydrojet 140
Saxon 104, 160
Scammell
  Explorer 166
  Pioneer 17
Scimitar 25
Scorpion 25, 119
Screw threads 16, 27
Sentinel aircraft tugs 184, 185 *see also Tugmaster*
Service record, engines 43, *40*
Sewell, Charles (Rex) 56
Silver Dawn 23
Silver Ghost 16
Silver Wraith 23

Simms 17
  generators 41
  starter motors 41
Slip, fluid flywheel 39
SMMT 5, 9
Snippet engines 23
Snow ploughs, Sno-Flyr 186
Sno-Flyr 179, *183*, 186 see also specific entries
Society of Motor Manufacturers and Traders *see SMMT*
Solex carburettors 32, *35*
SP 12-3 Schutzenpanzer Lang 23
Spark plugs *39*, 41
Spartan 25, 104, 160
Special tools, engines 43
Specified repairs, engines 43
Speed limiters 42
Spencer, Reg 14, 17, 18, 176
Stalwart 39, 118, 125, 137-148, *140-143*, 159, 179, *180* see also specific entries
Standardisation, design 8
Standardised
  engines 10
  vehicles 5
Starter motors *39*, 41, 70
Steering gear
  Abbot 161
  Albion 5 ton 190
  Cambridge 194
  Champ 63
  Douglas fire appliances 185
  Ferret 85
  FV432 161
  Humber 1 ton 96
  Land Rover 70
  Martian 170
  Nubian 187, 196
  Pig 108
  Saladin 121
  Salamander 181, 182
  Saracen 133
  Sno-Flyr 186
  Stalwart 145
  Thornycroft LMD 178
  Tugmaster 184
Stowage
  Cambridge 194
  Champ 64
  Ferret 85, 88
  Humber 1 ton 98
  Pig 109
  Saladin 122
  Saracen 134
Straussler wheels, Champ *61*
Striker 25, 93, 104
Stromberg carburettors 24
Sultan 25, 130
Sump design 35
Sun Engineering, fire-fighting equipment 185, 187
Suspension
  Abbot 161
  Albion 5 ton 190

INDEX

BOC/Tasker oxygen plant 192
Cambridge 194
Champ 63
Douglas fire appliances 185
Ferret 85
FV432 161
Humber 1 ton 96
Land Rover 70
Martian 170
Nubian 187, 196
Pig 108
Saladin 121
Salamander 180, 182
Saracen 133
Stalwart 145
Thornycroft LMD 178
Tugmaster 184
Vauxhall 3 ton 197
Swingfire 93
  Ferret 82, *83*, 86
  Saladin 119, *119*
  Saracen 132
  Stalwart 144

T

Tecalemit oil filters 34
Technical data, engines 27
Technical manuals
  Auto Diesels 10kVA generator 74
  Cambridge 195
  Centurion ARV's 196
  Centurion bridgelayer 73
  Champ 65
  engines 44
  Ferret 88
  FV432 162
  Humber 1 ton 100
  Jones KL66 crane 73
  Martian 174
  Nubian 187
  Pig 111
  Saladin 124
  Saracen 136
  Sno-Flyr 187
  Stalwart 147
  Thornycroft LMD 178
  Tugmaster 185
Technical problems
  Champ 58
  Humber 1 ton 92
  Saladin 118
  Saracen 129
  Stalwart 142
  Vauxhall 3 ton 197
Testing, engines 15, 17, 43
Thermostats 38
Thornycroft
  commercial trucks 24
  LMD 175-178, *177* see also specific entries
  Nubian *see* Nubian
Timing gears 31
Tools, special 43
Torque convertors 38

Tracks
  Abbot 161
  Cambridge 194
  FV432 161
Transmission
  Abbot 161
  Albion 5 ton 190
  Cambridge 194
  Champ 63
  Douglas fire appliances 185
  Ferret 84
  FV432 161
  GM-Allison TX200 158, 161
  Hobbs 194
  Humber 1 ton 96
  Land Rover 70
  Martian 169
  Nubian 187, 196
  Pig 107
  Saladin 120
  Salamander 180, 182
  Saracen 132
  Sno-Flyr 186
  Stalwart 144
  Thornycroft LMD 177
  Tugmaster 184
  Vauxhall 3 ton 197
  Wilson pre-selective 39, 84, 120, 132, 184, 194
Trojan *see FV432*
Tropicalisation, engines 18
Tug, motor 23
Tugmaster 179, *181*, 184 see also specific entries
Turner winches
  Champ 65
  Humber 1 ton 99
  Pig 110
Turrets
  Ferret 85
  Saladin 121, 122
  Saracen 134

U

UBRE 144
UNC screw threads 16, 27
UNF engines 27
UNF screw threads 16, 27
Unit bulk replenishment equipment 144
Universal carrier 11, 157, 192
Unleaded fuels 32
Unreliability 9
Uprating
  Ferret 83
  Saladin 119
Utility body, Champ 60, *60*

V

Valve configuration 15
Valve gear 31
Valve guides 31
Valves
  exhaust 31
  inlet 31

Vanden Plas 4 litre 'R' 24
Vauxhall 3 ton 8, 9, 24, 189, *193*, *194*, 197 see also specific entries
  FV1300 series *8*
Vehicles
  category 'A' 6
  category 'B' 6
  category 'C' 6
  CL 6
  combat 6
  commercial 6
  CT, discontinuation 10
  CT 6, 10
  general service 6, 9
  GS 6, 9
  plan for standardised range 5
  types 5
Ventilation equipment
  Abbot 162
  FV432 162
  Pig 111
  Saracen 128
Vickers 71 *see also* Abbot
Vigilant 81, 93
  Ferret 86
Vixen 80
Volvo 23
Vulcan Sinclair Fluidrive 186

W

Wading
  Champ 42, 64
  engines 17
  Humber 1 ton 95, 99
  Jones KL66 crane 42
  Martian 173
  Mudlark *40*, *62*
  Pig 110
  Saracen *40*, 128, *131*
War Office Policy Committee 5
War Office Policy Statement '26' 139, 159
Warrior 160
Water pumps 35, *35*
Waterproofing, engines 17, 42
Wearing sleeves 28
Weather equipment
  Champ 64
  Land Rover 70
  Stalwart 146
Weight
  Abbot 159
  Albion 5 ton 191
  Auto Diesels 10kVA generator 74
  BOC/Tasker oxygen plant 192
  Cambridge 195
  Centurion ARV's 196
  Centurion bridgelayer 72
  Champ 57
  Douglas fire appliances 185
  engines 29
  Ferret 79
  FV432 159
  Humber 1 ton 91

Jones KL66 crane 73
Land Rover 68
Martian 165
Nubian 187, 197
Pig 103
Saladin 117
Salamander 181, 183
Saracen 127
Sno-Flyr 186
Stalwart 139
Thornycroft LMD 176
Tugmaster 185
West German Army 119, 141
Wharton Engineers 104
Wheels
  Abbot 161
  Albion 5 ton 190
  BOC/Tasker oxygen plant 192
  Champ 63
  Douglas fire appliances 185
  Ferret 85
  FV432 161
  Humber 1 ton 97
  Land Rover 70
  Martian 171
  Nubian 187, 196
  Pig 108
  Saladin 121
  Salamander 181, 183
  Saracen 133
  Sno-Flyr 186
  Stalwart 145
  Thornycroft LMD 178
  Tugmaster 184
Wilkes, Maurice 67
Wilson pre-selective gearboxes 39
  Cambridge 194
  Ferret 84
  Saladin 120
  Saracen 132
  Tugmaster 184
Winches
  Centurion ARV's 195
  Champ 64
  Darlington 185
  Humber 1 ton 99
  Martian 172
  Pig 110
  Stalwart 147
  Tugmaster 184
  Turner 65, 99, 110
Wolseley Mudlark 57, 68
WOPC 5
WOPS '26' 139, 159
Wright, Derek 15
Wynn's, hoverlift trailer 24

Z

ZB 298 radar
  Ferret 83, *84*
  Saladin 120